C000229129

Cruise Ships – The Small Scale Fleet

Maritime books by the same Author:

Action Imminent
Arctic Victory
Battle of Midway
Battles of the Malta Striking Forces
Battleship *Royal Sovereign*
British Battle Cruisers
Cruisers in Action
Cruise Ships
Destroyer Action
Destroyer Leader
Eagle's War
Fighting Flotilla
Hard Lying
Heritage of the Sea
HMS *Royal Sovereign* and her sister ships
HMS *Wild Swan*
Into the Minefields
Midway Dauntless Victory
Naval Warfare in the English Channel
Offshore Ferry Services
Pedestal; the Convoy that saved Malta
Royal Navy Ships' Badges
Task Force 57
The Battle-Cruiser HMS *Renown*
The Great Ships Pass

Cruise Ships – The Small Scale Fleet
A Visual Showcase

Peter C. Smith

Pen & Sword
MARITIME

First published in Great Britain in 2014 by
Pen & Sword Maritime
An imprint of
Pen & Sword Books Ltd
47 Church Street
Barnsley
South Yorkshire
S70 2AS

Copyright © Peter C. Smith 2014
www.dive-bombers.co.uk

ISBN 978 1 78159 281 6

The right of Peter C. Smith to be identified as Author of this work
has been asserted by him in accordance with the Copyright, Designs
and Patents Act 1988.

A CIP catalogue record for this book is
available from the British Library

All rights reserved. No part of this book may be reproduced or transmitted in any form
or by any means, electronic or mechanical including photocopying, recording or by any
information storage and retrieval system, without permission from the Publisher in writing.

Typeset in 10pt Palatino by Mac Style, Bridlington, East Yorkshire
Printed and bound in India by Replika Press Pvt Ltd.

Pen & Sword Books Ltd incorporates the Imprints of Pen & Sword Aviation, Pen & Sword Maritime,
Pen & Sword Military, Wharncliffe Local History, Pen & Sword Select, Pen & Sword Military Classics,
Leo Cooper, Seaforth Publishing and Frontline Publishing

For a complete list of Pen & Sword titles please contact
PEN & SWORD BOOKS LIMITED
47 Church Street, Barnsley, South Yorkshire, S70 2AS, England
E-mail: enquiries@pen-and-sword.co.uk
Website: www.pen-and-sword.co.uk

Contents

Foreword and Acknowledgements

Cruising as a popular holiday as we know it today may be said to have been originated in 1900 by Albert Ballin the then general manager of the Hamburg–America Line. He commissioned the first ship built specifically for what we now call cruise tourism from the German shipbuilder Blohm und Voss, and it was a 4,409-GRT German vessel christened the *Prinzessin Victoria Luise*. This vessel was equipped with more than one hundred first-class cabins and in order to keep these high-paying customers entertained throughout their journey it was fitted with a gymnasium, a library and a film-developing darkroom. She proved most successful and carried a succession of wealthy Germans industrialists and their families to such destinations as the West Indies, the Black Sea and the Mediterranean, locales that still feature highly on the itineraries of cruise ships today. Ballin was ahead of his time in foreseeing the demand for such holidays among the newly rich but even he would have been amazed at the results of his experiment. Just over one hundred years later the cruise line industry was booming and the international tourism was a world-wide tourist phenomena with some small island states almost totally reliant upon it for their income.

In the last three decades the growth of the cruise line industry has been a remarkable event. The sheer size of the market, dominated by North America, has astonished many, even in the industry itself, and until comparatively recently there seemed no end to the phenomenal acceleration both of numbers and the size of the ships being built to cater for them. At its pre-recession peak, 2007, more than 12.5 million took a cruise vacation, as against 3.7 million in 1990, a remarkable leap by any standards. By 2008 the UK cruise industry alone expanded by 11 per cent, while even Spanish interest was almost double that percentage over the same period.

Events since 2008 have slowed, but not halted, this expansion. But even before the world downturn many discerning cruise enthusiasts were more drawn to the smaller ships rather than the giants of the deep with the disaster of the *Costa Concordia*, which brought in its wake many significant changes and costs.

Strangely enough this tragedy, although it had some initial impact and demand in the immediate aftermath, has not, in the end, fatally weakened the allure of cruising as many feared it might. In 2012 a total of twenty-two new leviathans were on the order books, holding between them some 66,831 new berths to be filled and the total order book was a staggering US$14,919,800,000. Certainly, Michelle Fee, founder of Cruise Planners, remained upbeat, stating that the *Concordia* affair was, '...a non-issue' as far as cruise business was concerned. 'Something like that hasn't happened since the *Titanic*, over one hundred years ago,' she is reported as saying. 'Cruising was, and still is, one the safest modes of travel.'

The large vessels have more and more facilities and allure, but if one is to 'get away from it all' then the fact that these colossal ships appear to take it all with them, with malls, amusement centres and sports facilities, some travellers prefer the idea that fewer people is a better option. And the smaller cruise liners do not stint on luxury, quite the contrary with the Seabourn, Silver and Le Ponant flotillas, among many others, having breathtaking ships and restaurants and casinos that defy comparison in opulence and class. Even those smaller cruise ships that offer the barest of essentials can offer what many much larger vessels cannot, besides exclusivity, and that is access to ports, harbours and destinations that the big ships cannot reach. Exotic islands and ports of call, with shallow, shelving coastlines or limited harbour access, offer the traveller a unique series of experiences beyond the reach of their brethren embarked in the larger ships. As the world shrinks and the unspoilt areas become more pedestrian, small cruise ships open up parts of the world still largely untainted and unsullied for the delight of their guests. They evoke the original wonder of the first quests and offer a different facet on our beautiful world.

Thus, this book celebrates the smaller of these wonderful pleasure ships, those of 40,000 GRT or less, in all their beauty and style, and illustrates not only their external appearance but also how they are conceived, designed, built and utilized. It is the intention of the author and publisher that the book will be regularly updated and become a basic reference tool for lovers of the ultimate in maritime magnificence.

This volume acts as a companion to the first *Cruise Ships*, which covered those cruise ships of more than 40,000 GRT, of which, despite the world-wide recession, there is an even larger number, with many more on the stocks at the time of writing. But, if big is beautiful, then small is select and those vessels covered here have their own special merits and attractions.

There are also many other facets to the story, which can only be touched on here for lack of space. There are the very popular major river cruise ships, large vessels that probe the breathtaking scenery of Europe, from the Scottish Highlands and the Thames to the Rhine, Danube and other major rivers and waterways of Europe and also that probe the Mississippi, Alaskan coastline and the great American wilderness and others in Burma and beyond. Just a taste of these is included here, although it is hoped a whole book will be devoted to them soon. There are the casino ships, mainly in the Far East, that cruise beyond the jurisdiction of the nearby lands to enable gambling of all types; there are hotel ships in the Middle East and accommodation ships for world-wide exhibitions and Expos, including in 2012 on the Thames for the most successful London Olympics. Again, a few are listed here as examples of a growing trend. Purists may turn up their noses at their inclusion, but they exist and are increasing so cannot be ignored and most were genuine cruise ships not so long ago – and their present employment is a better alternative to ship lovers than the welder's torch in an Indian scrapyard.

Finally, two important points need to be emphasized right at the start. Firstly, there is inevitably some repetition here, not only because some ships have had many different owners and operators down very long lives, but also with Volume One of *Cruise Ships*, which dealt with the larger vessels, because many lines own, or have owned, both large and small ships. While the history of such owners is the same in both volumes, emphasis has naturally been placed on the smaller vessels in this volume, but duplication is unavoidable for not every person who reads this volume will necessarily read the other and vice versa. The reader of both is asked to be indulgent on this point. Secondly, tracking ship history through the labyrinthine maze of ships owners, operators, holding companies, LLCs, charters, leases, take-overs, amalgamations and name-changes requires a lot of patience and considerable time. I am acutely aware that I may not have covered every base in this quest.

The gap of time between final proofread and publication is quite large and much can happen but any errors will be rectified in future updated editions to reflect the continuous changes in the cruise world that occur almost daily and with increasing complexity.

A book of this kind would be impossible without the kind and dedicated help from numerous people connected with the ships and the industry. I fully acknowledge my debt to the following individuals and organizations who gave me the utmost assistance in tracking down details and photographs and answering my many questions. In alphabetical order then, let me sincerely thank the following:

P. Adonelos, Majestic International Cruises, Inc. Athens, for information, permission to use images and assistance; Anja Allnoch, TransOcean Kreuzfahrten GmbH & Co., Bremen for images of *Astor*; Kate Ashman, *Coral Princess*; Claudia Babl, Deilmann Public Relations; K. G. Bailey, PG Cruises; Neil Bleach, EC2i Ltd, Southend-on-Sea; V. Baranov, Head of Marine Directorate, Russian Maritime Register of Shipping, St Petersburg, Russia; Elizabeth Bell, Celebrity Cruises; Signe Bjorndal, Azamara Club Cruises; Peter Blossom, American Cruise Lines; Julie Blount, Blount Boats; Vanessa Bloy, Paul Gauguin Cruises for images of their fleet; Ronald Bruegmann, Caterpillar Marine Power Systems, Hamburg, Germany, for information and for permission to reproduce some of their original images; Ivonne Brown, Vice President Sales & Marketing, All Discovery Cruising for permission to use images and information; Sharon Buckland, Brand Communications; Trey Byus, Lindblad Expeditions; Jill Channing, Fred Olsen Cruise Lines, London, for permission to reproduce their original images; Daniel Chui for information and for his permission to reproduce images of *Oriental Dragon*; Linda Cochrane, Noble Caledonia; Sarah Cogswell, Saga; Michael Corbett, Orion Expedition Cruises for images of *Orion*; Anne Cowne, Information Officer, Corporate Communications,

Lloyd's Register Group Services, Ltd, London, for enormous help and information during my several research visits to the Library at Fenchurch Street and her patience at my many questions; Laurent Darcy, Pacific Beachcomber; Lynsey Devon, Heaven Publicity and Quark Expeditions for images of the Quark Expeditions Fleet; Patty Disken-Cahill, Expeditions for information and images of *National Geographic Endeavour*; Diana Ditto, Travel Dynamics International, New York, NY; Rachel Edmed, Saga Picture Desk for Quest for Adventure images; Chris Dunham, Polar Latitudes for information and permission to use images of Sea Explorer; Rachael Edmed, Saga Picture Desk, Saga Cruises for images of their fleet; Julie Ellis, Newman PR for information and images of Star Ships; Annette Engelke, Director Communications, TUI Cruises GmbH, Hamburg, Germany; Jill Faulds, Hapag-Lloyd Cruises; Donald Ferguson, Rooster, for Costa images; Mary Frances, Early Interest Services; Claudio Galbo of Fincantieri Spa, for his kind permission to use photos and materials appertaining to that company and the ships they construct; Paul Gauguin Cruises; Julie Giraud, Four Communications for images of Compagne du Ponant fleet; Amanda Graham, Windstar Cruises; Werner Goes, Scheepvaartwest for images of *Albatross*, *Louis Cristal*, *Nautica* and *The Calypso*; Leanne Gosford, PR Siren Communications; Management/PR Star Clippers Americas; Angela Hackman for image of *Voyager*; Peter Hackmann, Head of Corporate Communications, Meyer Werft GmbH, Papenburg, Germany, for information and for permission to reproduce their original images; Rachel Hilton, Vice-President, Quark; Rachel Jackson, Fred Olsen Cruises for permission to use their images and information; Christine Jacobs, Thomson Cruises, Crawley, for permission to reproduce their original images; Gene Kause, Vice President Business Development, Allen Marine Inc; Marjo Keiramo, Communications Manager, Cruises & Ferries, STX Europe, Turku, Finland, for information and for permission to reproduce their original images; Andrew Knox for permission to use some of his outstanding photographs; Cecilia Kolga, Wallenius Lines for information on *Boheme*; Marissa Kowlessar of Compagne du Ponant for information and images of their fleet; John Kuehmayer, AMEM Cruise Ship Database, Salzburg, Austria, for much valuable information and permission to reproduce certain original images; Andreas Gotaut, Marketing Manager; Reederei Peter Deilmann GmbH for permission to use images of *Deutschland* and *Sea Cloud* ships; Jussu Laine, Shipping Manager, Salmaa Travel Ltd, for information and images of *Brahe*; Karen Lamon, Kalos Golf, Chapel Hill, North Carolina; Sara Larmer, SilverSea Cruises, for information and permission to use images of the Silver Fleet; Andy Lovering, Director Sales and Marketing, Star Clippers; Anna Lüftner, Lüftner Cruises, for information and permission to use images of *Amadeus Diamond*; Kristian Lundgren of Klubb Maritim Hesingborg for permission to use image of *Costa Voyager*; Caroline Lynas, Corporate Communications, Belfast City Council, Chief Executive's Department, Belfast; Lauren Maayle, Siren Communications and Swan Hellenic for *Minerva* images; Steven Macaskill for permission to use his photographs of *Kristina Katarina*; Marc at Thomson Cruises PR for permission to use images of their fleet; Peter Margerison, Fotoseeker Image Library, for access to the Fred Olsen images; Daniel Mears, Saga Holidays; Peter Meisel, MAN AG, München, Germany; Sandra Millerkinge, Birka Cruises for images of the Birka fleet; Christian Mueller, FTI Touristik GmbH, Munich; Carlos Moreno for image of Coral; Manuel Moreno for permission to use many of his fine images; Norbert Nagel; Romy Nandelstadt, Hapag-Lloyd Cruises, Hamburg; Craig Naugle, C N Design Group for images of *Alaskan Dream*; John Newth, Clydesights for image of *Amadea*; Britta Oldermann, Cassenwerft GmbH; Goeran Olsson, Klubb Maritim Helsingborg; Courtnay Oswin, Quark Tours; Antti Partanen, Development Manager, Kristina Cruises Oy Ltd for information and images of *Katarina Kristina*; Rachel Peters, Voyages of Antiquity, Oxford; Florian Piper, Oceanwide Expeditions for images of *Plancius* and *Ortelius* and information; Anna-Leena Pohjanpalo, Wärtsilä Corporation, Helsinki, for photographs and information; Britt Rabinovici, American Cruise Lines for information and permission to reproduce some of their original images; Andrea Richartz, Gruene-Segel for photos of *Alexander von Humboldt*; Madeleine Roast, Roast Public Relations Ltd for images of the Hurtigen fleet; Melissa Rubin, Redpoint; Glenn Ryerson and Allinson for images of the *Bahamas Celebration*; Regina Schudrowitz, Stellvertretende Bereichsleitung Marketing for images of *Astor*; Michael Schulze, Director of Cruising, Phoenix Reisen GmbH for kind information and permission to use images of *Amadea*, and *Albatros*; Sarah Scoltock, Director of Communications, Un-Cruise Adventures (formerly Innersea Discoveries and American Safari Tours); Anita Sondern, Adventure Life; Gessica Sortino, MAN Diesel AG, Augsburg, Germany, for information and for permission to reproduce some of their original images; Stacey Stockwell of Siren Communications and Celebrity Cruises for permission to use images of *Celebrity Xpedition*; Monika Sundem, Adventure Life; Meekam Tam, Hong Kong, for image of *China Star*; Franz Truyens for permission to use images of *Louis Cristal* and *Louis Olympia*; Ruud Peter van der Duin for images of *Sea Adventurer*; Matthew Vince of Orion Cruises for images of *Orion*; Dimitra Vlachou, Louis Cruise Line for permission to use images of their fleet; Romana Voet, Hapag-Lloyd Cruises Press office; Christina Wenzel Majestic International Cruises Inc. Athens, for images of *Ocean Countess* and *Ocean Majesty*; Michael N. Wien, Vice-President Sales and& Marketing, Alaskan Dream Cruises, Sitka, Alaska; Katie Wright, Siren Communications for images of *Minerva*; Theodorou Xenia, Salamis Tours (Holdings) Public Ltd; Rebecca Zapfe, Siemens AG, Industry Solutions Division, Press Office, Erlangen, Germany, for information and for permission to reproduce some of their original images; Mrs Christina Zografou, Advertising Manager, Salamis Cruise Lines for images of *Salamis Filoxenia*; and finally my former, much-missed long-time editor, the late Peter Coles of Pen & Sword Maritime, for his original backing of this project from my original conception, for helping me drive it forward to completion and for making it something of special quality. Special thanks to my Editor, Ting Baker.

NB – In this book all tonnages are Gross Registered Tonnage (GT – formerly GRT) unless otherwise stated. GT is not the ship's displacement tonnage but a calculation of its size to the formula 1000 cu/ft of permanently enclosed revenue-generating space = one gross ton. Engine-rooms, fuel and water-bunkerage are discounted under this equation, but food and supply storage is included.

Peter C. Smith
Riseley, Bedford, 2013

The Author aboard the *Thomson Celebration*.

Part One

The Ships

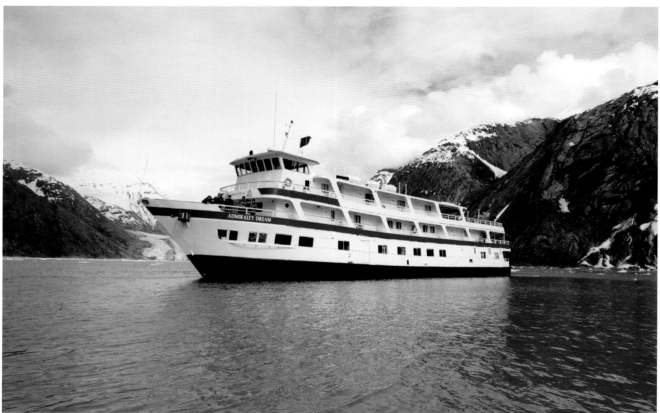

Ship: *ADMIRALTY DREAM*
IMO: 8963727
MMSI: USCG 614006
Callsign: WDF7628
Operator: Alaskan Dream Cruises, Sitka, AK/Allen Marine Tours
Tonnage (GRT): 514
Dimensions (length × beam × draught): 43.5 m (143 ft) × 8.53 m (28 ft) × 1.9 m (6.5 ft)
Constructor & Yard Number: Eastern Shipping, Gulf Coast, Panama City, Florida. **Yard No:** NS-225
Motive Power: 2 × GM12V71 diesel = 700 hp; 1 propeller
Speed (knots): 10
Launched/Floated out: 1979
Christened by: Mrs Jane Blount
Passenger Cabins: 33
Passenger Decks: 4
Passengers/Crew Numbers (max.): 66/20
Class: Coastal Cruise
Registered: Juneau, Alaska
Former Names: *NEW SHOREHAM II/ SPIRIT OF COLUMBIA*

(Courtesy of AlasKan Dream Cruises via C N Design)

Ship: *ADONIA*
IMO: 9210220
MMSI: 310530000
Callsign: ZCDV2
Operator: P&O Cruises, Southampton, UK
Tonnage (GRT): 30,277
Dimensions (length × beam × draught):
 180.45 m (592 ft) × 25.46 m (83 ft 6 in) ×
 6 m (19 ft 8 in)
Constructor & Yard Number: Chantiers
 de l'Atlantique, St Nazaire, France.
 Yard No: Z31
Motive Power: 4 × Wärtsilä 12V32 diesels
 = 13,500 kW; 2 propellers
Speed (knots): 18
Launched/Floated out: 2000
Christened by: Dame Shirley Bassey
 (re-christening May 2011)
Passenger Cabins: 355
Passenger Decks: 8
Passengers/Crew Numbers (max.):
 710/373
Class: R (Renaissance)
Registered: Hamilton, Bermuda
Former Names: *R EIGHT/MINERVA II/
 ROYAL PRINCESS*

(Courtesy Trondheim Port Authority)

13

Ship: *AEGEAN ODYSSEY*
IMO: 7225910
MMSI: 248541000
Callsign: 9HA2404
Operator: Voyages to Antiquity/ Samos Island Maritime Co. Ltd, Pireaus
Tonnage (GRT): 11,503
Dimensions (length × beam × draught): 140.51 m (461 ft) × 20.42 m (67 ft) × 6.10 m (20 ft)
Constructor & Yard Number: Santierul Galatz, Romania. **Yard No:** 617
Motive Power: 2 × Pielstick-Crossley 14 cyl diesel = 10,296 kW; 2 × C/P propellers; Denny-Brown stabilizer; 1000 kW bow thruster
Speed (knots): 16
Launched/Floated out: 1973
Passenger Cabins: 280
Passenger Decks: 7
Passengers/Crew Numbers (max.): 380/180
Class: Originally Ro-Ro ferry
Registered: Valletta, Malta
Former Names: *NARCIS/ALKYON/ AEGEAN DOLPHIN/DOLPHIN/ AEGEAN 1*

(Courtesy Voyages to Discovery)

Ship: *AEGEAN PARADISE*
IMO: 8902333
MMSI: 309877000
Callsign: C6UU6
Operator: Hainan Cruise Enterprises SA, Hong Kong/ Etstur, Istanbul, Turkey
Tonnage (GRT): 23,287
Dimensions (length × beam × draught): 174 m (570 ft 8 in) × 24 m (78 ft 7 in) × 6.7 m (21. ft 6 in)
Constructor & Yard Number: Ishikawajima Harima Heavy Industries Co. Ltd (IHI), Tokyo, Japan.
Yard No: 2987
Motive Power: 2 × 12-cyl Pielstick 12PC2 = 6V diesel = 13,316 kW; 2 C/P propellers
Speed (knots): 21
Launched/Floated out: 26 January 1990
Re-christened by: Katrin Harkmann
Passenger Cabins: 325
Passenger Decks: 8
Passengers/Crew Numbers (max.): 650/250
Class: Germanischer Lloyd/BV
Registered: Nassau, Bahamas
Former Names: *ORIENT VENUS/CRUISE ONE/DELPHIN VOYAGER/HAINAN EMPRESS/HAPPY DOLPHIN*

(Copyright Norbert Nagel)

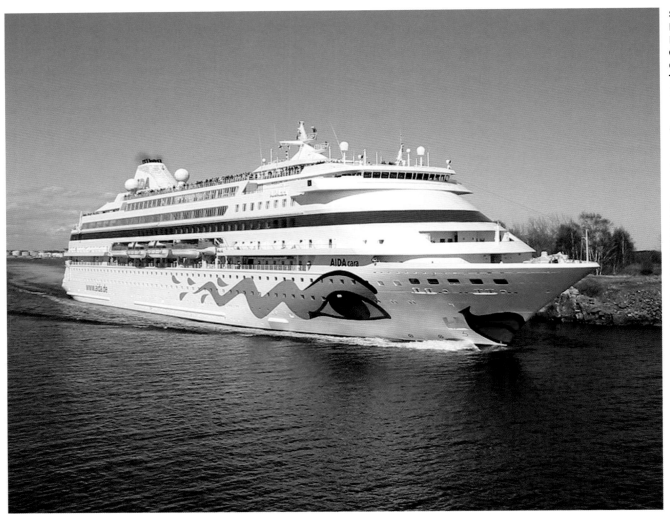

Ship: *AIDAcara*
IMO: 9112789
MMSI: 247117300
Callsign: IBNR
Operator: Aida Cruises
Tonnage (GRT): 38,531
Dimensions (length × beam × draught):
193.30 m (634.2 ft) × 27.58 m (90.5 ft) ×
6.19 m (20.3 ft)
Constructor & Yard Number: Kvaerner
Masa-Yards, Turku, Finland.
Yard No: 1337
Motive Power: 2 × MAN B7W CL48/60
diesel-electric = 21,720 kW twin-pitch
props
Speed (knots): 20
Launched/Floated out: 16 February 1996
Christened by: Christiane Herzog
Passenger Cabins: 593
Passenger Decks: 9
Passengers/Crew Numbers (max.):
1,186/360
Class: Clubschiff
Registered: Genoa, Italy
Former Names: *AIDA*

(Courtesy Aida Cruises)

Ship: *ALBATROS*
IMO: 7304314
MMSI: 308784000
Callsign: C6CN4
Operator: Phoenix Reisen GmbH, Bonn,
Germany
Tonnage (GRT): 28,518
Dimensions (length × beam × draught):
205.46 m (674.2 ft) × 25 m (82 ft) ×
7.30 m (23.9 ft)
Constructor & Yard Number: Wärtsilä,
Helsinki, Finland. **Yard No:** 397
Motive Power: 4 × Wärtsilä-Sulzer 9zh
40/48 diesel = 13,240 kW
Speed (knots): 21
Launched/Floated out: 19 January 1973
Christened by: Vesla Darre Hirsch
Passenger Cabins: 442
Passenger Decks: 8
Passengers/Crew Numbers (max.):
812/340
Class: Det Norske Veritas
Registered: Nassau, Bahamas
Former Names: *ROYAL VIKING SEA/
ROYAL ODYSSEY/NORWEGIAN STAR 1/
CROWN*

(Copyright Werner Goes Scheepvaartwest)

17

Ship: *AMADEA*
IMO: 8913162
MMSI: 308445000
Callsign: C6VE9
Operator: Phoenix Reisen, Bonn, Germany
Tonnage (GRT): 28,856
Dimensions (length × beam × draught):
192.82 m (632 ft 7 in) × 24.70 m (81 ft) ×
6.20 m (20 ft 4 in)
Constructor & Yard Number: Mitsubishi
Heavy Industries, Nagasaki, Japan.
Yard No: 2050
Motive Power: 2 × MAN-Mitsubishi
7L58/64 diesel = 17,300 kW; 2 propellers
Speed (knots): 21
Launched/Floated out: 6 April 1991
Christened by: Keiko Kishi
Passenger Cabins: 303
Passenger Decks: 8
Passengers/Crew Numbers (max.):
624/292
Class: N/A
Registered: Nassau, Bahamas
Former Names: *ASUKA*

(Courtesty John Newth, Clydesights)

Ship: *AMADEUS DIAMOND*
IMO: 04807380 (European ID Nor.)
MMSI: 211443640
Callsign: DB 5333
Operator: Luftner Cruises of Austria/Danuia Kreuzfahrten, GmbH, Vienna, Austria
Tonnage (GRT): 1,566
Dimensions (length × beam × draught): 110 m (360 ft) × 11.40 m (37 ft) × 1.6 m (5 ft 3 in)
Constructor & Yard Number: Shipyard de Hoop Foxal, Lobith, The Netherlands.
Yard No: NB428
Motive Power: 2 × Caterpillar = 782 kW
Speed (knots): 11.9
Launched/Floated out: December 2008
Christened by: Martina Lüfner
Passenger Cabins: 74
Passenger Decks: 4
Passengers/Crew Numbers (max.): 148/40
Class: Hotel ship
Registered: Passau, Germany
Former Names: N/A

(Courtesy Dr. W. Luftner Reisen GmbH)

Ship: *AMERICAN GLORY*
IMO: 8972338
MMSI: 366858820
Callsign: WDA8860
Operator: American Cruise Lines, Guilford, Connecticut, USA
Tonnage (GRT): 1,480
Dimensions (length × beam × draught): 53 m (174 ft) × 12.30 m (40.5 ft) × 1.98 m (6.5 ft)
Constructor & Yard Number: Chesapeake Shipbuilding, Salisbury, Maryland, USA. **Yard No:** 88
Motive Power: diesel; 2 Caterpillar 3406E diesel = 650 hp; 2 propellers
Speed (knots): 10.2
Launched/Floated out: 2002
Passenger Cabins: 31
Passenger Decks: 4
Passengers/Crew Numbers (max.): 49/22
Class: Boutique ship
Registered: Wilmington, Delaware, USA
Former Names: N/A

(Courtesy of American Cruise Lines)

Ship: *AMERICAN SPIRIT*
IMO: 9283124
MMSI: 367023690
Callsign: WDC4371
Operator: American Cruise Lines, Guilford, Connecticut, USA
Tonnage (GRT): 1,955
Dimensions (length × beam × draught): 67 m (220 ft) × 14m (46 ft) × 2.5 m (8.2 ft)
Constructor & Yard Number: Chesapeake Shipbuilding, Salisbury, Maryland, USA. **Yard No:** 52
Motive Power: 2 × MTU 16v-2000 diesel = 1100 hp; Thrustmaster bow thruster; 2 propellers
Speed (knots): 12.6
Launched/Floated out: 14 October 2003
Passenger Cabins: 51
Passenger Decks: 4
Passengers/Crew Numbers (max.): 92/27
Class: Boutique ship
Registered: Wilmington, Delaware, USA
Former Names: N/A

(Courtesy of American Cruise Lines)

Ship: *AMERICAN STAR*
IMO: 9427615
MMSI: 367184740
Callsign: WDD7311
Operator: American Cruise Lines, Guilford, Connecticut, USA
Tonnage (GRT): 1,973
Dimensions (length × beam × draught): 67 m (220 ft) × 14 m (46 ft) × 2.5 m (8.2 ft)
Constructor & Yard Number: Chesapeake Shipbuilding, Maryland, USA. **Yard No:** 89
Motive Power: 2 D Caterpillar C-32 diesel – 1,250 hp; Thrustmaster bow thruster; 2 propellers
Speed (knots): 12.4
Launched/Floated out: 2007
Christened by: Karen Baldacci
Passenger Cabins: 52
Passenger Decks: 4
Passengers/Crew Numbers (max.): 100/27
Class: Boutique ship
Registered: Wilmington, Delaware, USA
Former Names: N/A

(Courtesy of American Cruise Lines)

Ship: *AMUSEMENT WORLD*
IMO: 6620773
MMSI: 572243000
Callsign: T2JA2
Operator: New Century Tours Corporation
Pte Ltd, Singapore/Universal Ship
Management, Singapore
Tonnage (GRT): 12,764
Dimensions (length × beam × draught):
141.2 m (463 ft) × 22.5 m (74 ft) × 5.75 m
(19 ft)
Constructor & Yard Number: Lindholmen
Varv A/B, Gothenburg, Sweden.
Yard No: 1095
Motive Power: 4 × Pielstick-Lindholmen
6PC2-2L400 diesel = 7,415 kW; 2 × V/P
propellers; 2 bow thrusters
Speed (knots): 13.3
Launched/Floated out: 29 September
1966
Christened by: Svenska Lloyd
Passenger Cabins: 250
Passenger Decks: 3
Passengers/Crew Numbers (max.):
900/200
Class: Casino ship
Registered: Tuvalu Palau
Former Names: *PATRICIA/STENA*
OCEANICA/STENA SAGA/LION
QUEEN/CROWN PRINCESS/CROWN
PRINCESS VICTORIA/PACIFIC STAR/
SUN FIESTA/PUTRI BINTANG

(Copyright Frank Katzer)

Ship: *ASTOR*
IMO: 8506373
MMSI: 311348000
Callsign: C6JR3
Operator: Astor Premicon
  Hochseekreuzfahten, Germany/
  Transocean, Bremen
Tonnage (GRT): 20,606
Dimensions (length × beam × draught):
  176.50 m (579 ft) × 22.61 m (74.1 ft) ×
  6.10 m (20 ft)
Constructor & Yard Number:
  Howaldtswerke-Deutsche Werft, Kiel,
  Germany.
Yard No: 218
Motive Power: 4 × Sulzer-Wärtsilä 6ZAL40
  diesel = 13,200 kWw + 2 × 8zal40 =
  8,800 kW; 2 C/P propellers
Speed (knots): 16.5
Launched/Floated out: 30 May 1986
Christened by: Inta Gleich
Passenger Cabins: 285
Passenger Decks: 7
Passengers/Crew Numbers (max.):
  578/278
Class: E1
Registered: Nassau, Bahamas
Former Names: *ASTOR/FEDOR
  DOSTOEVSKIY*

*(courtesy Astor Premicon
Hochseekreuzfahten)*

Ship: *ATHENA*
IMO: 5383304
MMSI: 255801380
Callsign: CQRV
Operator: Classic International Cruises, Neutral Bay, Australia
Tonnage (GRT): 16,144
Dimensions (length × beam × draught): 160.10 m (525.2 ft) × 21.04 m (68.8 ft) × 7.6 m (24.9 ft)
Constructor & Yard Number: Götaverken, Gothenburg, Sweden. **Yard No:** 611
Motive Power: 2 × Wärtsilä 16V32 diesel = 10,700 kW; 2 propellers
Speed (knots): 19
Launched/Floated out: 9 September 1946
Passenger Cabins: 277
Passenger Decks: 8
Passengers/Crew Numbers (max.): 580/240
Class: RINA
Registered: Funchal, Madeira, Portugal
Former Names: *STOCKHOLM/ VOLKERFREUND SCHAFT/VOELKER/ FRIDTJOF NANSEN/ITALIA I/ITALIA PRIMA/VALTUR PRIMA/CARIBE*

(Courtesy and copyright Andrew Knox)

Ship: *AZAMARA JOURNEY*
IMO: 9200940
MMSI: 256204000
Callsign: 9HOB8
Operator: Azamara Club Cruises
Tonnage (GRT): 30,277
Dimensions (length × beam × draught):
181 m (593.7 ft) × 29 m (95.1 ft) × 5.85 m
(6 ft)
Constructor & Yard Number: Chantiers
de l'Atlantique, Nantes Saint Nazare,
France. **Yard No:** Y31
Motive Power: 4 × Wärtsilä 12V32 diesel =
18,600 kW; 2 × GEC Alsthom electric @
6,750 kW; 2 propellers
Speed (knots): 18.5
Launched/Floated out: 17 January 2000
Passenger Cabins: 338
Passenger Decks: 9
Passengers/Crew Numbers (max.):
694/408
Class: R
Registered: Valletta, Malta
Former Names: *R SIX/BLUE DREAM*

(Courtesy and copyright Manuel Moreno)

Ship: *AZAMARA QUEST*
IMO: 9210218
MMSI: 256216000
Callsign: 9HOM8
Operator: Azamara Club Cruises
Tonnage (GRT): 30,277
Dimensions (length × beam × draught):
    180.4 m (591.8 ft) × 30 m (96 ft) × 5.8 m
    (19 ft)
Constructor: Chantiers de l'Atlantique,
    Nantes, Saint Nazaire, France.
Yard No: Y31
Motive Power: 4 × Wärtsilä 12V32 diesel =
    18,600 kW; 2 × GEC Alsthom electric @
    6,750 kW; 2 propellers
Speed (knots): 18.5
Launched/Floated out: 23 May 2000
Passenger Cabins: 358
Passenger Decks: 9
Passengers/Crew Numbers (max.):
    777/306
Class: R
Registered: Valletta, Malta
Former Names: *R SEVEN/DELPHIN
    RENAISSANCE/BLUE MOON*

(Courtesy and copyright Manuel Moreno)

Ship: *BAHAMAS CELEBRATION*
IMO: 7904891
MMSI: 3110113000
Callsign: C6XJ3
Operator: Celebration Cruise Line, Plantation, Florida, USA
Tonnage (GRT): 35,855
Dimensions (length × beam × draught): 205.25 m (673 ft 5 in) × 24 m (78 ft 9 in) × 6 m (19 ft 8 in)
Constructor & Yard Number: Howaldtswerke-Deutsche Werft, Kiel, Germany. **Yard No:** 164
Motive Power: 4 × Stork-Wärtsilä 9FEDH240 diesel; 2 × Stork-Wärtsilä 9FEDH240G = 36,356 kW; 2 C/P propellers
Speed (knots): 21
Launched/Floated out: 31 July 1980
Christened by: Princess Ragnhild of Norway/Glenn Ryerson Allinson
Passenger Cabins: 499
Passenger Decks: 7
Passengers/Crew Numbers (max.): 1,200//312
Class: Ice 1B
Registered: Nassau, Bahamas
Former Names: *PRINCESS RAGNHILD*

(Courtesy Celebration Cruise Line)

Ship: *BARANOF DREAM*
USCG doc No: 628951
MMSI: WBF9253
Callsign: WBF9523
Operator: Alaskan Dream Cruises, Sitka,
   AK/Allen Marine Tours
Tonnage (GRT): 97
Dimensions (length × beam × draught):
   43.5 m (143.5 ft) × 8.6 m (28.5 ft) ×
   2.2 m (7.5 ft)
Constructor & Yard Number: Blount
   Marine Corp., Warren, Rhode Island.
   Yard No: AP234
Motive Power: 2 × Deutz BF12M 716
   diesels @ 700 b hp; 1 propeller
Speed (knots): 12
Launched/Floated out: 1980
Christened by: Eleanor Shockley
Passenger Cabins: 39
Passenger Decks: 4
Passengers/Crew Numbers (max.):
   66/21
Class: Coastal Cruise
Registered: Portland, Oregon
Former Names: *PACIFIC NORTHWEST
   EXPLORER/SPIRIT OF ALASKA*

*(Courtesy and copyright Admiralty Dream
Cruises via C.N. Design)*

Ship: *BIRGER JARL*
IMO: 5044893
MMSI: 265078000
Callsign: SIAU
Operator: Åndinlinjen, Stockholm, Sweden/
Rederi Birger Jarl AB
Tonnage (GRT): 3,564
Dimensions (length × beam × draught):
95.50 m (303 ft 6 in) × 14.28 m (46 ft
10 in) × 5.50 m (18 ft 1 in)
Constructor & Yard Number: Finnboda
Varv, Nacka, Sweden. **Yard No:** 351.
Motive Power: 1 × MAN B&W 4SA diesel
= 2,795 kW; 1 propeller; 1 bow thruster
Speed (knots): 10.2
Launched/Floated out: 15 January 1953
Christened by: Margit Hagander
Passenger Cabins: 156
Passenger Decks: 6
Passengers/Crew Numbers (max.): 369
Class: Olympia
Registered: Stockholm, Sweden
Former Names: *BORE NORD/MINISEA/
BALTIC STAR*

(Copyright Andin Linjen)

Ship: *BIRKA PARADISE*
IMO: 9273727
MMSI: 230962000
Callsign: SIJW
Operator: Birka Cruises/ Birka Line, Stockholm, Sweden
Tonnage (GRT): 34,924
Dimensions (length × beam × draught): 177 m (580 ft) × 43 m (141 ft 1 in) × 9.40 m (30 ft 10 in)
Constructor & Yard Number: Aker Finnyards, Rauma, Finland. **Yard No:** 442
Motive Power: 4 × Wärtsilä 6L46 diesels = 23,400 kW; 4 × Wärtsilä 6l32 diesels = 11,400 kW; 4 propellers
Speed (knots): 21
Launched/Floated out: 16 April 2004
Christened by: Arja Saijonmaa
Passenger Cabins: 734
Passenger Decks: 10
Passengers/Crew Numbers (max.): 1800/181
Class: Ice
Registered: Stockholm, Sweden
Former Names: N/A

(Courtesy Birka Cruises)

Ship: *BLACK WATCH*
IMO: 7108930
MMSI: 311166000
Callsign: C6RS5
Operator: Fred Olsen Cruise Lines, Ipswich, Suffolk, UK
Tonnage (GRT): 28,388
Dimensions (length × beam × draught): 205.47 m (674.1 ft) × 25.20 m (82.6 ft) × 7.55 m (24.7 ft)
Constructor & Yard Number: Wärtsilä Helsinki New Shipyard, Helsinki, Finland. **Yard No:** 395
Motive Power: 4 × MAN UL32/40 diesel = 14,000 kW; 2 C/P propellers
Speed (knots): 18.5
Launched/Floated out: 12 May 1971
Christened by: Mrs Thor Heyerdahl
Passenger Cabins: 423
Passenger Decks: 8
Passengers/Crew Numbers (max.): 804/330
Class: Royal Viking
Registered: Nassau, Bahamas
Former Names: *STAR ODYSSEY/ WESTWARD/ROYAL VIKING STAR*

(Courtesy of Fred Olsen Lines)

Ship: *BRAHE*
IMO: 5345065
MMSI: 230197000
Callsign: OIEC
Operator: Saimaan Matkaverkko Oy, Lappeenranta
Tonnage (GRT): 1,105
Dimensions (length × beam × draught): 56.80 m (186 ft 4 in) × 10.8 m (33 ft 1 in) × 3.30 m (10 ft 10 in)
Constructor & Yard Number: Pullman Standard Car Manufacturing, Chicago, Illinois, USA. **Yard No:** 254
Motive Power: 2 × Caterpillar diesel = 66 kW
Speed (knots): 14
Launched/Floated out: 13 June 1943
Christened by: Kristina Brahe
Passenger Cabins: 45
Passenger Decks: 4
Passengers/Crew Numbers (max.): 132/18
Class: Admirable Patrol Craft Escort (USN PCE)
Registered: Helsinki, Finland
Former Names: *USS PCE830/HMS KILCHRENNAN/SUNNHORDLAND/ KRISTINA BRAHE*

(Courtesy Saimaan Matkavekko Oy)

Ship: *BREMEN*
IMO: 8907424
MMSI: 308429000
Callsign: C6JC3
Operator: Hapag-Lloyd (Bahamas) Ltd, Hamburg, Germany
Tonnage (GRT): 6,752
Dimensions (length × beam × draught): 111.5 m (365.8 ft) × 17 m (55.7 ft) × 4.8 m (15.7 ft)
Constructor & Yard Number: MHI Kobe Shipyard & Machinery Works, Kobe, Japan. **Yard No:** 1182
Motive Power: 2 × 8DKM-32 diesel = 4,884 kW; 2 propellers
Speed (knots): 16.5
Launched/Floated out: 20 June 1990
Christened by: Ute Wedemeier
Passenger Cabins: 82
Passenger Decks: 6
Passengers/Crew Numbers (max.): 164/100
Class: Ice
Registered: Nassau, Bahamas
Former Names: *FRONTIER SPIRIT*

(Courtesy Hapag-Lloyd (Bahamas) Ltd, Hamburg)

Ship: *CALEDONIAN SKY*
IMO: 5631587
MMSI: 235254000
Callsign: ZN9RZ
Operator: Noble Caledonian, UK/
Caledonian Sky Shipping Inc, Bahamas
(Salen Ship Management AB,
Gothenburg, Sweden)
Tonnage (GRT): 4,200
Dimensions (length × beam × draught):
90.6 m (297 ft 3 in) × 15.3 m (44 ft 3 in) ×
5.85 m (19 ft 2 in)
Constructor & Yard Number: Nuovi
Cantieri Apuania, MaRINA Di Carrara,
Italy. **Yard No:** 1145
Motive Power: 2 × MAN B&W 8L28/32A-
FHO diesel = 1,760 kW; 2 F/P propellers
Speed (knots): 16
Launched/Floated out: 17 January 2000
Christened by: HRH Anne Princess Royal
Passenger Suites: 57
Passenger Decks: 5
Passengers/Crew Numbers (max.):
114/71
Class: Renaissance
Registered: Nassau, Bahamas
Former Names: RENAISSANCE SIX/
SUNRISE/HEBRIDEAN SPIRIT/
MEGASTAR CAPRICORN/SUN VISTA II

(Copyright Rick Tomlinson)

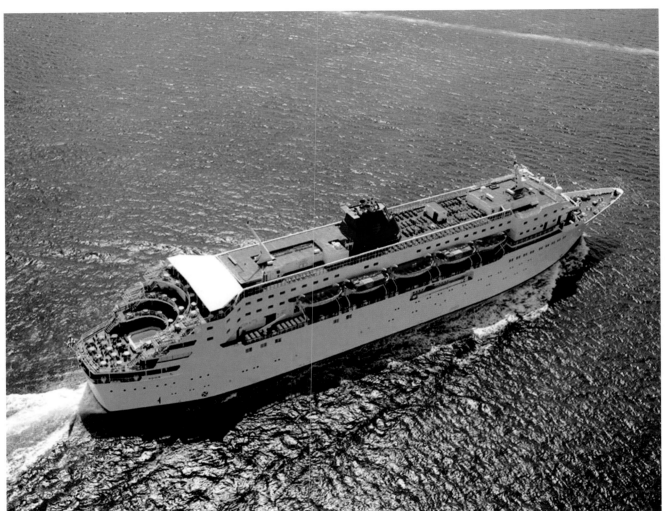

Ship: *CALYPSO, THE*
IMO: 6715372
MMSI: 240627000
Callsign: SVSY
Operator: Thomson Cruises/Louis Cruise
Lines
Tonnage (GRT): 360
Dimensions (length × beam × draught):
135.4 m (444 ft 3 in) × 19.2 m (63 ft) ×
6.3 m (20 ft 8 in)
Constructor & Yard Number: Italcantieri
SpA, Castellammare Di Stabia, Italy.
Yard No: 645
Motive Power: 2 × FIAT 7-cylinder FIAT
diesel; 2 × Wärtsilä 12V32D diesel =
11,900 kW; 2 C/P propellers
Speed (knots): 18.5
Launched/Floated out: 12 September
1967
Passenger Cabins: 243
Passenger Decks: 8
Passengers/Crew Numbers (max.):
740/220
Class: Canguro
Registered: Cyprus
Former Names: *CANGURO VERDE/
DURR/IONIAN HARMONY/SUN
FIESTA/REGENT JEWEL/CALYPSO*

(Courtesy Louis Cruise Lines)

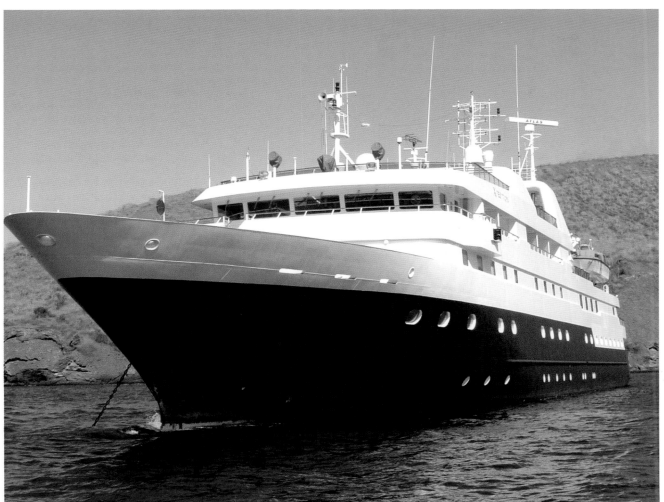

Ship: *CELEBRITY XPEDITION*
IMO: 9228368
MMSI: 735023483
Callsign: HC2083
Operator: Celebrity Cruises/Islas
  Galapagos Turismo y Vapores Ca, Quito,
  Ecuador
Tonnage (GRT): 2,842
Dimensions (length × beam × draught):
  90.2 m (296 ft) × 13 m × 43 ft 6 in) ×
  3.5 m (11.4 ft)
Constructor & Yard Number: Cassens C
  Schiffswerft, Emden, Germany.
  Yard No: 228
Motive Power: 2 × MaK 6-cyl 6M25 diesel
  = 3,700 kW, 2 propellers
Speed (knots): 15
Launched/Floated out: 2001
Christened by: Senta Berger
Passenger Cabins: 45
Passenger Decks: 6
Passengers/Crew Numbers (max.):
  90/68
Class: Sun
Registered: Guayaquil, Ecuador
Former Names: *SUN BAY I*

(Courtesy Celebrity Cruises)

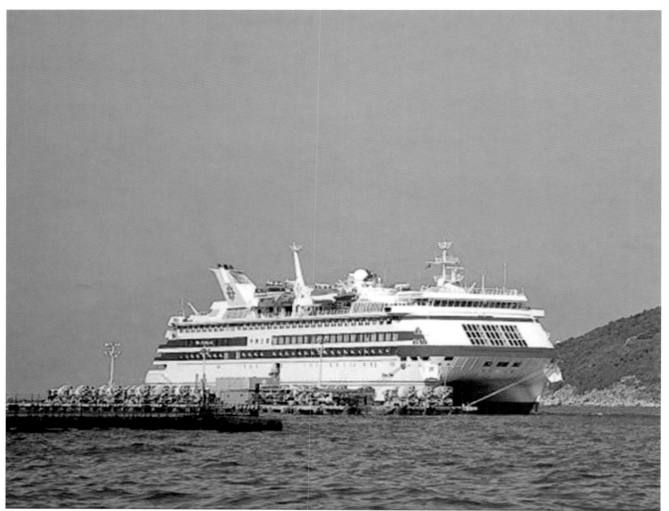

Ship: *CHINA STAR*
IMO: 9008407
MMSI: 309788000
Callsign: C60P6
Operator: China Cruise Company, Hong Kong/Wenzhou, Zhejiang, China
Tonnage (GRT): 20,295
Dimensions (length × beam × draught): 131.2 m (430 ft) × 31.96 m (104.9 ft) × 7.6 m (25 ft)
Constructor & Yard Number: Rauma Finnyards, Helsingfors, Finland.
Yard No: 310
Motive Power: 2 × Wärtsilä 8432E; 2 × Wärtsilä 6R323 diesel = 11, 340 kW
Speed (knots): 12.5
Launched/Floated out: 20 June 1991
Christened by: Dame Kiri Te Kanawa
Passenger Cabins: 177
Passenger Decks: 12
Passengers/Crew Numbers (max.): 354/200
Class: Swath
Registered: Nassau, Bahamas
Former Names: *RADISSON DIAMOND/ OMAR STAR/ASIA STAR*

(Copyright Meekana Tam, Hong Kong)

Ship: *CLIPPER ODYSSEY*
IMO: 8800195
MMSI: 301913000
Callsign: C60ZZ3
Operator: International Shipping Partners, Miami, Florida/Zegrahm Expeditions
Tonnage (GRT): 5,218
Dimensions (length × beam × draught): 102.97 m (337.8 ft) × 15/42 m (50.6 ft) × 4.13 m (13.5 ft)
Constructor & Yard Number: Nippon Kokan Co., Tsu, Japan. **Yard No:** 112
Motive Power: diesel-electric – 2 × Wärtsilä V22HF diesel = 5,192 kW; 2 propellers
Speed (knots): 17.6
Launched/Floated out: 31 October 1988
Passenger Cabins: 64
Passenger Decks: 5
Passengers/Crew Numbers (max.): 128/52
Class: Sea Goddess
Registered: Nassau, Bahamas
Former Names: *OCEANIC GRACE/ OCEANIC ODYSSEY*

(Copyright Trondheim Port Authority)

Ship: *CLUB HARMONY*
IMO: 6910544
MMSI: 538004519
Callsign: V7XN2
Operator: Polaris Shipping, Seoul, Republic
  of Korea/ Harmony Cruises
Tonnage (GRT): 25,558
Dimensions (length × beam × draught):
  174.3 m (571.8 ft) × 25.8 m (84.6 ft) ×
  8.5 m (27 ft 10.5 in)
Constructor & Yard Number: Wärtsilä
  Turku Shipyard, Turku, Finland.
  Yard No: 1169
Motive Power: Wärtsilä Piestick 16PC2-V
  diesel = 19,136 kW; 2 propellers
Speed (knots): 19.5
Launched/Floated out: 16 January 1969
Christened by: Anette Funicello
Passenger Cabins: 386
Passenger Decks: 8
Passengers/Crew Numbers (max.):
  1,005/356
Class: Johnson
Registered: Majuro, Marshall Islands
Former Names: *AXEL JOHNSON/*
  REGENT SUN/ITALIA/COSTA MARINA/
  HARMONY PRINCESS

(Copyright J.O.)

Ship: *CLUB MED 2*
IMO: 9007491
MMSI: 227194000
Callsign: FNIR
Operator: Club Méditerranée Cruises, Paris/V Ships Group, Monaco
Tonnage (GRT): 14,983
Dimensions (length × beam × draught): 187.10 m (613.8 ft) × 20 m (65.6 ft) × 5 m (164/4 ft)
Constructor & Yard Number: Snach (Sociéte Nouvelle des Ach), Le Havre, France.
Yard No: 282
Motive Power: 5 × 67.5 m (221 ft) tall masts with 7 × computer controlled sails = 2,500 m^2 (26,910 sq ft). 4 × diesel electric engines = 9,120 kW; 2 propellers
Speed (knots): 10/15
Launched/Floated out: July 1991
Christened by: Hervé Novelli
Passenger Cabins: 185
Passenger Decks: 8
Passengers/Crew Numbers (max.): 409/214
Class: Trident
Registered: Mata-Utu, Wallis & Futuna
Former Names: N/A

(Courtesy and copyright Manuel Moreno)

Ship: *COLUMBUS 2*
IMO: 9156462
MMSI: 538001663
Callsign: V7DM2
Operator: Hapag-Lloyd
Tonnage (GRT): 30,277
Dimensions (length × beam × draught):
180.96 m (593.7 ft) × 25.46 m (83.5 ft) ×
5.95 m (19.5 ft)
Constructor & Yard Number: Chantiers
de l'Atlantique, St Nazaire, France.
Yard No: H31
Motive Power: 4 × Wärtsilä 12V32 diesel
= 13,500 kW; 2 C/P propellers; 2 ×
stabilizers
Speed (knots): 18
Launched/Floated out: 24 June 1998
Christened by: Carmen Riu-Güell
Passenger Cabins: 342
Passenger Decks: 9
Passengers/Crew Numbers (max.):
698/377
Class: Regatta
Registered: Majuro, Marshall Islands
Former Names: *R ONE/INSIGNIA*

(Courtesy of Hapag-Lloyd, Bremen)

Ship: *CORAL*
IMO: 7046936
MMSI: 2848347000
Callsign: 9HA2326
Operator: Louis Hellenic Cruises, Piraeus, Greece
Tonnage (GRT): 14,194
Dimensions (length × beam × draught): 148.10 m (485 ft 10 in) × 21.5 m (70.5 ft) × 6.1 m (20 ft)
Constructor & Yard Number: De Rotterdamsche Droogdok, Rotterdam, the Netherlands. **Yard No:** 329
Motive Power: 4 × Stork-Werkspoor 12-cyl diesel = 19,860 kW; 2 propellers
Speed (knots): 21.5
Launched/Floated out: 2 February 1971
Christened by: President Mireya Moscoso
Passenger Cabins: 718
Passenger Decks: 7
Passengers/Crew Numbers (max.): 945/265
Class: N/A
Registered: Valletta, Malta
Former Names: *CUNARD ADVENTURER/ SUNWARD II/ TRITON*

(Courtesy and copyright Manuel Moreno)

Ship: *COSTA VOYAGER*
IMO: 9183506
MMSI: 2473128000
Callsign: ICSW
Operator: Costa Crociere, Genoa, Italy
Tonnage (GRT): 24,391
Dimensions (length × beam × draught):
180.7 m (593 ft) × 25.6 m (84 ft) × 7.4 m
(24 ft 3 in)
Constructor & Yard Number: Blohm +
Voss, Hamburg, Germany. **Yard No:** 961
Motive Power: Wärtsilä 9OL46D diesel =
37,800 kW
Speed (knots): 28
Launched/Floated out: 14 July 1999
Christened by: His Excellency
Konstantinos Stefanopoulos
Passenger Cabins: 416
Passenger Decks: 6
Passengers/Crew Numbers (max.):
927/353
Class: Voyager
Registered: Genoa, Italy
Former Names: *OLYMPIC VOYAGER/*
GRAND VOYAGER

*(Copyright Kristian Lundgren/Klubmoritim,
Helsingborg)*

Ship: *DELPHIN*
IMO: 7347536
MMSI: 308658000
Callsign: C6VV2
Operator: Vishal Cruises Pvt Ltd, Quatre Bornes, Mauritius/Passat Cruises Ltd, Hamburg
Tonnage (GRT): 16,214
Dimensions (length × beam × draught): 156.27 m (512 ft 6 in) × 21.9 m (71.8 ft) × 6.20 m (20.3 ft)
Constructor & Yard Number: Oy Wärtsilä Ab, Turku, Finland. **Yard No:** 1212
Motive Power: 2 × Pielstik-Wärtsilä 18RPC2V @6,625 kW, 2 C/P propellers
Speed (knots): 21.5
Launched/Floated out: 6 March 1974
Christened by: Katrin Hackman
Passenger Cabins: 236
Passenger Decks: 7
Passengers/Crew Numbers (max.): 554/234
Class: Belorussiya
Registered: Nassau, Bahamas
Former Names: *KAZAKHSTAN II/ BELORUSSIYA*

(Copyright Trondheim Port Authrrity)

Ship: *DEUTSCHLAND*
IMO: 9141807
MMSI: 211274670
Callsign: DMMC
Operator: Peter Deilamnn Reederei
Tonnage (GRT): 22,186
Dimensions (length × beam × draught):
  175.30 m (575 ft 2 in) × 23 m (75 ft 6 in)
  × 5.79 m (19 ft0
Constructor & Yard Number:
  Howaldtswerke-DeutscheWerft.
Yard No: 328
Motive Power: 2 × MaK DMR 8M32 diesel;
  2 × MaK DMR 6M32 diesel N = 12,320
  kW, 2 propellers
Speed (knots): 20
Launched/Floated out: 16 January 1998
Christened by: Richard von Weizsacker
Passenger Cabins: 292
Passenger Decks: 7
Passengers/Crew Numbers (max.):
  513/270
Class: N/A
Registered: Neustadt in Holstein, Germany
Former Names: N/A

(Courtesy Peter Deilmann Reederei)

Ship: *DISCOVERY SAILAWAY*
IMO: 7108514
MMSI: 310382000
Callsign: ZCDG2
Operator: Cruise & Maritime Voyages (Cmv)/All Leisure Group, Burgess Hill/V-Ships, Monaco
Tonnage (GRT): 20,186
Dimensions (length × beam × draught): 168.74 m (553.6 ft) × 24.6 m (80 ft 8 in) × 7.49 m (24 ft 7 in)
Constructor & Yard Number: Rheinstahl-Nordsee Werke GmbH, EMDEN, Germany. **Yard No:** 414
Motive Power: 4 × FIAT GMT C421OSS diesel @ 18000 hp; 2 × Kamewa C/P propellers; Denny-Brown AEG D stabilizers
Speed (knots): 18
Launched/Floated out: 6 March 1971
Christened by: Jennie Smith
Passenger Cabins: 343
Passenger Decks: 8
Passengers/Crew Numbers (max.): 698/350
Class: Princess
Registered: Hamilton, Bermuda
Former Names: *ISLAND VENTURE/ISLAND PRNCESS/HYUNDAI PUNGAK/PLATINUM/DISCOVERY/ANDAMAN VICTORY/DISCOVERY*

(*Copyright* **Cruise & Maritime**)

Ship: *EUROPA*
IMO: 9183855
MMSI: 308007000
Callsign: C6QK8
Operator: Hapag-Lloyd Cruises/Hapag-Lloyd (Bahams) AG, Hamburg, Germany
Tonnage (GRT): 28,890
Dimensions (length × beam × draught): 198.60 m (651.6 ft) × 24 m (79 ft) X6 m (20 ft)
Constructor & Yard Number: Kvaerner, Masa Yards, Hietalahti Shipyard, Helsinki, Finland. **Yard No:** 495
Motive Power: 2 MAN B&W 7ZYL40/54 diesel; 2 × 8ZYL40/54 diesel = 21,6000 kW; 2 ABB Azipod = 13,300 kWh; 2 11m^2 Finantieri bow thrusters
Speed (knots): 21
Launched/Floated out: 5 March 1993
Christened by: Gabriel Frentzel
Passenger Cabins: 204
Passenger Decks: 7
Passengers/Crew Numbers (max.): 408/264
Class: N/A
Registered: Nassau, Bahamas
Former Names: N/A

(Copyright and courtesy Andrew Knox)

Ship: *EUROPA 2*
IMO: 9616230
MMSI: 209197000
Operator: Hapag-Lloyd Cruises/Hapag-Lloyd (Bahams) AG, Hamburg, Germany
Tonnage (GRT): 39,500
Dimensions (length × beam × draught): 225.38 m (739 ft 5 in) × 26.70 m (87 ft 7 in) × 6.30 m (20 ft 8 in)
Constructor & Yard Number: STX, Europe, St Nazaire, France.
Yard No: H33
Motive Power: 4 × MaK diesel/Mermaid pods = 24,000 kW; 2 × PWM MV7000 converters
Speed (knots): 21
Launched/Floated out: 6 July 2012
Christened by: Dana Schweiger
Passenger Suites: 251
Passenger Decks: 11
Passengers/Crew Numbers (max.): 516/370
Class: N/A
Registered: Nassau, Bahamas
Former Names: N/A

(Courtesy Hapag-Lloyd, Hamburg)

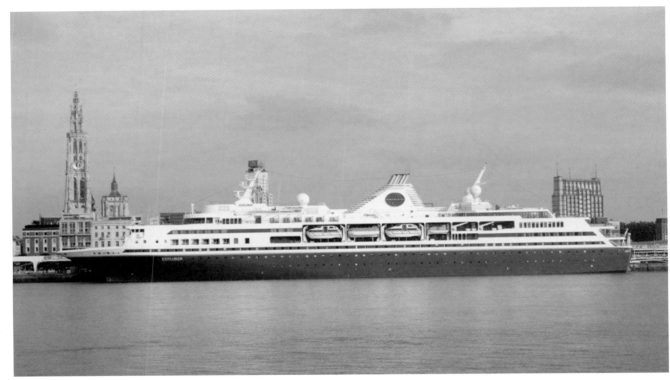

Ship: *EXPLORER*
IMO: 9183518
MMSI: 311705000
Callsign: C6TN4
Operator: Institute for Shipboard Education/Semester at Sea for V Ships Leisure S A M, Monaco /Stella Maritime S A /Explorer Maritime LLC
Tonnage (GRT): 24,318
Dimensions (length × beam × draught): 180.45 m (592 ft) × 25.50 m (83 ft 8 in) × 7.250 m (23 ft 9.5 in)
Constructor & Yard Number: Blohm und Voss GmbH, Hamburg, Germany.
  Yard No: 962
Motive Power: 4 × Wärtsilä 9L46C NSD diesel = 37,800 kW: 2 × Kamewa C/P propellers
Speed (knots): 27
Launched/Floated out: 19 May 2000
Christened by: Vangelis (Evangelos Odysseas Papathanassiou)
Passenger Decks: 8
Passengers/Crew Numbers (max.): 920 /353
Class: N/A
Registered: Nassau, Bahamas
Former Names: *OLYMPIA EXPLORER/ OLYMPIC EXPLORER*

(Copyright and courtesy Frans Tryens)

Ship: *FIFTY YEARS OF VICTORY*
(50 LET POBEDY)
IMO: 9152959
MMSI: 273316240
Callsign: UGYU
Operator: Rostatom State Nuclear Energy
Group/Russ Government, Moscow/
Quark Expeditions
Tonnage (GRT): 23,439
Dimensions (length × beam × draught):
159.60 m (523 ft 7 in) × 30 m (98 ft 5 in)
× 11.08 m (36 ft 4 in)
Constructor & Yard Number: Baltiskiy
Zavod, St Petersburg, Russia.
Yard No: 05705
Motive Power: 2 × OK-900A nuclear
reactors = 342M2; 3 × nuclear turbo
electric; 3 fixed propellers
Speed (knots): 21.4
Launched/Floated out: 29 December
1993
Passenger Cabins: 64
Passenger Decks: 6
Passengers/Crew Numbers (max.):
128/140
Class: Arktika nuclear icebreaker
Registered: St Petersburg, Russia
Former Names: *URAL*

(Courtesy Quark Expeditions)

Ship: *FINNMARKEN*
IMO: 9231951
MMSI: 259210000
Callsign: LDBE
Operator: Hurtigruten ASA, Narvik, Norway
Tonnage (GRT): 15,690
Dimensions (length × beam × draught):
18.509 m (456 ft) × 21.5 m (70 ft 6.5 in) ×
4.9 m 16 ft 1 in)
Constructor & Yard Number: Kvaerner
Kleven, Ulsteinvik, Norway. **Yard No:** 292
Motive Power: 4 × Wärtsilä 9L3/6L32
diesel = 13,838 kW; 2 C/P propellers;
2 × stabilizers, 3 × thrusters (2 × bow,
1 × stern)
Speed (knots): 18
Launched/Floated out: 15 September
2001
Christened by: Torhild Skogsholm
Passenger Cabins: 274
Passenger Decks: 7
Passengers/Crew Numbers (max.):
1,000/100
Class: Ro-Ro/Pax
Registered: Tromsø, Norway
Former Names: N/A

(Courtesy Hurtigruten ASA)

Ship: *FORMOSA QUEEN*
IMO: 7005190
MMSI: 530003398
Callsign: 3FLU9
Operator: Formosa Queen Corporation,
Taipei, Taiwan/Asia Star Cruise
Management Operations, Taipei,
Formosaø
Tonnage (GRT): 22,945
Dimensions (length × beam × draught):
194.32 m (637.53 ft) × 23.96 m (78.61 ft)
× 6.70 m (21.98 ft)
Constructor & Yard Number: Oy Wärtsilä
Ab, Vasa, Helsinki, Finland.
Yard No: 392
Motive Power: 4 × Sulzer-Wärtsilädiesel =
13,248 kW; 2 C/P propellers
Speed (knots): 18
Launched/Floated out: 2 December 1969
Christened by: Magnhild Borton
Passenger Cabins: 540
Passenger Decks: 5
Passengers/Crew Numbers (max.)
1196/423
Class: N/A
Registered: Panama City, Panama
Former Names: *SONG OF NORWAY/*
SUN DREAM/DREAM PRINCESS/
DREAM/CLIPPER PEARL/CLIPPER
PACIFIC/FESTIVAL/OCEAN PEARL

(Courtesy Formasa Queen Corporation,
Taipei)

Ship: *FRAM*
IMO: 9370018
MMSI: 258932000
Callsign: LADA7
Operator: Hurtigruten ASA, Narvik, Norway
Tonnage (GRT): 11,647
Dimensions (length × beam × draught):
114 m (374 ft) × 20.2 m (66 ft 3 in) × 5.1 m (16 ft 9 in)
Constructor & Yard Number: Fincantieri Monfalcone, Monfalcone, Italy.
Yard No: 6144
Motive Power: 4 × diesel-electric @1,973 kW; 2 × electrical motors = 2,310 kW directional propellers
Speed (knots): 16
Launched/Floated out: 18 November 2006
Christened by: Crown Princess Mette Marit of Norway
Passenger Cabins: 175
Passenger Decks: 8
Passengers/Crew Numbers (max.):
400/280
Class: Ice 1B
Registered: Tromsø, Norway
Former Names: N/A

(Courtesy Hurtigruten ASA)

Ship: *FREEWINDS*
IMO: 6810811
MMSI: 354993000
Callsign: H9CK
Operator: Flagship Service Organization, Willemstad, Curacao/San Donato Properties, Miami, Florida
Tonnage (GRT): 10,328
Dimensions (length × beam × draught): 134.32 m (440 ft 8 in) × 21.04 m (69 ft) × 5.74 m (18 ft 10 in)
Constructor & Yard Number: Wärtsilä Turku Shipyard, Turku, Finland.
Yard No: 1161
Motive Power: 2 × Wärtsilä-VASA 2SA8; 2 × D814KVV diesel = 10,444 kW; 2 propellers
Speed (knots): 20
Launched/Floated out: 12 February 1968
Christened by: Margareta Walllenius-Kleberg
Passenger Cabins: 290
Passenger Decks: 5
Passengers/Crew Numbers (max.): 380/280
Class: Finnhansa
Registered: Cartegena, Columbia
Former Names: *PRINS ALBERT/ BOHEME*

(Copyright Annelis)

Ship: *FTI BERLIN*
IMO: 7904889
MMSI: 248277000
Callsign: 9HA2295
Operator: Berlin Shipping Ltd, Munich, Germany/FTI Cruises, Munich, Germany
Tonnage (GRT): 9,570
Dimensions (length × beam × draught): 139.30 m (457 ft) × 17.52 m (57.5 ft0 × 4.8 m (15.7 ft)
Constructor & Yard Number: Howaldswerke Deutsche AG, Jiel, Germany.
Yard No: 163
Motive Power: 2 × MaK 12M453AK = 7,060 kW; 2 C/P propellers
Speed (knots): 18
Launched/Floated out: 12 January 1980
Christened by: Ute Wedemeier
Passenger Cabins: 206
Passenger Decks: 6
Passengers/Crew Numbers (max.): 470/168
Class: N/A
Registered: Valletta, Malta
Former Names: *BERLIN/PRINCESS MAHSURI/ORANGE MELODY/SPIRIT OF ADVENTURE*

(Copyright Berlin Shipping Ltd, Munich)

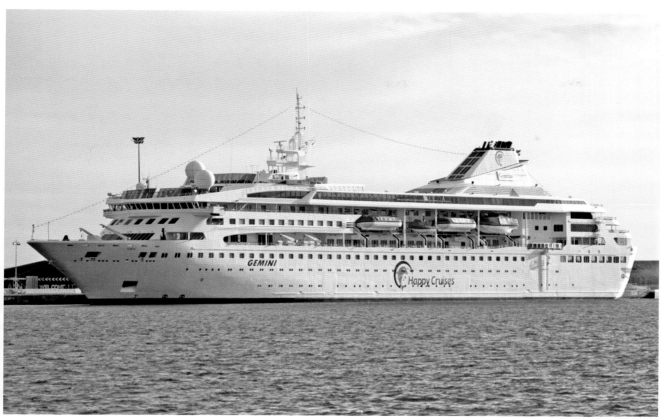

Ship: *GEMINI*
IMO: 9000687
MMSI: 352133000
Callsign: 3FLY7
Operator: Jewel Owner Ltd, Nassau, Bahamas/International Shipping, Miami
Tonnage (GRT): 19,093
Dimensions (length × beam × draught): 163.81 m (537 ft 5 in) × 22.5 m (73 ft 10 in) × 5.40 m (17 ft 9 in)
Constructor & Yard Number: Union Navale De Levante, Valencia, Spain.
Yard No: 197
Motive Power: 4 × Wärtsilä 8R32 diesels; 2 Kamewa C/P propellers; 2 × bow thrusters
Speed (knots): 19
Launched/Floated out: 30 May 1991
Christened by: Diana Ross
Passenger Cabins: 400
Passenger Decks: 7
Passengers/Crew Numbers (max.): 916/580
Class: Crown
Registered: Majuro, Marshall Islands
Former Names: *CROWN JEWEL/ CUNARD CROWN JEWEL/ SUPERSTAR GEMINI/VISION STAR*

(Copyright and courtesy Manuel Moreno)

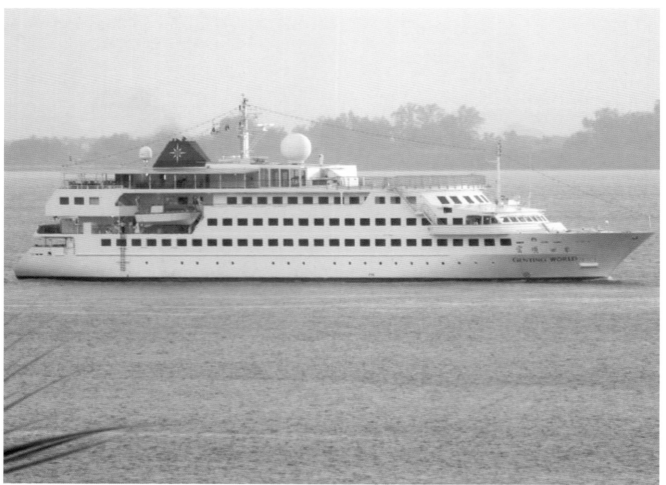

Ship: *GENTING WORLD*
IMO: 8705278
MMSI: 353013000
Callsign: 3FMD4
Operator: Star Cruises, Kuala Lumpur, Malaysia
Tonnage (GRT): 3,341
Dimensions (length × beam × draught): 85.3 m (279.7 ft) × 14 m (45.9 ft) × 3.3 m (10.7 ft)
Constructor & Yard Number: Flender Werft AG, Lübeck, Tyskland.
Yard No: 647
Motive Power: 2 × Klöckner-Humboldt Deutz TBD6048V16 = 3,356 kW; 1 × Rolls-Royce bow thruster; 2 × C/P propellers
Speed (knots): 19
Launched/Floated out: 7 April 1988
Passenger Cabins: 33
Passenger Decks: 5
Passengers/Crew Numbers (max.): 179/136
Class: N/A
Registered: Panama City, Panama
Former Names: *LADY DIANA/AURORA I/ MEGASTAR ARIES*

(Courtesy Star Cruises)

Ship: *GOLDEN IRIS*
IMO: 7358573
MMSI: 371771000
Callsign: CFZK4
Operator: Mano Maritime, Haifa, Israel/Mint Maritime Ltd, Marshall Islands
Tonnage (GRT): 17,095
Dimensions (length × beam × draught): 163.56 m (536 ft 7 in) × 22.84 m (75 ft) × 6.02 m (19 ft 9 in)
Constructor & Yard Number: Burmaister & Wain, Skibsbyggen A/S, Copenhagen, Denmark (Hull)/ Navali Mechaninche Afini, La Spezia, Italy (Machinery).
Yard No: 859
Motive Power: 2 × B&W 7U50HU diesel = 15,444 kW; 2 C/P propellers
Speed (knots): 21.5
Launched/Floated out: December 1976
Christened by: Princess Grace Of Monaco
Passenger Cabins: 405
Passenger Decks: 8
Passengers/Crew Numbers (max.): 959/350
Class: RINA
Registered: Panama City, Panama
Former Names: *CUNARD CONQUEST/ CUNARD PRINCESS/MSC RHAPSODY*

(Copyright and courtesy Manuel Moreno)

Ship: *HAMBURG*
IMO: 9138329
MMSI: 309908000
Callsign: C6OX6
Operator: Plantours GmbH Bremen, Germany
Tonnage (GRT): 15,067
Dimensions (length × beam × draught): 144 m (472 ft) × 22 m (72 ft) × 5.6 m (18 ft 4.5 in)
Constructor & Yard Number: Nordic Yards Wismar, Wismar, Germany.
Yard No: 451
Motive Power: Wärtsilä 6L32 diesel = 10,560 kW; Blohm und Voss stabilizers; 2 C/P propellers
Speed (knots): 18.5
Launched/Floated out: 30 October 1996
Christened by: Carol Veit
Passenger Cabins: 205
Passenger Decks: 6
Passengers/Crew Numbers (max.): 423/170
Class: N/A
Registered: Nassau, Bahamas
Former Names: *C. COLUMBUS*

(Copyright Trondheim Port Authority)

Ship: *HANSEATIC*
IMO: 9000168
MMSI: 309577000
Callsign: C6KA9
Operator: Hapag-Lloyd Cruises Ag, Hanover, Germany/Bunnys Adventure And Cruise Shipping Co. Ltd, Nassau, Bahamas
Tonnage (GRT): 8,378
Dimensions (length × beam × draught): 122.80 m (403 ft 7 in) × 18 m (55 ft 9 in) × 4.91 m (15 ft 9 in)
Constructor & Yard Number: Rauma Repola, Rauma, Finland.
Yard No: 306
Motive Power: MaK 8M453 diesel = 5,880 kW; 2 propellers; bow thrusters and stabilizers
Speed (knots): 16
Launched/Floated out: 5 January 1991
Christened by: Dagmar Berghoff
Passenger Cabins: 92
Passenger Decks: 6
Passengers/Crew Numbers (max.): 184/125
Class: Ice E4
Registered: Nassau, Bahamas
Former Names: *SOCIETY ADVENTURER*

(Courtesy Hapag-Lloyd, Cruises AG)

Ship: *HEBRIDEAN PRINCESS*
IMO: 6409351
MMSI: 232649000
Callsign: GNHV
Operator: Hebridean Island Cruises/ All Leisure Holidays Ltd
Tonnage (GRT): 2,112
Dimensions (length × beam × draught): 72 m (226 ft) × 14 m (46 ft) × 3 m (10 ft)
Constructor & Yard Number: Hall Russell & Co, Aberdeen, UK. Engines Crossley Brothers Ltd, Manchester, UK.
Yard No: 912
Motive Power: 2 × SCSA 8-cyl diesel = 1,790 kW; 2 × propellers; 1 × bow thruster
Speed (knots): 12
Launched/Floated out: 12 March 1964
Christened by: Lady Craigton
Passenger Cabins: 30
Passenger Decks: 5
Passengers/Crew Numbers (max.): 49/38
Class: N/A
Registered: Glasgow, UK
Former Names: *COLUMBIA*

(Copyright and courtesy Andrew Knox)

Ship: *ISLAND SKY*
IMO: 8802894
MMSI: 311743000
Callsign: C67Q2
Operator: Noble Caledonia, London/ Ship Management AB, Gothenburg, Sweden
Tonnage (GRT): 4,280
Dimensions (length × beam × draught): 90.6 m (297.2 ft) × 15.3 m (50.1 ft) × 2.95 m (12.9 ft)
Constructor & Yard Number: Nuovi Cantieri Apuania SpA, Carara, Italy. **Yard No:** 1147
Motive Power: 2 × MAN 8L28/32A-A10 diesel = 5,000 kW; 2 propellers
Speed (knots): 16
Launched/Floated out: 20 July 1991
Passenger Cabins: 61
Passenger Decks: 5
Passengers/Crew Numbers (max.): 116/71
Class: R (Regatta)
Registered: Nassau, Bahamas
Former Names: *RENAISSANCE EIGHT/ RENAI II/SKY*

(Courtesy Noble Caledonia)

Ship: *KAPITAN DRANITSYN*
IMO: 7824405
MMSI: 273138300
Callsign: UCJP
Operator: Murmansk Shipping Company
(Fesco), Murmansk, Russia/Quark
Expeditions
Tonnage (GRT): 19,919
Dimensions (length × beam × draught):
122.5 m (423.3 ft) × 26.54 m (87.1 ft) ×
8.50 m (27.9 in)
Constructor & Yard Number: Wärtsilä,
Helsinki New Shipyard, Helsinki, Finland.
Yard No: 413
Motive Power: 6 × Wärtsilä-Sulzer
9ZL40/48 diesels = 24,000 kW; 3 four-
bladed propellers
Speed (knots): 19
Launched/Floated out: 2 December 1980
Passenger Cabins: 53
Passenger Decks: 6
Passengers/Crew Numbers (max.):
113/90
Class: Ice RMRS LL3
Registered: Murmansk, Russia
Former Names: N/A

(Courtesy Quark Expeditions)

Ship: *KONG HARALD*
IMO: 9039119
MMSI: 257200000
Callsign: LGIY
Operator: Hurtigruten ASA, Narvik, Norway
Tonnage (GRT): 11,204
Dimensions (length × beam × draught):
 121.8 m (399 ft 7 in) × 19.2 m 63 ft) ×
 4.9 m (16 ft 1 in)
Constructor & Yard Number: Volkswerft
 GmbH/ P S Werten Stralsund, Stralsund,
 Germany.
Yard No: 101
Motive Power: 2 × Krupp MaK 6M552C
 diesel = 8991 kW;2 × C/P propellers
.**Speed (knots):** 18
Launched/Floated out: 28 November
 1992
Christened by: Hjordis Opseth
Passenger Cabins: 227
Passenger Decks: 6
Passengers/Crew Numbers (max.):
 490/60
Class: Ro-Ro/Pax
Registered: Tromsø, Norway
Former Names: N/A

(Courtesy Hurtigruten, ASA)

Ship: *KRISTINA KATARINA*
IMO: 7625811
MMSI: 230614000
Callsign: OJOH
Operator: Kristina Cruises, Kotka, Finland
Tonnage (GRT): 12,825
Dimensions (length × beam × draught):
    138 m (453 ft) × 22 m (72 ft) × 5.6 m
    (18.4 ft)
Constructor & Yard Number: Stocnia
    Szczecinska Imadolfa, Warskieo,
    Szczecin, Poland.
Yard No: 49203
Motive Power: 4 × Sulzer 6L2 40/48 diesel
    = 12,800 kW; 2 propellers; 1 × bow
    thruster
Speed (knots): 18
Launched/Floated out: 17 April 1981
Passenger Cabins: 231
Passenger Decks: 7
Passengers/Crew Numbers (max.):
    750/150
Class: N/A
Registered: Kotka, Finland
Former Names: *KONSTANTIN SIMINOV/*
    FRANCESCA/THE IRIS

(Courtesy and copyright Steven Macaskill)

Ship: *L'AUSTRAL*
IMO: 9502518
MMSI: 578000700
Callsign: FLTU
Operator: Ponant Cruises/Compagnie du Ponant, Marseille, France
Tonnage (GRT): 10,700
Dimensions (length × beam × draught): 142.10 m (467 ft) × 18 m (59 ft) × 4.70 m (15 ft 8.5 ft)
Constructor & Yard Number: Fincantieri Cantierie Navali Italiani SpA, Ancona, Italy.
Yard No: 6193
Motive Power: 4 × Wärtsilä 8L20 diesel = 6,400 kW; 2 × ABB @ 2,300 kW; 1 × Rolls-Royce bow thruster @ 800 kW; 2 propellers
Speed (knots): 18.5
Launched/Floated out: 8 April 2011
Christened by: Florence Rousset
Passenger Cabins: 132
Passenger Decks: 6
Passengers/Crew Numbers (max.): 264/136
Class: N/A
Registered: Mata-Utu, Wallis and Futuna Islands
Former Names: N/A

(Courtesy Ponant Cruises)

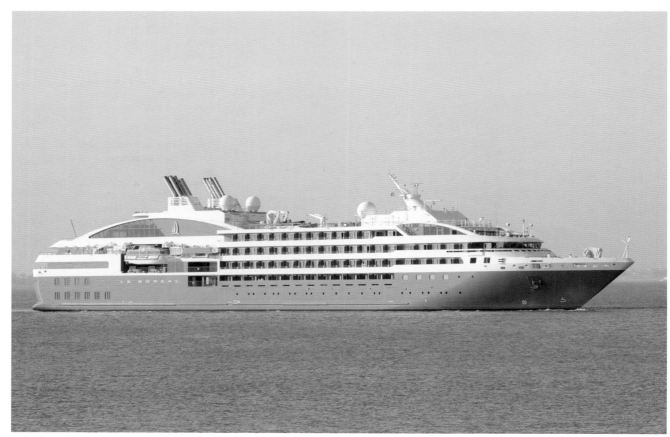

Ship: *LE BOREAL*
IMO: 9502506
MMSI: 578000500
Callsign: FLSY
Operator: Ponant Cruises/Compagnie du Ponant, Marseille, France
Tonnage (GRT): 10,700
Dimensions (length × beam × draught): 142.10 m (467 ft) × 18 m (59 ft) × 4.70 m (15 ft 8.5 in)
Constructor & Yard Number: Fincantieri Canatieri Navali Italiani SpA, Ancona, Italy.
Yard No: 6192
Motive Power: 4 × Wärtsilä 8L20 diesel = 6,400 kW; 2 ABB @ 2,300 kW; 1 × Rolls-Royce bow thruster @ 800 kW; 2 propellers
Speed (knots): 18.5
Launched/Floated out: 1 May 2009
Christened by: Veronique Saade
Passenger Cabins: 132
Passenger Decks: 6
Passengers/Crew Numbers (max.): 264/136
Class: N/A
Registered: Mata-Utu, Wallis and Futuna Islands
Former Names: N/A

(Courtesy Ponant Cruises)

Ship: *LEISURE WORLD*
IMO: 6921828
MMSI: 572282000
Callsign: T2LE2
Operator: New Century Tours Corporation
Pte Ltd, Singapore
Tonnage (GRT): 15,653
Dimensions (length × beam × draught):
161 m (528 ft) × 23 m (74 ft) × 7 m
(23 ft ft)
Constructor & Yard Number: AG Weser,
Bremerhaven, Germany.
Yard No: 942
Motive Power: 2 × MAN V8V 40/54 =
12,789 kW; 2 propellers
Speed (knots): 16
Launched/Floated out: 28 June 1969
Christened by: Lin Arrison
Passenger Cabins: N/A
Passenger Decks: 6
Passengers/Crew Numbers (max.):
850/250
Class: Casino ship
Registered: Tuvalu, Marshall Islands
Former Names: *SKYWARD/SHANGRI-
LA WORLD/ASEAN WORLD/FANTASY
WORLD/CONTINENTAL WORLD*

*(Courtesy New Century Tours Corporation,
Singapore)*

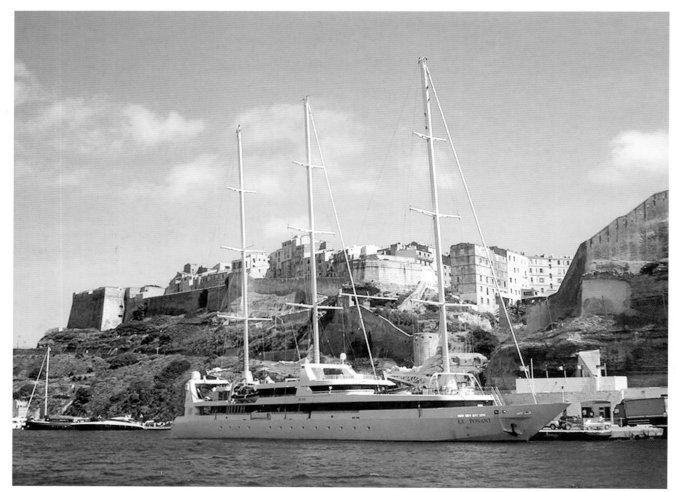

Ship: *LE PONANT*
IMO: 8914219
MMSI: 227186000
Callsign: FGZZ
Operator: Ponant Cruises/Compagnie du Ponant, Marsaille, France
Tonnage (GRT): 1,489
Dimensions (length × beam × draught): 88 m (288 ft 9 in) × 12 m (39 ft 4 in) × 4 m (13 ft 1 in)
Constructor & Yard Number: Française de Construction Navale, Villeneuve la Garenne, France.
Motive Power: 3 masts = 1,500 m² (16,140 sq ft) sail area; 1 Deutz AG Werk, Mannheim 1,680 kW; 1 propeller
Speed (knots): 14/6
Launched/Floated out: 1 January 1991
Christened by: March Pajot, Marie-Claire Pauwels, Jen-Louis Foulquier, Bernard Giraudeau, Régis Faucon, Bernard Mabille
Passenger Cabins: 32
Passenger Decks: 3
Passengers/Crew Numbers (max.): 67/30
Class: N/A
Registered: Mata-Utu, Wallis and Futuna Islands
Former Names: N/A

(Courtesy Ponant Cruises/Philip Plisson)

Ship: *LE SOLEAL*
IMO: 9641675
MMSI: 316006887
Callsign: FLSY
Operator: Ponant Cruises/Compagnie du Ponant, Marseille, France
Tonnage (GRT): 10,944
Dimensions (length × beam × draught): 142.10 m (467 ft) × 18 m (59 ft) × 4.70 m (15 ft 8.5 in)
Constructor & Yard Number: Fincantieri Canatieri Navali Italian SpA, Ancona, Italy.
Yard No: 6229
Motive Power: 4 × Wärtsilä 8L20 diesel = 6,400 kW; 2 ABB @ 2,300 kW; 1 × Rolls-Royce bow thruster @ 800 kW; 2 propellers
Speed (knots): 18.5
Launched/Floated out: 6 December 2012
Passenger Staterooms/Cabins: 132
Passenger Decks: 6
Passengers/Crew Numbers (max.): 264/136
Class: N/A
Registered: Mata-Utu, Wallis and Futuna Islands
Former Names: N/A

(Courtesy Ponant Cruises)

Ship: *LOFOTEN*
IMO: 5424562
MMSI: 258477000
Callsign: LIXN
Operator: Hurtigruten ASA, Narvik, Norway
Tonnage (GRT): 2,621
Dimensions (length × beam × draught):
    87.4 m (286 ft 9 in) × 13 m (42 ft 8 in) ×
    4.6 m (15 ft 1 in)
Constructor & Yard Number: Akers Verft,
    Oslo, Norway.
Yard No: 547
Motive Power: 1 × B&W 742 DM VT 2BF-
    90 diesel = 2445 kW
Speed (knots): 15
Launched/Floated out: 7 September
    1963
Christened by: Asbjorn Bergsmo
Passenger Cabins: 67
Passenger Decks: 5
Passengers/Crew Numbers (max.):
    410/40
Class: Ro-Ro/Pax
Registered: Tromsø, Norway
Former Names: N/A

(Courtesy of Hurtigruten, ASA)

Ship: *LORD OF THE GLENS*
IMO: 8966470
MMSI: 23500295
Callsign: ZQOE9
Operator: Magna Carta Steamship
    Company Ltd, London
Tonnage (GRT): 729
Dimensions (length × beam × draught):
    45 m (147 ft 9 in) × 10.48 m (30 ft 4.5 in)
    × 2.7 m (8 ft 10 in)
Constructor & Yard Number: Greece
Motive Power: 2 Cummins Marine V12kt-
    38-m = 588 kW
Speed (knots): 11.2
Launched/Floated out: 1985
Passenger Cabins: 27
Passenger Decks: 4
Passengers/Crew Numbers (max.):
    54/18
Class: N/A
Registered: Inverness, UK
Former Names: *VICTORIA/VICTORIA II*

(Copyright and courtesy Andrew Knox)

Ship: *LOUIS CRISTAL*
IMO: 7827213
MMSI: 240695000
Callsign: SWQ1
Operator: Louis Cruise Lines
Tonnage (GRT): 25,611
Dimensions (length × beam × draught): 158.88 m (521 ft 3 in) × 25.20 m (82 ft 8 in) × 5.60 m (18 ft 4 in)
Constructor & Yard Number: Wärtsilä, Turku, Finland.
Yard No: 1247
Motive Power: Pielstick diesel = 19,120 kW; 2 propellers, 2 bow thrusters, 1 stern thruster
Speed (knots): 19
Launched/Floated out: 4 January 1980
Christened by: Liza Minnelli
Passenger Cabins: 476
Passenger Decks: 9
Passengers/Crew Numbers (max.): 1,409/400
Class: N/A
Registered: Nassau, Bahamas
Former Names: *VIKING SAGA/SALLY ALBATROSS/LEEWARD/SUPERSTART TAURUS/SIJA OPERA/OPERA*

(Courtesy Louis Cruise Lines)

Ship: *LOUIS MAJESTY*
IMO: 8814744
MMSI: 248124000
Callsign: C60Y4
Operator: Louis Cruise Lines
Tonnage (GRT): 40,876
Dimensions (length × beam × draught):
207.1 m (679 ft) × 32.3 m (106 ft ft) × 14
m (45 ft 11 in)
Constructor & Yard Number: Wärtsilä
Marine Turku Shipyard, Turku, Finland /
Kvaenner Masa Yard, Finland.
Yard No: 1312
Motive Power: 4 × Wärtsilä 6R46 diesel =
21,120 kW; 2 × C/P propellers
Speed (knots): 20.5
Launched/Floated out: 15 November
1991
Christened by: Liza Minnelli
Passenger Cabins: 730
Passenger Decks: 9
Passengers/Crew Numbers (max.):
1,970/620
Class: Ice 1A Super
Registered: Valletta, Malta
Former Names: *BIRKA QUEEN/ROYAL
MAJESTY/NORWEGIAN MAJESTY/
THOMSON MAJESTY*

(Courtesy Louis Cruise Lines)

Ship: *LOUIS OLYMPIA*
IMO: 7927984
MMSI: 209691000
Callsign: P3US9
Operator: Louis Cruise Lines, Cyprus
Tonnage (GRT): 37,773
Dimensions (length × beam × draught):
214.51 m (703 ft 9 in) × 28.41 m (93 ft
3 in) × 6.8 m (22 ft 4 in).
Constructor & Yard Number: Wärtsilä
Hietalahti, Helsinki, Finland.
Yard No: 431
Motive Power: 4 × Sulzer-Wärtsilä diesel =
17,060 kW; 2 propellers
Speed (knots): 21
Launched/Floated out: 26 November
1981
Christened by: Beverly Sills
Passenger Cabins: 725
Passenger Decks: 12
Passengers/Crew Numbers (max.):
1664/540
Class: N/A
Registered: Limassol, Cyprus
Former Names: *SONG OF AMERICA/
SUNBIRD/THOMSON DESTINY*

(Copyright Frans Trugens)

Ship: *MARCO POLO II*
IMO: 6447097
MMSI: 308693000
Callsign: C6J27
Operator: Cruise & Maritime Voyages,
  Dartford, Kent, UK/ Global Maritime,
  Houston, Texas, USA
Tonnage (GRT): 22,080
Dimensions (length × beam × draught):
  176.28 m (578 ft 35 in) × 23.55 m (77 ft
  26 in) × 8.20 m (26.9 ft)
Constructor & Yard Number: VEB
  Mathias-Thesen Werft, Wismar, Germany.
  Yard No: 126
Motive Power: 2 × Sulzer-Cegielski
  7RND76 diesels = 15,447 kW; 2
  propellers
Speed (knots): 16.5
Launched/Floated out: 26 April 1964
Passenger Cabins: 425
Passenger Decks: 8
Passengers/Crew Numbers (max.):
  820/356
Class: Ivan Franko
Registered: Nassau, Bahamas
Former Names: *ALEXANDR PUSHKIN*

(Copyright Cruise & Maritime Voyages)

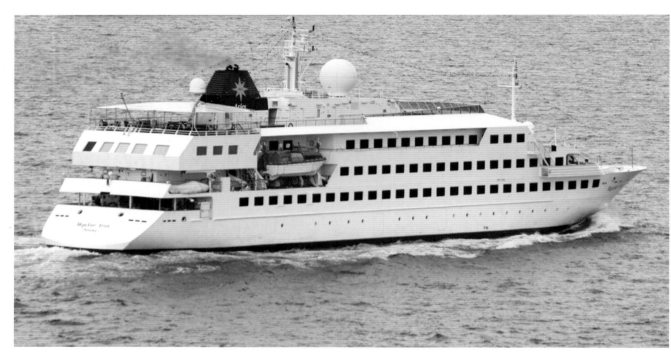

Ship: *MEGASTAR TAURUS*
IMO: 8705266
MMSI: 354264000
Callsign: 3FPT4
Operator: Star Cruises, Kuala Lumpur, Malaysia
Tonnage (GRT): 3,341
Dimensions (length × beam × draught): 85.3 m (279.7 ft) × 14 m (45.9 ft) × 3.3 m (10.7 ft)
Constructor & Yard Number: Flender Werft AG, Lübeck, Tyskland.
Yard No: 648
Motive Power: 2 × Klöckner-Humboldt Deutz TBD6048V16 = 3,356 kW; 1 × Rolls-Royce bow thruster; 2 × C/P propellers
Speed (knots): 19
Launched/Floated out: 24 February 1989
Passenger Cabins: 33
Passenger Decks: 5
Passengers/Crew Numbers (max.): 179/136
Class: N/A
Registered: Panama City, Panama
Former Names: *LADY SARA/AURORA II*

(Courtesy Star Cruises)

Ship: *MIDNATSOL*
IMO: 9247728
MMSI: 258595000
Callsign: LMDH
Operator: Hurtigruten ASA, Narvik, Norway
Tonnage (GRT): 16,151
Dimensions (length × beam × draught):
  135.70 m (445 ft 2.5 in) × 21.50 m 70 ft
  6.5 in) × 5.1 m (16 ft 9 in)
Constructor & Yard Number: Fosen
  Mekanisk Verksteder, Rissa, Norway.
Yard No: 73
Motive Power: 2 × Wärtsilä 9L32 and 2 ×
  Wärtsilä 6L32 diesel = 13,800 kW; 2 C/P
  propellers; 2 bow thrusters
Speed (knots): 18
Launched/Floated out: 26 April 2002
Christened by: Rut Brandt
Passenger Cabins: 291
Passenger Decks: 9
Passengers/Crew Numbers (max.):
  1000/150
Class: N/A
Registered: Tromsø, Norway
Former Names: N/A

(Courtesy Hurtigruten ASA)

Ship: *MINERVA*
IMO: 9144196
MMSI: 309477000
Callsign: C6NP5
Operator: Swan Hellenic Cruises, Burgess Hill, Sussex, UK
Tonnage (GRT): 12,892
Dimensions (length × beam × draught): 135.1 m (436.3 ft) × 16.6 m (65.6 ft) × 5.8 m (19 ft)
Constructor & Yard Number: Okean, Oktyabrskoye Nikolayev, Ukraine/Mariotti, Genoa, Italy.
Yard No: 001/595
Motive Power: 2 × MAN-B+W PO2-6E diesel = 3,480 kW; 2 C/P propellers; stabilizers
Speed (knots): 14
Launched/Floated out: 1989
Christened by: HRH Duchess of Gloucester
Passenger Cabins: 178
Passenger Decks: 6
Passengers/Crew Numbers (max.): 350/160
Class: N/A
Registered: Nassau, Bahamas
Former Names: *OKEAN/ALEXANDER VON HUMBOLDT/EXPLORER II/SAGA PEARL*

(Courtesy Swan Hellenic Cruises)

Ship: *MSC MELODY*
IMO: 7902295
MMSI: 353157000
Callsign: 3FB7
Operator: Lotus Mine, South Korea/China International Travel Service, Beijing, China
Tonnage (GRT): 35,143
Dimensions (length × beam × draught): 204.81 m (670 ft 11 in) × 27.36 m (89 ft 9 in) × 7.80 m (25 ft 7 in)
Constructor & Yard Number: CNIM, La Seyne, France.
Yard No: 1432
Motive Power: 2 × 10-cyl GMT-FIAT = 22,070 kW; 2 propellers
Speed (knots): 23
Launched/Floated out: 9 January 1981
Christened by: Sophia Loren
Passenger Cabins: 549
Passenger Decks: 9
Passengers/Crew Numbers (max.): 1600/535
Class: N/A
Registered: Panama City, Panama
Former Names: *ATLANTIC/STARSHIP ATLANTIC/MELODY*

(Copyright Arno Esturhuizen)

Ship: *NATIONAL GEOGRAPHIC ENDEAVOUR*
IMO: 6611863
MMSI: 308182000
Callsign: C6BE4
Operator: Lindblad Expeditions, New York, NY/Etica, Guayaquil, Ecuador
Tonnage (GRT): 3,132
Dimensions (length × beam × draught): 89.20 m (292.6 ft) × 14.03 m (46 ft) × 6.6 m (20.5 ft)
Constructor & Yard Number: AG Weser, Seebeckwerft, Bremen, Germany.
Yard No: 917
Motive Power: 2 × MaK 8M582AK diesel @ 1,618 kW; 1 propeller
Speed (knots): 11.5
Launched/Floated out: June 1966
Christened by: Pamela Fingleton
Passenger Cabins: 67
Passenger Decks: 6
Passengers/Crew Numbers (max.): 96/64
Class: Boutique ship
Registered: Guayaquil, Ecuador
Former Names: *MARBURG/ LINDA R/ LINDMAR/NORTH STAR/CALEDONIAN STAR/ENDEAVOUR*

(Courtesy and copyright Lindblad Expeditions/Michael S. Nolan)

Ship: *NAUTICA*
IMO: 9200938
MMSI: 538001665
Callsign: V7DM4
Operator: Oceania Cruises, Miami, Florida, USA
Tonnage (GRT): 30,277
Dimensions (length × beam × draught): 181 m (593 ft 10 in) × 25.46 m (83 ft 6 in) × 5.95 m (19 ft 6 in)
Constructor & Yard Number: Chantiers de l'Atlantique, St Nazaire, France.
Yard No: P31
Motive Power: 4 × Wärtsilä 12V32 diesel = 13,500 kW; 2 propellers
Speed (knots): 18
Launched/Floated out: 31 July 1999
Christened by: Fana Holtz
Passenger Cabins: 342
Passenger Decks: 9
Passengers/Crew Numbers (max.): 824/386
Class: Regatta
Registered: Majuro, Marshall Islands
Former Names: *R-FIVE/BLUE DREAM*

(Courtesy Oceania Cruises, Miami)

Ship: *NORDKAPP*
IMO: 9107772
MMSI: 259330000
Callsign: LASQ
Operator: Hurtigruten Group ASA, Narvik, Norway
Tonnage (GRT): 11,386
Dimensions (length × beam × draught): 123.30 m (404.53 ft) × 19.50 m (63.98 ft) × 4.9 m (16.08 ft)
Constructor & Yard Number: Kvaener-Kleven Verft Ulsteinvik, Norway.
Yard No: 265
Motive Power: 2 × MaK 6M552C, 6-Cyl diesel = 9,000 kW; 2 propellers; bow thrusters
Speed (knots): 18
Launched/Floated out: 18 August 1995
Christened by: Queen Sonja of Norway
Passenger Cabins: 490
Passenger Decks: 6
Passengers/Crew Numbers (max.): 479/69
Class: Nordkapp
Registered: Narvik, Norway
Former Names: N/A

(Courtesy Hurtigruten ASA)

Ship: *NORDLYS*
IMO: 9048914
MMSI: 259139000
Callsign: LHCW
Operator: Hurtigruten ASA, Narvik, Norway
Tonnage (GRT): 11,204
Dimensions (length × beam × draught):
121.8 m (399 ft 7 in) × 19.2 m (63 ft) ×
4.9 m (16 ft 1 in)
Constructor & Yard Number: Volkswerft
GmbH/ P + S Werten Stralsund, Stralsund
GmbH, Germany. **Yard No:** 102
Motive Power: 2 × Krupp MaK 6M552C
diesel = 8991 kW; 2 × Kamewa C/P
propellers
Speed (knots): 18
Launched/Floated out: 13 August 1993
Christened by: Kirsti Kolle Grøndahl
Passenger Cabins: 224
Passenger Decks: 7
Passengers/Crew Numbers (max.): 691/
55
Class: Ro-Ro/Pax
Registered: Tromsø, Norway
Former Names: N/A

(Courtesy Hurtigruten ASA)

Ship: *NORDNORGE*
IMO: 9107784
MMSI: 259371000
Callsign: 3YGW
Operator: Hurtigruten Group ASA, Narvik, Norway
Tonnage (GRT): 11,286
Dimensions (length × beam × draught): 123.30 m (404.53 ft) × 19.50 m (63.98 ft) × 4.9 m (16.08 ft)
Constructor & Yard Number: Kvaerner-Kleven Verft Ulsteinvik, Norway.
Yard No: 266
Motive Power: 2 × MaK 6M552C, 6-Cyl diesel = 9,000 kW; 2 propellers
Speed (knots): 18
Launched/Floated out: 6 July 1996
Christened by: Sissei Ronbeck
Passenger Cabins: 490
Passenger Decks: 6
Passengers/Crew Numbers (max.): 6911/57
Class: Nordkapp
Registered: Narvik, Norway
Former Names: N/A

(Courtesy Hurtigruten ASA)

Ship: *OCEAN COUNTESS*
IMO: 7358561
MMSI: 255724000
Callsign: CQRH
Operator: Maximus Navigation Ltd,
  Madeira/Cruise & Maritime Voyages,
  Dartford, Kent
Tonnage (GRT): 17,593
Dimensions (length × beam × draught):
  163 m (537 ft) × 22 m (75 ft) × 6.3 m
  (20 ft 8 in)
Constructor & Yard Number: Burmeister
  & Wain, Copenhagen, Denmark (hull)/
  Navali Meccaniche Affini, La Spezia, Italy.
Yard No: 858
Motive Power: 4 × B&W 7U50HU diesel =
  15.447 kW; 2 propellers
Speed (knots): 18.5
Launched/Floated out: 20 September
  1974
Christened by: Mrs Janet Armstrong
Passenger Cabins: 400
Passenger Decks: 7
Passengers/Crew Numbers (max.):
  800/350
Class: N/A
Registered: Funchal, Madeira, Portugal
Former Names: *CUNARD COUNTESS/
  AWANI DREAM II/OLYMPIA
  COUNTESS/OLYMPIC COUNTESS/LILI
  MARLEEN/RUBY*

(Courtesy Majestic International Cruises Inc.)

Ship: *OCEAN DIAMOND*
IMO: 7325629
MMSI: 578101000
Callsign: FMAQ
Operator: Quark Expeditions, Waterbury, Vermont, USA/CMA CGM, Marseille, France
Tonnage (GRT): 8,282
Dimensions (Length × Beam × Draught): 124.19 m (407.4 ft) × 16.03 m (52.6 ft) × 4.9 m (16 ft)
Constructor & Yard Number: Kristiansand N/V A/S, Mekaniske Verksted, Kristiansund, Norway.
Yard No: 220
Motive Power: 4 × Wichmann Motorfabrik WX 28V10 = 2150 kW; 2 × CP propellers
Speed (knots): 14.5
Launched/Floated out: 1 February 1974
Passenger Cabins: 99
Passenger Decks: 6
Passengers/Crew Numbers (max.): 198/140
Class: Ice 1D
Registered: Nassau, Bahamas
Former Names: *BEGONIA/FERNHILL/ EXPLORER STARSHIP/SONG OF FLOWER/LE DIAMANT*

(Courtesy Quark Expeditions)

Ship: *OCEAN DREAM*
IMO: 7915096
MMSI: 256666000
Callsign: 9H2Y8
Operator: Peace Boat, Shinjuku, Tokyo, Japan
Tonnage (GRT): 36,265
Dimensions (length × beam × draught):
 204.76 m (671 ft 9 I) × 26.4 m (86 ft 9 in) × 7 m (23 ft)
Constructor & Yard Number: Aalborg Vaerft, Alborg, Denmark.
Yard No: 234
Motive Power: 2 × Sulzer 7RND68m diesel = 19,560 kW; 2 × C/P propellers
Speed (knots): 21
Launched/Floated out: 31 October 1980
Christened by: Sarah Davies
Passenger Cabins: 511
Passenger Decks: 10
Passenger/Crew Numbers (max.):
 1,412/550
Class: RINA
Registered: Valletta, Malta
Former Names: *TROPICALE/COSTA TROPICALE/PACIFIC STAR*

(Courtesy Pulmantur)

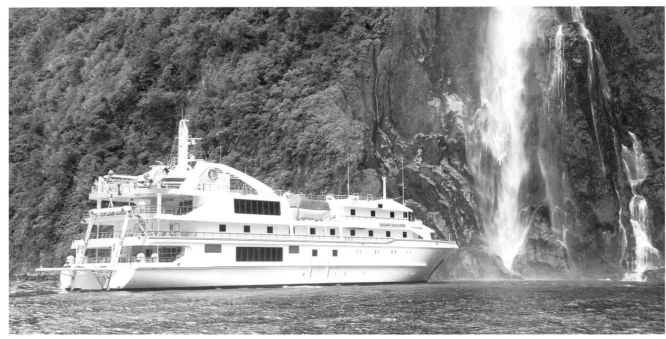

Ship: *OCEANIC DISCOVERER*
IMO: 9292747
MMSI: 503492000
Callsign: VMQ8808
Operator: Coral Princess Cruises, Cairns, Queensland, Australia
Tonnage (GRT): 1,838
Dimensions (length × beam × draught): 63.02 m (206 ft 9 in) × 13 m (42 ft 8 in) × 3 m (9 ft 10 in)
Constructor & Yard Number: NQEA (North Queensland Engineers And Agents) Australian Pty, Cairns (AIMTEK). Yard No: 220
Motive Power: 2 × Caterpillar BRN diesel = 2,236 kW; 2 F/P propellers
Speed (knots): 14
Launched/Floated out: January 1988
Christened by: Vicki Briggs
Passenger Cabins: 36
Passenger Decks: 4
Passengers/Crew Numbers (max.): 72/25
Class: N/A
Registered: Cairns, Australia
Former Names: *OCEANIC PRINCESS*

(Courtesy Coral Princess Cruises)

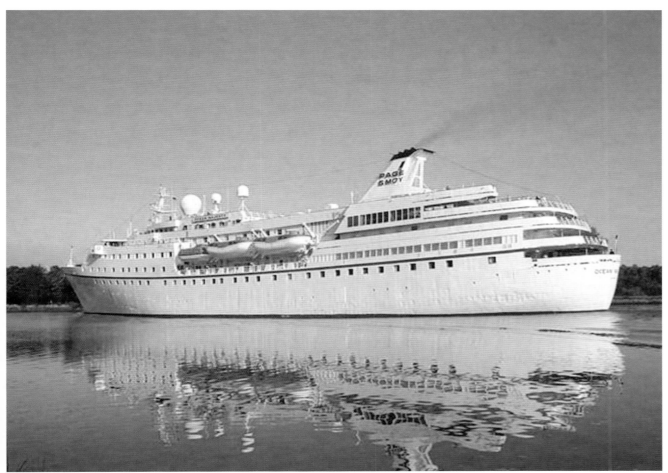

Ship: *OCEAN MAJESTY*
IMO: 6602898
MMSI: 255717000
Callsign: CQSC
Operator: Majestic International/Hansa Touristik, Bremen
Tonnage (GRT): 10,417
Dimensions (length × beam × draught): 135 m (443 ft) × 15. 8m (52 ft) × 6.2 m (20 ft 4 in)
Constructor & Yard Number: Union Naval de Levante. **Yard No:** 498
Motive Power: 2 × Wärtsilä 1V32D diesel = 13,200 kW; 2 propellers
Speed (knots): 18
Launched/Floated out: 4 December 1965
Christened by: Lady Carmen Delgado
Passenger Cabins: 274
Passenger Decks: 8
Passengers/Crew Numbers (max.): 621/257
Class: ABS
Registered: Madeira, Portugal
Former Names: *JUAN MARCH/SOL CHRISTINA/KYPROS STAR/OCEAN MAJESTY/HOMERIC*

(Courtesy Majestic International)

Ship: *OCEAN PRINCESS*
IMO: 9187899
MMSI: 310505000
Callsign: ZCDS4
Operator: Princess Cruises Line, Valencia, California, USA
Tonnage (GRT): 30,277
Dimensions (length × beam × draught): 181 m (593 ft 10 in) × 25.46 m (83 ft 6 in) × 5.80 m (19 ft0
Constructor & Yard Number: Chantiers de l'Atlantique, Nantes, St Nazaire, France.
Yard No: O31
Motive Power: 4 × Wärtsilä 12V32 diesel = 18,600 kW; 2 × F/P propellers
Speed (knots): 18
Launched/Floated out: 24 December 2002
Christened by: Virtual christening on-line by donors December 1999
Passenger Cabins: 344
Passenger Decks: 9
Passengers/Crew Numbers (max.): 826/373
Class: Regatta
Registered: Hamilton, Bermuda
Former Names: *4-FOUR/TAHITIAN PRINCESS*

(Copyright Pjor Mahhonin)

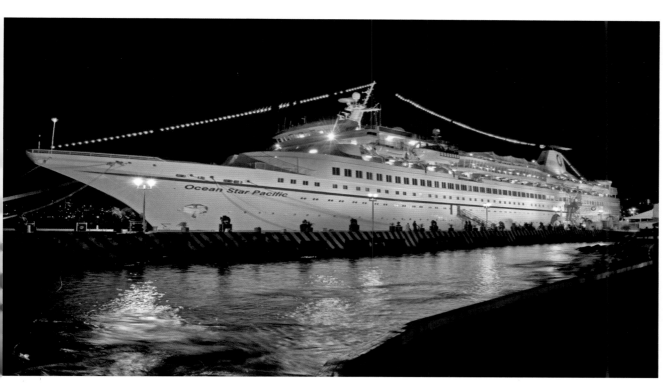

Ship: *OCEAN STAR PACIFIC*
IMO: 7027411
MMSI: 356643000
Callsign: 3FCR
Operator: ALAS/PV Enterprises
    International inc. Fort Lauderdale,
    FLORIDA/Peter Villiotis
Tonnage (GRT): 23,149
Dimensions (length × beam × draught):
    193.65 m (635.3 ft) × 24.01 m (78.8 ft) ×
    6.72 m (22 ft)
Constructor & Yard Number: Oy Wärtsilä
    Ab, Helsinki New Shipyard, Helsinki,
    Finland.
Yard No: 393
Motive Power: 4 × Wärtsilä-Sulzer
    9ZH40/48 diesel = 14,560 kW; 2 C/P
    propellers
Speed (knots): 17.5
Launched/Floated out: 9 July 1970
Christened by: Ingrid Bergman
Passenger Cabins: 525
Passenger Decks: 7
Passengers/Crew Numbers (max.):
    1,231/ 432
Class: N/A
Registered: Panama City, Panama
Former Names: *NORDIC PRINCE/
    CAROUSEL/AQUAMARINE/ARIELLE/
    AQUAMARINE*

(Courtesy Ocean Star Cruises)

Ship: *ORIENT QUEEN*
IMO: 6821080
MMSI: 538003557
Callsign: 9HA2738
Operator: Louis Cruises Cyprus, Nicosia, Cyprus/Teal Shipping, Greece/Abou Merhi Cruises, Beirut, Lebanon
Tonnage (GRT): 15,781
Dimensions (length × beam × draught): 160.30 m (525.9 ft) × 22.84 m (74.9 ft) × 6.86 m (22.5 ft)
Constructor & Yard Number: Seebeckwerft/AG Weser, Bremerhaven, Germany.
Yard No: 288
Motive Power: 2 × MAN V8V40/54 diesel – 12,784 kW; 2 × C/P propellers; 6 × Bergen auxiliary engines; 1 bow thruster
Speed (knots): 17
Launched/Floated out: 21 June 1968
Passenger Cabins: 370
Passenger Decks: 7
Passengers/Crew Numbers (max.): 850/400
Class: N/A
Registered: Valletta, Malta
Former Names: *STARWARD/BOLERO*

(Courtesy Louis Cruises)

Ship: *ORIENT QUEEN*
IMO: 8701193
MMSI: 373703000
Callsign: 3FDJ9
Operator: Orient Queen Shipping Ltd, Valletta, Malta/A Boumerhi Cruises, Beirut, Lebanon
Tonnage (GRT): 7,478
Dimensions (length × beam × draught): 120.8 m (396 ft) × 16.7 m (55 ft) × 4.9 m (14 ft 9 in)
Constructor & Yard Number: Union Naval Valencia, Valencia, Spain. **Yard No:** C175
Motive Power: 2 × Wärtsilä Iberica S.A. 12V22HF-D diesel @1,950 kW; 2 × C/P propellers
Speed (knots): 16.5
Launched/Floated out: 1 December 1988
Passenger Cabins: 152
Passenger Decks: 6
Passengers/Crew Numbers (max.): 320/110
Class: RINA
Registered: Panama City, Panama
Former Names: *VISTAMAR*

(Courtesy Louis Cruise Lines)

Ship: *ORIENTAL DRAGON*
IMO: 7125861
MMSI: 353669000
Callsign: 3FDZ8
Operator: Capital Dragon Global Holdings
Ltd, Hong Kong, China/Oceanic Group
(International) Ltd, Hong Kong, China
Tonnage (GRT): 18,455
Dimensions (length × beam × draught):
171.69 m (563 ft 3.5 in) × 23.98 m (78 ft
8 in) × 6.7 m (22 ft)
Constructor & Yard Number: Oy Wärtsilä
AB, Helsinki, Finland.
Yard No: 394
Motive Power: 4 × Wärtsilä 9ZH 40/48 –
14,560 kW; 2 C/P propellers
Speed (knots): 20.5
Launched/Floated out: 27 November
1971
Passenger Cabins: 271
Passenger Decks: 8
Passengers/Crew Numbers (max.):
600/300
Class: N/A
Registered: Panama City, Panama
Former Names: *SUN VIKING/*
SUPERSTAR SAGITTARIUS/HYUNDAI
PONGNAE/ PONGNAE/OMAR III/
LONG JIE

(Courtesy Daniel Chui, Oceanic Group)

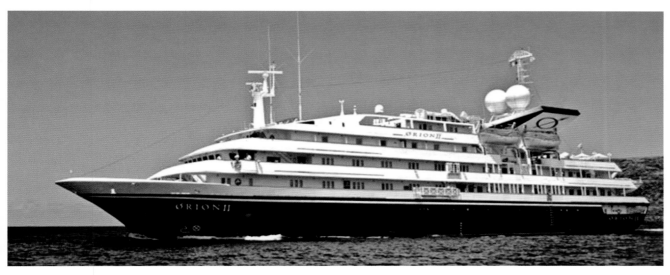

Ship: *ORION II*
IMO: 9273076
MMSI: 311603000
Callsign: C6TE3
Operator: Explorer Maritime/KSL Capital
Partners, Denver, USA
Tonnage (GRT): 3,984
Dimensions (length × beam × draught):
103 m (338 ft) × 14.25 m (46 ft 9 in) ×
3.83 m (12.6 in)
Constructor & Yard Number: Cassens
Shipyard, Emden Germany.
Yard No: 236
Motive Power: 1 × MaK 8M25 diesel
= 3,2K65 kW; bow & stern thrusters;
Blohm und Voss stabilizers; 1 c/p
propeller
Speed (knots): 15
Launched/Floated out: 1 November 2003
Christened by: SaRINA Bratton/Jill
Bennette/Laurel Norris/ Shirley Turtie
Passenger Cabins: 53
Passenger Decks: 5
Passengers/Crew Numbers (max.):
120/75
Class: N/A
Registered: Majuro, Marshall Islands
Former Names: N/A

(Courtesy of Orion Expeditions)

Ship: *PAUL GAUGUIN*
IMO: 9111319
MMSI: 311652000
Callsign: C6TH9
Operator: Paul Gauguin Cruises/Pacific Beachcomber, Taihiti
Tonnage (GRT): 19,170
Dimensions (length × beam × draught): 153.66 m (513.4 ft) × 21.60 m (72 ft) × 5.2 m (16.8 ft)
Constructor & Yard Number: Chantiers de l'Atlantique, Nantes, St Nazaire, France.
Yard No: G31
Motive Power: 2 × MAN 6L32ST diesel & 2 × MAN 9L32 diesel = 17.846 kW; 2 propellers
Speed (knots): 18
Launched/Floated out: 25 April 1996
Christened by: Carole Pdylo
Passenger Cabins: 165
Passenger Decks: 7
Passengers/Crew Numbers (max.): 332/211
Class: N/A
Registered: Nassau, Bahamas
Former Names: N/A

(Courtesy Paul Gauguin Cruises)

Ship: *PEARL MIST*
IMO: 9412701
MMSI: 316013870
Callsign: ANCDE
Operator: Pearl Seas Cruises, Guildford, Connecticut, USA
Tonnage (GRT): 8,700
Dimensions (length × beam × draught): 102.10 m (335 ft) × 17.06 m (56 ft) × 3.657 m (12 ft)
Constructor & Yard Number: Irving Shipbuilding, Shelburne Shipyard, Halifax, Nova Scotia, Canada.
Yard No: 6092
Motive Power: 2 × Caterpillar 3516C diesels = 6,300 hp
Speed (knots): 17
Launched/Floated out: March 2008
Passenger Staterooms: 108
Passenger Decks: 6
Passengers/Crew Numbers (max.): 210/65
Class: RINA
Registered: Majuro, Marshall Islands
Former Names: N/A

(Copyright Dennis G. Jervis)

Ship: *POLARLYS*
IMO: 9107796
MMSI: 259322000
Callsign: LHYG
Operator: Hurtigruten ASA, Narvik, Norway
Tonnage (GRT): 11,341
Dimensions (length × beam × draught):
   123 m (403 ft 6.5 in) × 19.5 m (64 ft) ×
   4.9 m (16 ft 1 in)
Constructor & Yard Number: Ulstein Verft,
   Ulsteinvik, Norway.
Yard No: 223
Motive Power: 2 × Normo-Ulstein BRM 9
   &2 Normo-Ulstein KRG9 diesel = 11,690
   kW; 2 F/P propellers
Speed (knots): 18.5
Launched/Floated out: 26 April 2002
Christened by: Ann-Kristin Olsen
Passenger Cabins: 226
Passenger Decks: 6
Passengers/Crew Numbers (max.):
   497/70
Class: Ro-Ro/Pax
Registered: Tromsø, Norway
Former Names: N/A

(Courtesy Hurtigruten ASA)

Ship: *POLYNESIA*
IMO: 5023564
MMSI: N/A
Callsign: 3CM2027
Operator: Pascoal & Filhos SA, Gafanha Da Nazare, Aveiro
Tonnage (GRT): 430
Dimensions (length × beam × draught): 75.5 m (248 ft) × 10.9 m (36 ft) × 5.4 m (18 ft)
Constructor & Yard Number: De Hoop Scheepswerf Heusden, the Netherlands.
Yard No: 206
Motive Power: 4 masts, 1, 672.2 m² (18,000 sq ft) sail area; 1 × MAN diesel
Speed (knots): 6
Launched/Floated out: 20 May 1938
Passenger Cabins: 55
Passenger Decks: 4
Passengers/Crew Numbers (max.): 122/45
Class: Topsail Schooner
Registered: Grenada, Leeward Islands. Purchased by Pascoal & Fiohos in 2009 – docked at Aveiro for conversion back to private yacht
Former Names: *ARGUS/POLYNESIA 1/ OISEAU DE POLYNESIA*

(Copyright Mike Schninkel)

Ship: *PRINSENDAM*
IMO: 8700280
MMSI: 244126000
Callsign: PB8H
Operator: Holland America Line
Tonnage (GRT): 37,983
Dimensions (length × beam × draught):
   203.9 m (674.2 ft) × 32.3 m (91.8 ft) ×
   7.2 m (23 ft 6 in)
Constructor & Yard Number: Oy Wärtsilä
   AD, ABO, M Finland.
Yard No: 1296
Motive Power: 4 × Wärtsilä-Sulzer
   8ZAL40S diesel = 21,120 kW; 2
   propellers; 2 × LIAAEN bow thrusters
Speed (knots): 21.5
Launched/Floated out: 17 March 1998
Christened by: Gloria Hatrick Stewart
Passenger Cabins: 396
Passenger Decks: 9
Passengers/Crew Numbers (max.):
   835/470
Class: N/A
Registered: Rotterdam, the Netherlands
Former Names: *ROYAL VIKING SUN/
   SEABOURN SUN*

(Courtesy of Holland America Line)

Ship: *QUEST FOR ADVENTURE*
IMO: 8000214
MMSI: 311348000
Callsign: C6SI2
Operator: Saga Cruises/Enbrook Cruises
  Ltd, Folkestone, UK
Tonnage (GRT): 18,627
Dimensions (length × beam × draught):
  164.35 m (539 ft 2.5 in) × 22.60 m (74 ft
  1.5 in) × 6.3 m (20 ft 8 in)
Constructor & Yard Number:
  Howaldtswerke-Deutsche Werft AG,
  Wekross, Hamburg, Germany.
Yard No: 165
Motive Power: 4 × Wärtsilä 6L40/45 diesel
  = 15,400 kW; 2 × C/P propellers
Speed (knots): 21.4
Launched/Floated out: 18 December
  1980
Christened by: Emma Soames
Passenger Cabins: 252
Passenger Decks: 6
Passengers/Crew Numbers (max.):
  446/252
Class: N/A
Registered: Nassau, Bahamas
Former Names: *ASTOR/ARKONA/
  ASTORIA/SAGA PEARL II (reverts to
  SAGA PEARL II in 2014)*

(Courtesy Saga Cruises)

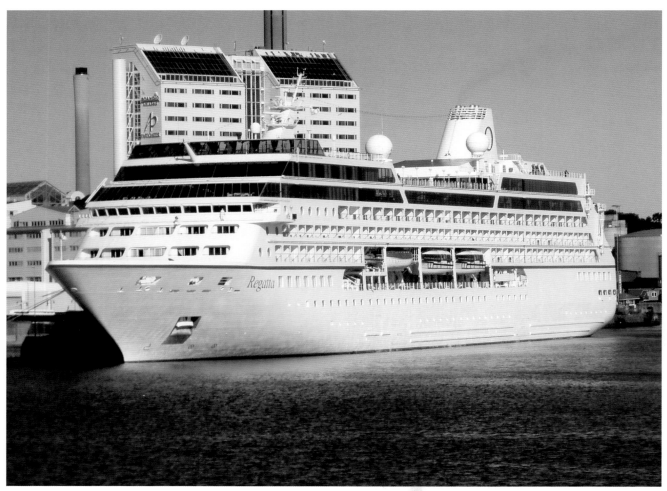

Ship: *REGATTA*
IMO: 9156474
MMSI: 538001664
Callsign: V7DM3
Operator: Oceana Cruises/ Prestige Cruise Holdings Company/Hapag Lloyd Cruises
Tonnage (GRT): 30,277
Dimensions (length × beam × draught): 180.45 m (594 ft) × 25.73 m (83.6 ft) × 6 m (19.5 ft)
Constructor & Yard Number: Chantiers de l'Atlantique, Nantes, St Nazaire, France.
Yard No: I31
Motive Power: 4 × 2A45SILA 12V32 diesel = 18,596 kW; 2 propellers
Speed (knots): 18.5
Launched/Floated out: 22 May 1998
Christened by: Virginia Watters
Passenger Cabins: 342
Passenger Decks: 9
Passengers/Crew Numbers (max.): 702/386
Class: R
Registered: Majuro, Marshall Islands
Former Names: *R TWO/INSIGNIA*

(Copyright Kalle Id)

Ship: *RICHARD WITH*
IMO: 9040429
MMSI: 258500000
Callsign: LGWH
Operator: Hurtigruten ASA, Narvik, Norway
Tonnage (GRT): 11,204
Dimensions (length × beam × draught):
  121.8 m (399 ft 7 in) × 19.2 m 63 ft) ×
  4.9 m (16 ft 1 in)
Constructor & Yard Number: Volkswerft
  GmbH/ P+ S Werften Stralsund GmbH,
  Stralsund, Germany.
Yard No: 103
Motive Power: 2 × Krupp MaK 6M552C
  diesel = 8991 kW; 2 C/P propellers
Speed (knots): 18
Launched/Floated out: 14 February 1993
Christened by: Ashild Hauan
Passenger Cabins: 224
Passenger Decks: 7
Passengers/Crew Numbers (max.): 691/
  55
Class: Ro-Ro/Pax
Registered: Tromsø, Norway
Former Names: N/A

(Courtesy Hurtigruten ASA)

Ship: *ROYAL CLIPPER*
IMO: 8712178
MMSI: 215813000
Callsign: 9HA2796
Operator: Star Clippers Ltd, Monaco/
  Luxembourg Shipping Services
Tonnage (GRT): 4,425
Dimensions (length × beam × draught):
  133.74 m (438 ft 9.5 in) × 16.28 m (53 ft
  5 in) × 6.2 m (20 ft 4 in)
Constructor & Yard Number: Stocznia,
  Gdanska, Poland/ Shipyard ihc de
  Merwde, The Netherlands.
  Yard nos: B811/01/681
Motive Power: 5 63m masts, 42 sails,
  56,000 m^2 (5,204 sq ft) sail area; 2 ×
  Caterpillar 3516 B diesel – 3,730 kW.
Speed (knots): 17
Launched/Floated out: 28 July 2000
Christened by: HM Queen Silvia of
  Sweden
Passenger Cabins: 114
Passenger Decks: 4
Passengers/Crew Numbers (max.):
  227/106
Class: DNV
Registered: Valletta, Malta
Former Names: *GWAREK*

(Courtesy Star Clippers Ltd, Monaco)

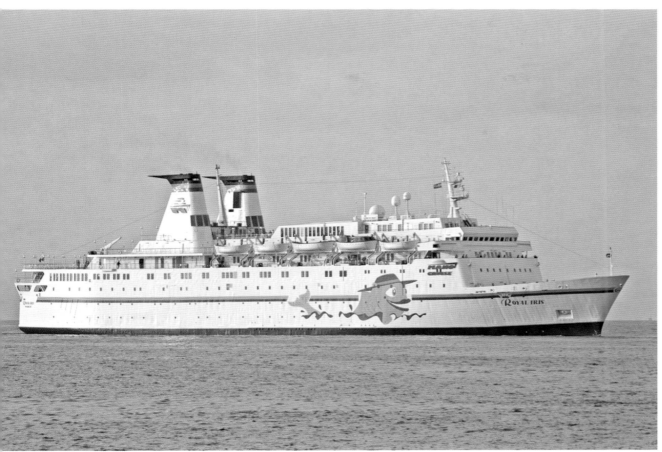

Ship: *ROYAL IRIS*
IMO: 7032997
MMSI: 354952000
Callsign: 3EPR5
Operator: Mano Maritime, Haifia, Israel
Tonnage (GRT): 14,717
Dimensions (length × beam × draught): 141.79 m (465 ft 2.5 in) × 21.90 m (71 ft 8 in) × 5.5 m (18 ft)
Constructor & Yard Number: Dubigeon-Normandie, Nantes, France. **Yard No:** 123
Motive Power: 2 × Pielstick-Atlantique 12PC3 diesel = 16.035 kW; 2 propellers
Speed (knots): 23
Launched/Floated out: 16 October 1970
Christened by: Edith Morkelman
Passenger Cabins: 361
Passenger Decks: 7
Passengers/Crew Numbers (max.): 770/350
Class: N/A
Registered: Panama City, Panama
Former Names: *EAGLE/AZUR/THE AZUR/ELOISE*

(Courtesy and copyright Manuel Moreno)

Ship: *SAFARI ENDEAVOUR*
IMO: 8963698
MMSI: 33892300
Callsign: WDG2742
Operator: Un-Cruise Adventures, Seattle, Washington, USA
Tonnage (GRT): 96
Dimensions (length × beam × draught): 70.71 m (232 ft) × 11.27 m (37 ft) × 3.50 m (11.5 ft)
Constructor & Yard Number: Jeffboat, Jefferson, Indiana, USA. **Yard No:** 82-2542
Motive Power: 2 × Caterpillar diesel = 1,875 hp
Speed (knots): 10
Launched/Floated out: September 1983
Christened by: Margaret Propper
Passenger Cabins: 43
Passenger Decks: 4
Passengers/Crew Numbers (max.): 86/35
Class: N/A
Registered: Seattle, Washington, USA
Former Names: *SPIRIT OF ENDEAVOUR/ SEA SPIRIT*

(Courtesy Un-Cruise Adventures)

Ship: *SAFARI EXPLORER*
IMO: 8964654
MMSI: 336339000
Callsign: WCY5674
Operator: Un-Cruise Adventure Tours, Seattle, Washington, USA
Tonnage (GRT): 97
Dimensions (length × beam × draught): 44.19 m (145 ft) × 11 m (36 ft) × 2.59 m (8.5 ft)
Constructor & Yard Number: Freeport Shipbuilding inc. Freeport, Florida.
Yard No: 151
Motive Power: 2 × Lugger diesel 6170 = 1,400 hp
Speed (knots): 10
Launched/Floated out: 1998
Christened by: Margaret Propper
Passenger Cabins: 18
Passenger Decks: 3
Passengers/Crew Numbers (max.): 36/15
Class:
Registered: Juneau, AK, USA
Former Names: *RAPTURE*

(Couresy Un-Cruise Adventure Tours)

Ship: *SS LEGACY*
IMO: 8963703
MMSI: 366933000
Callsign: WBR4896
Operator: Un-Cruise/Innerseas Discoveries Seattle, Washington, USA
Tonnage (GRT): 1,472
Dimensions (length × beam × draught): 58.52 m (192 ft 1 in) × 12.19 m (40 ft) × 2.89 m (9.4 ft)
Constructor & Yard Number: Bender Shipbuilding and Repair (Signal Ship Repair), Mobile, Alabama, USA.
Yard No: 140
Motive Power: 2 × Caterpillar diesel = 2,100 bhp; 1 propeller; 1 300 hp bow thruster
Speed (knots): 11
Launched/Floated out: 12 December 1984
Christened by: Mrs Fredrick Scudder
Passenger Cabins: 45
Passenger Decks: 4
Passengers/Crew Numbers (max.): 88/34
Class: Steamer
Registered: Seattle, Washington, USA
Former Names: *PILGRIM BELLE/ VICTORIAN EMPRESS/COLONIAL EXPLORER/SPRIT OF '98/SAFARI LEGACY*

(Couresy Un-Cruise Adventure Tours)

Ship: *SAGA RUBY*
IMO: 7214715
MMSI: 248563000
Callsign: 9HA2415
Operator: Saga Cruises/ Saga Shipping
Company, Folkestone, Kent, UK (to be
retired December 2013)
Tonnage (GRT): 24,492
Dimensions (length × beam × draught):
191.09 m (626 ft 11 in) × 25 m (82 ft) ×
8.23 m (27 ft)
Constructor & Yard Number: Swan
Hunters, Wallsend, Tyne and Wear, UK.
Yard No: 39
Motive Power: 2 × Sulzer 9RD68 diesel =
17,650 kW; 2 propellers
Speed (knots): 20
Launched/Floated out: 15 May 1972
Christened by: Virginia Goodsell
Passenger Cabins: 376
Passenger Decks: 9
Passengers/Crew Numbers (max.):
655/380
Class: DNV
Registered: Valletta, Malta
Former Names: *VISTAFJORD/CARONIA*

(Courtesy Saga Cruises)

Ship: *SAGA SAPPHIRE*
IMO: 7822457
MMSI: 256208000
Callsign: 9HOF8
Operator: Saga Cruises/ Saga Shipping Company, Folkwestone, Kent, UK
Tonnage (GRT): 37,301
Dimensions (length × beam × draught): 199.63 m (654.9 ft) × 28.60 m (93.8 ft) × 8.42 m (27.6 ft)
Constructor & Yard Number: Bremen Vulkan, Bremen, Germany.
Yard No: 1001
Motive Power: 2 × MAN-Bremer Vulkan diesel – 21,270 kW; 2 propellers
Speed (knots): 19
Launched/Floated out: 22 December 1980
Christened by: The Britannia Club members
Passenger Cabins: 376
Passenger Decks: 10
Passengers/Crew Numbers (max.): 706/406
Class: GL
Registered: Valletta, Malta
Former Names: *EUROPA/SUPERSTAR EUROPE/SUPERSTAR ARIES/HOLIDAY DREAM/BLEU DE FRANCE*

(Courtesy Saga Cruises)

Ship: *SALAMIS FILOXENIA*
IMO: 7359400
MMSI: 209167000
Callsign: 5BUY2
Operator: Salamis Cruise Lines, Limassol,
Cyprus/Mana Shipping Co Ltd, Cyprus
Tonnage (GRT): 15,402
Dimensions (length × beam × draught):
15627 m (512 ft 8 in) × 22.05 m (72 ft
4 in) × 5.92 m (19.5 ft)
Constructor & Yard Number: Oy Wärtsilä
AB, Turku, Finland.
Yard No: 1213
Motive Power: 2 × Pilstick Wärtsilä
18PC2V diesel = 13,240 kW; 2 propellers
Speed (knots): 20
Launched/Floated out: 18 October 1974
Christened by: Elena Hadjitheopossiou
Passenger Cabins: 255
Passenger Decks: 8
Passengers/Crew Numbers (max.):
795/250
Class: Belorussia
Registered: Limassol, Cyprus
Former Names: *CLUB I/ODESSA SKY/
GRUZIYA/VAN GOGH*

(Courtesy Salamis Cruise Lines)

Ship: *SEA ADVENTURER*
IMO: 7391422
MMSI: 309997000
Callsign: C6PG6
Operator: International Shipping Partners (Isp), Miami, Florida/Quark Expeditions, Norwalk, Connecticut
Tonnage (GRT): 4,376
Dimensions (length × beam × draught): 100.58 m (330 ft) × 16.31 m (53.5 ft) × 4.72 m (15.5 ft)
Constructor & Yard Number: Titov Brod, Gradjliste, Kraljevica, Croatia.
Yard No: 408
Motive Power: – 2 × MAN B&W diesel= 5,280 shp; 2 × C/P propellers; 1 × 500 hp bow thruster; stabilizers
Speed (knots): 12
Launched/Floated out: 19 April 1975
Passenger Cabins: 61
Passenger Decks: 6
Passengers/Crew Numbers (max.): 122/72
Class: Mariya
Registered: Nassau, Bahamas
Former Names: *ALLA TARASOVA/ CLIPPER ADVENTURR*

(Copyright Roud Peter Van Der Duirn)

Ship: *STAR LEGEND*
IMO: 9008598
MMSI: 311085000
Callsign: C6FR6
Operator: Windstar Cruises
Tonnage (GRT): 9,961
Dimensions (length × beam × draught):
1114.9 m (377 ft) × 118.98 m (62.3 ft) ×
5.2 m (16.5 ft)
Constructor & Yard Number: SSW
Schicha u Seebeck Shipyard,
Bremerhaven, Germany.
Yard No: 1071
Motive Power: BMV Bergen diesel A/V
diesel = 7280 kW; 2 propellers
Speed (knots): 19.2
Launched/Floated out: May 1991
Christened by: Linn Brynestad
Passenger Cabins: 106
Passenger Decks: 6
Passengers/Crew Numbers (max.):
208/164
Class: N/A
Registered: Nassau, Bahamas
Former Names: *ROYAL VIKING QUEEN/*
QUEEN ODYSSEY/SEABOURN
LEGEND

(Courtesy of Windstar Cruises)

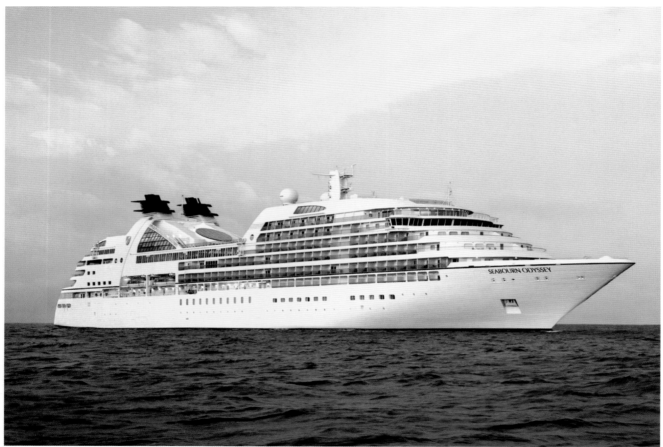

Ship: *SEABOURN ODYSSEY*
IMO: 9417086
MMSI: 309416000
Callsign: C6XC6
Operator: Seabourn Cruise Line, Seattle, Washington, USA/Carnival Corporation
Tonnage (GRT): 23,346
Dimensions (length × beam × draught): 197 m (648 ft) × 26 m (84 ft) × 6.4 m (21 ft)
Constructor & Yard Number: Cimolai-Mariotti Yard, Genova, Italy.
Yard No: MAR 062
Motive Power: 4 × Wärtsilä SpA NI2V32B3 = 2300 kW; 2 propellers
Speed (knots): 21
Launched/Floated out: 25 June 2009
Christened by: Inaugural cruise guests
Passenger Cabins: 225
Passenger Decks: 8
Passengers/Crew Numbers (max.): 450/330
Class: Odyssey
Registered: Nassau, Bahamas
Former Names: N/A

(Courtesy of Seabourn Cruise Line, Seattle)

Ship: *STAR PRIDE*
IMO: 8707343
MMSI: 311084000
Callsign: C6FR5
Operator: Windstar Cruises USA
Tonnage (GRT): 9,975
DIMENSIONS (**length × beam × draught)**); 133.40 (437 ft 8 in) × 20.50m (67 ft 3 in) × 5.415m (17 ft 9.5 in)
Constructor & Yard Number: SSW Schichau Seebeck Shipyard GmbH, Bremerhaven, Germany.
Yard No: 1065
Motive Power: 2 × Normo-Bergen KVMB 712 = 7,280 kW; 2 C/P propellers
Speed (knots): 15
Launched/Floated out: 22 July 1988
Christened by: Shirley Temple Black
Passenger Cabins: 106
Passenger Decks: 6
Passengers/Crew Numbers (max.): 208/164
Class: N/A
Registered: Nassau, Bahamas
Former Names: SEABOURN PRIDE

(Courtesy Windstar Cruises)

Ship: *SEABOURN QUEST*
IMO: 9483126
MMSI: 311038900
Callsign: C6Y25
Operator: Seabourn Cruise Line, Miami, Florida, USA
Tonnage (GRT): 32,346
Dimensions (length × beam × draught): 198 m (647 ft 7 in) × 25.6 m (84 ft) × 6.4 m (21 ft)
Constructor & Yard Number: Cimolai-Mariotti SpA, Construzioni Navali, San Giorgio di Nogaro, Italy.
Yard No: MAR-64
Motive Power: 4 × Wärtsilä 12V32B3 diesel = 23,020 kW; 2 propellers
Speed (knots): 19
Launched/Floated out: 20 June 2011
Christened by: Blythe Danner
Passenger Cabins: 225
Passenger Decks: 8
Passengers/Crew Numbers (max.): 450/330
Class: Odyssey
Registered: Nassau, Bahamas
Former Names: N/A

(Courtesy Seabourn Cruise Line)

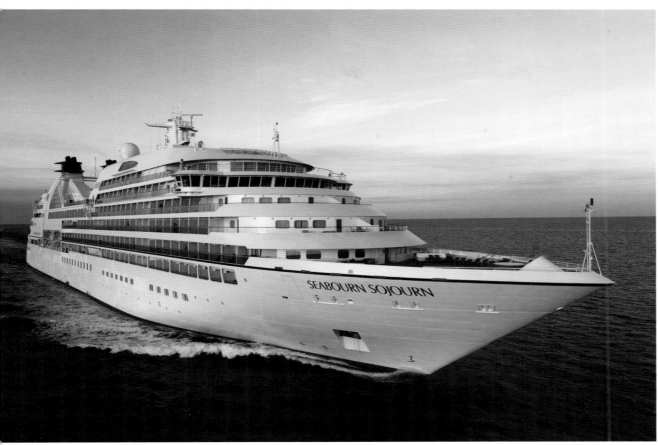

Ship: *SEABOURN SOJOURN*
IMO: 9417098
MMSI: 311027100
Callsign: C6YA5
Operator: Seabourn Cruise Line, Seattle, Washington, USA
Tonnage (GRT): 32,345
Dimensions (length × beam × draught): 198 m (650.1 ft) × 25.60 m (84 ft) × 6.40 m (21 ft 3 in)
Constructor & Yard Number: Cimolai-Mariott SpA, Genoa, Italy.
 Yard No: MAR-0 63
Motive Power: 4 × Wärtsilä 12V32B3 diesel = 23,040 kW; 2 propellers
Speed (knots): 22
Launched/Floated out: 25 July 2009
Christened by: Twiggy (Leslie Hornby)
Passenger Cabins: 225
Passenger Decks: 10
Passengers/Crew Numbers (max.): 450/335
Class: Odyssey
Registered: Nassau, Bahamas
Former Names: N/A

(Courtesy Seabourn Cruise Line, Seattle)

Ship: STAR*
IMO: 8807997
MMSI: 311085000
Callsign: C6FR4
Operator: Windstar Cruises
Tonnage (GRT): 9,975
Dimensions (length × beam × draught: 133.40 m (437 ft 8 in) × 20.5 m (67 ft 3 in) × 5.515 m (18 ft 1 in)
Constructor & Yard Number: SSW Schichau Seebeck Shipyard AG GmbH, Bremerhaven, Germany. **Yard No:** 1070
Motive Power: 2 × BMV Bergen Normo KVMB-12 + 2 KVM8 = 7,280 kW; 2 C/P propellers
Speed (knots): 16
Launched/Floated out: 17 March 1989
Christened by: Aagot Brynestad
Passenger Cabins: 106
Passenger Decks: 6
Passengers/Crew Numbers (max.): 2108164
Class: N/A
Registered: Nassau, Bahamas
Former Names: *SEABOURN SPIRIT*

* New name unallocated at time of going to press.

(Courtesy of Windstar Cruises (as Seabourn Spirit*))*

Ship: *SEACLOUD*
IMO: 8843446
MMSI: 256084000
Callsign: 9HOMZ
Operator: Sea Cloud Cruises GmbH, Hamburg, Germany/Hansa Treuhand Holding AG, Hamburg
Tonnage (GRT): 2,532
Dimensions (length × beam × draught): 109.50 m (359 ft 3 in ft) × 14.99 m (49 ft 2 in) × 5.8 m (19 ft)
Constructor & Yard Number: Krupp Germaniawerft Shipyard, Howaldtswerke-Deutsche Werft) Kiel, Germany.
Yard No: 519
Motive Power: 4 masts, 30 sails 3,000 mm² (32,292 sq ft); diesel = 4,4K76 kW; 2 propellers
Speed (knots): 10.3/7.6
Launched/Floated out: 25 April 1931
Christened by: Marjorie Merriweather Post as *Hussar II*
Passenger Cabins: 34
Passenger Decks: 3
Passengers/Crew Numbers (max.): 69/60
Class: Barque
Registered: Valletta, Malta
Former Names: *HUSSAR/WPG-284/IX-99/ANGELITA/PATRIA/ANTARNA/IX-99/CAYMAN/SEA CLOUD OF GRAND CAYMAN*

(Courtesy Sea Cloud Cruises GmbH, Hamburg)

Ship: *SEA CLOUD II*
IMO: 9171292
MMSI: 248953000
Callsign: 9HUE6
Operator: Sea Cloud II Cruises GmbH, Hamburg, Germany/Hansa Treuhand Holding AG, Hamburg
Tonnage (GRT): 3,849
Dimensions (length × beam × draught): 105.90 m (347 ft 5 in) × 16 m (52 ft 6 in) × 5.18 m (17 ft)
Constructor & Yard Number: Astilleros Gondani, SA, Figueras-Castropol (Astorias) Spain.
Yard No: 519
Motive Power: 3 masts, 3000 m² (32,150 sq ft) sail area; 2 × Krupp MaK 8M20 diesel = 2,480 kW; 1 C/P propeller; 1 bow thruster
Speed (knots): 13
Launched/Floated out: 10 March 1999
Christened by: Sabine Christiansen
Passenger Cabins: 48
Passenger Decks: 4
Passengers/Crew Numbers (max.): 96/56
Class: Barque
Registered: Valletta, Malta
Former Names: N/A

(Courtesy of Sea Cloud II Cruises GmbH, Hamburg)

Ship: *SEA EXPLORER*
IMO: 8802882
MMSI: 538004274
Callsign: V7WD8
Operator: Polar Latitudes, USA/Travel Dynamics Inc, New York, NY
Tonnage (GRT): 4,200
Dimensions (length × beam × draught): 90.6 m (297.2 ft) × 15.30 m (50.1 ft) × 2.95 m (12.9 ft)
Constructor & Yard Number: Nuovi Cantieri Apuania, SpA, Carrara, Italy. **Yard No:** 1146
Motive Power: 2 × MAN B7W 8L28/32AFHO diesel= 3,514 kW; 2 propellers; bow thruster, stabilizers.
Speed (knots): 14.5
Launched/Floated out: 13 April 1991
Passenger Cabins: 61
Passenger Decks: 6
Passengers/Crew Numbers (max.): 114/70
Class: Ice 1C
Registered: Marshall Islands
Former Names: *REN 7/REGINA RENAISSANCE/RENAISSANCE VII/RENA1/SUN/ISLAND SUN/ CORINTHIAN II*

(Courtesy of Polar Latitudes)

125

Ship: *SEA SPIRIT*
IMO: 8802868
MMSI: 309224000
Callsign: C6PJ8
Operator: International Shipping Partners, Miami, Florida, USA/TN CRUISE K/S
Tonnage (GRT): 4,200
Dimensions (length × beam × draught): 90.36 m (298.5 ft) × 15.30 m (49 ft 2 in) × 4.2 m (13 ft 9 in)
Constructor & Yard Number: Nuovi Cantieri Apuania MaRINA di Carrara, Italy.
Yard No: 1144
Motive Power: 2 × MAN B+W Alpha 8L28/32A-FHO diesel = 3,518 kW; 2 C/P propellers; 1 × bow thruster
Speed (knots): 14.5
Launched/Floated out: 13 February 1990
Passenger Cabins: 57
Passenger Decks: 5
Passengers/Crew Numbers (max.): 114/72
Class: Ice 1D
Registered: Nassau, Bahamas
Former Names: *HANSEATIC RENAISSANCE/RENAISSANCE V/SUN VIVA/MEGASTAR SAGITTARIUS/SPIRIT OF OCEANUS*

(Coutesy Seabourn Cruises)

Ship: *SEVEN SEAS NAVIGATOR*
IMO: 9064126
MMSI: 311050600
Callsign: C6ZI9
Operator: Regent Seven Seas Cruises,
Miami, Florida, USA
Tonnage (GRT): 28,550
Dimensions (length × beam × draught):
172.5 m (566 ft) × 24.6 m (80 ft 8.5 in) ×
7.5 m (24 ft 7 in)
Constructor & Yard Number:
Sudostroiteiny Zavod, Rybisnk, Admiralty
Wharves, St Petersburg, Russia/T
Mariotti, Genoa, Italy.
Yard No: 6125/1
Motive Power: 3 × Wärtsilä 8L38 diesels =
21,000 kW; 2 C/P propellers
Speed (knots): 19.5
Launched/Floated out: 23 August 1991
Christened by: Barbara Carlson Gage
Passenger Cabins: 245
Passenger Decks: 8
Passengers/Crew Numbers (max.):
490/345
Class: RINA
Registered: Hamilton, Bermuda
Former Names: *AKADEMIK NIKOLAY
PILYUGIN/BLUE NUN/BLUE SEA/
RADISSON SEVEN SEAS*

*(Courtesy Regent Seven Seas Cruises,
Miami)*

Ship: *SILVER CLOUD*
IMO: 8903923
MMSI: 309027000
Callsign: C6MQ5
Operator: Silversea Cruises, Monaco
Tonnage (GRT): 16,927
Dimensions (length × beam × draught): 156.7 m (514 ft) × 21.5 m (70.62 ft) × 5.5 m (18 ft)
Constructor & Yard Number: Cantieri Navali Francesco, Visentini, Trieste, Italy/ Mariotti Yard, Genoa.
Yard No: 775
Motive Power: 2 × Wärtsilä 6R46 diesel – 10,600 kW; 2 C/P propellers
Speed (knots): 17.5
Launched/Floated out: 20 June 2008
Christened by: Lindsey Wilkerson
Passenger Cabins: 146
Passenger Decks: 6
Passengers/Crew Numbers (max.): 296/212
Class: N/A
Registered: Nassau, Bahamas
Former Names: N/A

(Courtesy Silversea Cruises, Monaco)

Ship: *SILVER EXPLORER*
IMO: 8806747
MMSI: 311562000
Callsign: C67A8
Operator: Silversea Cruises, Monaco
Tonnage (GRT): 6,072
Dimensions (length × beam × draught):
108 m (354 ft 4 in) × 15.6 m (51 ft 2 in) ×
4.38 m (14 ft 4 in)
Constructor & Yard Number: Rauma-
Repola Oy, Rauma, Finland.
Yard No: 304
Motive Power: 2 × Wärtsilä/Vasa 8RD32
diesel = 4,500 kW; 2 C/P propellers
Speed (knots): 14
Launched/Floated out: 3 February 1989
Christened by: Leena Matomäki
Passenger Cabins: 66
Passenger Decks: 5
Passengers/Crew Numbers (max.):
132/117
Class: Ice 1A
Registered: Nassau, Bahamas
Former Names: *DELFIN CLIPPER/
SALLY CLIPPER/BALTIC CLIPPER/
DELFIN STAR/DREAM 21/WORLD
DISCOVERER/WORLD ADVENTURER/
PRINCE ALBERT II*

(Courtesy Silversea Cruises, Monaco)

Ship: *SILVER GALÁPAGOS*
IMO: 8708660
MMSI: 735057575
Callsign: HC4403
Operator: Silversea Cruises, Monaco
Tonnage (GRT): 4.077
Dimensions (length × beam × draught):
    88.16 m (289 ft 3 in) × 15.3 m (50 ft 2.5
    in) × 4.012 m (13 ft 2 in)
Constructor & Yard Number: Cantieri
    Navali Ferri-Signani, La Spezia, Italy.
Yard No: 45
Motive Power: 2 × MAN-B&W diesel =
    7,028 kW 2 C/P propellers
Speed (knots): 17
Launched/Floated out: 1990
Passenger Cabins: 53
Passenger Decks: 5
Passengers/Crew Numbers (max.):
    100/70
Class: Renaissance
Registered: Nassau, Bahamas
Former Names: *RENAISSANCE THREE/*
    GALÁPAGOS EXPLORER II

(Courtesy of Silversea Cruises, Monaco)

Ship: *SILVER SHADOW*
IMO: 9192167
MMSI: 308628000
Callsign: C6FN6
Operator: Silver Sea Cruises, Monaco
Tonnage (GRT): 28,258
Dimensions (length × beam × draught):
186 m (610 ft) × 24.8 m (81 ft 4 in) × 6 m
(19 ft 8 in)
Constructor & Yard Number: Francisco
Visentini Shipyard, Trieste (Hull)/ T
Mariotti SpA, Genoa, Italy.
Yard No: 304/981
Motive Power: 2 × Wärtsilä 8L46B diesel =
15,700 kW; 2 C/P propellers
Speed (knots): 17.5
Launched/Floated out: 1 September
2000
Christened by: Janet Burke
Passenger Cabins: 194
Passenger Decks: 7
Passengers/Crew Numbers (max.):
382/295
Class: RINA
Registered: Nassau, Bahamas
Former Names: N/A

(Courtesy Silversea Cruises, Monaco)

Ship: *SILVER SPIRIT*
IMO: 9437866
MMSI: 311022500
Callsign: C6XU6
Operator: Silversea Cruises, Monaco
Tonnage (GRT): 36,009
Dimensions (length × beam × draught):
198.5 m (642 ft) × 26.2 m (86 ft) × 6.2 m (20.3 ft)
Constructor & Yard Number: Fincantieri, Ancona, Italy.
Yard No: 6178
Motive Power: 4 × Wärtsilä W9L38B diesel = 26,100 kW 2 F/P propellers
Speed (knots): 20.3
Launched/Floated out: 27 February 2009
Christened by: Mrs Silvia Lefebvre O'Vidio
Passenger Cabins: 270
Passenger Decks: 8
Passengers/Crew Numbers (max.):
540/376
Class: RINA
Registered: Nassau, Bahamas
Former Names: N/A

(Courtesy Silversea Cruises, Monaco)

Ship: *SILVER WHISPER*
IMO: 9192179
MMSI: 308322000
Callsign: C6FN7
Operator: Silversea Cruises, Monaco
Tonnage (GRT): 28,258
Dimensions (length × beam × draught):
186 m (610 ft) × 24.9 m (8.8 ft) × 6 m
(19.6 ft)
Constructor & Yard Number: Cantieri
Navali Francisco Visentini, Donada,
Italy(Hull)/T Mariotti Yard, Genoa.
Yard No: 982
Motive Power: 2 × Wärtsilä 8L46B =
15,700 kW; 2 C/P propellers
Speed (knots): 21
Launched/Floated out: 1 July 2001
Christened by: Mrs Marzia Lefebvre
D'Ovidio
Passenger Cabins: 194
Passenger Decks: 7
Passengers/Crew Numbers (max.):
382/295
Class: RINA
Registered: Nassau, Bahamas
Former Names: N/A

(Courtesy Silversea Cruises, Monaco)

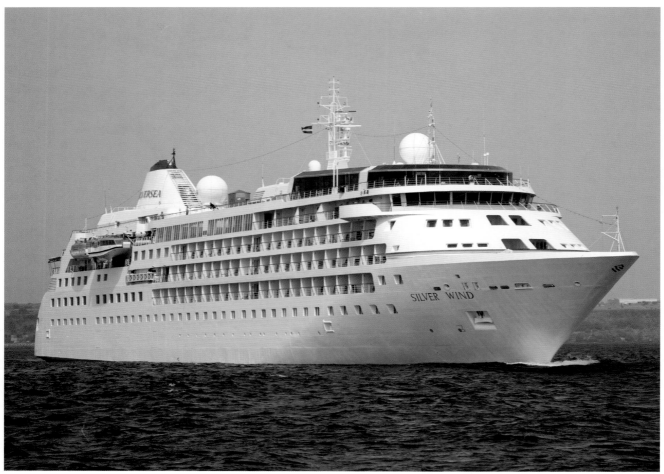

Ship: *SILVER WIND*
IMO: 8903935
MMSI: 308814000
Callsign: C6FG2
Operator: Silversea Cruises, Fort Lauderdale, Florida, USA
Tonnage (GRT): 17,400
Dimensions (length × beam × draught): 156.7 m (514 ft) × 21.5 m (70.62 ft) × 5.5 m (18 ft)
Constructor & Yard Number: Francisco Visentini Yard Donada, Italy (Hull) /Mariotti Yard, Genoa, Italy.
Yard No: 776
Motive Power: 2 × Wärtsilä 6R46 =10,600 kW; 2 C/P propellers
Speed (knots): 20.5
Launched/Floated out: 19 October 1993
Christened by: Patrizia Lefebvre D'Ovidio
Passenger Cabins: 157
Passenger Decks: 6
Passengers/Crew Numbers (max.): 298/212
Class: RINA
Registered: Nassau, Bahamas
Former Names: N/A

(Courtesy Silversea Cruises, Monaco)

Ship: *STAR CLIPPER*
IMO: 8915445
MMSI: 248786000
Callsign: 9HA2513
Operator: Star Clippers, Monaco
Tonnage (GRT): 2,298
Dimensions (length × beam × draught):
  111.57 m (366.5 ft) × 15.14 m (49 ft 9 in)
  × 5.9 m (18.5 in)
Constructor & Yard Number:
  Scheepswerven Van Langerbrugge,
  Ghent, Belgium. **Yard No:** 2184
Motive Power: 4 × masts = 3,344.5 m²
  (36,000 sq ft) sail power; 1 × Caterpillar
  3512 DITA diesel = 1,030 kW; 1 C/P
  propeller
Speed (knots): 17
Launched/Floated out: 1 April 1992
Christened by: Marie Krafft
Passenger Cabins: 85
Passenger Decks: 4
Passengers/Crew Numbers (max.):
  170/72
Class: Barquentine
Registered: Valletta, Malta
Former Names: N/A

(Courtesy and copyright Manuel Moreno)

Ship: *STAR FLYER*
IMO: 8915433
MMSI: 248785000
Callsign: 9HA2512
Operator: Star Clippers, Monaco
Tonnage (GRT): 2,298
Dimensions (length × beam × draught):
  115 m (366 ft 1 in) × 15.14 m (49 ft 8 in)
  × 5.5 m (18 ft 6 in)
Constructor & Yard Number:
  Scheepswerven Van Langerbrugge,
  Ghent, Belgium. **Yard No:** 2183
Motive Power: 4 masts, 16 sails, 3,365
  m² (36,221 sq ft) sail area; 1 × Caterpillar
  3512 diesel = 1,030 kW; 1 propeller
Speed (knots): 11.6/8.4
Launched/Floated out: 27 April 1991
Christened by: Ann Krafft
Passenger Cabins: 85
Passenger Decks: 4
Passengers/Crew Numbers (max.):
  170/72
Class: Barquentine
Registered: Valletta, Malta
Former Names: N/A

(Courtesy and copyright Manuel Moreno)

Ship: *TERE MOANA*
IMO: 9159830
MMSI: 228043000
Callsign: FNGC
Operator: Pacific Beachcomber (Paul Gauguin Cruises), Tahiti/Thomas P Gohagan & Co., Chicago, Illinois
Tonnage (GRT): 3,504
Dimensions (length × beam × draught): 100 m (328 ft) × 14 m (45.9 ft) × 3.50 m 11.4 ft)
Constructor & Yard Number: Alstrom Leroux Naval, St Malo, France.
Yard No: 625
Motive Power: Wärtsilä 9L20 diesel = 4,038 bhp; 2 C/P propellers; 1 × bow thruster
Speed (knots): 17
Launched/Floated out: 29 December 2012
Christened by: Mireille Bailey
Passenger Cabins: 45
Passenger Decks: 5
Passengers/Crew Numbers (max.): 90/50
Class: Boutique
Registered: Mata-Utu, Wallis and Futuna Islands
Former Names: *LE LEVANT*

(Courtesy Paul Gauguin Cruises)

Ship: *THOMSON CELEBRATION*
IMO: 8028298
MMSI: 249544000
Callsign: 9HUI9
Operator: Louis Cruise Line/Thomson
Cruises
Tonnage (GRT): 33,933
Dimensions (length × beam × draught):
214.66 m (704 ft 3 in) × 27.26 m (89 ft
5 in) × 7.50 m (24 ft 7 in)
Constructor & Yard Number: Chantiers
de l'Atlantique, Nantes, St Nazaire,
France.
Yard No: X27
Motive Power: 2 × Sulzer RLBD66 diesels
= 22,400 kW; 2 C/P propellers
Speed (knots): 21
Launched/Floated out: 21 May 1983
Christened by: Mrs van den Walt Bake-Van
Der Vorm
Passenger Cabins: 627
Passenger Decks: 10
Passengers/Crew Numbers (max.):
1,254/520
Class: N/A
Registered: Valletta, Malta
Former Names: *NOORDAM*

(Copyright Peter C. Smith)

Ship: *THOMSON SPIRIT*
IMO: 8024014
MMSI: 209594000
Callsign: P3SK9
Operator: Louis Cruise Lines, Limassol,
Cyprus/Thomson Cruises
Tonnage (GRT): 33,930
Dimensions (length × beam × draught):
214.66 m (704 ft 3 in) × 27.26 m (89 ft
5.5 in) × 7.32 m (24.5 ft)
Constructor & Yard Number: Chantiers
de l'Atlantique, Nantes, St Nazaire,
France.
Yard No: V27
Motive Power: 2 × Sulzer RLB66 diesel =
22,400 kW; 2 × C/P propellers
Speed (knots): 21
Launched/Floated out: 20 August 1982
Christened by: HRH Princess Margaret
Passenger Cabins: 627
Passenger Decks: 9
Passengers/Crew Numbers (max.):
1,254/520
Class: N/A
Registered: Limassol, Cyprus
Former Names: *NIEUW AMSTERDAM/
PATRIOT*

(Courtesy Thomson Cruises)

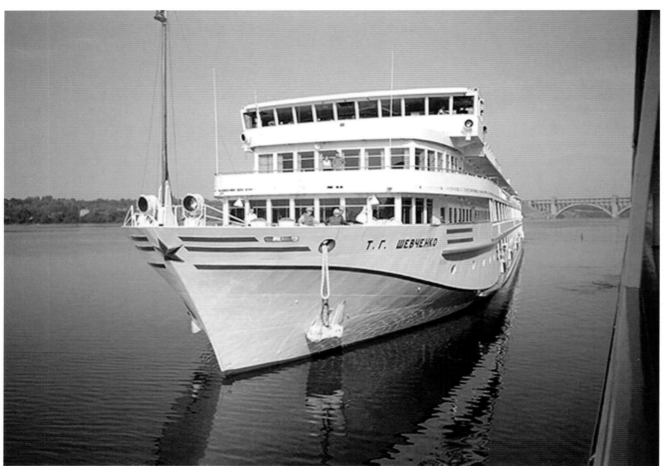

Ship: *T G SHEVCHENKO*
IMO: 8925036
MMSI: 272445000
Callsign: URMK
Operator: Caspiy Ak Jhelken Llp, Kazakhstan.
Tonnage (GRT): 5,475
Dimensions (length × beam × draught): 129.10 m (423.6 ft) × 16.7 m (55 ft) × 2.75 m (9.5 ft)
Constructor & Yard Number: Elbewerft Boizenburg GmbH, Boizenburg, Germany/DMS AG, Deutschen Maschinen-und-Schiffbau AG, Germany.
Yard No: 303
Motive Power: 3 × 64PH diesel @ 736 kW; 3 propellers
Speed (knots): 13.7
Launched/Floated out: 1 January 1991
Passenger Cabins: 140
Passenger Decks: 5
Passengers/Crew Numbers (max.): 238/98
Class: Dmitriy Furmanov
Registered: Aktau, Kazakhstan
Former Names: *TARAS SHEVCHENCKO*

(Courtesy Caspiy Ak Jhelken LLP)

Ship: *TROLLFJORD*
IMO: 9233258
MMSI: 25047500
Callsign: LLVT
Operator: Hurtigruten ASA, Narvik, Norway
Tonnage (GRT): 16,140
Dimensions (length × beam × draught):
135.75 m (445 ft 4.5 in) × 21.5 m (70 ft
6.5 in) × 4.9 m (17 ft)
Constructor & Yard Number: Fosen
Mekaniske Verksteder AS, Norway.
Yard No: 72
Motive Power: 2 × Wärtsilä 9L32 diesel =
8,280 kW; 3 × Brunvoll AP thrusters; 2 ×
Rolls-Royce Oy Ab azimuth thrusters
Speed (knots): 16.2
Launched/Floated out: 10 October 2001
Christened by: Kari Bremnes
Passenger Cabins: 293
Passenger Decks: 9
Passengers/Crew Numbers (max.):
1,000/150
Class: Ro-Ro/Pax
Registered: Tromsø, Norway
Former Names: N/A

(Courtesy Hurtigruten ASA)

Ship: *VESTERÅLEN*
IMO: 8019368
MMSI: 258478000
Callsign: LLZY
Operator: Hurtigruten ASA, Narvik, Norway
Tonnage (GRT): 6,261
Dimensions (length × beam × draught):
   108.51 m (357 ft) × 16.5 m 54.5 ft) ×
   4.6 m (21 ft)
Constructor & Yard Number: Kaarbos,
   Mek, Verksted, Norway.
Yard No: 101
Motive Power: 2 × Normo-Bergen KVMB-
   16 diesel = 4,708 kW; 2 × C/P propellers
Speed (knots): 17.5
Launched/Floated out: 18 September
   1982
Christened by: Elsie Kobro
Passenger Cabins: 146
Passenger Decks: 7
Passengers/Crew Numbers (max.):
   510/50
Class: Ro-Ro/Pax
Registered: Tromsø, Norway
Former Names: N/A

(Courtesy Hurtigruten ASA)

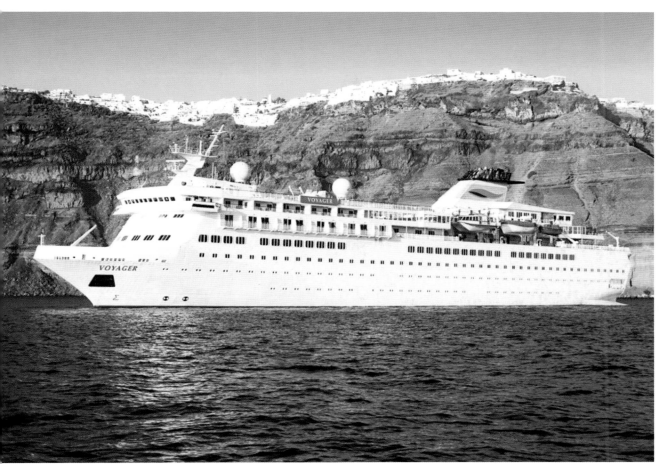

Ship: *VOYAGER*
IMO: 8709573
MMSI: 309695000
Callsign: 9HQN5
Operator: Voyages Of Discovery Ltd, UK/
All Leisure Group
Tonnage (GRT): 15,271
Dimensions (length × beam × draught):
152.20 m (500 ft 3.5 in) × 20.60 m (67 ft
7 in) × 5.8 m (19 ft 4 in)
Constructor & Yard Number: Union
Navale de Levante, Valencia, Spain.
Yard No: 185
Motive Power: 4 × Bergen BRM diesel –
13,340 kW; 2 C/P propellers
Speed (knots): 18
Launched/Floated out: 30 October 1989
Passenger Cabins: 278
Passenger Decks: 7
Passengers/Crew Numbers (max.):
556/215
Class: Voyager
Registered: Nassau, Bahamas
Former Names: *CROWN MONARCH/*
CUNARD CROWN MONARCH/
NAUTICAN/WALRUS JULES VERNE/
ALEXANDER VON HUMBOLDT

(Courtesy Voyages of Discovery)

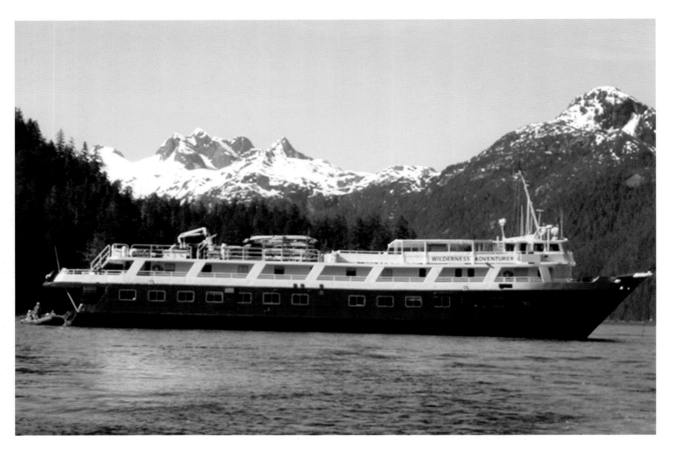

Ship: *WILDERNESS ADVENTURER*
IMO: 8978667
MMSI: 303361000
Callsign: WDF 6885
Operator: Un-Cruise Adventures, Seattle
Tonnage (GRT): 89
Dimensions (length × beam × draught):
 47.55 m (156 ft) × 11.58 m (38 ft) × 1.95 m
 (6.4 ft)
Constructor & Yard Number: Blount
 Marine Corporation, Warren Rhode
 Island, USA.
Yard No: LIB-250
Motive Power: Cummins KTA-10M diesel -
 680 hp; American bow thruster; 1 × 44 ft
 Michigan propeller
Speed (knots): 9.5
Launched/Floated out: 1983
Passenger Cabins: 30
Passenger Decks: 3
Passengers/Crew Numbers (max.):
 60/25
Class: Expedition ship
Registered: Seattle, WA
Former Names: *CARIBBEAN PRINCE*

(Courtesy of Un-Cruises Adventures)

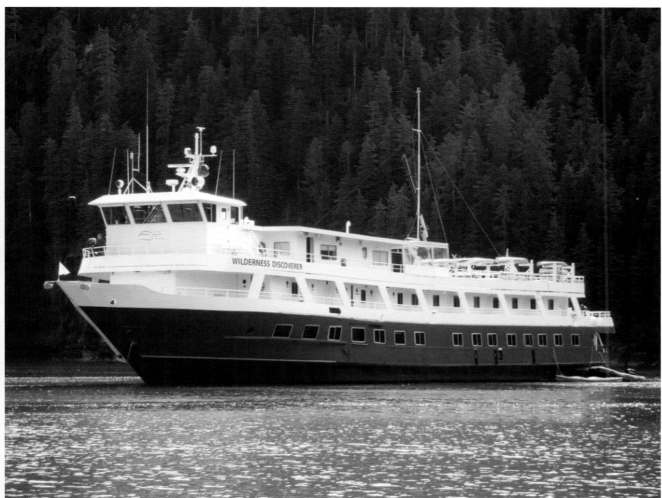

Ship: *WILDERNESS DISCOVERER*
IMO: 8859689 USCG NBR: 952722
MMSI: 366746920
Callsign: WDF7009
Operator: Akaska's Glacier Bay Tours &
Cruises/Un-Cruise Adventures
Tonnage (GRT): 99
Dimensions (length × beam × draught):
53.64 m (176 ft) × 11.89 m (39 ft) ×
2.95 m (9.7 ft)
Constructor & Yard Number: Blount
Boats, Warren Rhode Island, USA.
Yard No: MP-280
Motive Power: Cummins KTA-10M diesel –
680 hp; American bow thruster; 1 × 44 ft
Michigan propeller.
Speed (knots): 10
Launched/Floated out: 1976
Christened by: Naomi Sture
Passenger Cabins: 38
Passenger Decks: 3
Passengers/Crew Numbers (max.):
76/26
Class: Expedition ship
Registered: Juneau, Alaska
Former Names: *MAYAN PRINCE*

(Courtesy Of Un-Cruises Adventures)

145

Ship: *WILDERNESS EXPLORER*
IMO: 7641413
MMSI: 367167190
Callsign: WDG 2904
Operator: Akaska's Glacier Bay Tours & Cruises/Innerseas Discoveries, Seattle, Washington, USA
Tonnage (GRT): 94
Dimensions (length × beam × draught): 43.83 m (143.8 ft) × 10.97 m (36 ft) × 3.535 m (11.6 ft)
Constructor & Yard Number: Eastern Shipbuilding, RI.
Yard No: 1
Motive Power: 2 × Caterpiller diesels; 1 × propeller; 2 bow thrusters
Speed (knots): 10
Launched/Floated out: 1 January 1976
Christened by: Linda Reist
Passenger Cabins: 38
Passenger Decks: 3
Passengers/Crew Numbers (max.): 76/26
Class: N/A
Registered: Seattle, Washington, USA
Former Names: *INDEPENDENCE/SPIRIT OF DISCOVERY/COLUMBIA*

(Courtesy Un-Cruise Adventures)

Ship: *WIND SPIRIT*
IMO: 8603509
MMSI: 309056000
Callsign: C6CY9
Operator: Windstar Cruises, USA
Tonnage (GRT): 5,736
Dimensions (length × beam × draught):
134.02 m (439 ft 8 in) × 15.83 m (52 ft) × 4.10 m (13 ft 5 in)
Constructor & Yard Number: Ateliers & Chantiers du Havre, Nouvelle Havre, Le Havre, France.
Yard No: 0272
Motive Power: 4 masts = computer controlled sails 1,996 m² sail area; 3 × Wärtsilä 6R32E diesel = 1,050 kW; 1 C/P propeller
Speed (knots): 15.8
Launched/Floated out: 13 July 1987
Christened by: Clara van de Vorm
Passenger Cabins: 75
Passenger Decks: 5
Passengers/Crew Numbers (max.):
148/88
Class: MSY
Registered: Nassau, Bahamas
Former Names: N/A

(Courtesy Windstar Cruises)

Ship: *WIND STAR*

IMO: 8420978

MMSI: 309163000

Callsign: C6CA9

Operator: Windstar Cruises, Seattle, Washington, USA/TAC Cruise/Xanterra Holding Corp, Greenwood, Colorado

Tonnage (GRT): 5,703

Dimensions (length × beam × draught): 134.20 m (440.3 ft) × 15.80 m (52 ft) × 4.11 m (13.5 ft)

Constructor & Yard Number: SOC Nouvelle Des Ateliers & Chantiers du Havre, Le Havre, France.

Yard No: 0269

Motive Power: 4 × 62 m masts, computer-controlled sails 1,966 m² sail area; 3 × Wärtsilä-Femmart Schner diesel-electric = 2,964 kW, 2 × C/P propellers; 1 × 350 kW bow thruster; 2 × ACH Engineering stabilizers

Speed (knots): 10 (engines)/14 (wind & engines)

Launched/Floated out: 13 July 1987

Christened by: Louise Andren

Passenger Cabins: 74

Passenger Decks: 5

Passengers/Crew Numbers (max.): 148/88

Class: MSY

Registered: Nassau, Bahamas

Former Names: N/A

(Courtesy Windstar Cruises)

Ship: *WIND SURF*
IMO: 8700785
MMSI: 309242000
Callsign: C6106
Operator: Degrees Ltd, USA/TAC Cruise (Xanterra Holding Corp, Greenwood Village, Colorado)
Tonnage (GRT): 14,745
Dimensions (length × beam × draught): 187.2 m (617 ft) × 20.2 m (66 ft 3 in) × 5.01 m (16 ft 5 in)
Constructor & Yard Number: Soc Nouvelle des Ateliers Chantiers, du Havre, Le Havre, France.
Yard No: 274
Motive Power: 5 × masts, 7 × computer-operated sails, 2,600m² sail area; 4 × Wärtsilä-Duvant Crepelle diesel-electric = 9,120 kW, 2 × C/P propellers
Speed (knots): 12 (engines)/15 (engines and wind)
Launched/Floated out: January 1989
Passenger Cabins: 187
Passenger Decks: 8
Passengers/Crew Numbers (max.): 312/191
Class: MSY
Registered: Nassau, Bahamas
Former Names: *LA FAYETTE/CLUB MED1*

(Courtesy Windstar Cruises)

Ship: *YAMAL*
IMO: 9077549
MMSI: 273132400
Callsign: UCOT
Operator: Poseidon Arctic Voyages,
  Huntington, New York, NY, USA/
  Murmansk Shipping Company
Tonnage (GRT): 23,445
Dimensions (length × beam × draught):
  150 m (492.1 ft0 × 30 m (98.4 ft) × 11 m
  (36 ft)
Constructor & Yard Number: Baltic
  Shipyard & Engineering, Baltiyskiy Zavod,
  St Petersburg, Russia.
Yard No: 704
Motive Power: 2 × OK-900 171 MW
  Nuclear-powered turbo-electric = 55,950
  kW; 3 propellers
Speed (knots): 20.6
Launched/Floated out: 28 October 1992
Passenger Cabins: 56
Passenger Decks: 4
Passengers/Crew Numbers (max.):
  100/155
Class: N/A
Registered: Murmansk, Russia
Former Names: *OKTKYABRSKAYA*
  REVOLYOTSIYA

(Copyright Rosatom/ NAF)

Ship: *YORKTOWN*
IMO: 8949472
MMSI: 368373000
Callsign: WDG3446
Operator: Travel Dynamics International, New York, NY
Tonnage (GRT): 2,354
Dimensions (length × beam × draught): 78.30 m (257 ft) × 11.30 m (38 ft) × 2.43 m (8 ft)
Constructor & Yard Number: First Coastal Shipbuilding, Green Cove, Coral Springs, Florida, USA.
Yard No: 1
Motive Power: 2 × General Motors diesel = 1,332 kW; 2 propellers; 1 bow thruster
Speed (knots): 12
Launched/Floated out: as *Yorktown Clipper*, completed in April 1984
Passenger Cabins: 69
Passenger Decks: 4
Passengers/Crew Numbers (max.): 138/40
Class: Clipper
Registered: New York, NY
Former Names: *YORKTOWN CLIPPER/ SPIRIT OF YORKTOWN*

(Courtesy Travel Dynamics International)

Part Two

Behind the Ships

Chapter One

SOLAS (Safety of Life at Sea)

The SOLAS Convention in its successive forms is generally regarded as the most important of all international treaties concerning the safety of merchant ships. The first version was adopted in 1914, in response to the *Titanic* disaster, the second in 1929, the third in 1948, and the fourth in 1960. The 1974 version includes the tacit acceptance procedure – which provides that an amendment shall enter into force on a specified date unless, before that date, objections to the amendment are received from an agreed number of parties.

As a result the 1974 Convention has been updated and amended on numerous occasions. The Convention in force today is sometimes referred to as SOLAS, 1974, as amended.

Technical Provisions

The main objective of the SOLAS Convention is to specify minimum standards for the construction, equipment and operation of ships, compatible with their safety. Flag states are responsible for ensuring that ships under their flag comply with its requirements, and a number of certificates are prescribed in the Convention as proof that this has been done. Control provisions also allow contracting governments to inspect ships of other contracting states if there are clear grounds for believing that the ship and its equipment do not substantially comply with the requirements of the Convention – this procedure is known as port state control. The current SOLAS Convention includes articles setting out general obligations, amendment procedure and so on, followed by an annex divided into twelve chapters.

Chapter I – General provisions

Includes regulations concerning surveying the various types of ships and the issuing of documents signifying that ships meet the requirements of the Convention. The chapter also includes provisions for the control of ships in ports of other contracting governments.

Chapter II-1 – Construction – Subdivision and stability, machinery and electrical installations

The subdivision of passenger ships into watertight compartments must be such that after assumed damage to the ship's hull the vessel will remain afloat and stable. Requirements for watertight integrity and bilge pumping arrangements for passenger ships are also laid down as well as stability requirements for both passenger and cargo ships.

The degree of subdivision – measured by the maximum permissible distance between two adjacent bulkheads – varies with a ship's length and the service in which it is engaged. The highest degree of subdivision applies to passenger ships.

Requirements covering machinery and electrical installations are designed to ensure that services that are essential for the safety of the ship, passengers and crew are maintained under various emergency conditions.

'Goal-based standards' for oil tankers and bulk carriers were adopted in 2010, requiring new ships to be designed and constructed for a specified design life and to be safe and environmentally friendly, in intact and specified damage conditions, throughout their life. Under the regulation, ships should have adequate strength, integrity and stability to minimize the risk of loss of the ship or pollution to the marine environment due to structural failure, including collapse, resulting in flooding or loss of watertight integrity.

Chapter II-2 – Fire protection, fire detection and fire extinction
This includes detailed fire safety provisions for all ships and specific measures for passenger ships, cargo ships and tankers.

They include the following principles: division of the ship into main and vertical zones by thermal and structural boundaries; separation of accommodation spaces from the remainder of the ship by thermal and structural boundaries; restricted use of combustible materials; detection of any fire in the zone of origin; containment and extinction of any fire in the space of origin; protection of the means of escape or of access for fire-fighting purposes; ready availability of fire-extinguishing appliances; minimization of the possibility of ignition of flammable cargo vapour.

Chapter III – Life-saving appliances and arrangements
This Chapter includes requirements for life-saving appliances and arrangements, including requirements for life boats, rescue boats and life jackets according to the type of ship. The International Life-Saving Appliance (LSA) Code gives specific technical requirements for LSAs and is mandatory under Regulation 34, which states that all life-saving appliances and arrangements shall comply with the applicable requirements of the LSA Code.

Chapter IV – Radiocommunications
This Chapter incorporates the Global Maritime Distress and Safety System (GMDSS). All passenger ships and all cargo ships of 300 gross tonnage and upwards on international voyages are required to carry equipment designed to improve the chances of rescue following an accident, including satellite emergency position indicating radio beacons (EPIRBs) and search and rescue transponders (SARTs) for the location of the ship or survival craft.

Regulations in Chapter IV cover undertakings by contracting governments to provide radiocommunication services as well as ship requirements for carriage of radiocommunications equipment. The Chapter is closely linked to the Radio Regulations of the International Telecommunication Union.

Chapter V – Safety of navigation
Chapter V identifies certain navigation safety services that should be provided by contracting governments and sets forth provisions of an operational nature applicable in general to all ships on all voyages. This is in contrast to the Convention as a whole, which only applies to certain classes of ship engaged on international voyages.

The subjects covered include the maintenance of meteorological services for ships; the ice patrol service; routeing of ships; and the maintenance of search and rescue services.

This chapter also includes a general obligation for masters to proceed to the assistance of those in distress and for contracting governments to ensure that all ships shall be sufficiently and efficiently manned from a safety point of view.

The chapter makes mandatory the carriage of voyage data recorders (VDRs) and automatic ship identification systems (AIS).

Chapter VI – Carriage of cargoes
This Chapter covers all types of cargo (except liquids and gases in bulk) 'which, owing to their particular hazards to ships or persons on board, may require special precautions'. The regulations include requirements for stowage and securing of cargo or cargo units (such as containers). The Chapter requires cargo ships carrying grain to comply with the International Grain Code.

Chapter VII – Carriage of dangerous goods
The regulations comprise three parts:

Part A – Carriage of dangerous goods in packaged form – includes provisions for the classification, packing, marking, labelling and placarding, documentation and stowage of dangerous goods. Contracting governments are required to issue instructions at national level and the Chapter makes mandatory the International Maritime Dangerous Goods (IMDG) Code, developed by IMO, which is constantly updated to accommodate new dangerous goods and to supplement or revise existing provisions.

Part A-1 – Carriage of dangerous goods in solid form in bulk – covers the documentation, stowage and segregation requirements for these goods and requires reporting of incidents involving such goods.

Part B covers construction and equipment of ships carrying dangerous liquid chemicals in bulk and requires chemical tankers to comply with the International Bulk Chemical Code (IBC Code).

Part C covers construction and equipment of ships carrying liquefied gases in bulk and gas carriers' requirement to comply with the requirements of the International Gas Carrier Code (IGC Code).

Part D includes special requirements for the carriage of packaged irradiated nuclear fuel, plutonium and high-level radioactive waste on board ships and requires ships carrying such products to comply with the International Code for the Safe Carriage of Packaged Irradiated Nuclear Fuel, Plutonium and High-Level Radioactive Wastes on Board Ships (INF Code).

The chapter requires carriage of dangerous goods to be in compliance with the relevant provisions of the International Maritime Dangerous Goods Code (IMDG Code).

Chapter VIII – Nuclear ships

This Chapter cites basic requirements for nuclear-powered ships and is particularly concerned with radiation hazards. It refers to the detailed and comprehensive Code of Safety for Nuclear Merchant Ships, which was adopted by the IMO Assembly in 1981.

Chapter IX – Management for the safe operation of ships

This Chapter makes mandatory the International Safety Management (ISM) Code, which requires a safety management system to be established by the ship owner or any person who has assumed responsibility for the ship (the 'Company').

Chapter X – Safety measures for high-speed craft

The Chapter makes mandatory the International Code of Safety for High-Speed Craft (HSC Code).

Chapter XI-1 – Special measures to enhance maritime safety

The Chapter clarifies requirements relating to authorization of recognized organizations (responsible for carrying out surveys and inspections on the behalf of administrations); enhanced surveys; ship identification number scheme; and port state control on operational requirements.

Chapter XI-2 – Special measures to enhance maritime security

Regulation XI-2/3 of the chapter enshrines the International Ship and Port Facilities Security Code (ISPS Code). Part A of the Code is mandatory and Part B contains guidance as to how best to comply with the mandatory requirements. Regulation XI-2/8 confirms the role of the Master in exercising his professional judgement over decisions necessary to maintain the security of the ship. It says he shall not be constrained by the company, the charterer or any other person in this respect.

Regulation XI-2/5 requires all ships to be provided with a ship security alert system. Regulation XI-2/6 covers requirements for port facilities, providing among other things for contracting governments to ensure that port facility security assessments are carried out and that port facility security plans are developed, implemented and reviewed in accordance with the ISPS Code. Other regulations include detention, restriction of operations including movement within the port, or expulsion of a ship from port), and the specific responsibility of companies.

New regulations came into force on 1 July 2010 and are summarized by the IMO thus:

Revised passenger ship safety standards

The package of amendments to SOLAS were the result of a comprehensive review of passenger ship safety initiated in 2000 with the aim of assessing whether the current regulations were adequate, in particular for the large passenger ships now being built.

The work in developing the new and amended regulations has based its guiding philosophy on the dual premise that the regulatory framework should place more emphasis on the prevention of a casualty from occurring in the first place and that future passenger ships should be designed for improved survivability so that, in the event of a casualty, persons can stay safely on board as the ship proceeds to port.

The amendments include new concepts such as the incorporation of criteria for the casualty threshold (the amount of damage a ship is able to withstand, according to the design basis, and still safely return to port) into SOLAS chapters II-1 and II-2. The amendments also provide regulatory flexibility so that ship designers can meet any safety challenges the future may bring. The amendments include:

- alternative designs and arrangements;
- safe areas and the essential systems to be maintained while a ship proceeds to port after a casualty, which will require redundancy of propulsion and other essential systems;
- on-board safety centres, from where safety systems can be controlled, operated and monitored;
- fixed fire detection and alarm systems, including requirements for fire detectors and manually operated call points to be capable of being remotely and individually identified;
- fire prevention, including amendments aimed at enhancing the fire safety of atriums, the means of escape in case of fire and ventilation systems; and

- time for orderly evacuation and abandonment, including requirements for the essential systems that must remain operational in case any one main vertical zone is unserviceable due to fire.

Verification and Classification

Lloyd's Register in London, The American Bureau of Shipping and the Norwegian Det Norske Veritas (DNV) are the thee principal companies involved in the classification and verification of the cruise industry with regard to the safeguarding of life, property and the environment. Some smaller American vessels received similar classification from the United States Coastguard Service.

Det Norske Veritas (DNV)

The DNV is an independent foundation established in 1864 exclusively to inspect Norwegian shipping. It was established by some Norwegian insurance companies as a national alternative to Lloyd's but from 1867 it had itself become an international organization and the widespread introduction of steam vessels accelerated that expansion. By 1883 the Norwegian merchant fleet had become the world's third largest and by the turn of the century ships owned by Scandinavian companies still dominated the DNV listings.

Following the shock of the loss of the *Titanic* in 1912 and the International Convention for the Safety of Life at Sea two years later, which coincided with outbreak of the Great War with its unprecedented mercantile shipping losses, expansion was inevitable. In 1940 the German occupation of Norway forced a shift to England and necessitated close liaison with Lloyd's of London, which continued until 1952. From 1967 expansion was marked as was a wider mix of ship owners, which the establishment of the International Association of Class Society (IACS) the following year aided as did the rapid growth of the offshore oil field in Norwegian waters with its associated subsidiaries of pipelines, pumping stations and exploration. The ISO standards were published in 1987 and by the new millennium a complete turnaround from its original stance had been achieved with over 70 per cent of shipping classified by DNV being international.

Nowadays DNV has some three hundred offices in one hundred countries, including since 2009 China, employing 11,000 people for eighty-five different nations. Currently the organization has three major operating companies.

DNV Maritime and Oil & Gas specializes in classification, verification, risk management and offers technical advisory services for both the maritime and the oil and gas industries, which include safety on offshore rigs. Most relevant to the cruise industry are of course the Ship Classification Rules developed over a century and half. Thus DNV, with its Classification Rules establishes demanding standards, verifies correct and continued compliance with them through approvals, surveying and regular testing and issues survey reports and certificates on a regular basis to record such standards have been attained and are being upheld.

DNV KEMA is a worldwide consultancy, test and certification service organization providing these services across the spectrum of renewable energy, power generating, transmission and distribution and the increasing prominent carbon reduction and energy efficiency standards of such industries.

DNV Business Assurance provides certification, assessments and also provides training programmes to guarantee efficient and effective compliance across such industries.

Additionally, DNV established a research facility to study and enhance best-practice standards and pioneer new bench-marks internationally in all these areas.

New builds

Due to the economic downturn the dizzy pace of new cruise liner building has slowed somewhat in recent years, and this applies as much, indeed more so, to the smaller classes. Conversely, the higher end of the market, as typified by the Seabourn and Silver fleets with *Seabourn Odyssey*, *Seabourn Sojourn*, *Seabourn Quest* and *Silver Spirit* appeared to flourish. At the time of writing only the following vessels of 40,000 GT or less are underway on the building slips.

Shipyard	Cruise ship	Est. GRT	Passengers	Date	Cruise line
STX Europe	*Europa 2*	39,500	516	2013	Celebrity Cruises
Fincantieri	*La Soleal*	10,700	264	2013	Carnival Cruise Line
Factoria Naval de Marin, Marin	*Sea Cloud Hussar*	4,228	136	2013	

Ships to come?

Due to the current economic downturn many planned cruise ships may be delayed or even cancelled. The situation at the time of writing is very fluid and a ship confirmed one day could easily disappear from the order books the next.

The Fincantieri/Wärtsillä collaboration project, *XVintage*, designed by Pastrovich may be the future for small-ship cruising. She combines maximum comfort, interior and exterior beauty and environmentally-friendly power via a dual fuel/power and propulsion system base on the Wärtsillä 20DF dual-fuel engine, already IMO Tier-III compliant.

Chapter Two

The Owners, the Operators and the Ships

The current make-up of the cruise line market is a result of many decades of boom, take-overs, mergers and labyrinthine ship-exchanges as companies have either been created from long-established shipping empires with long and proud histories, suddenly having to adapt to the rise of airline travel and the decline of the traditional passenger market, or brand-new companies that have sprung up from nowhere to meet the unprecedented demand for the cruise product, principally in the United States and Europe, but, more recently in the New World also.

The cold winds of the recession have, from 2008 onward, blown coldly around this seemingly unstoppable surge, resulting in a spate of cancellations, sell-offs and laying-up of vessels so optimistically launched scant years before. It may turn out to be a re-run of the infamous 'tanker bubble' of an earlier decade, or it may be no more than a temporary blip in the relentless advance, but whatever the future, many of these giants will grace the world's oceans for decades to come.

It is a particular feature of the smaller cruise line market that it is even more fragmented and transitory than the complex weave of the larger owners, which when analysed come down to just a few huge conglomerates. At the smaller end of the scale one encounters a dizzying kaleidoscope of owners, charter companies and tour operators, or combinations of all three with subsidiary operators and management companies, whose involvement is sometimes brief, even just one season, and sometimes prolonged, but which can involved temporary re-naming of ships in a frenetic merry-go-round. Here we take a brief look at some of the companies behind the vessels listed in part one, but it can, perforce, only be a mere snapshot in time and the musical chairs continue to move around constantly. The ephemeral nature of many of these small concerns also makes a certain amount of duplication unavoidable.

AIDA Cruises

With more than a third of a million passengers and many thousands of staff worldwide AIDA Cruises is far-and-away the largest cruise company catering for mainly German-speaking customers and has one of most modern fleet of ships afloat. Its specialist and highly-successful marketing brand of 'Club Cruising', tailored for the younger and less formal end of the market, has proven highly popular and has spawned imitations, notably the Ocean Village concept in the UK. Now part of the enormous Carnival Corporation, AIDA still has its main base located at Rostock, Germany, where it began almost half a century ago. It is at Rostock that the administration, financial, marketing, operation and sales divisions are based, while at Hamburg the joint venture with Schmidt's Tivoli had an all-embracing and seamless input of all aspects of on-board entertainment from SeeLive Tivoli Entertainment & Consulting GmbH. By 2010 it was expected that the AIDA cruise fleet would have available 9,400 beds served by 2,400 staff in twenty-five countries.

This highly successful organization has seen major expansion over the last decade, but AIDA's roots are to be found in the former Communist state of East Germany. Back in the 1960s this strictly controlled regime was the antithesis of the burgeoning capitalist company of today, and everything was state controlled, including the national shipping company Deutsche Seereederei. The liner *Stockholm* was bought from its then Swedish-American owners (who were happy to be rid of her after the collision with the *liner Andrea Doria)*, and given the less-than-inspiring name of *Volkerfreundschaft* (which translates as 'Friendship Between Peoples'). She was used to reward those selected Communist Party officials deemed worthy, by giving them refreshing cruises. This vessel served for almost two decades before being replaced by the four-year-old custom-built cruise ship *Arkona*, formerly the *Astor*, which her West German owners had failed to make pay. The *Arkona*, like her predecessor, combined pleasure cruising for state-approved workers with charter work with Western operators until the fall of the Berlin Wall and the reunification of Germany. The privatization of the operating company as DSR in 1991 followed and her new German owners chartered her to Seetours.

By 1996 DSR had introduced a new concept to the cruise franchise, the 'Club Ship', based upon targeting a more youthful audience than the then 'traditional' cruise customer, with a more casual, laid-back and far less formal regime in which the emphasis was on a healthy and active fitness-based lifestyle, combined with a casual etiquette, which saw rigid dress codes abandoned and regulated dining largely abandoned in place of round-the-clock buffet meals. TUI's Robinson Club had been the inspiration and the idea was to prove as attractive afloat as it had been ashore. The idea caught the mood of the moment

and proved highly popular with young upwardly mobile Germans, and was encapsulated in the custom-built *Aida* (renamed as *AIDAcara* in 2001) constructed in Finland between 1994 and 1996 by Kvaerner Masa-Yards for the company. DSR had also acquired Seetours from TUI and marketed its cruises under this brand-name, either as charter ships or as direct operations. This German-based and orientated success attracted the attention of major operators further afield and P&O Princess Cruises acquired Seetours in 1999 and proceeded to expand the franchise both inside and outside Germany. The new owners placed orders for two new cruise ships, the *AIDAvita* and *AIDAaura*, built at Aker MTW Werft on the Baltic Coast and entering service in 2002 and 2003 respectively, and also sold off the *Arkona* and purchased the *Crown Princess*, which was renamed *A'Rosa Blu*. In the United Kingdom the 'Club' concept was marketed as Ocean Village with two customized ships and proved equally successful, although recent decisions have seen the abandonment of the concept in Britain.

The German-speaking market continued to thrive and *A'Rosa Blu* became *AIDAblu*, and Seetours was rebranded as AIDA Cruises, now part of the huge Carnival conglomerate that had incorporated the P&O Princess group. Two even larger ships were ordered by Carnival, built to a new design by Meyer Werft, but still featuring the basic 'Club' concept albeit on an even grander scale, the first of which, the 69,203-ton *AIDAdiva*, commenced operations in 2007, with *AIDAbella* joining the fleet a year later. These were followed by orders for two further ships, *AIDAluna* in 2009 and a 71,100-ton ship due in 2010, a new *AIDAblu*, the original having become *Ocean Village* in the interim and then P&O Australia's *Pacific Jewel*. Two further 'new generation' vessels are on order from Meyer Werft, which has orders totalling 945,000,000 euros.

AIDA ships have expanded from the Baltic origins and operate as far afield as the Canary Islands, the Mediterranean, the Caribbean and Central

America and German-speaking passenger numbers were expected to rise to one million in 2010 according to the president of the company, Michael Thamm. The company is now registered in Genoa, Italy, with its ships Italian-flagged ships, and is described as the German subsidiary of Carnival Corporation's Costa Crociere but both the ships themselves and their engines, as well as their customers, remain German, with the Caterpillar Groups MaK medium-speed diesel engines being selected as the prime movers for the diesel-electric and propulsion plants of the new ships; Siemens supplies the power generation, electric propulsion machinery and marine automation units, and the Nacos navigation and command systems are provided by SAM Electronics.

AIDAcara remains the smallest ship in the fleet, and the only one to qualify for entry here. She was originally built as *Aida* for *Deutsche Seetouristik/Arkona Reisen*, but when in 1999 P&O Cruises acquired that company she was the first of the new Aida brand, and renamed *AidaCara* in 2001. In March 2011 she was given a large refit at the Hamburg yard of Blohm und Voss and refurbishment, which has brought her right up to date with the modernization of her spa and sauna, as well as complete replacement of her carpets and tiling. A three-dimensional golf simulator was also added and the hull of the ship was given a new silicone coating. She now accommodates 1186 guests over nine decks (3 to 11) in a variety of balcony/outside/inside staterooms, outside comfort staterooms and junior suites. Her facilities include the Calypso and Markt Restaurants, both with open-seat buffet dining, the Rossini Restaurant, which is an extra tariff à la carte, waiter service dining establishment at extra tariff, the large Das Theatre for shows, the Aida Bar and the Anytime Disco. There is a promenade deck, a pool deck with a volleyball/basketball court, Aida golf, which is a golf simulator and indoor putting green, and the Body and Soul spa and fitness centre.

The *AidaCara* is registered in Genoa, Italy.

ALAS (PV International Holdings, Inc.)

This ship management and cruise services corporation was founded as PV Holdings Inc. by Peter Villiotis. In 1998 the company acquired the Delaware yacht and ship management organization Saenz Corporation, of Portside Yachting Center, 1850 SE 17th Street Causeway, Fort Lauderdale, Florida. This gave PV International control of their worldwide ferry, passenger and overnight cruise base. Peter Villiotis had previous cruise ship experience with Regency and Carnival. The aim was to enter the Latin American ferry operations while establishing a single-ship cruise ship company. In December 2011 PV Enterprises Inc. was 'reversed-merged' into ALAS Holdings. It is headquartered at Clearwater, Florida. Peter Villiotis remains Chairman and Chief Executive Officer, and David W Turner is Chief Financial Officer and Board member. Saenz was recently re-positioned as a Bahamas-based daily luxury fun club providing cruise ship clientele with small luxury yacht services.

ALAS/PV Enterprises initially intended to buy the Louis Cruise ship *Emerald*, which was laid up, the aim being to employ her as a hotel/accommodation ship for the South Korean Yeosu Expo 2012, but this plan fell through and the *Emerald* went to an Indian breakers yard. In her place another idle Louis Line ship, the *Aquamarine*, was targeted and acquired by the company in May 2012 as the *Ocean Star Pacific*. She managed to obtain Short Term SOLAS Certificates from Det Norske Veritas valid until July 2012 for her to make a single 'empty-ship' voyage to Mexico in order to complete Conditions of Class for outstanding deficiencies, the first step to full SOLAS certification after a major investment into her.

The 23,149-GT *Ocean Star Pacific* was originally built in 1971 by Oy Wärtsilä, Finland, as the *Nordic Prince* for Royal Caribbean. In June 1980 she was lengthened by 26 m at Wärtsilä. She continued serving as a worldwide cruise vessel until March 1995 when she was sold to Sun Cruises and received a refit and the new name *Carousel*. She was sold to Louis Cruise Lines in July 2004 and given another refit. They also renamed her *Aquamarine* and used her for Mediterranean cruising working from Genoa. In April 2006 Louis Cruise Lines, after another refit in 2007, chartered her out to Transocean Tours, who operated her

The Wärtsilä 38 engine is one of the most popular power plants in use today, being the lightest and most compact heavy duty engine this international company now produces. While incorporating the latest technology this engine contains fewer individual parts, so requires less maintenance. It has been designed for low fuel consumption, reduced emission levels and is fully compliant with the IMO Tier II exhaust emissions regulations. (*Courtesy and copyright of Wärtsilä*)

until 2008 as the *Arielle*. She returned to the Louis Cruise Lines fold and resumed her previous name of *Aquamarine* once more but she suffered hull damage in May and had to undergo repair. In December 2010 Louis Cruise Lines sold *Aquamarine* to the Mexican Corporación de Cruceros Nacionales for $23,375,000 and she was renamed *Ocean Star Pacific* in April 2011 and operated by Ocean Star Cruises, Mexico City, with ownership by ALAS/PV Enterprises International Inc., Fort Lauderdale, Florida. Work commenced to restore her to full service; however, she was incapacitated by a severe engine room fire in her engine room while at Huatulco, Mexico. After the damage had been repaired at Salina Cruz, further problems arose in July 2011 with the new cooling and air conditioning generators that had been recently fitted. She remained anchored off Mazatlán, Mexico, for the whole of 2012.

She can accommodate 1,231 guests across eight passenger decks. She is registered at Panama City, Panama.

laskan Dream Cruises

This company's operations were commenced in May 2011 by the boat-building company Allen Marine a year after Chuck West's Cruise West cruise company went into bankruptcy and two of its former vessels were acquired. The company's address is Sawmill Creek Road, Sitka, Alaska, and the company President and Chief Executive Officer is David Allen. The company can trace its roots back to Alaskans, Bob and Betty Allen, who restored a laid-up tour boat and renamed her *St Michael*, a name that reflected the couple's Russian Orthodox beliefs. Later their five children and then their grandchildren joined and expanded the business into Allen Marine Tours and it remains a family company. Allen Marine is the complete package, designing, building and operating the boats on day trips, whale-watching forays and inshore operations for the guests of the large cruise companies in Alaskan waters. Alaska Dream Cruises operates out of Siska. When Cruise West failed Allen Marine acquired several of its boats and the Alaskan Dream Cruises operation got under way in earnest. The company is locally owned and orientated with members of the Kaagwaantaan Clan with their strong ties with the Tlingit community, with whom they co-operate in shore excursions and local crewing, and also with the National Park Service ashore who also provide guest lecturers. Operating small vessels means accessing areas off the beaten track to most tourist companies, such as Kake, Icy Strait, Point Adolphus, Hobart Bay, Tracy Arm, Kasaan and other small communities in the Glacier Bay region of South-East Alaska. Nor does the size of the vessels prevent them serving excellent cuisine, champagne and wines aboard. Nonetheless, the company operates a sustainable and green tourism policy and has on-board educational programmes and locally sourced organic foods. Currently the fleet comprises two cruise ships and a catamaran.

The 514-GT *Admiralty Dream* was built in 1979 by Eastern Shipping as the *Columbia*. She later became the *Independence* and then *Spirit of Columbia* for Cruise West. She was refitted in 2012. She is owned by General Electric Credit, Delaware, and is on charter to Alaskan Dream Cruises. She can carry sixty-six guests in thirty-three cabins. The suites are named Kootznahoo, Tenakee, Chilkoot, Katlian, Lituya, Taku, Lazaria, Yakobi, Lisianski, Chichagof and there is an owner's suite forward. She has a sun deck, the Admiralty dining room, with galley and the forward lounge and bar.

The 97-GT *Baranof Dream* was built in 1980 by Nichols Blount Marine, Warren, Rhode Island, for Cruise West as the *Pacific Northwest* but became the *Spirit of Alaska* with Cruise West. She was refitted in 1991. She has four decks, bridge, upper, main and lower, and can accommodate fifty-eight guests in thirty-one cabins. The suites are named Tebenkov, Wrangell, Alexander, Verstovia, Frederick, Kruzov, Lydonia, Chatham and Shelikof. She has a sun deck, the Baranof dining room, galley and the Explorer's lounge and bar plus a bow viewing area.

The aluminium-constructed catamaran is the 490-GT *Alaskan Dream* (IMO 8978679) built in 1986 by Nichols Brothers Shipyard as the *Contessa* for Glacier Bay Marine Services. She was later owned by EEX Acquisition LLC and then Contessa Boat LLC before being renamed *Executive Explorer*. She was refitted in 2011. She has capacity for forty-two guests in twenty-three cabins including the owner's suite and two vista view suites. She has four passenger decks, observation, bridge, upper and main. She has an open deck, the vista view lounge and Sitka Rose dining room.

American Cruise Lines (ACL)

Founded in 1991, American Cruise Lines has its HQ on the Boston Post Road, Guildford, Connecticut, USA. The Chairman and CEO is Charles A. Robertson, with Vice-Presidents Timothy Beebe and Paul Taiclet (Hotels). The company currently owns six new-build luxury river cruise ships, *American Glory, American Spirit, American Star, Independence, Queen of the Mississippi* and *Queen of the West*. Another vessel, *American Eagle*, is currently laid up at Salisbury, Maryland, and for sale. The company itinerary is a wide one, and on the whole it tends to concentrate on the Mississippi region, New England and Alaska, also stating that it offers 'thirty-five cruise options in twenty-eight states'. An earlier vessel, *American Eagle*, now registered to American River Cruises, is currently up for sale at Salisbury.

American Glory, American Spirit and *American Star*, along with the earlier *American Eagle*, now discarded, are all similar vessels. All were of welded steel construction, with Caterpillar diesel engines with two Aquamet shafts with two five-bladed Nibral propellers and a 175hp

Caterpillar engine aboard *American Eagle*. (*ACL official*)

Thrustmaster bow thruster, and were custom-built for ACL by the Chesapeake Shipbuilding Corporation, Salisbury, Maryland, between 2000 and 2008. Dimensions vary a little between ships but all are built to carry both daytime and overnight guests, the latter ranging from forty-nine to 102. The newer *Independence* is a larger version of these vessels but with larger dimensions is more comfortable and is fitted with Rolls-Royce stabilizers. She has overnight accommodation for 104 guests. All have four main decks, observation, Carolina, lounge and main. The target audience is mainly more mature passengers and the amenities reflect a more leisurely type of cruise with bingo, bridge and

board games. There are guest lecturers in the evenings who act as guides during the daytime, and at ports of call local musicians and entertainers sometimes provide on-board concerts and shore-excursions are arranged. There is one grand dining room, and there is one large lounge, known as the Nantucket lounge on *American Glory* and the Chesapeake lounge aboard the others. All vessels have a library/lounge, midships lounge, and main lounge. There are either putting greens or an exercise area on the observation deck along with sun loungers and shades.

All four vessels are registered in Wilmington, Delaware.

The company also operates two new-build river cruisers that are very spacious and comfortable replicas of the old-time stern-wheelers, the *Queen of the West* and *Queen of the Mississippi*, but these fall outside the range of this book.

Åndin Linjen/Rederi Allandia AB

First established in the 1970s, the company has changed owners several times since then. Sold to Rederei AB Ållandia it now has its HQ at Vasagatan 6, Stockholm, and is now a subsidiary of Ingenjörsfirma Strauch Aktieb. It conducts daily cruises from the Old Town Wharf, near the Tessin Palace, in central Stockholm to Mariehamn and back and has done for many years. It has only used single vessels in that time, commencing with the *Artemis K* in 1973, then the *Achillies* from 1974 to 1979 and since 1979 the veteran *Birger Jarl*. The company is owned by the Strauch brothers Micael and Magnus Hans-Axel.

The *Birger Jarl* was first built with this name and served thus until January 1977. She was built at the Finnboda Varv in Nacka, near Stockholm, in 1953 for Stockholm's Rederi AB Svea. She was constructed as a conventional passenger-steamer, could carry 369 passengers and had a quadruple-expansion steam power plant, class-divided accommodation. She served the Stockholm to Helsinki ferry link in summer with the Finnish *Aallotar* and *Bore III* of similar construction. In the winter months she cruised to Turku and was maintained by Svea. The three concerns eventually merged into the Silja Line. In 1971 the company introduced new ice-breaking Ro-Ro type ferries and *Birger Jarl* was utilized for the first time for cruising between Stockholm and Mariehamn. In 1973 she was acquired by Jakob Lines, Jakobstad, Finland, and she was given a major reconstruction, which converted her with her own Ro-Ro car deck, and was renamed *Bore Nord*, owned by Steamship Company Bore, Turku, Finland. From 1977 to 1978 she was owned by Minicarriers of Mariehamn and was used on various Baltic ferry routes. She also served as an accommodation ship at Stavanger, Norway, between 1976 and 1977, and was given the name *Minisea* in January 1977 for the year to January 1978.

She was acquired by the London-based Caribbean Shipping Company and underwent another reconstruction in 1978–79 when she was again converted to work as a cruise ship, and was renamed as *Baltic Star* and was registered in Panama. Under her new owners, Åndin Linjen, she returned in this new guise to Baltic working. In 1982 her old steam engines were finally replaced by a MAN B&W 4SA diesel. In 2002, the ship got back her original name and again became registered in Sweden. Also between January 1978 and March 2002 she transported guests to Mariehamn in Aland, Finland and also made occasional voyages to Tallinn, Slite, Riga, Saaremaa, Ventspils and Klaipeda.

In 2002 the ship was sold to Åndin-Linjen/Rederi Allandia AB. To commemorate Stockholm's 750-year anniversary, and her return the Swedish flag, she was given the name *Birger Jarl*. For the past twenty-four years she has been continuously in service.

The *Birger Jarl's* biggest threat is not lack of customers but, like many veterans, the ramifications of SOLAS 2010. This saw her laid up at Stockholm in October 2010 for a period when the new regulations came in. She is an old vessel with many wooden combustible fitments, which renders her vulnerable as a fire hazard under the new regulations. She has been awarded many six-monthly special exemptions or 'stay of executions' from the Swedish and Finnish authorities since 2011, and has been laid up at Stockholm for periods awaiting final decisions but, at the time of writing, having been 'technically upgraded', is still faithfully plying her route. As always cost is the deciding factor, but tempered by sentimentality as she is acknowledged as having a unique cultural value by her longevity alone. In fact in acknowledgement of this the Swedish State Maritime Museum placed her on their 'K' Listing as a historically important ship in May 2010. The options available to keep her running have been listed as the removal of all wood fittings and fixtures and totally reconstructing her internally – a very expensive exercise; a cheaper alternative is to apply special fireproofing treatments internally, but whether this would suffice is problematical; installing extra fire sprinklers and other protective measures; or sending *Birger Jarl* to the scrapyard and either replacing her or ceasing the service. In the end a temporary solution was found when she was dry-docked in August 2011 and refitted while retaining her wooden fittings. However, the owners have announced that she is due for replacement as soon as a suitable vessel is found. She might therefore become a museum ship on display but unable to trade.

The *Birger Jarl* has 156 cabins, 'every one different' and is too small to boast too many amenities but while in service she has the Roslagen Restaurant and smorgasbord dining, the Sky Bar and cocktail bar, a perfumery and a duty-free shop.

Azamara Club Cruises

The company was founded in 2007 as Azamara Cruises and was intended to be part of subsidiary Celebrity Expeditions' branding but, instead,

165

was given its own distinctive status. It further re-positioned itself and became Azamara Club Cruises in April 2010. It remains a subsidiary of Royal Caribbean Cruises (RCC) and is located at Caribbean Way, Miami, Florida. The Chairman and Chief Executive Officer is Richard D. Fain of Royal Caribbean Cruises Ltd, the President and Chief Executive Officer of Azamara Club Cruises is Larry Pimentel, appointed in July 2009 and the Executive Vice President and Chief Financial Officer is Brian J. Rice of RCC. Edie Bornstein is Vice President, Sales and Marketing, Bert Van Middendorp is Assistant Vice President, Hotel Operations, Signe Bjorndal is Marketing Director, Anita Carson is Director of National Accounts and Bruce G. Setloff is Global Director, Charters & Incentive Sales. The company has positioned itself as a high-end cruise operator. Currently it operates two ships, the 30,277-GT sisters *Azamara Journey* and *Azamara Quest* whose cruises feature 'Destination Immersion' by offering longer overnight stays at ports of call and linking high-quality hotel venues. This ethos is reflected in their new tag line 'You'll love where we take you' and where they will take you is to 150 different destinations in fifty countries. Among the overnight locations are St Tropez, France; Istanbul, Turkey; Sorrento, Italy, including the Amalfi Coast and Capri; extended stays in St Petersburg, Russia, on Azamara's Scandinavia and Russia Itineraries; London, which requires time due to its vastness and range of venues; and in the Mediterranean and Black Sea areas there are visits to Dubrovnik, Croatia; an evening gondola ride in Venice; Odessa, Ukraine; Livorno (Florence), Italy; and Warnemunde for visiting Berlin. In the Far East locations included multiple overnight stays in Ho Chi Minh City, Bangkok, Singapore and Hong Kong. There are two-night packages allowing travellers to journey from the ship berthed at Bangkok to Laos; similarly from Hiroshima to Osaka via the famed Bullet train; in India guests can travel over a three-night experience from Mumbai to the Taj Mahal. In the Middle East similar overnight packages can be found for Israel from Ashdod; High Tea at the Burj al Arab Hotel in Dubai and there is the Grand Egypt tour that incorporates both Cairo and Luxor.

Both ships recently underwent $25 million makeovers at Sembawang Shipyard, Singapore, which introduced LCD televisions in staterooms, more comprehensive public access areas, new carpets, decor, mattresses and fittings. The Casino bar was also expanded and enhanced with new furniture, the already famous spa and fitness centre was given a new steam room and showers, plus new state-of-the-art 'Life Fitness' cardio equipment. Another improvement was the inclusion of special complimentary boutique-produced wines. A new hull colour was introduced termed by the Navantia Shipyard that carried out the refurbishment 'Azamara Blue'. A new logo was adopted. The upgrading also brought in the Le Club Voyage loyalty programme.

Both ships were built by Chantiers de l'Atlantique in 2007 as the Renaissance vessels *R Six* and *R Seven* respectively. When Renaissance folded Cruise Invest leased *R Seven* to the German Delphin Seereisen Company in June 2003, they renamed her *Delphin Renaissance* until she was sold in May 2006 to Pullmantur who gave her the new name *Blue Moon*. It was only a short period, however, before she became the *Azamara Quest* from September 2003. Similarly, *R Six* became the Celebrity Expeditions vessel *Celebrity Journey* and it was planned for her to become a Galapagos tourist ship, but she never sailed under that name. Instead, in October 2006, she was transferred to Pullmantur and became their *Blue Dream* in January 2007 before joining Azamara as the *Azamara Journey*.

They both have nine passenger accessible decks (3 to 11) and can accommodate 694 guests in a range of suites – Club Ocean, Club Continental, Club Deluxe, Club Ocean, Club Continental,

Club Deluxe, Veranda, Club Veranda Accessible, Club Oceanview Accessible, Club Veranda, Club Oceanview, Club Interior Accessible and Club Interior. For dining options there are two speciality restaurants, the Aqualina and the Prime C Steakhouse; there are also the Wine Cellar, Discoveries Restaurant, the Pool Grill, Mosaic Café, the Martini Bar, and Windows Café. For entertainment there is the Casino Luxe, the cabaret lounge, the Looking Glass lounge and the Discoveries lounge, There are also the drawing room and the sun deck with shuffleboard. For more active participation there is a jogging track and the thalassotherapy pool. Shopaholics have the choice of The Journey Shop, La Boutique and Indulgences, while there is a hair salon and a medical facility.

Both ships are registered at Valletta, Malta.

Birka Cruises

Working out of Stockholm, Sweden Birka Cruises is currently part of the Ålandian-based Rederiaktiebolaget Eckerö but was originally established as long ago as 1971 as a ferry company plying the route to Mariehamn. The first ship was the former DFDS Line vessel *Prinsessen*, renamed as *Prinsessan* and the following year a second sister ship, the *Olav*, became the *Baronessan*. After a short-lived venture working to Helsinki and Leningrad with two further ferry purchases failed in 1973, new vessels were added on the original route and by 1986 the company refocused its efforts with a new build, the *Birka Princess*, which shifted the emphasis more from ferry operations to cruise operating and Birka Cruises was created. Four years later the company bought into United Shipping and a second cruise vessel was ordered, the *Birka Queen*. However, during her construction the Finnish shipyard Wärtsilä Turku, went into receivership and the cost of her completion proved too high for Birka to continue. Instead, a cheaper option was followed

and, in 1992, the *Sunward* was bought from Norwegian Cruise Line as a prudent alternative and given the name *Birka Queen* with the intent to cruise the Baltic to St Petersburg and Riga. Again, this proved a short-lived episode, although the ship sailed under NCL charter for a further five years.

The *Birka Princess* herself underwent a total re-construction in 1999, resulting in increased accommodation and updated facilities and, by 2002, conditions had so improved that another new vessel was ordered, the *Birka Paradise*, this time from the Aker Finnyards at Rauma. Birka took delivery of this ship in 2004 but, once more, the climate had changed and they were again forced to sell her two years later to Louis Cruises. Financial difficulties resulted in the purchase of just under half the company by Rederiaktiebolaget Eckerö and in 2007 this holding was enlarged bringing control of Birka to Eckerö Line.

Carnival Cruise Lines

Carnival itself grew from humble beginnings to become the huge organization it is today, embracing as it does not just the Carnival branding but also the Holland America (American orientated), AIDA (German), Costa (Italian), Cunard (British), Iberocruceros (Spanish), P&O (British) and Princess (American) Lines, which mainly sail larger and larger cruise lines the world over. It also has embraced down the years a number of smaller ship operators, some of which it still oversees. Among them are a number described in these pages, including at one time Windstar Cruises' *Minerva* and *Peace Boat* and it still controls today HAL's *Prinsendam*.

The whole cruise world cannot possible ignore Carnival and nor can I, having spent my Golden Wedding anniversary aboard the *Carnival Liberty* in the Caribbean in 2012. So I make no excuses for repeating the interesting history and vicissitudes of that giant again here.

Minerva, bows and bridge. (*Swan Helenic Minerva official*)

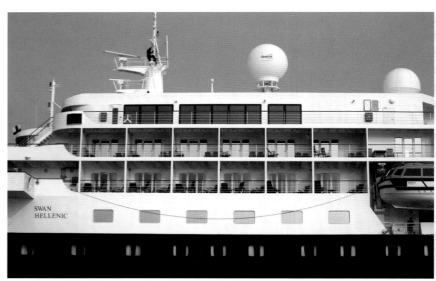

Minerva, close-up port view. (*Swan Helenic Minerva official*)

The Carnival Corporation is a truly unique organization. Growing from a tiny seed, by brilliant marketing and sagacious marketing it has blossomed to become the Cruise Lines' mega-giant, absorbing into its ample bosom all manner of cruise line companies and shipping lines, both new and old, into one vast conglomerate. However, rather than extinguish these famous brands by merging them into one mammoth brand, the trend by Carnival overall has been to retain them as quasi-autonomous companies, each playing to its particular market, strength and customer appeal. This has proved, so far anyway, a wise decision and is being strengthened by the concentration on an ethnic or national series of brands relating to each sector of the market. This policy can be illustrated by listing Carnival Corporation's brands and their principal customer base.

The potentially enormous Chinese market has not escaped attention either; one of the older and smaller Costa ships, the 28,430-ton *Costa Allegra* has, since 2006, been experimentally working for winter periods out of Shanghai with a Chinese name, on cruises to Japan and Korea and there is talk of her being joined by a second vessel.

Carnival Corporation & plc is headquartered in Miami, Florida, and its subsidiary companies currently run 92 cruise ships of all sizes, with 13 more ships on order with approximately 80,000 employees worldwide. Revenue in 2008 was $US 14.6 billion. This huge empire originated from one man's vision, that man being Theodore Arisohn, born in Tel Aviv, Palestine, in 1924. After moving to Miami in 1966, he started a partnership that founded what would later become NCL. They only had single ship but had a new philosophy, short-haul pleasure packed cruises, with the ships' amenities themselves a main part of the packages' attraction.

The combining of P&O Princess Cruises made it the world's largest vacation group by some way, and the parent company became Carnival Corporation & plc. Other cruise lines followed in rapid succession, Seabourn in 1992, Costa Crocierein 1997, Cunard in 1998 and the German AIDA.

The four smaller *Spirit*-class ships, *Carnival Legend*, *Carnival Miracle*, *Carnival Pride* and *Carnival Spirit*, and the five *Conquest*-class 110,000 tonners, *Carnival Conquest*, *Carnival Freedom*, *Carnival Glory*, *Carnival Liberty* and *Carnival Valor* all made their debuts in the early twenty-first-century, and the upward trend continued with the 113,300-ton *Carnival Splendor* in July 2008, originally designed for the Costa brand, while 2009 saw the introduction of the 130,000-ton *Carnival Dream*, with her sister *Carnival Magic* arriving in June 2011. New builds have continued apace, but all far too enormous to be included in this volume.

Caspiy AK Jhelken LLP

Caspiy AK Jhelken Ltd is a Russian Ship Management Agency whose HQ is at Microdistrict 8, Building 38, Offices 401–404 Aktau c., 130000 Mangistau Region, Republic of Kazakhstan. The company was awarded an ISO 9002 Certificate in 2010 and although this did not replace the more normal ISM which is the shipping trade's equivalent, it gave added gravitas to the company when working with engineering groups in offshore projects and the like. The Coordinator for Foreign Economic Affairs is Natalia Gribanova. Caspiy AK Jhelken LLP with its river cruise

fleet currently works closely in conjunction with partner companies such as Silverburn Shipping with Arkship, whose Marketing and Client Development Manager, Vito Scalogna, is mainly based at Aktau, Kazakhstan. Silverburn Shipping provides accommodation vessels. Since 2010 the company has acquired several river cruise vessels to utilize as accommodation vessels or hotel ships on big projects.

The *T G Shevchenko* was original built by the German shipbuilding company Elbewerft Boizewburg GmbH, Boizenburg (now part of the Deutschen Maschinen-und-Schiffbau AG) for the Dnepr Shipping Company as the *Taras Shevchencko*.

Reception staff aboart *T.G. Shevchenko*. (*Inflot*)

She can accommodate 140 guests in ten suites, ten single cabins, 112 twin cabins and eight quad cabins. She has five decks, sun, boat, upper, main and lower. She has two restaurants, the Odessa on the boat deck and the Kyiv on the upper deck, and also two bars, the Odessa and the Panorama. She also has a large lounge, a conference hall and a souvenir shop.

In 2010 she was acquired by Caspiy AK Jhelken LLP, who renamed her *T G Shevchencko,* and she is currently in use as a floating accommodation ship for the Kurmangazy Oilfield development project in the Caspian Sea.

Celebrity Cruises

When the North American public began flocking to cruise ships in ever increasing numbers there seemed to many existing shipping companies a perfect way to turn around their waning fortunes as conventional passenger transit declined sharply. One such family company to seize the opportunity and optimize the new wave was the Chandris family from the Aegean island of Chios, Greece. John D. Chandris, Snr had founded this shipping dynasty back in 1915 with the purchase of a single sailing vessel, the *Dimitrios,* with which he traded around the Eastern Mediterranean. In the glut of post-war shipping he was able to build up his fleet by adding three steamships, which also carried cargoes to Levant ports. In 1922, Chandris moved into the passenger market with the *Chimara* and plied a regular route between Piraeus and Corinth. Growth was gradual and the next acquisition did not occur until 1936, when a British-built, French-owned steamer, the *Corte II* (ex-*Bloemfontein Castle)* was purchased and renamed *Patris.* Based principally at Venice, and with a single-class capacity of 161, *Patris* ran combined passenger/cruise routes up and down the Adriatic and around the Aegean as far as Haifa. The Second World War intervened, Greece being invaded first by Italy in 1940 and then by Germany in 1941, when many citizens were forced to flee and *Patris* herself was bombed and sunk.

During the war the death of the company's founder left his two London-based sons, Anthony and Dimitri, in charge and, with the coming of peace, they steadily began to re-build the company. A ready-made market was available in the mass exodus from the rubble and near famine of war-torn Europe of people seeking a new and better life in North and South America and Australia. Among the companies to service this need was Chandris. Two ex-Canadian Train ferries, which had served as auxiliary warships in the Royal Navy during the war and were surplus to requirement, were the 6,892-ton sisters, *Prince Robert* and *Prince David.* In 1948 these ships became the Charlton Line's *Charlton Monarch* and *Charlton Sovereign* respectively, and underwent conversion to cruise vessel in Belgium in 1946. The Chandris brothers had purchased this company and these two ships became the nucleus of what was to become the largest Greek shipping line of the post-war period. They voyaged from Bremerhaven, Germany to Sydney, Australia and similar destinations packed with refugees from Stalin's occupation of Eastern Europe as far apart as Lithuania and the Ukraine.

Back in Greece the fleet was steadily increased as similar older ships were added and converted to passenger/cruise capacity, and routes grew. The *Britanis* (the former Union-Castle liner *Kenya Castle*) inaugurated a migrant route from Piraeus to Australia in 1961 and two years later *Ellinis* extended this via the Panama Canal to a global service. By 1976 the Chandris line was running thirteen ships and carrying half-a-million people. The distinctive house-style featured blue funnels with the upper-case rendition of the Greek alphabetical character 'Chi', used in both Chios and Chandris, which takes the shape of an 'X' and which still forms one of today's most immediately recognizable ship markings. Attention had also been turned toward the American market where the examples of others had shown a demand and, by the 1980s, as the passenger-liner was clearly in decline, a conscious decision was made to move over to the cruise market. The *Amerikanis* (previously the Matson Line's ship *Monterey*) joined the newly established Miami-based Chandris Fantasy Cruises, which had been set up to serve the Caribbean trade. The ship, along with others of the fleet, enjoyed considerable popularity with the bottom-end of the cruise market, despite being rather elderly ladies. However, it became increasingly obvious that with rival companies such as Carnival building radically new and exciting ships, the days of the Chandris 'makeover' fleet were numbered.

A move 'upmarket' was clearly indicated and the opportunity arose when, early in 1988, one of the companies holding special government of Bermuda contracts for two special berthing rights at Hamilton for the prestigious New York to Bermuda seven-day cruise ships, was absorbed by HAL, who declined to take up that option. Bermuda would only sanction the highest-quality applicants, which seemingly ruled Chandris Fantasy out of the running, but this requirement met with the company's own desire to re-position itself at the high end of the market. Rather than attempt to re-grade a brand that was already firmly established as a low-cost operation, in 1989 John D. Chandris, the founder's grandson, announced the inauguration of a totally new company, which he named Celebrity Cruises, a name that reflected the new aspirational status of the line.

Chandris presented the concept to Bermuda, who, convinced by its potential, awarded the new company a two-ship contract for an initial five-year period to run from 1990. In order to meet this deadline, one new ship was ordered and one of the existing vessels, the 30,440-ton *Galileo*, (formerly the Lloyd Triestino's *Galileo Galilei*) was earmarked for a multi-million dollar upgrade to bring her up to the new required standard. This total refurbishment was carried out at Lloyd Werft shipyard, Bremerhaven, at a cost $50 million, and, upon completion in February 1990, she was renamed *Meridian*. She made her new maiden voyage from Port Everglades in April 1990 and then moved north to New York to join the brand-new *Horizon*, which had arrived there on 12 May to commence the two-ship, week-long service to Hamilton as scheduled for the high season, with the ships working the Caribbean during the fall and winter period.

For the first ship of the planned new-image fleet, far more original and imaginative ships than the *Meridian* were demanded. Future Celebrity ships would reflect quality by both their external and internal style and especially by their elegant cuisine and exceptionally high on-board standards. Starting from scratch a whole design team was assembled from the best exponents of flair and brio. The noted and revolutionary London-based naval architect Jon Bannenberg was commissioned and he came up with an distinctive and outstanding design like no other, with raking, angular lines, and dark blue and white contrasting colours that accentuated the impression of speed and grace with a raw excitement that hit the 'right-on note' with the rich young New Yorkers that were the target audience. The ship 'looked right' and felt right, and once aboard the guests found that the interiors were similarly styled in an up-to-the-moment raciness that nonetheless revealed grace and space with modernity. The whole vessel struck the optimistic note of the time and was coupled with a dedicated attention to on-board service. This revolutionary ship was the 46,811-ton $US 185 million *Horizon*, which was built by the Joe L. Meyers shipyard in Germany to the teams' most exacting standards. The company's 'safe hands' who was the overseer of this, and indeed of all Celebrity new builds since the 1960s, was Vice-President Demetrios Kaparis who ensured that the board's wishes were adhered to throughout the construction.

With the first ships up-and-running and with the verdict of success achieved, *Horizon's* sister ship, the 47,225-ton *Zenith,* joined her in April 1992.

Good and popular as the two new ships were, they were third-generation ships in what was becoming a fourth-generation world and the newer builds of their competitors saw tonnages pushed up sharply to increase passenger numbers. Clearly Celebrity had to follow suit, and so the next stage of the plan called for even larger vessels, and even more flair from the same teams that had produced *Horizon* and *Zenith,* and these ships became known collectively as the *Century* class. The lead ship, *Century,* was financed partly through a joint venture deal with the New York-based Overseas Ship holding Group (OSG), which was agreed in October 1992, which raised $US 220 million capital in exchange for a 49 per cent slice of Celebrity. Thus bankrolled, Celebrity went ahead the following year and placed an order for two further new vessels of this class of vessel with Meyers, *Century* and *Mercury*.

The lead ship was delivered on 30 November 1995. She was a 70,606-ton ship with a passenger capacity of 1,778.

She had been christened by John's wife, Tina, the previous October. Compared with the *Horizon* the *Celebrity* had 50 per cent extra space for 25 per cent more guests, giving even more luxury per client and hallmarking the Celebrity style. This extra elbow-room was matched with vastly increased shipboard technology, outstanding for its day. The Sony Corporation of America Company was brought into the design team to add its high-tech input to what was already an impressive ship. *Century* thus featured one of the first inbuilt, fully interactive cabin communications systems afloat and this was coupled with impressive audio-visual public area suites. The *Century* and slightly enlarged 76-522-ton *Mercury* followed, giving the company a totally modern fleet of five outstanding vessels, and the older ships were discarded, while the old Chandris Fantasy brand had long-since faded into oblivion. Celebrity expanded into other areas, the Alaskan market being served by *Galaxy* and *Horizon* while *Celebrity* made an experimental foray into the multilingual Europe scene.

All this was well and good, however, despite this growth, larger rivals such as Carnival, RCCI and P&O Princess, were expanding even more rapidly and it was clear that, excellent as the brand was, it needed more support to survive in the cut-throat world of cruising. In June 1997 came the announcement that Royal Caribbean International had bought Celebrity from the Chandris family for $US 1.3 billion in cash and equities, the two companies merging to become Royal Caribbean Cruises Ltd, headquartered at Miami, and with Celebrity remaining a separate subsidiary brand in the group, and John D. Chandris and OSG's President, Morton Hyman, receiving seats on the parent company's board.

Thus further financially buttressed, Celebrity was able to press ahead yet further with new ships and new ideas, and the result was the ground-breaking *Millennium* class, the 90,280-ton *Millennium Infinity, Summit* and *Constellation,* the lead ship appropriately enough entering service in 2000 with the others joining the two following years. These huge ships obviously presented yet more scope for the unique Celebrity product, being longer and wider than any of their predecessors, but even more space was gained by the adoption, for the first time, of a pair of General-Electric (GE) gas turbines in place of diesel engines to generate power for her prime-mover electric motors. The 'aeroderivative' gas turbine is quieter by far, more economical in cost as well as space and is more environmentally friendly, a bonus in an era in which this was becoming more-and-more an issue. There is also a small 12,000-hp steam turbine as part of GE's COGES integrated propulsion package. Once adopted, these assets quickly ensured that hey were made standard for all new-build vessels. Another innovative feature was the employment of a pair of the Mermaid fully azimuthal pod-propulsion system developed by Cegelec/Kamewa. Construction of the class was switched from Germany to St Nazaire, France, and the shipyard of Chantiers de l'Atlantique.

As part of the updating of the brand these new additions adopted an all-blue hull, with the 'Chi' outlined in yellow to give a new emphasized appeal. During 2007–2008, in a similar manner to other lines, the word 'Celebrity' was added as a prefix to all the ships in commission and this was continued with the next class of super-ship that Celebrity ordered in 2005, the *Solstice* class, five of which have been ordered to date. These are 122,000-tonners built by Meyer Werft, Papenburg, once again, being the largest cruise ships constructed so far in Germany, of which *Celebrity Solstice*, *Celebrity Equinox* and *Celebrity Eclipse* have so far been delivered.

At a cost of $US 750 million, the *Solstice* class is another quantum leap, and the ships' 2,850 guests are serviced by a crew of 1,500 and spread over nineteen decks. Power is provided once more by a quartet of Wärtsilä diesel engines, with propulsion by a pair of 20.5 MW pods to give a top speed of 24 knots. The hulls of the new ships have reverted to all-white once more, while the 'Chi' has been re-located several times and is now affixed to both sides of the forward funnel. In addition to the now traditional Celebrity offerings amenities, some 90 per cent of the staterooms have outside views and 85 per cent have verandas. There is a new AquaClassTM spa accommodation added to the six different stateroom types, and a lawn club where croquet and golf putting can be practised on a half-acre of real growing turf! Like all Celebrity ships they are Malta-registered.

These magnificent vessels should ensure the Celebrity brand remains at the forefront of cruising. For the future, both *Celebrity Solstice* and *Celebrity Equinox* have been assigned to the European area of operations, *Celebrity Mercury* is to be based at Baltimore and Charleston while the Bermuda route, abandoned for a long while after the departure of *Zenith*, is due to be re-opened with *Celebrity Summit*.

The *Celebrity Xpedition* is the only vessel that concerns us here. She was the first 'Mega Yacht' and was built in Germany by Cassens C Schiffswerft of Emden as the *Sun Bay* in January 2001 and was chartered out by Travel Dynamics of New York in May 2001 for the next four years. She was positioned principally for the German-speaking market but when it did not meet expectations she was offered up for sale by the Frankfurt-based Kreditanstalt für Wiederaufbau (KfW) Bank and purchased by Royal Caribbean International for their Celebrity Cruises arm.

She became the *Xpedition* in 2004 and, after a big refit, is currently owned by Islas Galápagos Turismo y Vapores CA, with HQ at Sunyana Corporate Tower, La Carolina, Quito, Ecuador, and operated by Celebrity Cruises from Puerto Ayora, Sana Cruz, Galápagos. Exclusively, her tours are around the Galápagos Islands, retracing the footsteps of Charles Darwin.

Her facilities include: on deck 6 is a hot tub, an exercise room and a massage room; on deck 5 there are The Blue Finch Bar and the Panorama deck; on deck 4 there is the Discovery lounge, the Beagle Grill, a library and an internet café and on deck 3 the Darwin's Rest, the Beach Club and a gift shop. She is registered in the Bahamas.

Celebration Cruise Line

This company owns the Bahamas Celebration and is part of Celebration Cruise Holdings Inc. with its office registered at Suite 203, 33308 East Commercial Boulevard, Fort Lauderdale, Florida. The ship is managed by International Shipping Partners Ltd at Biscayne Boulevard, Miami, Florida, and she are registered in Nassau, Bahamas.

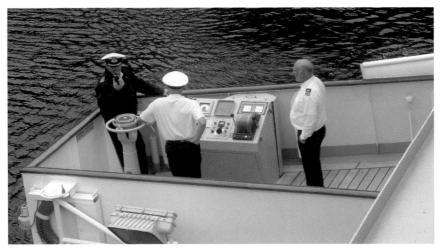

The captain supervising the docking of the *Thomson Celebration* from the bridge wing. (*Peter C. Smith*)

The *Bahamas Celebration* was built for the Norwegian Jahre Line in 1981 by Howaldtswerke-Deutsche Werft AG, Kiel, Germany, as a Type 410 car ferry and named *Princess Ragnhild* and used on the Oslo–Kiel route. She originally had 896 berths but this was later increased to 1,006. The name of the company was changed to Color Line in 1991. She was totally re-built at Astilleros Espaoles Cadiz, Spain, shipyard in 1992, being lengthened by over 25 metres, emerging in 1992 with a capacity of 1,876 berths. She continued to serve with Color. In 1999 she suffered an engine-room fire with the loss of one passenger to a heart attack. The crew put the fire out and she reached port. She was repaired by Blohm und Voss, Hamburg. She was again extensively refitted in 2003 and sailed from Bergen to Stavanger and later Oslo again to Hirtshals

until 2008 when she was sold for $23 million. She was handed over at Sandefjord, south-east Norway, that same October.

On-board facilities are comprehensive and include: for meal choices, The Crystal Dining Room, Trattoria Di Gerry for Italian food, Rio's for buffet dining and the exclusive venue The Cove; for entertainment the Wynmore Casino is popular and there is The View for shows, the Sports Bar for gaming while you drink and Pub 411 is an English-themed public house and there is also the Ocean Breeze Lounge. Health-wise there are two jacuzzis, the sun deck, the Fountain of Youth Spa and salon, the Mussel Beach Gym and the poolside side. For younger guests aged three to nine there is Club Coconuts, ten to fourteen-year-olds can have fun at Club Wave while older teens can chill at Open Water. There is the inevitable internet café, the Treasure Coast gift shop and a photo gallery. Cruises are usually two-day trips out to the Bahamas and back but can be combined with a five or seven-day shore stay at associated hotels in Nassau.

China Cruises Company Ltd (CCCL)

This company is located at Wenzhou, Zhejiang, China, and the CEO is Huang Weijian. The cruise ships are managed by the shipping services company Conning Shipping Ltd. The company is based at China Merchants Tower, Shun Tak Centre, Hong Kong.

The *China Star* was originally built by Oy Wärtsilä AB, Rauma, Finland, in 1992 for a Finnish Banking consortium under the name of Diamond Cruises and chartered to Radisson Seven Seas Cruises between then and June 2005 as *Radisson Diamond*, when she was initially leased to Carlson Companies, which was the parent company of Radisson Hotels. She was an experimental vessel, one that has yet to be repeated on this scale. She was the first ever (and to date, the only) cruise ship constructed with a twin-hull (not really a catamaran because the two hulls extend into the water not straight but with marked bulges) configuration. SWATH (Small Waterplane Area Twin Hull) technology. She was equipped with four stabilizers, two on the inner surface of each hull. Being double-hulled was considered desirable as it gives additional stability to a comparatively small vessel but it increased maintenance. The two hulls are joined forward by the bridge and the large Windows Lounge forward and the Grand Restaurant aft, while aft the considerable gap enables cabin windows on both inward-facing stern areas of the hull. The ship has a four-deck atrium with backing staircases and a dance floor and stage area below. Aft of this she has a portable water-sports platform that can be lowered into place in the space between the hulls at suitable opportunities.

She was actually christened at Greenwich on the River Thames in London that June 1982 and commenced cruises in the Caribbean. The following year Diamond Cruse and Seven Seas Cruises merged as Radisson Seven Seas Cruises. This period of her life ended after thirteen years' service in 2005 when Radisson Seven Seas Cruises sold *Radisson Diamond* to Macau Casino owner Stanley Ho and she sailed for Hong Kong in June to become the casino ship *Omar Star* in June.

She was given a major reconstruction to fill her new mission and In October 2005 *Omar Star* was renamed *Asia Star*.

Asia Star operated as a successful gambling ship with ownership listed as Ocean Treasure Ltd, switching her base of operations from Hong Kong to Singapore in 2009. After operating thus for six years she was sold.

China Cruise bought the vessel for $45 million in October 2011 for a $20 million conversion to a luxury cruise ship and renamed her *China Star*. Balconies were added to the cabins, which were targeted at the high-end business and entertainment market. While Western-style food, drink and entertainment remain aboard the Chinese guests are also offered green tea and local fish cakes and other delicacies. The ship features a theatre, a wine and cigar bar, a library, a theatre, as business centre, karaoke room, gaming centre, two Chinese spas and duty-free outlets. The ship's home port is Zhoushan and she operates four or five-day cruises to Kaohsiung and Keeling, Taiwan and longer trips to Vietnam, Korea and Japan. She is registered in the Bahamas.

The company also announced further expansion plans with a view to acquiring two or three 1,500-guest capacity cruise ships

Classic International Cruises (CIC)

Classic International Cruises was founded in 1985 by George P. Potamianos whose family had shipping experience dating back to the mid nineteenth-century and involvement with the Greek Epirotiki Line, Sun Line and Royal Olympia Cruises. Potamianos then went his own way and started afresh in Lisbon. He once described CIC as 'a group of companies using a common trading name'. With Arcalia Shipping, established in Cyprus in 1985, as owners, World Cruises Agency at Lisbon as marketing, and CIC as operators, he expanded with a series of popular cruise vessels, all of which were former vintage liners of a high standard. George died in May 2012 and his twin sons were appointed directors. The company is based at Avenida 24 de Julho, Lisbon, and *Athena* operates from Neutral Bay, Sydney, NSW, Australia, with the main branches in London and other cities worldwide.

The first liner the company acquired under the Arcalia Shipping Company Ltd branding was the *Funchal*, which was purchased at an auction in August 1985. She remained the sole operating vessel until 1988 when a second ship, the 23,000-GT *Infante Dom Henrique* was obtained and similarly converted, becoming the *Vasco da Gama*. She was sold to Cruise Holdings in 1995 and became the *Seawind Crown*. To replace her the 16,335-GT *Baltica*, was purchased in February 1996. She was originally built at the Swan Hunter shipyard in 1955 as the *Port Melbourne* for Port Line and later served as the *Danae, Starlight Princess* and then *Baltica*. Once converted she became the *Princess Danae*. In 1999 the 1965-built *Istra* was obtained, re-built and renamed *Astra 1* in May 2000. She was rebuilt and became the *Arion* was in 1999, the *Athena* in 2005 and the *Princess Daphne* in 2008.

The 9,536-GT *Funchal* was built in 1961 and was a former Portuguese passenger liner and served as the Portuguese Presidential Yacht. She cruised from Australia from 2009 and in 2010 was refitted to become SOLAS compliant and a further refit followed in 2011 at Lisbon Shipyard. The 5,888-GT *Arion* was built by Brodogradiliste Uljanik, Pula, Croatia, in 1965 and was the former Yugoslavian passenger vessel *Istra*. She was purchased by ASC, Lisbon, as *Astra*; her upperworks were completely re-fashioned to make her into a cruise vessel. The 15,833-GT *Princess Daphne* was built in 1955 as the *Port Sydney* for the Cunard subsidiary, Port Line for use on the New Zealand route. She later had a string of owners and names, being in turn the *Akrotiri Express, Daphne, Switzerland* and *Ocean Odyssey* and she was rebuilt in 1972.

Athena was built by Götaverken-Sweden shipyard in Gothenburg as the Swedish America Line's (SAL) 12,165-GT ocean liner *Stockholm* as long ago as 1948. She sailed with the company for twelve years. She achieved considerable notoriety in July 1956 when she collided in thick fog off Nantucket Island with the *Andrea Doria*, resulting in the loss of the latter vessel. *Stockholm* remained seaworthy and reached New York where her bows were repaired.

In 1960 she became the *Volkerfreundschaft*, owned and operated by the East German Communists as a Party cruise ship with the VEB Deutsche Seereederei, Rostock. When that state-run organization merged with an commercial international freighting outfit, Internationale Befrachtung,

she began operating in conjunction with Stena Line during the winter season, and she served thus until 1985.

In 1985/86 she became the *Volker* owned by the Panama-based company Neptunus Rex Enterprises and was laid up at Southampton. In 1986 she was moved to Oslo and used as an accommodation vessel for the influx of refugees into Norway and was dubbed *Fridtjof Nansen*, owned by StarLauro but out of commission.

In 1989 she was sold to an Italian consortium and moved to Genoa where she was to have been named *Surriento*, but instead was taken under charter by Nina Cia di Navigazione who named her *Italia-I*. In 1993 she went into dock at Varco Chiapella, Italy, to undergo a full conversion to a cruise ship. She emerged as a 15,614-GT vessel, with a capacity for 556 guests, over seven passenger decks and retained many of the most desirable features of her liner days, including marble bathrooms and the like, and, on re-entering service in 1994, received the new identity *Italia Prima* and was operated between 1995 and 1998 by the German company Neckermann Seereisen. In 1998 she became the *Valtur Prima* and was operated under the Valtur Tourist banner by Air Martiim Seereisen, until laid up again in Havana, Cuba. She was renamed the *Caribe* in 2002 with the intention of adding her to the Festival Cruises fleet, but they collapsed and she was never used by them.

Classic International bought her in 2005 and again renamed her *Athena*. Her registered owner was First Quality Cruises Inc., Portugal, and she was operated by Classic under the name Arcalia Shipping, Portugal. She survived a mass attack of piracy in the Gulf of Aden in 2008. In April 2009 she was chartered to the German Phoenix Reisen for a period. She later operated cruises from both Freemantle and Perth, Western Australia, for nine years most successfully. She was extremely popular with the Aussies with a wide-range of amenities, including the

Olissipo Restaurant and Lotus Pool Grill for dining, the Muses Night Club, Captain's Club, Circe's Casino, Calypso Show Lounge, and the Tychon card room for entertainment, with Sirene's Bar, Elpinor Bar and Aeolos Bar for drinking venues. She also featured a sauna, fitness centre, swimming pool, and barbecue as well as a beauty salon, photo shop, chapel and medical centre.

On 17 September 2012 the *Athena*, at the time chartered to the Belgian tour firm All Ways, was impounded at the port of Marseille for non-payment of fuel bills and complaints from her crew that they had not been paid. The passengers were repatriated to Belgium. In October CIC collapsed with heavy debts and went into administration. Attempts by Grant Hunter, the Managing Director of CIC Australia, to obtain the *Delphin* as a replacement to honour those who had booked on *Athena* in 2012 failed when the ship could not be made available on time.

Three other ships of the CIC fleet shared *Athena*'s fate; the *Princess Danae* was also arrested at Marseille, the *Arion* was held at Kotor, Montenegro, and the *Princess Daphne*, on charter to German cruise line Ambiente Kreuzfahrten with 169 passengers embarked, was seized at Souda Bay, Crete, on 2 October 2012. The fourth vessel, *Funchal*, was laid up at Lisbon awaiting refurbishment to bring her in line with SOLAS requirements at the time of the crash. It was hoped that the company could be re-structured but in December 2012 the company went into liquidation.

Club Méditerranée Cruises

The French Club Méditerranée concept was conceived and founded by Gérard Blitz, a Belgian water-polo player back in 1950 in Mallorca. In 1961 Baron Edmond de Rothschild bought the company and under the direction of Gilbert Trigano it has been developed into a global company featuring high-class holiday all-inclusive subscription resorts, among the first of their kind, which have since expanded into a worldwide organization and into cruising. It is headquartered in Paris and in Miami, Florida, and has staff exceeding 20,000. The present Board Chairman is Henri Giscard d'Estaing, with Michel Wolfovski as Executive Vice Chairman and Chief Finance Officer.

The 14,983-GT *Club Med 2* is one of a pair of vessels originally designed and built as enlarged high-tech sailing cruise ships, with five masts with seven computer-controlled sails and special diesel engines for dual power, built for the Windstar organization. Her sister ship, *Wind Surf*, and two smaller half-sisters still sail with that brand.

She was constructed at Ateliers et Chantiers du Havre, Le Havre, France, in 1996. In October 2008 she was totally refurbished at Genoa. She carries 386 guests with a crew of 214. Her 185 suites were re-designed and ten new cabins built in. She installed a Carita spa, and a new Club Med gym was fitted. The two restaurants were also made over and became Le Méditerranée and Le Magellan and a re-vamped lounge, the Salon Pacific, was installed. She is registered at Mata-Utu in the Wallis and Futuna Islands.

Compagnie du Ponant

This renowned top-end French cruise company, the leading cruise operator for French-speaking customers, was first established in Nantes 1988 by a group of mercantile marine officers led by Philippe Videau, and Jean-Emmanuel Sauvée. In 2011 the line carried 20,000 passengers and had revenue of 80 million euros.

In 2006 the company was acquired by CMA-CGM (Compagnie Maritime d'Affrètement – Compagnie Général Maritime), the large shipping and container transport group based at Marseille, who moved the Compagnie du Ponant headquarters to that city.

In 2012 Compagnie du Ponant was discarded by CMA-CGM and was sold again via its parent company, Mérit, this time to Bridgepoint Capital. Bridgeport is a private equity investor in a whole range of businesses across the UK and Europe, with its headquarters in Warwick Street, Soho, London, and was the former NatWest Equity Partners but in May 2000 was bought out by the management. Existing Ponant management including Jean-Emmanuel Sauvée and Véronique Saadé are expected to continue in their posts.

Compagnie du Ponant currently operates a fleet of three ships with a fourth under construction. *Le Ponant* is a barque built in 1991 that carries sixty-four guests accommodated in thirty-two cabins, with a crew of thirty-two. *Le Boréal*, built in 2009, has room for 264 guests in 132 cabins and suites, with 140 crew members. *Le Boréal* was awarded the 'Best Newcomer of the Year – GOLD' award by the European Cruiser Association (EUCRAS). *L'Austral, a* sister ship to *Le Boréal*, completed in 2011. A third sister is under construction at Fincantieri with delivery due in 2013.

The company also owned *Le Diamant,* the former *Song of Flower* conversion, whose details are included in the Quark Expeditions entry. Another former Compagnie du Ponant vessel was *Le Levant,* a large yacht built in 1998, which could carry ninety guests in forty-five cabins with a crew of fifty-five. It was sold to Paul Gauguin Cruises and became its *Moana* in 2012.

Destinations served currently include the Aegean, the Adriatic, the Black Sea, Corsica, Croatia, Italy, Portugal and Spain in Europe and, further afield, the Persian Gulf and the Red Sea in the Middle East; the Maldives, various Asian ports, Central and South America and Antarctica.

Coral Princess Cruises

The company was founded by Tony Briggs in 1984 and he still remains the CEO along with wife Viki. It has its present HQ at Redden Street, Portsmith, Queensland, Australia. The company was the first to cruise the Great Barrier Reef, utilizing a 102-BRT, 115-ft former World War II Navy Fairmile D motor gun boat, converted to peacetime use and carrying twenty-four guests in pretty basic conditions. In the following thirty years it has steadily built up its operations from Cairns running cruises between Townsend and Lizard Island and earned for itself many accolades. The company now runs two 135 m catamarans, *Coral Princess* and *Coral Princess II* with a guest capacity of fifty and forty-four passengers respectively, but the flagship is the *Oceanic Discover*.

Oceanic Discover was built in 2005 by North Queensland Engineers & Agents (NQEA) and Australian Pty (Aimtek), at Cairns as the *Oceanic Princess* and cost A$30 million. On 12 October 2006 her name was changed to *Oceanic Discoverer* because there were so many cruise ships with 'Princess' in the name visiting Australia at that time.

She carries seventy-two guests housed in thirty-six staterooms on the bridge, promenade and main decks. Her amenities include a sundeck and pool, a lecture lounge with plasma TV screens, two cocktail bars, a gift shop, a library, Wi-Fi, scuba diving facilities and gear, Zodiac inflatables, and the Xplorer excursion vessel capable of carrying all the guests if required.

Her itineraries include Australia's 'Top End' and Kimberley, Papua New Guinea, Melanesia and New Zealand. In 2013 the ship made an inaugural sailing to Indonesia and West Papua. *Oceanic Discoverer* is one of three vessels in the Coral Princess Cruises fleet, operating alongside *Coral Princess* and *Coral Princess II*, and 50 passenger catamarans operating weekly sailings on Australia's World Heritage-listed Great Barrier Reef.

Costa Crociere SpA

This famous Italian company has for many years now been a part of the huge Carnival Corporation Empire, who took over this old-established cruise operator in 1997. However, Costa managed to preserve a certain degree of autonomy for the original Costa family in the running and management.

The Costas can trace their history back several centuries and first sprang to prominence as the producers and suppliers of the Dante Olive Oil product, which was refined at Genoa. The company gradually diversified and expanded into many other areas of activity, including shipping and mechanical engineering. In order to bulk ship its most famous product back to the refinery from all over the southern and eastern Mediterranean it was part of this natural progression that the company should purchase its own cargo ships. The first vessel so bought was a small, ancient (1888) Scottish-built steamer named *Ravenna*, which was purchased on 7 August 1924. She was the first of the Costa fleet and during the late 1920s and on into the 1930s, this expanded rapidly. As the number of ships grew, so the family started naming their vessels after family members, firstly the three brothers, *Federico*, *Eugenio* and *Enrico* and then the ladies, *Antionietta*, *Beatrice* and *Giacomo Costa* respectively.

By the time Italy declared war on Great Britain in June 1940 the fleet had grown considerably and the first custom-built ship was ordered, despite the fact that heavy losses were being taken by the British naval and submarine operations. This vessel, the 8,000-ton motor-ship *Caterina C* was finally launched in April 1942, but had only a brief career before being blown up at Naples the following year. The armistice that followed found only a solitary survivor, the *Langano*. Despite her age and limited accommodation Giacomo Costa put her into service ferrying passengers in 1945 and, in a similar boom to that following the

Great War, the post-war Italy to South America emigration boom gave scope for another expansion, and two large war-built Liberty Ships, renamed as the *Eugenio C* and *Enrico C* respectively, were among those purchased in 1947. A third such vessel was added in 1953 and named *Frederico Costa*.

In March 1948 a milestone was reached with the *Maria C* commencing the first regular transatlantic service in 1947, and the following year the purchase of two more vessels, the former British *Southern Prince* and the American *Robert Luckenbach*, which became the *Anna C* and *Andrea C* respectively. The flood of Italian emigrants to Argentina, Venezuela, Colombia and Brazil was matched with similar waves to Canada and Australia so demand grew and Costa flourished.

By 1958 Costa had taken delivery of its first 'proper' liner, the *Fedrico C*, This 20,416-ton vessel was constructed at the Ansaldo yard at Genoa Sestri, and featured both first, cabin and tourist class passenger accommodation reflecting the changing market, with touring replacing emigration in the 1950s. *Fedrico C* was the first large liner to be equipped with the Denny-Brown stabilizers for passenger comfort and started her long career on the Genoa to South Americas run.

This ship was followed by the *Franca C* and she may be said to have in many ways initiated the Costa Cruise tradition as we know it today. She was constructed totally with the rich American tourist market in mind. She was originally the *Roma*, which herself had been virtually re-built from the 1914-built US fruit-carrying freighter *Medina*. The Giacomo Costa fu Andrea acquired her as bankrupt stock and re-constructed her with new decks, new engines et *al*, and commenced her first cruise to the West Indies in the winter of 1957/58. A further reconstruction took place in 1959 when she became on single-class cruise ship with air-conditioning, a lido, and a range of refurbished cabins and facilities, with the distinctive Italian flair and styling of Nino Zoncada who transformed her into a floating symbol of elegance and style. From her base at Fort Lauderdale the *Franca C* cruised the Caribbean and the Bahamas and opened up this lucrative market in a big way.

By 1968 further sophistication was achieved with the launch of what is now known as the fly / cruise concept when Costa Line Inc. was set up in the United States whereby customers were flown from Florida to San Juan to embark for their Caribbean cruises. Until 1986 Costa Armatori SpA had continued its hitherto catholic embracing of nautical transport running freighters and liners in addition to its cruise ships, which had now much expanded, but from August that year the company metamorphosed into today's Costa Crociere SpA concentrating solely on its ever-growing cruise clientele, this firm becoming a public company in 1989 but still under the direction of the Costa family.

What might be called the final phase of the long and distinguished background activity to today's company came with the arrival of four dedicated cruise ships, *Costa Allegra, Costa Classica, Costa Marina*, and *Costa Romantica*, with the addition in 1995 of the former Croisières Paquet vessel *Pearl*, named the *Costa Playa* in 1995. Again the emphasis was on Italian styling with designs for both exterior and interior by Ivana Porfiri and Pierluigi Cerri, typified by a diverse range of marble, art and sculpture, which on *Costa Romantica* includes titanium and synthetic fibre work by Susumu Shingu, the renowned Japanese artist. She was followed by the, what was then enormous, 76,000-ton *Costa Victoria*. The twin yellow funnels with the worldwide famed Costa 'C' emblazoned gave this leviathan grace and beauty coupled with a solid appearance. She, perhaps, may be said to have initiated the so-called 'arms race' between the companies for larger and more grand ships, each huge acceleration in tonnage and dimension being soon overtaken as the building programmes gathered pace in the 1990s and early twenty-first century. Built in prefabricated sections in German yards of Schichau Seebeckwerft at Bremerhaven and Bremer Vulkan Werft und Maschinenfabrik GmbH and then towed for final assembly at Vegesack, Weser, before fitting out at Lloyd Werft, this vessel and all subsequent Costa ships, broke new ground for sheer sumptuousness. The planned sister ship, *Costa Olympia*, had to be suspended for a while when Vulkan became bankrupt and eventually became *Norwegian Sky*.

Costa itself continued to go from strength-to-strength, and the AIDA Cruise Company established for German guests was part of that growth. The half-a-century of cruise experience has resulted in a dozen of the world's greatest cruise liners that between them reach out from Europe all over the world, with offices in twenty-seven countries and a total guest number in 2005 of more that 6½ million per day. Costa was the first company to be given permission to cruise from Chinese ports. The mighty *Concordia* class ships of the current construction, based on parent company's *Conquest* type ships but enlarged and modified, seemed to ensure that Costa Crociere maintained a leading position in the cruise fleets of the world. RINA's Green Star for environmental excellence certification for every ship in the fourteen-strong fleet only appeared to emphasize that.

With the tragedy of the *Costa Concordia*, which ran aground on Giglio Island after hitting offshore rocks at speed on 13 January 2012, with the loss of thirty-two lives, all this magnificent and hard-won acclaim appeared to be placed in jeopardy at a stroke, more by the whole manner in which the whole affair was handled than by the subsequent salvage and the prolonged legal ramifications and the huge costs involved in both. Six months after the accident Costa started discounting prices and this spread to other cruise lines. Numbers began to pick up slowly.

Sadly, any thoughts of shrugging off this disaster were, incredibly, marred when the *Costa Allegra* suffered an engine room fire in February 2012 while some two hundred miles south-west of the Seychelles. The fire, which broke out in the electric generator room was confined to that area, and there were no casualties or injuries. The *Allegra* was *en route* from Diego Suarez and Victoria, Mahé, with 636 guests and 413 crew. She was adrift for three days without power, or air conditioning and hot food had to be transported in by helicopter. Tugs were sent and she was got into Victoria on 28 February and remained there for a full inspection while her passengers were flown home. The *Costa Voyager* replaced her from 18 March. By 25 March the *Costa Allegra* was brought home to Savona under her own power and then to Genoa, but Carnival already had her up for sale and decided she was not worth repair. Ownership was transferred to Themis Maritime Ltd, Dubai, who renamed her *Santa Cruise* and registered her in Freetown, Sierra Leone, for the voyage to the ship-breakers at Aliaga, Turkey, in September 2012. She had gone but this second blow to the Costa brand in under a year had not been good publicity.

This loss means the only medium-size ship that currently remains operational with the Costa fleet at the time of writing is the *Costa Voyager* but her future is also limited, Carnival putting her up for sale in 2012. Currently she is owned by Grand Cruise Investments (Costa Crociere SpA).

Cruise & Maritime Voyages

Based at Dartford, Kent, Cruise & Maritime Voyages is part of CMV Holdings London Travel & Leisure Group, with offices at both Purfleet, Essex, and at Fort Lauderdale, Florida. Founded in 2009, the company describes itself as Britain's newest privately owned cruise line.

In 2012 the company was awarded the accolade 'Best Values Cruise Line' and 'Cruise Line of the Year' at the Cruise International Magazine Awards and 'Favourite Cruise Line' at the Globe Travel Awards, in conjunction with *Mail Newspapers* and *Travel Weekly* in 2013.

The popular 22,080-GT *Marco Polo* was built as the second of the four vessels of the Soviet *Ivan Franko* class, her sisters being *Ivan Franko*, *Shoto Rustavelli* and *Taras Shevchencko* and long since sunk or departed to the breakers yards. She was built by VEB (Volkseigener Betrieb) Mathias Thesen Werft, at the Baltic port of Wismar, Mecklenburg-Vorpommern (now Nordic Yards) in what was then Communist-controlled East Germany (German Democratic Republic) in 1965. She was designed for Atlantic passenger service for the Baltic Shipping Company of what was then Leningrad (St Petersburg). In 1991 the *Pushkin* was sold to Gerry Herrod's Shipping & General Ltd, UK, and was renamed *Marco Polo*. She immediately underwent a full refit at the Neorion and Perama Shipyard, located just west of Piraeus Commercial Port, Athens, Greece, on conclusion of which she was allocated to the Herrod's newly-established Orient Line. She was refitted in 1993. In 1998 Norwegian Cruise Line bought Orient Line and *Marco Polo* and she underwent another makeover in 2006.

In 2007 Global Cruises acquired *Marco Polo*, and equally important, at additional cost, the right to the name itself, from NCL. She was yet again refitted in 2008 and Global Cruises took delivery at Lisbon in March of that year. The intention was to charter her out to Transocean Cruises, Germany, for two years, but in 2009 Transocean failed and she was idle for a period after another refit. In 2010 the newly established Cruise & Maritime signed a five-year charter option. She is currently owned by Story Cruises Ltd, Greece, which is affiliated to Global Cruises, Greece.

The *Marco Polo* can accommodate 820 guests in a selection of 425 cabins, with combinations of twin/single, outside/inside, superior, premier, standard cabins and ocean-view, deluxe or junior suites. The *Marco Polo* has eight guest-accessible decks, Navigator, Columbus, Amundsen, Magellan, Pacific, Atlantic, Baltic and Caribic. The amenities and facilities include the Waldorf Restaurant, Marco's Restaurant, the

Palm Garden and Captain's Club, Scott's Bar, the pool and bar, the Marco Polo Lounge, Livingstone Library, Nansen Card Room , the Jade Wellness Centre, an internet café, boutiques, a beauty salon, three whirlpools and a hospital.

She is registered at Nassau, Bahamas.

The 20,186-GT *Discovery* was built at for Flagship Cruises as the *Island Venture* in 1972. From October 1972 to 1999 *Island Princess* was chartered out to Princess Cruises and cruised from Los Angeles to Mexico. *Princess* was bought by P&O in 1974. While with Princess Cruises she briefly 'starred' in the TV show *The Love Boat* standing in for her sister ship. From October 1986 she was based from time to time at Sydney, NSW, and cruised the south Pacific region. She was purchased by the Panama-registered company Ringcroft Investment Inc. in 1999, which chartered her out to South Korean Hyundai Merchant Marine Co. Ltd (HMM), Seoul. In the period 1999–2000 she became the *Hyundai Pungak* with Hyundai Merchant Marine during which time she conveyed pilgrims from South Korea to holy destinations in North Korea. She was sold in 2000 and spent the period 2000–2001 as the *Platinum* with Fiducia Shipping Company SA, also of Panama. She underwent a major refit and from 2002 onward became *Discovery for* Voyages of Discovery working from Harwich. During this period she was also chartered out as the *Andaman Victory* for voyaging the Pacific, Indian Ocean and similar locales. In 2013 she was replaced by *Voyager* and chartered to Cruise & Maritime Voyages and operated UK 'No Fly' holidays.

The *Discovery* can accommodate 698 guests in 354 cabins, either standard or superior inside and outside cabins, or junior and owner's suites. She has a crew of 350. She has eight passenger decks, Sky, Sun, Bridge, Promenade, Riviera, Pacific, Bali and Coral. Dining is at the Seven Continents Restaurant and there is a buffet. Relaxation can be had at the Carousel Lounge and bar, the Palm Court or the Discovery Lounge while other bars are the Hideaway, Explorer, lido and pool. Entertainment can be had at the Discovery Theatre, two swimming pools, the Yacht Club, the library, the health centre and gym, internet centre and bridge club. There is also a photo shop, a souvenir shop, a beauty salon and a medical centre.

She is registered at Hamilton, Bermuda

Danubia Kreuzfahrten GmbH/Lufter Cruises of Austria

Danubia Kreuzfahrten GmbH of Vienna, Austria, has its office on the Handelskai. The company was established in the 1980s and owns shipping lines and river transport and is a ship broker. The Amadeus fleet of high-quality river cruises is operated by Dr W Lüftner Reisen

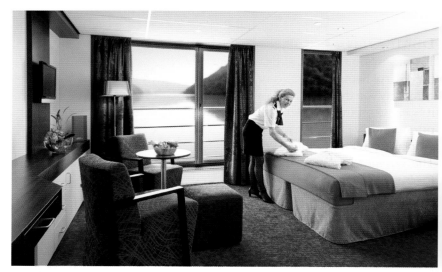

Amadeus Diamond suite. (*Courtesy of Dr. W. Luftner Reissen GmbH*)

GmbH, Menardi Centre, Innsbruck, Austria. The full fleet listing is *Amadeus Diamond, Amadeus Silver, Amadeus Elegant, Amadeus Princess, Amadeus Royal, Amadeus Symphony, Amadeus Classic, Danubia* and *Amadeus*. Their luxurious vessels run on the rivers Danube, Rhine, Main, Rhône, Saôn and cruise Europe from Amsterdam to Budapest.

The *Amadeus Diamond* is included as a typical such vessel (although they are so popular and numerous that they deserve a book to themselves). She can accommodate 148 guests in twelve Amadeus suites and sixty-two cabins, and she has a crew of forty. She has four decks, Sun, Mozart, Strauss and Haydn. Facilities and amenities include the Amadeus Club, Panorama Restaurant and Bar, a pool, the lido bar, a walking track, fitness room, massage parlour, a gift shop and a hairdresser.

The *Amadeus Diamond* is registered in Passau, Germany.

DSME-Oman

The Daewoo Shipbuilding & Marine Engineering Company Ltd (DSME) of Seoul, South Korea, with Jae-Ho Ko as the CEO, is the parent company for the *Veronica*. Founded at Okpo Bay, Geoje Island, in 1973, it became an independent company in October 2000. The *Veronica* was purchased by Daewoo Shipbuilding and Marine Engineering in October 2010 and after a year of refurbishments is now ready for her first guests. The *Veronica* serves as hotel accommodation in the Sultanate of Oman for business travellers coming to the Oman Drydock Company (ODC) and city of Duqm as well as regular travellers. The location of the hotel ship is Dry Dock, Duqm, Al Wusta. The registered local office is a PO box at Madinat Qaboos, Muscat, Oman.

The 26,670-GT *Veronica* was built as a dual-purpose ocean liner/cruise ship by the British John Brown & Company at Clydebank in 1966 for the Swedish America Line and named *Kungsholm*. She carried 713 passengers between Gothenburg and New York in the former role and 450 guests as a cruise vessel. The Swedish American Line failed in 1975 and the *Kungsholm* was purchased by Flagship Cruises and she became US-based. In 1978 P&O purchased her to replace the over-age *Arcadia* and she was extensively refitted at Bremen, the most obvious change being the loss of her fore-funnel. Her new owners renamed her *Sea Princess* and between 1979 and 1995 she cruised out of Australia initially, undergoing a refit in 1995 then from the UK and finally the USA under the Princess Cruises banner. On her return to P&O she was renamed again as *Victoria*. In the 1999/2000 she was briefly chartered to Union Castle and in 2002 she was sold to Bahamas-registered Leonardo Shipping (affiliated to Kyma Ship Management, Miami) and given the name *Mona Lisa*. As such she was chartered out to Holiday Kreuzfahten but when this company went bust in 2006 she was used for a period as an Asian Games accommodation ship and moored at Doha, Qatar, until January 2007. She was again renamed as *Oceanic II*; she was chartered out to both Louis Cruises and Pullmantur Cruises as *Oceanic II*. Under that name she also served for a period in a similar capacity as *The Scholar Ship*, and was utilized as a floating school vessel under Royal Caribbean Cruise Line's auspices. She embarked 796 students and their tutors for two sixteen-week cruises before financial difficulties caused the cessation of the scheme in June 2008. There followed a charter to the German-based Lord Nelson Seereisen for a Baltic cruise during which she grounded for three days off Riga, Latvia, and was docked at Ventspils. In 2008–2009 she was chartered by the Japanese Peace Boat group until 2010 under the name *Mona Lisa* and voyaged from Piraeus to Yokohama and then returned to her accommodation ship duties, this time for the 2010 Winter Olympics and Paralympics at Vancouver, British Columbia, and at Whistler. Further charters were followed by failure to meet the new SOLAS standards in October 2012. This brought her long career as a cruise ship to an abrupt termination, as it did so many other vessels.

Plans were on hand to convert her to a permanent floating hotel back in her old home port of Gothenburg and Stockholm, but these fell through and in 2011 she was purchased by Daewoo and became the hotel ship *Veronica*. She is under a five-year lease and is moored at Duqm, Sultanate of Oman.

The *Veronica* hotel is advertised as being equipped with 208 well furnished rooms; it also has a sports bar, several restaurants, karaoke rooms, an outdoor swimming pool, cafes, lounges, a business centre, a library, a theatre and a shopping arcade. The *Veronica* is equipped with significant office space, a spa and gym, a salon and a barbershop. Some recent reports from guests allege that not all these facilities were actually in use during their stay, however. A crew of 120 very polite staff care for guests.

Etstur Turkey

The ETS Group is Turkey's largest domestic tourist operator and was founded by the brothers Mehmet and Murat Ersoy in 1991 as Ersoy Tourist Services Inc. It has since grown into a whole network of hotels and resorts, and offers air, land and sea transport services in addition to overseas cultural and youth tours, ski holidays, thermal spas and tourism services with almost four thousand employees. It is headquartered at Kizitoprak, Istanbul, and the Board of Directors includes Ersoy Mehmet Nuri, Chairman, Ali Murat Ersoy, Deputy Chairman and M. Albas.

The Blue Cruise arm of the company purchased the 16,710-GT cruise ship *Venus*, which was originally built by Cantieri Navale del Tirreno, Italy, back in 1971 as the *Southward* for Norwegian Caribbean Line. Over her long history she has had many owners and many names. She became part of the Airtours fleet and became their Sun Cruises ship *Seawing* in 1994 and she was extensively refitted in 1995. In 2004 Louis Cruises acquired her and renamed her as the *Perla*, gave her another refit and chartered her to Golden Sun Cruises as *Aegean Pearl* sailing in the Aegean area and then the Far East, but this was not a success. The following year she returned to Louis Cruises as the *Aegean Pearl*, but in May 2010 Mano Maritime, Haifa, Israel, purchased her for $19.5 million and on delivery in June she was renamed *Rio* for Caspi Cruises. The owners were also reported as being Eagles Holding, registered in the Marshall Islands. While at the port of Ashdod the ship was seized. In September the *Rio* was sold to Acheon Akti Navigation Company Ltd, Cyprus, for $4.8 million to be operated by East Mediterranean Cruises SA and refitted. She was named *Venus* in March 2012 when she was laid up at Limassol. She was sold to Etstur in November 2012. Commencing from spring 2013 she has cruised in the Mediterranean and is almost exclusively marketed at Turkish guests.

Explorer Maritime/Institute for Shipboard Education

The concept of a 'floating university' can be traced back to psychology Professor James Edwin Lough of New York University and the first example of it in practice was a circumnavigation of the globe from Hoboken, New Jersey, with 504 students and 63 teachers and staff aboard the Holland America Line (HAL) liner *Ryndam* in September 1926. However, it was not until Bill Hughes, a Californian businessman, revived the idea in 1963 that the idea really took off with the chartering of the HAL cruise ship *Seven Seas* with 275 students embarked. Dr M.A. Griffiths became Dean of the World Campus Afloat in 1969 and another HAL vessel, also the *Ryndam*, served as host ship until HAL withdrew in 1970.

C.Y. Tung Chao Yung (Tung Chao Yung) was a famous Chinese shipping chief and a supporter of the Chinese Republic's ruling Kuomintang under Chiang Kai-shek who the Communist forces drove out to Taiwan. In 1947 C.Y. Tung founded the first line with an all-Chinese crew, the Orient Overseas Line, which over the decades grew into one of the world's great fleets and which, in 1969, became the present-day Orient Overseas Container Line (OOCL). Tung was a great exponent of education; his belief was that 'Ships could transport more than cargo, they could carry ideas.' He used his vast wealth to promote his dream of a floating United Nations University by setting up the Seawise Foundation, which provided a succession of ships, and the necessary management team to run them efficiently, for the World Campus Afloat. When World Campus Afloat ceased operations Tung and Griffiths lent their support to the founding of The Institute for Shipboard Education. The mutual beneficial liaison eventually parted and Tung himself died in 1982, but his ideals live on.

On-board education was conducted under the term University of the Seven Seas, which later became World Campus Afloat and since 1977 has been titled Semester at Sea. The Institute began what it terms 'Enrichment Voyages', which last about one hundred days during the circumnavigation of the world interspersed with sixty-five-day cruises to specific regions. Their guests are undergraduate students from participating US-based universities and they have on-board lecturers and a diverse and controversial list of international guest speakers. The Institute is headquartered at Charlottesville, Virginia, with the University of Virginia as academic sponsor.

Since its original establishment a succession of ships has acted as host vessel to the courses.

Seven Seas formerly the 13,500-on aircraft carrier USS *Long Island* (*CVE-1*). This old ship, the US Navy's first ever escort carrier, was built in 1941 and served in the Atlantic and Pacific during the war as a pilot trainer, aircraft transport and, once, in her designed role. She was sold for scrapping in 1946 but, instead, was bought by Canada-Europe Line and converted as an immigration carrier to and from Europe under the name *Nelly* until 1953. She was chartered by the German Europe-Canada Line as the *Seven Seas*. Burnt out in 1965 she was subsequently repaired and used as an accommodation ship for Rotterdam University until 1955 when she was finally scrapped.

Ryndam was the second liner of that name to be constructed for HAL. She had been laid down at the Wilton-Fijenoord Schiedam shipyard as the cargo ship *Dinteldyk,* but was altered whilst on the stocks to become a mainly tourist-class ship and completed in May 1951. After long service she was transferred to the Bremen-based Europa-Canada Line GmbH (later ECL Shipping Company) where she replaced the *Seven Seas* from October. She served as a school ship until 1971 then was sold in 1972 to World Wide Cruises SA (Panama), a subsidiary of Epirotiki Line who re-built her for the Aegean cruise market and named her *TSS Atlas.* She was frequently chartered out and cruised both sides of the Atlantic. Sold again in 1986 she ended her days as a floating Casino Ship at Gulfport, Mississippi, under the names *Pride of Mississippi, Pride of Galveston* and *Copa Casino* before sinking off the Dominican Republic in 2003 *en route* to the breakers yard.

Universe started her career as the freighter *Badger Marine,* which was constructed by Sun Shipbuilding & Dry Dock Company, Chester, Pennsylvania, in 1953. She was acquired by German-American shipping supremo Arnold Bernstein in 1957. He had founded American Banner Lines and he converted her into a 14,138-GT passenger cargo ship and renamed her *Atlantic* with over 90 per cent of her accommodation tourist class, albeit with private facilities, which was an innovation. Her inaugural route was on 11 June 2004 sailing from New York to

Amsterdam via Zeebrugge, Belgium. Unfortunately, this route began just as the jet airlines began to gain dominance as the North Atlantic's main carrier and by November 1959 *Atlantic* was laid up. In 1960 she was purchased by American Export Lines who retained the name and she cruised from America to Mediterranean destinations until 1968. Meanwhile, the famous old 1940s Cunard liner *Queen Elizabeth* was destined to be converted as the next floating school for the *Seawise University*, but during her conversion at Hong Kong burnt out and sank. A replacement was needed quickly and in 1971 the *Atlantic* was purchased by C.Y. Tung's Orient Overseas Lines for the job and renamed *Universe*. She was finally scrapped in 1996.

The next replacement vessel was the *Universe Explorer*. This was the former Moore-McCormack Lines liner *Brasil*, built for the South American Line in 1958. She served for fourteen years on this route. She was sold to HAL in August 1972 who renamed her *Volendam*. In 1975 she again changed ownership and became the Monarch Cruises Lines vessel *Monarch Sun*. She was re-purchased by HAL in 1978 and resumed the name *Volendam* once more and then in dizzying succession the *Island Sun, Liberté, Canada Star, Queen of Bermuda* and *Enchanted Seas*. At the end of the 1990s she was chartered to the Institute in association with the University of Pittsburgh. Meanwhile, the Institute and Seawise Foundation had gone their separate ways and when she was to have been named *Universe Explorer* Orient Overseas Line objected. By December 2004, the *University Explorer* was finally pronounced just too ancient to continue, being sold for scrapping at that graveyard of fine vessels, Alang, India. Yet another replacement was quickly found.

Originally built as the Royal Olympic Cruises vessel *Olympic Voyager* at the Blohm und Voss GmbH shipyard in Hamburg, she was completed in May 2001 as a sister ship to their *Olympic Voyager*, but the company refused to accept this second vessel. The company was forced to change its name (and the names of its ships) by the International Olympic Committee and both substituted the word 'Olympia' for 'Olympic' in 2002 and the same year *Olympia Explorer* was finally accepted into service. She cruised the Mediterranean and then was based at Port Canaveral, Florida, for touring the Caribbean and up the Amazon to Manaus. She also visited Hawaii and South America before returning to Piraeus. The 9/11 Islamic terrorist attacks affected sales and the company went bankrupt in 2004, the *Olympia Explorer* being impounded at Long Beach. She was bought by the Frankfurt-based German bank KfW (Kreditanstalt für Wiederaufbau) in March 2004 for $82.7 million and she was acquired as a floating university-cum-cruise ship by the Institute for Shipboard Education the same year for the Semester At Sea (SAS) Programmes on a fifteen-year lease, but was purchased totally in December 2007.

Explorer's accommodation features a wide range of staterooms and cabins for students over decks two, three and four, with economy cabins on deck three, while Lifelong Learners can choose from superior, deluxe or junior ocean-view suites or cabins on deck four. There are nine classrooms, a 380-seat Students' Union, a 9,000-volume Taormina Family Library housed in the former casino, and the Hudson Family Computer Center with free internet access. Other educational facilities include a variety of lounges used for lectures or cinemas. For entertainment there is The Piano Lounge and bar. Field Programs are held at each port of call. The two hundred officers and crew are supplied by the V Group's ship managerial services.

Far Eastern Shipping Company (FESCO)

This is an Open Joint Stock Company with its headquarters in Moscow and has over five thousand employees and more than fifty ships including Ro-Ro ships, container ships, cargo ships, bulk-carriers, timber ships and supply ships. The Executive Board of FESCO is headed by Yurky B. Gilts, President and CEO; with Alexey N. Grom, Vladimir N. Korchaanov, Sergey A. Blynda, Natalie N. Bondar and Sergey V. Kostyan as Vice Presidents, the latter of the Liner and Logistics arms and six further executives, making for a strong team. The company was original founded in 1880 at Vladivostok as The Volunteer Fleet Agency (*Dobroflot*) with the sailing of the *Moskwa* from Odessa to Vladivostok, Nikolaevsk and Sakhalin. Four years later the icebreaker *Silach* was the first to reach Vladivostok and start a continuous ice-free navigation route along the Egersheld Passage that same winter. Since then this vast conglomerate has expanded and expanded.

It is the non-nuclear icebreaking arm of this vast organization which is of prime interest here and FESCO is the largest operator of these vessels. Currently there are four in service, the *Kapitan Khlebnikov, the Admiral Makarov*, built in 1975, *Krasin* (1976) and *Magadan* (1982). The *Kapitan Khlebnikov* was launched in November 1980 at the Wärtsilä Helsinki New Yard, Finland, and in 1990 was given a refit to bring her up to cruise ship standards. From then until 2012 she has operated as a 'liner/icebreaker' for Quark Expeditions. Prior to that ten-year charter she performed usual icebreaker duties. In 1983 the *Kapitan Khlebnikov* participated in the rescue of the *Kolya Myagotin*, heavily damaged by ice in the Arctic during one of the most severe winters that region had recorded. The liner icebreakers *Krasin* and *Kapitan Khlebnikov* also commenced operations from De-Kastri via the Tatar Strait. She still retains Vladivostok as her home port.

The *Kapitan Khlebnikov* was first chartered out as an expedition ship in 1991 and was operational into 2012 with the aim of reverting her to normal icebreaker duties in the future. She made a number of major achievements during that time having circumnavigated the Antarctic continent on two occasions and made more penetrations of the Northwest Passage than any other vessel. The *Kapitan Khlebnikov* is well equipped for exploration having on-board helicopters for serial view flights over areas inaccessible to the ship, four fully enclosed lifeboats and a fleet of Zodiacs for close-up views and landings. On-board facilities include two dining rooms, a lounge, a bar, a theatre-type auditorium, exercise room and sauna, heated indoor swimming pool, gym, library, bar, gift shop and 24-hour lounge. She accommodates 112 guests in fifty-four suites and has cabins with private facilities and ocean views.

Formosa Queen Corporation/Asia Star Cruise Management

Formosa Queen Corporation is a new company founded at Taipei, Taiwan, in April 2011 to own the *Formosa Queen* while she is managed by the Asia Star Cruise Management Corporation, Alacra Store, Taipei City, Taipei, Taiwan, which includes Gary Chen on the management team. It is a subsidiary of Formosa Plastics Marine Corporation, with headquarters at Tung Hwa North Road, Taipei, which was founded in 1980 and is now a very large concern operating as ship owner, ship manager and liner operator.

She has operated since July 2012 from the port of Keelung and has a cruise schedule that takes her to Kaohsiung, Hualien or Taichung, travelling between these ports via International waters as a floating entertainment zone, enabling guests to shop, dine in restaurants, see shows or visit the night club in a very similar way as happens in the Xinyi District of Taipei City, that city's equivalent to Soho in London. Several other cruise companies had similar concepts either planned or in operation, including Star Cruise with its *Superstar Aquarius*; *Oriental Dragon* owned by Capital Dragon (Global) Ltd of Hong Kong, which operates to Okinawa and Ishigakjima, Japan; and Profit Summer Deluxe Cruise. *Formosa Queen* now has a night club under a glass dome in place of the former swimming pool.

The 22,945-GT *Formosa Queen* was built in 1997 as *Song of Norway*, but was taken over by Airtours/Sun Cruises (My Travel) by Wärtsilä-Finland as *Sundream*. In 2004 Tumaco Navigation Co. acquired her when Airtours stopped trading and renamed her as *Dream Princess,* but, due to the objections of Princess Cruises to that name, within two years she had moved on, becoming the Lance Shipping vessel *Dream*. She underwent a refit in Turkey ready to be chartered to Peace Boat, but this deal fell through. This much traded vessel was next obtained by Pearl Owner, a subsidiary of the Clipper Group and renamed as *Clipper Pearl* in 2007 and then as *Clipper Pacific* a year later. She was chartered out to Caspi Cruises between June and November 2009 as the *Festival,* then chartered to Quail from March 2010 and again in September 2011 to Happy Cruises, all as the *Ocean Pearl,* and was then taken out of service and moored at Tilbury on the River Thames, until she was sold to Asia Star and received her current identity. She was sailed to the Far East under ISP management and had her interior renovated and was altered as a five-star casino/cruise ship. She is registered in Panama City.

San Donato Properties SA/Monarch Cruise Line/Flag Ship Service Organization (FSSO)

The *Freewinds* is included in this book as a former cruise ship that still cruises extensively and has done for the Church of Scientology for more than two decades. Founded by L. Ron Hubbard, himself a former US Navy officer, the organization has always held a strong connection with the sea and down the years has operated a number of vessels, outlined below.

Apollo, the former 3,244-GT *Royal Scotman,* was built in 1936 by Harland & Wolf, Belfast, for Burns & Laird, a member of the Coast Lines group, for their Glasgow to Belfast ferry service. During World War II she was taken over by the Royal Navy as a Store Carrier and

subsequently in 1943 was converted to a Landing Ship Infantry (LSI) able to carry 830 soldiers into battle. She saw widespread action at North African landings in 1942, and at Sicily and Salerno in 1943. She was returned to her owners in 1945 and resumed service. The *Royal Scotsman* made her final Irish Sea crossing in September 1967 and was sold to Hubbard Exploration Ltd and renamed *Apollo*. She was sold in 1975 and finally scrapped in Texas in 1984.

Diana, the former *Enchanter*, a 280-ton, 65ft double-ended ketch, was acquired in August 1966 for the Hubbard Exploration Company as Hubbard's personal yacht and moored at Clearwater, Florida. She was original built in Holland and in 1967 was totally refitted at Las Palmas, Canary Islands. After his death in January 1986, his followers made attempts to make her a permanent memorial ashore at Clearwater.

Athena, was the former *Avon River* a former 145ft trawler, which became the first 'flagship' with Hubbard nominating himself as Commodore. These first three vessels forming the original flotilla were crewed by volunteers from his Sea Organization (*Sea Org*) and some seamen. There was also a catamaran named *Nekambia* and the following vessels were also utilized at various times:

The *Bolivar* was the former World War II 280-ton Patrol Craft *PC-1230* of the type of small submarine-chaser that Hubbard had briefly commanded in World War II. She had been built by Leathern D. Smith Shipbuilding Company, Wisconsin, in July 1943 and saw war service at the Peliliu Island invasion in 1944. Post-war she had been decommissioned in March 1946 and renamed USS *Grinnell* in 1956. She was sold to Western Milling Company in 1959 and served with the company until 1970 when she was bought by National Metals and Steel Company, California. In April 1971 she was acquired by Hubbard and renamed as *Bolivar* and was used for training. Later she reassumed the name *Grinnell* and docked at Terminal Island.

The *Excalibur* was another former US Navy vessel, a Patrol Craft Escort (Rescue), the *PCE(R)-855*. Of 850-tons, she was one of twelve such vessels and was built by Pullman-Standard Car Manufacturing Company, Chicago, in November 1944. She served at the Okinawa Campaign in 1945 rescuing survivors of two ships destroyed by Kamikazes, and subsequently in the Philippines and South China Sea. Post-war she became a maid-of-all work for the Navy Electronics Laboratory (NEL) at Terminal Island, San Diego, and became an Experimental Patrol Craft Escort (Rescue). She was named as the USS *Rexburg* in 1956 as a trials ship for new equipment in various electronics experiments and later served at Hawaii. She was sold out of service in 1970 and destined for the scrap yard but was rescued by being acquired by Hubbard in June 1971. She was renamed *Excalibur* and was used for training purposes until sold off in 1975.

Freewinds originated with the Lion Ferry of Sweden's order for two Ro/Pax ferries designed to operate between Bremerhaven and Harwich during the summer months and in the cruise ship role during the winter. They were to be built at Wärtsilä's Turku shipyard in Finland. The second vessel of the pair was to be named *Prins Albert*, but the order from Lion was cancelled while both ships were still on the stocks. Instead the ships were sold to the Swedish Wallenius Lines for completion as pure cruise ships and for charter to the newly established Commodore Cruise Line for their planned Caribbean itineraries. She was converted accordingly and Wallenius at Stockholm named the 10,328-GT vessel as *Bohème* and she was registered at Bremen.

Following an accident on her maiden voyage, she finally commenced service from Miami in December. She was refitted in 1970 to modify her air conditioning system, which had proved inadequate. In 1981 she was acquired by Rederi Ab Sally of Finland who bought out Commodore Cruise Line and from 1982–83 she was chartered to Saitecin Cruises in Brazil. The ship underwent a second large-scale refit at Bremerhaven in 1983, and after a brief period in the north Caribbean again, was chartered out to Sea Escape as its Freeport ferry ship during 1984–85. She briefly resumed operations with Commodore out of Saint Petersburg but Commodore sold her for $10million in September 1986.

The *Bohème* was acquired by San Donato Properties, SA, of Panama in 1985. Charter fees and cruise fees are originated by Majestic Cruise Lines, the latter using the revenue to pay interest and principal of the *Freewinds* mortgage to Transcorp Services of which San Donato is a wholly owned subsidiary. The Foundation Church of Scientology International (CSI) had formed the Flag Ship Trust for this purpose and on-board courses are run by the Flag Ship Service Organization (FSSO) aboard the *Freewinds*. Conversion resulted in the building of course rooms, a library, Sea Org facilities, the Religious Technology Center and similar internal organization areas, as well as a symbolic LRH office. She can accommodate a total of 540 devotees/students, over five decks. There is a restaurant, a lounge, swimming pool, cinema, beauty salon and cabaret. While in port concerts and conferences are held. In 2009 the ship was stripped of asbestos at Bonaire by a team of Polish shipyard workers contracted by Nordica amid considerable controversy.

She was DNA classified but is now classified at Lloyd's Register and is registered in Panama.

Fred Olsen Cruise Line

This is one of the smaller cruise lines, but one which, because of that fact, has one of the best customer/company relationships of them all. Although Fred Olsen Cruise Lines Ltd. is Norwegian in origin and ownership (now in its fifth generation), it is based in the UK, with headquarters in Ipswich, Suffolk, and Registration in London. The company is owned by Bonheur and Ganger Rolf, being a subsidiary of

189

the Fred Olsen Group, based in Oslo and Tenerife, which also included Fred Olsen Express/Lineas Fred Olsen and COMARIT. With offices worldwide, the group as a whole has interests in aviation, electronics, shipbuilding, hotels and property development. With currently five cruise ships operating the main European and American circuits, including the Baltic, Mediterranean and Caribbean, the emphasis is almost exclusively on British customers with whom it has a long-establish rapport with a strong loyal customer base.

The Fred Olsen group can trace its ancestry back to 1848 and the setting up of a small shipping company at Hvitsen, Norway, by Fredrik Christian Olsen, who gradually built up a fleet of small wooden coastal schooners trading along the Norwegian coast. His brothers Andreas and Petter also established similar sailing ships in the following decade. By 1896 a more ambitious expansion began with the establishment by Thomas Fredrik, a son of Petter Olsen, of A/S Bonheur, and the ordering of the first steamer, the *Bayard*. She proved the first of a long line of Olsen ships, and established the practice of naming the ships with the letter 'B'. Three years later the company offices were moved to Christianna (Oslo) to cope with the growing administration as the fleet expanded from coastal trade to International shipping. By 1901 the company had taken over the Faerder Steamship Company, whose principally cargo-carrying steamers also had provision for over a hundred passengers. The company's ships, identified by their black funnels with a red band and the family flag (a swallow tail with blue dot and diagonal bar) moved into the fruit trade transporting their perishable wares from southern Europe to northern ports, principally London. During the winter months in Europe Olsen marketed the attractions of the Canary Islands and Madeira for jaded northern Europeans, with considerable success, and thus established a small but steady cruise base.

After the Great War, this expansion continued and a notable milestone was the acquisition of the 100-passenger *Brabant* in 1926. Thomas Fredrik died in 1933 having built up the company to be a major shipping company that managed to survive the Great Depression intact. The fruit trade continued to be the company mainstay, the new era being represented by the change of the funnel colour to the now familiar yellow and the steady addition of new ships and, despite losses in the Second World War when Norway was occupied by the Nazis, the company went from strength to strength in the post-war era.

The real breakthrough on the cruising front came with the arrival of the famous *Black Prince* in 1966, with limited accommodation, which enabled the Fred Olsen and Bergen Line to establish a weekly passenger service on the Canary Island run, which quickly proved enormously popular. The 11,209-ton Bahamas-registered *Black Prince* was a car ferry with passenger accommodation, but her conversion reversed this and the emphasis was on providing quality accommodation for the new generation of younger travellers, themselves new to cruising. The ship was taken in hand and rebuilt with 125 new cabins and re-entered service in 1987. For the next ten years, under the command of Captain Thor Fleten, this ship established Olsen's reputation as a popular and caring company plying mainly the Canary Island, Madeira, Gibraltar route. She continued serving, after another refit, in 2005, until 2009. In 1996 a second vessel joined this circuit, the Olsen brothers purchasing former *Star Odyssey*, ex-*Royal Viking Star*, a custom-built ship of some 28,221 tons built in 1972. Again she underwent modernization to increase her passenger complement to a maximum of 843. Renamed the *Black Watch* after the famous Scottish regiment, she again quickly proved a highly popular and successful ship. A third acquisition was the *Crown Dynasty* in 2001, which was upgraded by Blohm und Voss, Hamburg, and especially designed to cater for the burgeoning seven-day Caribbean fly-cruise market. She became the *Braemar*. These medium-size ships, with their resulting intimacy, became the speciality of Fred Olsen Cruises, while other companies were steadily increasing the size of their individual vessels and fleets to cater to the explosion in worldwide demand for holidays afloat. A similar vessel was purchased in 1985, the 28,078-ton *Royal Viking Sky*, which duly became the *Boudicea*.

However, Fred Olsen could not forever remain immune to the upward trend in this type of ship, and, in November 2007, the former *Crown Odyssey*, ex-*Norwegian Crown*, was purchased as a major addition to the fleet. She is a 43,537-ton former Norwegian Cruise Line vessel that was put into dry-docks and had a 40-metre centre 'chop-and-stretch' extension added in addition to the usual refurbishment. She joined the fleet as *Balmoral* early in 2008. At the same time the company announced it was considering placing an order at STX's South Korean shipyard for construction of the hull of its first-ever custom-built 'new-build' ship, with Aker or a similar shipyard completing the outfitting of the vessel, which, again, may revert to a 'medium-size' vessel. Whether, in the harsh reality of present-day economic cutbacks, this rumoured project will ever come to fruition remains to be seen. Being a small fish among the whales seemingly makes Fred Olsen Cruise Line vulnerable to takeover it might seem, and the company has been involved in joint ventures with some of its bigger rivals. However, with company shares privately held, this popular line appears to have its independence safe for the time being.

While the *Balmoral* is featured in the first volume of *Cruise Ships* because she is marginally above 40,000-GT the other three vessels histories and attributes are as follows:

The 28,551-GT *Boudicca* is wholly Fred Olsen owned and was originally built by Wärtsilä Hietalahti, Helsinki, Finland as the *Royal Viking Sky* in 1973 for Nordenfjeldske Dampskibsselskab, Trondheim,

for Kloster Cruises. She served successfully on around-the-world cruises. In 1981 the ship was lengthened by 27.7m by the insertion of a midships section at the Bremerhaven shipyard of AG Weser. After service with Royal Viking Line Kloster she was then transferred to another of its companies, Norwegian Cruise Line, and she briefly became the *Sunward* between 1991 and 1992. She changed hands again in 1992 when acquired by Birka Cruises and cruised in the Baltic as the *Birka Queen* for another short season. She was chartered back to Norwegian Cruise Line once more between 1992 and 1993 again becoming the *Sunward*. Yet a further charter was arranged, this time to Princess Cruises and she was renamed as *Golden Princess* in its service from 1993 and 1996. When the charter was revoked Birka sold the vessel to Star Cruises who gave her the name *SuperStar Capricorn* but this only lasted until 1998 when she was chartered to Hyundai Merchant Marine who were running cruises up the Korean peninsula but this proved abortive in the political climate and soon ceased and so Star Cruises resumed operations with her under the *SuperStar Capricorn* once more. In 2004 this much-travelled ship received another change of ownership, being sold to the Spanish company Viajes Iberojet with the inevitable name change, this time becoming *Grand Latino*. Again, this was only of short duration for in 2005 Fred Olsen Cruise Line purchased her.

After a lengthy renovation at the German shipyard of Blohm und Voss, which involved much internal re-modelling and new gear boxes for her engines, she re-entered service in February 2006 as *Boudicca* [the fashionable 'new' name for what was, for centuries, represented as *Boadicea*, Queen of the Iceni of East Anglia and scourge of the Romans]. She again was extensively refurbished at Blohm und Voss in 2011 with the creation of seventeen new interior cabins by the re-location of the Fitness Centre to the Sun Deck. She currently carries 934 guests across eight passenger decks.

Currently *Boudicca*'s facilities include dining at the Four Seasons and Tintagel Restaurants, the Heligan Room and the Secret Garden buffet. Entertainment includes The Neptune Lounge for shows, and the Lido lounge, gaming tables, the Iceni Room, two swimming pools, two jacuzzis, a sauna and steam room, The Atlantis Spa and Salon, promenade, sun and lido decks, the observatory. She has a library, a card room, an arts and crafts room, fully equipped internet room, boutique, jewellery outlet, port shop and photo gallery, fitness gym, a medical centre, launderette. She is fully stabilized. She is registered in the Bahamas.

The 28,613-GT *Black Watch* is also a Fred Olsen-owned vessel, and built by Wärtsilä Helsinki New Shipyard, Helsinki, Finland, in 1972 as *Royal Viking Star* for the Royal Viking Line for whom she served until twenty years. She had her hull lengthened in 1981 by the insertion of a new 27.7m midships section in 1981, the work being carried out at Seebeckwerft, Bremerhaven. Following this she continued in service, being taken over by Kloster Cruises in 1984 without any change of name and continued thus until 1991. She was then moved over to Norwegian Cruise Line and renamed as the *Westward,* abandoning worldwide cruises for the Caribbean circuit out of New York. Three years on and another move saw her under the Royal Cruise Line banner with another new name, *Star Odyssey* and her routes switched to the Mediterranean. In 1996 the vessel was purchased by Fred Olsen becoming the *Black Watch*. Feeling her age she suffered some embarrassing breakdowns at sea and in 2005 was given a major fifty-seven day refit at Blohm und Voss, which involved the installation of a new set of four MAN 7L32/40 diesel engines, new gears, internal modifications resulting in an extra four new suites and a library. She was again refitted in 2009.

Black Watch now carries 868 guests in 423 suites and cabins over eight passenger decks. She is fully stabilized. Among her many amenities are the Neptune, Lido and the Observatory Lounges, the Marina Theatre and Pipers Bar. Dining options are the Glentanar Restaurant, the Orchid Room, the Braemar Café and the Marquee Bar. For entertainment there are the promenade and the sun deck with golf, two swimming pools, two jacuzzis, the Atlantis Spa and Salon, a fitness centre, sauna, library, card room and the Braemar Lounge. There is a medical centre, a lecture theatre, boutique, port shop, photo gallery and a launderette.

The *Black Watch* received the accolade of 'Best for Entertainment 'in the 2012 Cruise Critic 'Cruisers' Choice UK Awards. She is registered in the Bahamas.

Finally, the *Braemar* is owned by Capital Bank Leasing, Oslo, and managed by Fred Olsen Cruises after being acquired from the Commodore Cruise Line in 2001. She is the former *Crown Dynasty*, which was built in 1993 at Union Navale de Levante, Valencia, Spain, for Crown Cruise Line. They chartered her out to Cunard during 1993–1997 during which period she received the temporary title of *Cunard Crown Dynasty*.

She was renamed as *Crown Majesty* in 1997 for a brief period when she served with Majesty Cruise Line before transferring her to Norwegian Cruise Line, whereupon she became the *Norwegian Dynasty* between 1997 and 1999. She reverted to her original name, *Crown Dynasty*, once more between 1999 and 2001 with Commodore but in 2001 Fred Olsen took her over and renamed her *Braemar*.

In 2008 *Braemar* was also lengthened by 31.2m by inserting a new midships section and also lengthening the deck eight extremities at the Blohm und Voss yard at a cost of €60 million. This enabled more cabins, recreation space and swimming pools to be installed.

She now accommodates 929 guests in 485 suites and cabins over seven passenger decks.

Amenities and facilities include the Ballindalloch, Spey and Avon restaurants, the Palms Café and the Marquee bar for dining choices, The

Braemar Room, Coral Club and the Lido, Marquee Pool and Morning Light bars, the Neptune and Observatory lounges for entertainment. There is the promenade, the Braemar Lounge, an art gallery, arts and craft room, card room, the sun deck with golf, and a library. The *Braemar* has two swimming pools, two whirlpool jacuzzis, the Atlantis Spa Salon, a fitness centre, an internet centre and for shopping there are a boutique, jewellery showroom, port shop and photo gallery. She also has a 24/7 medical centre, and a laundrette.

FTI Cruises

With headquarters at the Landsberger Strasse in Munich, Germany, and offices in Austria and Switzerland, FTI (Frosch Touristik International) Touristik GmbH is a tour operator and was originally established as Frosch Touristik GmbH in 1983 and was at one time a subsidiary of MyTravel Group plc. Aged only twenty-one, Dietmar Gunz had, just two years earlier, founded LAL Sprachreisen, which specialized in selling English-language holidays to the German customer. The success of this venture enabled him to establish the new company as an offshoot, dealing principally with package holidays to Malta and in 1987 this became Frosch Touristik (Malta), which took over the long-haul operator CA Ferntouristik GmbH, which kick-started the worldwide operations. With a current turnover of around one billion euros, FTI is one of the leading German tourism organizations.

In April 2010 it changed its name. The group operates a worldwide tourist trade that encompasses as diverse a range of destinations as Australia, Bulgaria, the Caribbean, Egypt, Greece, Italy, Malta, Mauritius, Mexico, Namibia, New Zealand, Oman, South Africa, Spain, Tunisia, Turkey and the United Arab Emirates. The Chief Executive remains Dietmar Gunz, as CEO and Director, with Karlheinz Jungbeck, MD Finance, Boris Raoul, MD Tourism, and Turan Jenei, MD Corporate Development.

FTI Cruises was set up as a cruise arm of FTI Consulting, operating with the former Deilmann Cruises *ZDF Dreamboat*, now known as *FTI Berlin*, which is owned by Berlin Shipping Ltd, Greece, but under a long-term (to 2015) charter from the UK-based Saga Shipping (which had named her *Spirit of Adventure*). Cruises since 2011 have mainly been conducted to destinations in the Mediterranean area. The vessel was modernized and is designed to operate as a German-language ship catering for the 'fly-cruise' market under the marketing slogan 'Freestyle Elegant'.

Hainan Cruise Enterprises SA

This company has registered offices at Proton Capital Group HK Ltd building in Queen's Road Central, Hong Kong, and is a ship owner/manager. It is also an affiliated company of Enterprises Shipping and Trading SA, which has its HQ at Poseidonos Avenue, Athens. Founded in 1973, with M.G. Saris as President, it manages eighty-seven ships, including one cruise ship, and is a part of the Greek Restis Group.

Currently the single cruise ship operating for Hainan is the *Aegean Paradise*, which was built in 1990 at Ishikawajima Harima Heavy Industries Co. Ltd (IHI), Tokyo, as the *Orient Venus* for Venus Cruises, a subsidiary of Japan Cruise Line under Japan Charter Cruise. She served for fifteen years under this name, and was refitted by Hellenic Shipyard Perama, Greece, in 1990. She briefly became the First Cruise ship *Cruise One* in 2005. She was then acquired by Enterprise Shipping and Trading in 2005, when she underwent a massive refit, which involved considerable rebuilding of her upper works, and emerged vastly altered with additional balcony cabins, a disco and other updates. From May 2007 she started cruising for Delphin Kreuzfahrten as the

Delphin Voyager. In January 2011 she became the *Hainan Empress* but by that same May was the Happy Cruises (the resurrected Spanish Quail Cruises) vessel *Happy Dolphin*. When Happy Cruises in turn became bankrupt that very same September she was laid up at Piraeus. Hainan acquired her and chartered her to Etsur, Istanbul, and she was renamed *Aegean Paradise* in May 2012. She cruised from Izmir and then Istanbul during 2012 to the Aegean islands and also to Black Sea ports. She is registered in the Bahamas.

She can accommodate 748 guests in 325 cabins plus there is one owner's suite.

Hapag-Lloyd Cruises

Originally part of the giant Hapag-Lloyd transport conglomerate, whose early history is contained within the shipbuilders section, Hapag-Lloyd Cruises is now a subsidiary of the TUI AG travel group. Originally they came from two famous old German transatlantic liner operatives, based in Hamburg and Bremen respectively. The Hapag Company was first established in 1847, and had merged with North German Lloyd (NGL), while the Norddeutscher Lloyd (NDL) had been founded in 1856 and the two old firms had themselves been conjoined in 1970 as Hapag-Lloyd with HQ in Hamburg. This amalgamation was, in its turn, swallowed up by the Tourism giant TUI AG (Hanover) in 1998 and became a total subsidiary in 2002.

Hapag-Lloyd Cruises operated, and still operates, a mix of company-owned and chartered vessels.

The original *Europa* was built as a combination of ocean liner and cruise ship (then a novel concept), in 1953 at the De Schelde shipyard at Vlissingen, Netherlands, for the Swedish America Line as *Kingsholm* and served with them until 1965. When North German and Hapag merged the latter took her over. She had already been renamed as *Europa* and

she was operated by Hapag-Lloyd under that name until 1981. She was later sold to Independent Continental Lines, a Costa subsidiary, and she became the Costa Cruise Line ship *Columbus C* until an accident at Cadiz terminated her career prematurely in 1984 and she was scrapped at Barcelona the following year.

The *Finnstar* was built as a Baltic ferry by Wärtsilä Hietalahti, Helsinki, shipyard for the Finland Steamship Company in 1967. In 1975 she became the Finnlines vessel *Finnstar* and was partly converted by Wärtsilä at its Turku yard into a cruise/ferry ship in 1978–79. As such she was chartered by Hapag-Lloyd between 1979 and 1980 and cruised to Norway and the Mediterranean. In 1981 she was renamed as *Innstar* and, after a long career and seven more name changes, ended her days as the Hong Kong casino ship *Golden Princess* for Eurasian International before being sold for scrap in China in 2009.

Her replacement was a second *Europa*, which was custom-built for Hapag-Lloyd and the German cruise market in 1981 by Bremer Vulkan, Bremen, and delivered in December 1981. She was operated worldwide between 1982 and 1999. In 1998 she was in turn replaced, and was sold to Star Cruises, to become *SuperStar Europe*. Four changes of ownership and name and fourteen years later, she is still cruising, nowadays as the *Saga Sapphire*.

Another Hapag-Lloyd custom-built vessel was the 14,903-GT *C. Columbus*, which the company operated between 1997 and 2012. She was built at the MTW Schiffswerfte at Wismar, Germany, in 1997. She could carry 420 guests and had seven passenger decks. Oddly, her owners never referred to her by her given name, only as *Columbus*. She served unspectacularly until 2012 when she was transferred to Plantours and became the company's ship *Hamburg* and is still in service.

The current ships working with Hapag-Lloyd at the time of writing are outlined below:

The little 6,752-GT *Bremen* was first built as an arctic expedition vessel in 1990. She can carry 164 guests. She was constructed as the *Frontier Spirit* by Mitsubishi Heavy Industries in Japan for Frontier Cruises. When Frontier folded in 1993 the ship was acquired by Hapag-Lloyd. Her guest accommodation is eighteen balcony cabins and sixty-four ocean-view cabins. She has the advantage of having a helicopter deck and a sun deck with a panorama lounge, fitness room/massage and a pool. She carries twelve Zodiacs on deck six while the lido deck has the Bremen Club and a library. She is also equipped with an internet area, a cinema and the hospital. Dining is buffet-style in The Club or at The Grill on the lido deck. She has a small pool and a sauna. Her cruising takes her to Fiji, Tokyo, Mauritius, Cape Town and New Zealand among many diverse destinations.

Europa (28,600 GT) was built at Kvaerner Masa Yards, in Finland in 1999 and can carry 408 guests in great comfort. She is registered in Nassau, Bahamas. She boasts thirty-eight outside suites and 152 outside cabins, four spa suites, ten Penthouse Deluxe suits and two Grand suites. She has seven passenger decks, Penthouse, Bellevue, Lido, Sport, Atlantik, Pacifik and Europa. Restaurants are Dieter Müller, Europa and Venezia, plus the Lido Café. There are the Havana, Piano, Sand and Pool Bars. For entertainment there is the Clipper Lounge, Europa Lounge and stage, Club Belvedere, Magrodome, Teen Club and Kids' Club, and a boutique/jeweller. There is a gymnasium and fitness area, lido pool, golfing facilities, art workshop, ocean spa, whirlpool, and shuffleboard. She has a hospital, art gallery, library, carries thirteen Zodiacs for inshore work and one tender.

The 30,277-GT *Columbus 2* is the *Insignia*, built in 1998 at Chantiers de l'Atlantique, St Nazaire, France, as the *R-One* for Renaissance Cruises. She served until 2003, being chartered out for a period to TMR, France, and Oceania Incorporated of Prestige Cruise Holdings Company in the USA, but managed by Cruiseinvest. She then became the *Regatta* briefly before being renamed as *Insignia* from 2003 to 2012. She is under a two-year charter to Hapag-Lloyd before returning to Oceania. *Columbus 2* has passenger access on decks 3 to 10. She was fully renovated from 2010 to 2012 and her facilities are modern. For dining choices there is the Albert Ballin Restaurant and Ballin Bar, the Polo Grill, Toscana, the Lido Restaurant, Grill and Café, Sunburgers, She has an observation lounge, with dance floor and stage, a jogging track, pools, whirlpools, the Ocean Spa, fitness centre, sauna and steam room, putting green, the Wellness Oasis, and sun deck. Bars include the Pool, Martin's Bar and Club. She has a library, internet area, dance floor, lounge and stage, teens' club and kids' club. There is are also a boutique/jeweller, photographic/film shop and a hospital.

Europa 2 keel laying 21st century style on 1st March 2012. (Hapag-Loyd)

Europa 2 fitting out on 14th September 2012. (*Hapag-Loyd*)

The *Hanseatic* (8,378 GT) was built at the Rauma Repola Yards, Finland, in 1993 as the *Society Adventurer*. She has accommodation for 184 guests and is used as an expedition ship. She is owned by Bunnys Adventure & Cruise Shipping Company Ltd, of Nassau, Bahamas, and is on charter to Hapag-Lloyd until 2018. *Hanseatic* has six passenger decks, Observation, Bridge, Explorer, Marco Polo, Amundsen and Darwin. Amenities include the observation deck, Explorer Lounge, dance floor and bar, Darwin Hall, a library, the Marco Polo restaurant, Bistro Lemaire, three bars, a pool, whirlpool, sauna/ steam room, fitness room and there is a boutique, and a hair and beauty salon. She carries fourteen Zodiacs for inshore exploration and landings, and has a well-equipped hospital.

The new-build vessel is the 39,500-GT *Europa 2*, built by STX Europe, and completed in April 2013. She is owned by General Electric Energy's Converteam consortium. Hapag-Lloyd Kreuzfahrten has her on a long-term 'Bare Boat' charter arrangement. Rolls-Royce was awarded the contract for their Mermaid-podded propulsion systems for the vessel. Over decks 4–11 the *Europa 2*'s facilities are comprehensive. She can carry 516 guests in 251 suites of various categories – Owners, Grand Penthouse, Spa, Grand, Ocean and Family Apartments. She has many restaurants and eating outlets, the Weitmere, Serenissima, Elements, Tarragon, Sushi, and Yacht Club restaurants, a dining room, and even a culinary school. She has a wine bar, piano bar and pool bar. Entertainments include the jazz club, theatre, cinema, library, gallery, magrodome, belvedere, teen club and kids' club and there is shuffleboard, jacuzzi, a sun deck sauna, ocean spa, fitness room, golf a choice of pools, boutique/jeweller and a photo shop. She also carries twelve Zodiacs.

Hebridean Island Cruises

This company is now part of the All Leisure Holidays Group and was formed in 1989 by a Skipton, North Yorkshire, family who had previously operated a small canal boat company. They saw potential in cruises around the scenic Western Isles for top-end clientele. They bought the Oban-Mull ferry MV *Columba* from Scottish ferry operator Caledonian MacBrayne and she was totally refitted by George Prior Engineering of Great Yarmouth. On completion the ship was re-launched by the then-Duchess of York as the *Hebridean Princess* on 26 May 1989.

The *Hebridean Princess* itinerary was focused purely on the Scottish market and initially the ship retained its car spaces, but two years into its operation, the car deck was replaced with additional cabins and public rooms, raising the ship's passenger capacity to forty-nine and allowing it to carry a crew of thirty-seven. After nearly ten years of successful operation, the business was taken over by Altnamara plc in 1998. Its new managers decided to invest in a second ship and put it on far-flung international itineraries. She was joined by *the Hebridean Spirit* in 2001, the larger vessel enabling the company to expand to wider horizons with voyages to the Mediterranean, South Africa and into the Indian Ocean.

In 2001, the group acquired the 4,280-GT *Megastar Capricorn* from Star Cruises, refitted her and re-launched her as the eighty passenger, seventy-crew *Hebridean Spirit* on 3 July 2001. This vessel was the former *Renaissance VI*, later *Sun Viva II* built in 1991 and financed by a London Merchant Bank branch of a Scandinavian bank to take advantage of the Italian government's 86 per cent subsidy. Built by the Apuania shipyard, on completion she was acquired by Yachtship Cruise Line and operated by Renaissance Cruises as *Renaissance VI*. She worked the summer in the Mediterranean and the winter in the Far East from Singapore. In practice she proved too small for the requirement and in July 1998 she was sold to Sun Cruises, part of the Metro Holdings group, and was renamed as *Sun Viva II*, still working from Singapore. Sold again in February 2000 she was purchased by Star Cruises who renamed her *Megastar Capricorn* and ran cruises with her up the Malaysian coast, but she was almost immediately re-sold that October to Hebridean Island Cruise. She was transported back to the UK where, at the George Prior Engineering's shipyard at Great Yarmouth, she underwent a large modification to become *Hebridean Spirit*. She carried eighty passengers in forty-nine cabins with a crew of seventy and cruised in European waters during the summer and then the Mediterranean, South Africa and the Indian Ocean.

With a dwindling customer base, by 2009 the company sold the ninety-eight-passenger *Hebridean Spirit* via the yacht brokerage company Ocean Independence, due it was stated, to the effects of the recession

and the cost of operating internationally. The company concentrated solely on home water cruising, reverting to its original name.

Hebridean International Cruises and its sole ship, *Hebridean Princess*, were purchased in 1989 by UK-based All Leisure Group, which operates both Swan Hellenic and Voyages of Discovery. The line also reverted back to its original name, Hebridean Island Cruises.

The *Hebridean Queen* was originally built by Hall, Russell & Co., Aberdeen, for the Secretary of State for Scotland as a David MacBrayne-operated Ro-Ro/Pax car ferry and Royal Mail ship as the *Columbia*. She was of 2,112 GT and could carry 600, and from 1968, 870 passengers and fifty cars from the port of Oban out to the Western Isles, initially to the Isle of Mull. In 1972 and later she operated a variety of routes, latterly under the Caledonian MacBrayne (CalMac) banner. (See Peter C. Smith, *Offshore Ferry Services of England & Scotland*, Pen & Sword Maritime, 2012, for full details of her ferry service.) After a rebuild into a luxury cruise ship at the Great Yarmouth yard of George Prior Engineering in 1989, she commenced Western Island cruising under her present name. It was decided to do away with the car-carrying capacity and devote the extra space to luxury accommodation for guests and this was done by 1970. She carries fifty guests accommodated in thirty cabins, including ten singles, and has a crew of thirty-eight. Her Majesty Queen Elizabeth II has twice chartered the *Hebridean Princess* for family holidays. Following this she awarded the ship a coveted Royal Warrant.

Based at Oban on Scotland's west coast she celebrated her silver anniversary of inauguration and now cruises the Western Isles and lonely St Kilda, and as far north as the Orkney and Shetland islands, as well as circumnavigating the UK, visiting Irish ports and as far south as the Channel Islands and France.

On the promenade deck there is the Skye Deck and Skye Bar, the Look Out Lounge, library, conservatory, the Tiree Bar and the lounge.

The Princess deck houses the Columbia Restaurant and the Princess Shop, while the Waterfront Deck has a fully equipped gymnasium.

In addition to these two vessels, the company also conducts week-long European River Cruises along the Rhine, the Main and the Danube with the 2,721-GT *Royal Crown*, which was built in 1996 and given a major refit in 2010. She was deliberately styled for the 1930s and carried ninety passengers in forty-five spacious outside cabins with five classes, Junior, Superior, Deluxe, Premium and Royal, and had a crew of fifty-two. There were three passenger decks. She had a business centre, lounge/bar, sun deck, sauna, spa, fitness centre and hairdresser, library, restaurant with à la carte dining, a brasserie, a boutique and signature shop. She is now registered in the Netherlands and is operated by Select River Cruises, Germany.

Hellenic Seaways/Blue Ocean Cruises

Hellenic Seaways was founded in 2005 as Hellas Ferries, and is headquartered at Piraeus, Greece. The company was an amalgamation of Greek ferry operatives, Minoan Flying Dolphins, Hellas Flying Dolphins, Hellas Ferries, Saronikos Ferries and Sporades Ferries. They operate ten ferry ships, twelve Flying Dolphins and two Ro-Ro ships and provide fast passenger and freight ferry services out to the Greek Islands and the Adriatic. The CEO is Yannis S. Vardinoyannis. The parent company is ANEK Lines and the company is owned by Cyprus-based based Sea Star Capital plc. In August 2009 Hellenic Seaways purchased the single-ship, budget cruise line easyCruise from its founder Stelios Haji-Ioannou. In January 2011 the Heraklion, Crete-based Minoan Lines cancelled the sale of its one-third stake in Hellenic Seaways to ANEK.

Blue Ocean Cruises was a Greek company sub-leasing the ship with its head office at Old Kamani Chambers, R. Kamani Marg, Ballard Estate, Mumbai, India. The company was formed to operate the former easyCruise vessel *easyCruiseLife* under charter from September 2010, after the Greek ferry company Hellenic Seaways acquired easyCruise from easyGroup, the investment operation of Sir Stelios Haji-Ioannou, founder of easyJet. The take-over included the operating company and the easyCruise brand name as well as the ship and was Hellenic's first entry into the cruise market. Initially the new owners of easyCruise currently operated easyCruise Life in Eastern Mediterranean, re-naming her in 2010 as *Ocean Life*. Since April 2008, the owner had been registered as EasyCruiseLife Ltd, a wholly owned subsidiary of the Hellenic Seaways Management Company. Blue Ocean shut down early in 2011.

The 12,811-GT *Ocean Life* was originally built by Szczecin Stocznia, Poland, as the car ferry *Lev Tolsoi*. She was one of seven ships of the *Dmitriy Shostakokvich* class of ferries built in this ex-Stettin shipyard for the Soviet Union and was owned by Odessa-based Black Sea Shipping Company until 1995 and by Blasco UK from 1995 to 1998. She served for six years in this role before undergoing a complete re-build in 1986 in a German shipyard into a cruise vessel. Black Sea Shipping continued her ownership but chartered her out to various German tourist companies, in 1988 to Transocean as the *Natasha* and from 1998 to 2001 to Zenith Cruise Corporation as the *Palmira*. She underwent another refit in 2000 and in 2001 she was sold to Mano Cruises, part of the Mano Maritime empire, founded in Haifa, Israel, by Mordechai Mano. They renamed her *The Jasmine* and operated her until August 2006. She was refitted in the Neorion Yard, on the island of Syros, Greece and purchased by Salem International Trans[port Trading Company, owned by International Maritime Investments Company Ltd, and renamed again as *Farah* registered in Liberia and operating to the Far East. In 2008 she was acquired by easyGroup and became its budget cruise ship *easyCruiseLife* from 2008 to 2010. However, the concept that had worked so well for the easyJet airline failed to take hold when applied to cruising and the easyCruise's new owners, Hellenic Seaways, who had bought easyGroup from Stelios, was forced to cancel its 2010 sailings itineraries. The transfer to Blue Ocean, Mumbai, where she was scheduled to make a series of Indian-customer coastal cruises, duly followed, as noted above.

The *Ocean Life* accommodates a maximum of 574 passengers in 231 cabins, which include 35 suites, 121 outside and 75 inside staterooms. Most of the cabins can accommodate four passengers with a big discount for the third and fourth passenger in a cabin and children under five years of age could sail free. *Ocean Life's* assets included meals that reflected Indian cuisine combined with an international menu, and a tie-in with TAJ to serve both, including Jain meals. There is a large swimming pool, three hot tubs, as well as a spa and wellness zone. There is a casino, shops, a gaming zone, chill-out zone, a kids' zone and the pool bar restaurant. Blue Ocean had a 'tie-in' agreement with Air India for the promotion of 'Fly Cruise' packages from all regions of India.

To date her inaugural voyage for Blue Ocean, from Goa to Mumbai, with some 401 guests embarked and a crew of 134 was also her final one. On Monday 16 November 2010, when some seventeen miles out to sea on the return leg of her journey, a crack opened up in her port side hull, which quickly caused a thirty-five degree list and flooded some lower cabins. The Indian Navy and Coast Guard arrived in due course but initially took no action. Eleven hours later three tugs towed the ship into Mormugao port, Goa, at 0400 hours local time. During the rescue operation, passengers and the crew remained on board the vessel.

There were no casualties and initially MPT officials were confident that the cause of the problem could be quickly found and repaired.

However, *Ocean Life* was moved into the Western India Shipyard to be patched up and the guests were disembarked.

Ocean Life is registered at Valletta, Malta, but at the time of writing is still laid up in Greece. Speculation is divided between whether she will return to Indian waters as a cruise ship once more, or on her final voyage to the ship-breakers at Alang.

Holland America Line

One of the greatest of the old-established shipping lines, Holland America Line (HAL) has a history and a heritage that makes it a very special player on today's cruise scene. Since its founding back in 1873, this company has transported more than ten million guests around the globe. With that tradition of service the company, although now a Carnival Corporation subsidiary, has a firm base to draw upon in the twenty-first century and has one of most modern fleets afloat today. Holland America Line has placed particular emphasis on protecting the beautiful places it conveys its passengers to, in order to preserve them for future visitations. The company policy has been clearly stated by the President and Chief Executive Officer, Stein Kruse, who says 'Safeguarding our guests, crews, ships and the environment in which we live and operate is not only the right thing to do, it is essential to the successful conduct of our business.' This declared ethos, in the form of a company policy built upon and around continually improving environmental initiatives, extends right across the board and has resulted in the receipt of several prestigious awards including the NOAA Conservation Partnership Award 2006 for their Whale Strike Avoidance training programme; Kuoni Green Planet Award for three of its ships in 2206; the accolade 'Best Eco-Friendly Cruise Line' from *Porthole Cruise* magazine in 2006 and 2008 and Virgin Holidays Responsible Tourism Award 2008 as the Best Cruise Operator. In addition every ship holds the Lloyd's Register Quality Assurance (LRQA) certificate under ISO 14001.

In action this caring policy ensures that every ship has an Environmental Office aboard and is equipped with advanced waste water purification systems and water conservation low-flo systems fitted as standard and have dedicated waste management and recycling facilities. One new innovation is the unique 'Shore Power' renewable power supply fitted aboard the *Amsterdam*, *Noordam*, *Oosterdam* and *Westerdam* with reciprocal facilities ashore at Seattle to comply with the strict Alaskan rulings on sustainability. Nor are guests omitted in this thinking, and they are encouraged to follow simple guidelines to minimize waste and damage to wildlife both aboard and while away from the ships. In this modern take on an old problem HAL is doing no more than following its roots, for it has always been famed for the cleanliness of its ships, earning the accolade 'The Spotless Fleet' early on in its operations.

The original founding date of HAL as it is known worldwide was on 18 April 1873, when the existing Plate, Reuchlin & Co. was reorganized as the Nederlandsch-Amerikaansche Stoomvaart Maatschappij (Dutch-America Steamship Company) or NASM, at Rotterdam. The first vessel to sail under the house flag of this new shipping line was the *Rotterdam*, which already sailed under the old ensign from Holland to New York on 15 October 1872, taking over a fortnight to complete this maiden voyage. A New York terminal was established at Hoboken, New Jersey, in 1882 to meet the demand for its services on 15 June 1896. In deference to its principal Netherlands–America orientation, the line was officially re-christened as Holland Amerika Lijn. The suffix *-dam* became mandatory for the ships of the fleet, which, by 1898 had grown to six, following the explosive exodus of people from Europe to the United States that commenced in the 1880s.

Cruising became part of HAL's portfolio as early as 1895 when a new *Rotterdam*, a 3,300-ton steamer, conducted a short round-trip pleasure voyage via the newly-opened Kiel Canal to Copenhagen, Denmark. The experiment was not repeated until more than a decade later, when, in 1910, the 10,500-ton *Statendam* departed from New York taking American tourists back across the ocean and on through the Mediterranean to Palestine on a sight-seeing pilgrimage to the Holy Land. Following the hiatus of the Great War, when six of its vessels were destroyed, HAL was hard hit by the abrupt curtailing of immigration from 1921 onward and this was followed by the Great Depression in the early 1930s, when crew, staff and as many as twelve ships were shed. There had been a brief flourishing of cruising in 1926 when the *Rijndam* circumnavigated the globe as part of an educational enterprise and the 14,450-ton *Veendam* took American tourists around the Caribbean. By 1938, however, demand was increasing once more with the company sailing three dozen 'Vacation Cruises', but then World War II intervened. Again, losses were heavy, with sixteen out of the 1939 fleet of twenty-six being lost.

Post-war recovery was slow but by 1951 two new ships, *Maasdam* and *Ryndam*, were obtained and they were custom-tailored toward the new 'tourist class' passenger, with only a single deck allocated to upper class guests. Seven years later the 24,294-ton *Statendam* sailed from HAL's Hoboken terminal on a Grand World Voyage. From 1963 for the next six years, both *Ryndam* and the *Seven Seas*, a ship from the German Europa Canada Line, a HAL-owned company, made global cruises acting as the floating class-rooms and recreational area of the University of the Seven Seas and by 1966 the *Statendam* was employed totally as a cruise ship. She was joined thus in 1968 by the *Nieuw Amsterdam* and *Rotterdam*. The lido concept of alternative dining options was introduced on these vessels at this date. By the following year HAL was following other previously passenger-liner orientated companies and re-branded its fleet as Holland America Cruises, although the final transatlantic crossing was not made until 1971, when the famous *Nieuw Amsterdam* joined the Caribbean 10/11 day cruise rota, working out of Port Everglades, Florida, before being broken up in 1974.

Meanwhile, to supplement the West Indies, Bermuda and Indonesian (former Dutch East Indies) itineraries, HAL cruise liners, including the *Prinsendam*, commenced working the Inside Passage route from the north-west coast of the USA to open up the magnificent Alaskan wilderness as a tourist destinations, an area that would become increasingly popular in the years that followed, the *Veendam* joining the season in 1977. In the interim HAL had absorbed Westours to coordinate ship-and-shore based tourism seamlessly and by 1983 shifted its whole base out to Seattle as Holland America Line-Westours Inc. A third Alaskan cruiser was added with the arrival of *Rotterdam* in the summer of 1984, but next year it conducted a world cruise. Despite continued growth and success, in 1987 Carnival Cruise Lines acquired the company but continued to operate it as a separate subsidiary, and the *Westerdam* was also moved to the Alaska circuit.

As with all cruise companies the 1990s marked the biggest upsurge yet in the industry and HAL was among the many major lines that expanded enormously to meet the new demand. Four new ships were ordered from the Italian yard of Fincantieri, the *Statendam, Maasdam, Ryndam* and *Veendam*, bringing the fleet up to eight vessels, six of which are employed on the Alaskan Inside Passage route, two on the glacier route, with the *Westerdam* fully utilized in the Caribbean and *Maasdam* in European waters. To further boost tourist destinations HAL purchased the 2,450-acre Bahaman islet of Little San Salvador, re-dubbed Half Moon Cay, for almost $20 million US dollars and developed a complete 45-acre resort there to the highest standards. In November 199 this

expansion peaked with the ordering of no fewer than four 81,769-ton *Vista* class ships, each costing around US $400 million each with the capacity of 1,848 guests.

The twenty-first century saw seemingly no end to the boom and *Rotterdam, Zaandam, Volendam* and *Amsterdam* all entered service in 2000 followed by the *Prinsendam* in 2002, taking fleet numbers to 14, with three operating in European waters and Rotterdam breaking new ground by visiting Antarctica. That year saw the company change name once more to Holland America Line Inc., adopting dark blue hulls with all-white upper decks. Aboard the ships the 'Pacific Northwest' style of fine-dining, top-end restaurant concept, with the Pinnacle Grill, Neptune Lounge, Culinary Arts Center were introduced in conjunction with *Food & Wine* magazine. The same year saw the first of the magnificent Vistas arrive, with the *Zuiderdam*, being joined by her sister *Oosterdam* a year later and the adoption of the Signature of Excellence® code. 2004 saw the maiden voyage of *Westerdam*, while *Prinsendam* made history in the first HAL cruise up the river Amazon. The *Noordam* joined the fleet in 2006 and a new 86,723-ton, 2,044 passenger ship was announced for 2008, the *Eurodam*, along with option of a second vessel, *Nieuw Amsterdam*. Fine art joined fine dining in the HAL portfolio from 2006 with millions of dollars of paintings and sculptures installed aboard some of the ships along with a self-guided electronic art tour handheld device. The fleet currently stands at fourteen vessels, with a passenger throughput of almost three-quarters of a million annually) and visits seven continents. Carnival's chairman has announced a freeze on all new building for all its companies, including HAL.

The Prinsendam is a 37,983 GT vessel built by Wärtsilä at Turku, Finland, in 1988 for Royal Viking Line and named *Royal Viking Sun*. After eleven years' service she was bought by Seabourn Cruise Line in 1999 who fully renovated her renamed her *Seabourne Sun*. In 2002 she was transferred to Holland America to become *Prinsendam*. She was massively refurbished in 2010 at Freeport, Bahamas, as part of HAL's 'Signature of Excellence' upgrade at a cost of $525 million. Twenty-one new staterooms were added, the interior, including the Culinary Arts Center and the Wajanag Theatre, were made-over while the aft pool deck was extended and had a bar added. She can now host 835 guests.

For fine dining the ship has the La Fontaine and Lido Restaurants and the Pinnacle Grill. There is also the Culinary Arts Center. For entertainment there is the Neptune Lounge for Penthouse and Deluxe Veranda suite passengers and the Explorer's and Queen's lounges and the Casino. There is also the Crow's Nest Bar with disco, the Showroom Theatre, and the Ocean and Java bars. For teens there is Club HAL with a game room and The Loft. The ship has two freshwater swimming pools and three jacuzzi whirlpools. There is also the Greenhouse Spa and Salon with treatment room, sauna/steam room, beauty salon, hot tub and gym. There is a sports deck with jogging track, with bocce ball and croquet courts and golf simulator. Other features include an art gallery, photo gallery, card room, library, an internet café and a shopping arcade and medical centre. Her cruise schedule for 2013 included voyages to South America and Antarctica, the Mediterranean Baltic, North Cape, and Holy Land.

Hurtigruten ASA

The company can trace its roots back to 1893 and Richard With. He was the captain of the first coastal ferry to cover the whole 2,500-nautical mile Norwegian coastline from the populated south to remote Kirkenes in Norway's Arctic Circle region near the Russian border. The very first voyage was made by the *DS Vesteraalen*, with Richard With as her captain, in July 1893, which sailed from Trondheim to Hammerfest acting as an essential mail and trade link. Over the whole 120-year period since then, even during World War II, this service has been maintained and now encompasses not just a vital trade and travel route, with both passenger traffic and cargo transit, but takes in cruise tourism at its best, with locally run ships that visit ports and anchorages from Bergen to the Lofoten Islands and Kirkenes near the Russian border very rarely visited by outsider vessels. The cruising aspect of Hurtigruten ('Express Route') has gradually increased in importance over the last thirty years as air transport has shrunk the passenger requirement and many modern ships of the fleet no longer spend much time as pure ferries but operate worldwide in the pleasure market.

The company is now part of the Hurtigruten Group ASA (HRG), with Daniel Skjeldam as CEO replacing Olav Fjell in May 2012. This is now a nationwide transport and tourist group encompassing all facets of the industry, but the cruise section, which began life as the Tromsø-based Troms Fylkes Dampskibsselskap (TFDS) which was joined with the Stokmarknes-based ferry company Oftens og Vesteraalens Dampskibsselskab (OVDS) in 2006, and was until recently based at Havnegata 2, Narvik. In 2013 the Narvik headquarters was closed and operations concentrated at a new office complex at Tromsø once more after 120 years. They now have the sole responsibility for provision of the 'Coastal Express' sea link and the Chairman and Principal Owner is Trygve Hegnar, and Hurtigruten Board members include Berit Kjöll, Tone Moh-Haukland, Per Helge Isaksen and Haldor Moen as Directors.

The current fleet are outlined below.

The *Finnmarken* (15,690 GT) represents the new image. As the traditional passenger/cargo traffic steadily declined, along with profits, over the past two decades, the tourist market steadily expanded and the new ships of the Hurtigruten ASA fleet now reflect this trend. She still has the Ro-Pax capacity along with refrigeration storage for perishable cargoes, but her guest capacity has grown to one thousand in a wide variety of luxurious accommodations with two grand suites, twelve suites and a variety of mini-suites and cabins of varying sizes and four disability cabins for wheelchair access. She was built by Kleven Verft in 2001.

The *Finnmarken*'s public spaces include a restaurant, a bistro, bars and shops. She also has a conference zone with four separate lecture halls, the Brotoppen Panoramic Lounge, a wine bar, another panoramic lounge, an indoor/outdoor café, swimming pool, racquet court, gymnasium and the Aegir Fitness Centre. The internal decor is a reflection of Norwegian art and culture with paintings, sculptures and textiles in art deco (Jugend) style. The *Finnmarken* has three cargo holds capable of holding chilled and frozen goods, with individual temperature control and eight provisions rooms, six for chilled store rooms and two for freezer store rooms along with a thawing room and a cold room. Her normal routeing was from Bergen to Kirkenes. In 2010–2011, *Finnmarken* was chartered out as an accommodation ship and support vessel for the Gorgon Liquefied Natural Gas (LNG) Project at Barrow Island, Western Australia. She returned to Hurtigruten control at Singapore in November 2011.

She is registered at Tromsø.

The 11,647-GT *Fram* was built specifically as a polar expedition vessel by Fincantieri Monfalcone shipyard, Trieste, in 2006. She can carry 500 guests and has a specially reinforced ice-resistant hull. She made her maiden voyage to Greenland in May 2007. She is named in honour of the polar sailing vessel *Fram* in which Nansen carried out the earliest exploration of the ice caps. Artefacts from the original vessel are aboard her from the Fram Museum at Oslo. She accommodates 400 guests in 39 suites and 136 cabins and has a crew of 280.

She is well-equipped for her task with two lecture rooms, the Qilak (Sky) Observation Lounge, Imaq (Sea) Restaurant, bistro, the Nunami (Land) Lobby, library, shop, internet café, fitness room, sauna and jacuzzis. The decor includes paintings from Norwegian and Greenland artists.

She is registered at Tromsø.

The sister ships *Kong Harald*, *Nordlys* and *Richard With* (11,204 GT) were built between 1992 and 1994 at the German yard of Volkswerft GmbH/ and completed by PS Werften, Stralsund. They can accommodate 490 guests in 227 suites and cabins and have a crew of 60. In February 2005 the *Richard With* was sold to Kystruten KS, Oslo, but leased back by Ofotens Dampskibsselskab and Vesteraalens Dampskibsselskab (OVDS). Similarly, the Nordlys was sold to Kirberg Shipping KS, Bergen in 2003 but leased back by TFDS.

For food outlets the *Kong Harald* has the Martha Salen Dining Room with Continental and Norwegian cuisine and the Roald Amundsen Café with international cuisine.

For entertainment there is the Leif Eriksson Panoramic Lounge, the Ottar Viking Observation Lounge, the Fritjof Nansen Lounge, the Roald Amundsen Lounge and also the Snorre Sturlson Library.

She is registered at Tromsø.

The 16,151-GT *Midnatsol* and 16,140-GT *Trollfjord* are sister ships built by Fosen Mekanisk, Verksteder, Rissa, Norway, in 2001/2002. Their accommodation for their one thousand guests is spread across a range of suites – owner's, grand, suite and mini – and cabins – outside, inside and disabled. Their public areas include the sun deck, two jacuzzis, bar, Horsont Galleri, Hamson Room, library, internet café, Mysterier Bar, Paradis Bar, panorama lounge, Monatsol Restaurant, Midtsommer Café and a theatre. They have crews of 150.

They are both registered at Tromsø

The 11,386-GT *Nordkapp,* the 11,286-GT *Nordnorge* and the 11,341-GT *Polarlys* are sister ships, built by Kvaerner Kleven Verft Ulsteinvik in 1995,1996 and 2002 respectively for Ofotens og Vesteraalens Dampskibsselskab and since 2006 owned by Hurtigruten ASA. They carry 479 guests and have a crew of 57/70. Accommodation is in suites, junior suites and a variety of mainly ocean-view cabins with three wheelchair-access cabins.

Public areas include a 240-seater restaurant, a café, a bar, the panorama lounge, the salon/bar, the arcade, conference facilities, internet café, souvenir shop, library, card room, fitness centre/gym, sauna/steam room, beauty salon and two jacuzzis.

Nordnorge is decorated in art nouveau style with work by Norwegian artists on display. She is normally employed for Antarctic cruising where her guest numbers are restricted to 350, and she carries a flotilla of PolarCirkel inflatables. She helped rescue guests and crew from the *Explorer* in November 2007. In 2008/2009 she was chartered out as a hotel ship at Venice.

The trio are registered in Tromsø.

Two others older vessels are only utilized as reserve vessels when ships allocated to cruising need replacing in service; these are the *Lofoten* and the *Nordstjernen*.

The 2,191-GT *Nordstjernen* was built in 1956 and is the veteran of the fleet. Her days are clearly numbered and she only operates in the summer months on local cruses. She was built by Blohm und Voss, Germany, and has been refitted a number of times. In 1983 her original Blohm und Voss diesels were worn out and replaced by a MaK 8-cylinder generating 2,649 kW. She had refits in 1985, 1995 and 2003, in order to keep her active. She was withdrawn from coastal service and used for cruises to Svalbard until 2012 when she was put up for sale.

The 2,621-GT *Lofoten* was built by Ackers Verft, Oslo, and entered service in 1964. She is now one of the oldest ships in the fleet and whether she will continue to serve as reserve ship with the new retrenchments is uncertain. What is clear, however, is that she should be immune from the scrap yard as she is under the protection of the Norwegian Historic Monuments preservation order granted in 2000. She has been refitted several times during the course of her almost half-a-century of service, in 1980, 1985 and 2004, and is classed as a Ro-Pax ferry, but her size means her facilities are rudimentary. She has five passenger accessible decks, Boat, Saloon, A, B and C, with a wide range of cabins of various sizes. She has the *soldekk* (sundeck), the panorama lounge, a bar, a café, restaurant and lounge. Her main area of operation is around the Svalbard archipelago during the summer months and she makes a limited number of coastal voyages along the Norway coast during winter.

She is registered at Tromsø.

International Shipping Partners Inc. (ISP)

One of the premier cruise ship management services organizations, ISP was founded in March 2001 and now has its headquarters at Penthouse A, Biscayne Boulevard, Miami, Florida, and there is also a European base in Copenhagen, Denmark. Among the many 'one-stop' services they provide on a global scale are chartering, sales, conversions, port services, personnel, maritime insurance, purchasing, inspections and accounting. The President and CEO is Niels-Erik Lund, a former Finance Director of DFDS, Denmark, and President of Scandinavian World Cruises and SeaEscape, who formed Marne Investments Limited in 1988 with investors as a ship-owing company that acquired passenger vessels up for purchase, chartering them as 'bareboat' options to operators and selling them on. In 1990 a subsidiary was formed to manage the Marne Investment ships and this became International Shipping Partners, Inc. The logical expansion of this service to managing the ships of other owners duly followed successfully until a management buy-out saw

ISP become separate from its former parent company, which then continued the relationship as a client company. The largest client at the turn of the century was Premier Cruise Line, which had six large cruise ships under contract among the twenty being managed by ISP. The downturn that followed in 2000–2001 saw many of these clients go bankrupt, Premier, Cape Canaveral Cruise Line and Canyon Reach at Sea among them, more than halving the customer base in a single year following the 9/11 New York Islamic terrorist attacks in 2001. In 2005 it provided on-board services for the first time to *Island Sky*, and this side of the business expanded with the absorption of Triton Cruise Services in 2007 and the extension of this provision to *Ocean Nova*, *Clipper Adventurer*, *Clipper Odyssey* and, from 2008, *Regal Empress*. For a time the Sterling Casino's Casino ship *Ambassador II* was similarly managed. The company slowly built its way back and now manages more than twenty diverse cruise vessels once more.

The current Board of the company includes Kenneth Engstrom Executive Vice-President, Dietmar Wertanzl, Executive Vice-President of Hotel and Commercial Operations, Captain Sten Bergqvist, Captain Jorg Walczak and Heinz Steinhauser, all Vice-Presidents Special Projects, Emmanouil Vlahos, Senior Vice-President Technical Operations, Alan Freedman, Vice-President Quality Assurance, Jan-Otto Bergjlung, Vice-President Technical Operations, Nick Inglis, Senior Vice-President Marine Operations and Gary Kerr, Vice-President Marine Operations.

The ships ISP manages move in and out according to supply and demand, so any selection can only be a frozen moment in time of a continually changing operation, but, at the time of writing ISP has an impressive array of cruise vessels on its books, including the following diverse collection:

Akademik Ioffe (IMO 8507731) and *Akademik Sergey Vavilov* (IMO 8507729) are sisters ships of 6,450 GT and 6,344 GT respectively, built by Rauma shipyard, Finland, as a polar and oceanographical research vessel for P P Shirshov Oceanological Institute of the Russian Academy of Science in Kalingrad in 1988. They are ice-strengthened and operated as polar expedition ships for One Ocean Expeditions and Peregrine Adventures, when they were named *Peregrine Mariner* and *Peregrine Voyager*. The 35,855-GT *Bahamas Celebration* (IMO 7904891), formerly the Jahre Line and then Color Line vessel *Princess Ragnhild* was built at Howaldwerke Deutsche Werft, Germany in 1981. She is owned by Celebration Cruise Holdings, for the US-based Celebration Cruises. The 4,376-GT *Sea Adventurer* (IMO 7391422) was originally completed by the Tjtovo Brodogradiliste Kraljevica, Yugoslavia, in 1976 as the *Alla Tarasova*, as a Russian ferry, but in 1975 was converted to a cruise ship and renamed as *Clipper Adventurer* between 1997 and 2002. She sailed for Quark Expeditions, Norwalk, New Jersey.

The 5,218-GT *Clipper Odyssey* (IMO 8800195) was built in 1989 in the shipyard of Nippon Kokan Tsu, at Tsu, Japan, for the Showa Line and was named *Ocean Grace* and then *Ocean Odyssey*. She worked for Zegrahm Expeditions, Seattle, and was formerly with Clipper Cruises between 1999 and 2007 and is currently owned by Odyssey Owner Ltd, Bahamas. She is available for sale or charter. The 4,280-GT *Corinthian II* (IMO 8802882) is one of many ISP ships detailed elsewhere in these pages. She was built at Nuovi Cantiere, Apuania, Italy, as the 'mega-yacht' *Renaissance Seven* in 1992. She served as the *Rena 1* in 2000 to 2004, then as the *Sun* from 2001 to 2003, then the *Island Sun* from 2003 to March 2004 when she received her current name. She is registered to Corinthian II Owner Ltd for Clipper Cruises, Bahamas, and she is operated by Travel Dynamics International, New York.

The 9,780-GT *Freewinds* (IMO 6810811) is also described elsewhere and is the former *Boheme*, built in 1968 by Wärtsilä, Finland and currently registered to San Donato Properties S A, Panama. The 19,093-GT *Gemini*

(IMO 9000687) was built in 1992 at the Union Navale de Levante, Spain, and has carried the following names in her long career: *Crown Jewel* in 1992; *Cunard Crown Jewel* from 1993 to 1995; *Superstar Gemini* between 1998 and 2008; *Clipper Jewel* in 2009; *Vision Star* in 2009 and then *Braemar*. She is registered to Jewel Owner (Clipper International Dynamics), and has worked for Quail Cruises and Happy Cruises. She is currently laid up at Tilbury. The 12,288-GT icebreaker *Kapitan Khlebnikov* (IMO 7824417) was built for the Russian Far East Shipping Company by Wärtsilä Helsinki and worked for Quark Expeditions for many years on polar cruising trips. The 8,282-GT *Ocean Diamond* (IMO 7325629) was built in 1974 by KMV, Norway, as the *Begonia* and subsequently served as the *Fernill*, *Explorer Starship*, *Song of Flower* and *Le Diamant* to 2011 when she assumed her present identity. She is now registered to Explorer Partners Ltd (CMA CGM SA) and has also operated for Quark Expeditions. She is available for summer season charter. Likewise, the 12,798-GT *Ocean Atlantic* (IMO 8325432) has had several names. She was built as the Russian *Konstantin Chernenko* by the Polish shipyard of New Szczecin, Szczecin, in 1986 and served thus for three years before becoming the *Rus* between 1989 and 2010 and the *SC Atlantic* from 2010 to 2012. She is currently registered to Ocean Atlantic Partners and is available for sale or charter.

The 2,183-GT *Ocean Nova* (IMO8913916) was built by Orskov Christensen's yard in Denmark in 1992 as the *Sarpik Ittuk* and is now registered to Quark Expeditions. The 22,945-GT *Ocean Pearl* (IMO 7005190) was built in 1970 for the Royal Caribbean Cruise Line. Since then she has served with the following name changes: *Song of Norway* (1997), *Sundream* (1997), *Dream Princess* (2004), *Dream* (2006), *Clipper Pearl* (2007), *Clipper Pacific* (2008), *Festival* (2009) and *Ocean Pearl* (2010) and as *Formosa Queen* with Star Management, Taipei.

The 1,268-GT *Quest* (IMO 8913904) was built in 1992 by Orskov Christensen Staalskibverft, Frederikshavn, Denmark, as the *Saffit Ittuk*.

She has since carried the name *Disco II* and has been chartered to Polar Quest at Svalbard. She is now registered to Quest Owner Ltd, and is available for winter charter.

The 4,954-GT *Sea Discoverer* (IMO 921313) was built in 2004 as a coastal cruise ship by Atlantic Marine, Jacksonville, Florida, and carried the names *Cape Cod Light* for the now defunct American Classic Voyages until August 2007 and then *Clipper Discoverer* until December 2010. She is laid up at Tilbury at the time of writing available for sale or charter.

The 4,200-GT *Sea Spirit* (IMO 8802888) was built for Renaissance Cruises as the *Hanseatic Renaissance* in 1992 at the Marina di Carrara shipyard in Italy. She became the *Renaissance V*, the *Sun Viva 1*, the *Megastar Sagittarius* and then the *Spirit of Oceanus* before assuming her present name.

The 4,954-GT *Sea Voyager* (IMO 9213129) was built by Atlantic Marine, Jacksonville, Florida, as the *Cape May Light*, and later carried the names *Coastal Queen*, and then *Clipper Voyager* with Clipper Cruises. She is laid up at Charleston, South Carolina, awaiting sale or charter. The 11,457-GT Ro-Pax vessel *Warrior Spirit* (IMO 7902726) was built by Ateliers & Chantiers du Havre as the *Malta Express* and is currently registered to Achieva Shipping II Ltd.

Finally, ISP manages two river cruise vessels, the *Sound of Music* (ENI 2327687), built in 2006 and owned by River Advice AG, Basel, Switzerland, and working for Gate 1 Travel, Australia; and the *Rembrandt* (ENI 07001819), built by Grave BV, The Netherlands, in 2003 and operated by Waterway Rembrandt AG, Basel, Switzerland.

Kristina Cruises Oy

The company was first formed by the Partanen family as Rannikkolinjat in 1985 at Kotka, Finland, to provide cruise services to five designated ports in the Baltic Sea and adjacent areas as well as to the Mediterranean.

Initially the company acquired the 1943-built, former US Navy hospital ship *Solace* (PCE 830). *Kristina Brahe* was taken over from Fagerlines which were utilizing her as the *Sunnhorldland*, and cruised Finnish waters principally in the region of Lake Saimaa in the summer months and also Leningrad and Tallinn. Other destinations included cruises to Vyborg from Helsinki, Kotka and Lappeenranta.

The company enjoyed success and expanded its itineraries two years later by purchasing the 1960-built ferry ship.

Bore, a unique vessel built by Oskarshamns for Höyrylaiva Oy Bore-Angfartygs Ab Bore, combined the two-funnelled appearance of a miniature liner with Ro-Ro facilities. She had been laying idle at Turku, in south-west Finland, awaiting conversion to a cruise ship. She was renamed *Kristina Regina.* The ship was refitted at Wärtsila and given new diesel engines. From 1988 the *Kristina Regina* was working the Baltic circuit in the summer months only and the company was now known at Kristina Cruises. By 1990 the cruises included Norwegian ports and by 1999 had extended to the Mediterranean.

This latter vessel then tended to be mainly used for warm-water destinations as the company expanded its range of operations to more than seventy ports in the Baltic, Atlantic and Mediterranean. The tightening of the SOLAS regulations in 2010 meant that this elderly pair eventually failed to meet the necessary criteria and they were sold out. The *Bore* reverted to her former name and is now preserved at Turku. As a solitary replacement the 12,700-GT 1982-built *The Iris* (the former *Konstantin Simonov / Francesca*), built in Szczecin, Poland, for the Baltic Shipping Company, was purchased from Mano Cruises, Malta, in December 2009 and renamed *Kristina Katarina.* Her current facilities include three restaurants, three cafés and bars, a duty-free shop, saunas, gym, day-spa services and outside swimming pool, children's pool and jacuzzi.

The company remains independent and the current CEO is Mikko Partanen. Its 2013 schedules included cruises to France, Italy, Montenegro and Croatia; Greece, Turkey and Bulgaria, and Black Sea area ports in Georgia, the Ukraine, Romania and Bulgaria as well as Atlantic destinations such as France, Spain, Gibraltar, Morocco, Madeira, la Palma, Tenerife and Gran Canaria with a Western Europe cruise that also included the Netherlands and Belgium.

Linblad Expeditions

The founder of this New York-based company was Sven Olof Lindblad, son of the Swiss Antarctic traveller Lars-Eric Lindblad, who pioneered visits to Antarctica for layman travellers back in 1966 and to the Galápagos a year later. The company was founded in 1979 as Special Expeditions, becoming Lindblad Expeditions in 2000. Its philosophy was expounded by Lindblad as '...creating new possibilities for human experience and understanding' and its theme was 'Passport to Anywhere' reflecting its global range. The idea was to use small expedition vessels that were able to penetrate regions of the world that were inaccessible to normal cruising, to crew them with experts in the various fields of natural history and to also protect the sensitive environments in a responsible way.

The company conducts forays to Alaska, Antarctica, the Arctic, Baja California, Central American locations, the Galápagos and Scandinavia. Specialized photo expeditions also include guidance from leaders in the field of wildlife photography. The key to Lindblad is participation and active engagement. The team includes Vice President Ian Rogers, Chief Financial Officer and Peter Butz and Tey Byus, Chief Operating Officers.

In 2004 Lindblad undertook what was termed a strategic alliance with National Geographic to combine their strengths and the *National*

Suite aboard *National Geographic Endeavour* off Galapagos, 4th August 2010. (*Stewart Cohen/Lindblad Expeditions*)

Geographic Endeavour, the largest vessel of the fleet, has her own on-board flotilla of smaller craft, Zodiac landing craft, sea kayaks, a glass-bottom boat and an Remotely Operated Vehicle (ROV) for undersea video recording of exotic marine life, icebergs and even ship wrecks.

Lotus Mine

This is a new company formed in Seoul, South Koreas in July 2012 with the express purpose of operating the former *MSC Melody* cruise ship for the Asian market in conjunction with the Communist State-run China International Travel Services Limited (CITS) of Beijing, China's National Travel organization since 1954. The CEO is Mr Choi Won-Hoo.

The plan is to introduce a twice-weekly cruise to Shanghai, and Jeju (Cheju) Island, South Korea, commencing in February 2013 as the CL Cruise joint venture travel agency. The arrangement is that while Lotus Mine introduced and operated the cruise vessel, CITS would find some 100,000 customers per annum as potential passengers. The 1982-built, 35,000-GT *MSC Melody* was finally sold for a rumoured $60,000,000 after spending many seasons on the South African tour route, where she was popular due to the size of her 549 cabins which were, on average, 50 per cent larger than more modern ships. Whether these will survive the inevitable refit remains to be seen. She started life as the *Atlantic* of the Greek-based Homes Lines in 1982 and later served as *Starship Atlantic* with Premier Cruise Lines of Florida before being bought by MSC in 1997.

A new name and a new port of registry are inevitable but at the time of writing they have yet to be announced.

Magna Carta Steamship Company Ltd

The Magna Carta Steamship Company Ltd is a small independent travel agency company registered in London, with one director, Philip Morrell, appointed in April 1999, and one company secretary, Mrs Kim Morrell. They had formerly worked in the travel industry with the Thomson organization and through contacts with Lord Thomson of Fleet and through him the Chinese Vice President Chou en Lai, that enabled the vast China market to be opened up to tourism. Among the many innovations set up was Voyages Jules Verne. This successful expansion came to an abrupt halt in the worldwide revulsion at the Communist regime following the massacre in Tiananmen Square on 3 June 1989. Meanwhile, river cruising in both Europe and Egypt had featured in the Morrell portfolio of new ideas, which helped cushion the downturn in the East. By 1999 similar ideas closer to home came to fruition with the concept of exploring the Scottish Highlands by similar means and two vessels, the *Lord of the Glens* and the *Lord of the Highlands*, were built originally for this purpose.

The latter ship later moved to the Galápagos Islands, then opening up to tourism, and operated with Noble Caledonia after reconstruction in 2002 in various European locations. *Lord of the Glens* continues to be operated by Magna Carta in her original area, the Caledonian Canal and the Lochs of the Highlands, after a similar re-build in Spain.

Logic dictated that the rich heritage and enormously larger tourist potential of the River Thames could be similarly served and another, larger, vessel was obtained to fulfil this concept. Becoming the company's principal vessel, *Spirit of Chartwell*, of 485 GT, was classified as a luxury commercial passenger vessel when she was first built as a Rhine cruise ship, named the *Vincent van Gogh*, by Grave B.V. Grave, in the Netherlands in 1997. She was operated from 1997 by the Kooiman Group. When acquired by Philip Morrell in 2010 she was re-classified as a hotel barge.

In 2011 the planners of Her Majesty Queen Elizabeth II's Thames Diamond Jubilee Pageant selected her as the most suitable vessel to be made-over into the Royal Barge at the heart of the celebrations that included one thousand little boats on 3 June 2012. Her already lavish interior, based upon the luxury Côte d'Azur Pullman Express train and some famous old liners, was completely made-over to resemble, as far as possible, the barges that made the Royal Progresses along the Thames in the reign of the first Queen Elizabeth. The bow was given a jesmonite prow featuring Old Father Thames and lavish fittings, banners and a new paint job were topped up by masses of flowers for the occasion. She flew both the Royal Standard and the Royal Navy's White Ensign on the day and was widely acclaimed by all her saw her (apart from a rather inept BBC reporting team).

Unfortunately, despite the one million-pound makeover and the success of the event, plans for the resumption of *Spirit of Chartwell's* Thames cruises rapidly ran into the buffers. Due to the demands of the London Olympics, the company was unable to secure the central berth in London's docklands and also the Port of London refused to grant permission for her to pass under Richmond Bridge, deeming it a hazard. The company insisted that it was not a problem but it proved an impasse. Plans for a luxury route from Kent through Central London and into Surrey therefore became unviable. Other rivers were unsuitable due to lack of footfall. The 'superb boat' was therefore put up for sale and, at half the cost originally paid for her, in June 2012 was bought by Mário Ferreira's company Douro Azul She was towed away from Ramsgate harbour to become a cruise boat on the River Douro in Portugal.

Majestic International Cruises Inc.

The company was first established in the late 1980s by a group with interests in both the commercial and cruising shipping sectors. Its intention was to form a cruise line utilizing medium-size cruise ships to offer potential niche market long-term operators the option of chartering three-to-four star quality vessels and combine this with the necessary management and operational services that would equal the ships' high standards. The subsidiary organizations Maximus Navigation of Madeira and Monarch Classic Cruises formed part of the group.

In 1994 the first cruise ship selected was the 10,400-GRT *Ocean Majesty*, which had originally been built at Valencia by Union Naval de Levante SA, as a Spanish Balearic Islands ferry, the *Juan March*, as long ago as 1966. She subsequently worked under a variety of names in the Aegean and Adriatic but in 1989 was converted to a cruise ship for Majestic Cruises and first took the name *Ocean Majesty*. The refit lasted from 1989 until 1994 when she entered service but that same year she briefly carried the charter names *Olympic* and *Homeric* before reverting again in 1995. *Ocean Majesty* had 274 staterooms of the quality required. Some US$50 million was spent in renovating this vessel, and she was almost totally internally rebuilt, resulting in a cruise ship of the highest quality to meet the criteria set. She was first chartered to the British Page & Moy, operating for the company for about two-thirds of a year and up to 2009 was also being chartered for shorter periods to other charterers among them the Belgian AllWays Travel, the UK-based Voyages of Discovery, Spanish Halcyon and Templeton Tours in the USA. In mid-2010, after thirteen years of charter by Page & Moy, the *Ocean Majesty* was chartered by APEX Tours of Istanbul, who operated the vessel from Izmir on voyages ranging from three days to a week in the Aegean area and along the Dalmatian coast and this was repeated in 2011. She was again renovated in 2012/2013 at the Chalkis Yard, Greece, and is currently SOLAS 2010 compliant. From June 2010 she has been chartered to the Turkish Apex Tour sailing from Izmir to the Aegean and North Africa and for the 2013 season her charter is to the German-based Hansa Touristik, at Bremen

In 1998, after another $20 million conversion, the 20,000-GRT *Ocean Explorer* became the second vessel so utilized adding her 406 larger-than-average staterooms to the fleet. Originally built for the US War Department as the troopship *General W P Richardson* as long ago as 1944, this vessel served under a succession of names until purchased by Majestic Cruises. In this capacity she conducted several round-the-world cruises. She also proved most suitable due to her elegance to serve in the capacity of floating hotel at the Lisbon Expo 98 and the G8 Economic Conference in Genoa. This ship served for many years and then was laid up at Eleusis for a long period until April 2004 when she was sold for scrapping in India.

Meanwhile another vessel, the 15,800-GRT, *Ocean Monarch*, with 231 staterooms was brought into service in 2002 and, after a US$5 million renovation, was chartered to German Tour operator HANSA in 2003 and 2004 and later was chartered by Page & Moy, for a further three years in succession. In 2003 she had the distinction of hosting the Religion, Science and the Environment, of the Symposium V in the Baltic, entertaining for eight days the guests of His All Holiness Ecumenical Patriarch Bartholomew, the head of the Orthodox Church.

Ocean Countess shopping area on 28th April 2010. (*Majestic International Cruises Inc*)

During 2006/2007 *Ocean Monarch* operated three-to-four day cruises from Piraeus, Greece, before likewise being sold.

In February 2004 the 17,600-GRT Danish-built *Ocean Countess* was acquired by Maximus Navigation from Olympia Cruises. This 1971 vessel was originally ordered as one of eight ships for MGM as part of a diversification programme but this was abandoned after two ships were launched and she became the *Cunard Countess* as the first of many name changes. She brought her 400 staterooms to the Maximus scene, which, after a $5 million dollar upgrade was first used as a floating hotel and base at Piraeus, Greece, for the French television authority and the French Olympic Committee during the Olympic Games in 2004. The following year the ship was under charter to Travelplan of Spain, part of the Globalia Group of Companies, and operated out of the port of Valencia. In December 2005, she was under charter to first the German Tour operator Holiday Kreuzfahrten as *Lili Marleen* before it bacame bankrupt when she reverted to her former name in November 2006 before being used by Louis Cruises under the name *Ruby* for a period. In 2008 she conducted three- to four-day mini-cruises for Monarch Classic Cruises from Piraeus to the Greek islands and Turkey and this was followed that winter by sailing to South America for Travelplan. Between June 2009 and April 2010 she sailed as *New Pacific* for *Quail Cruises* of Spain, again reverting to *Ocean Countess* from April 2010 with UK-based Cruise and Maritime Voyages (CMV), cruising to the Norwegian fjords, the Baltic, around the UK and also in the Mediterranean. The last cruise for CMV is scheduled for October 2012 and she will be replaced by the refitted 20,636-GRT *Discovery*.

Headquartered in Athens, the executive team of Majestic International Cruises is headed up by Michael Lambros, with Costa P. Zalocosta and Theodore Kontesand. The trio between them have a combined 130 years experience in the cruising industry.

Mano Maritime

Part of the large Mano Holding Ltd group, which is not only one of the largest Israeli shipping concerns but that nation's only cruise line operator, this company was a direct descendant of Mediterranean Seaways, set up by Mordechai Mano in 1956 with the Ofer Brothers Group. The company operated four vessels, *Carmella*, *Eyal*, *Liora* and *Malkah*, the latter pair named after Mordechai's daughters. The partnership was wound up a decade later and Mano Maritime Ltd was founded shortly afterward. Since then it has gone from strength to strength.

The first cruise vessel operated was the 5,261-GRT Soviet cruise ship *Bashkiriya*, built in Germany by Mathias-Thesen, Wismar, in 1964 for the Black Sea Shipping Company. She was operated by the Odessa Cruise Line from 1991 as the *Odessa Song* and then became the *Royal Dream*. In 1998 Silver Star Shipping purchased her and as the *Silver Star* she ran for Mano Maritime until 2003 before being sold on.

In 2000 the 12,825-GRT 1982-built *Kristina Katrina* was re-named *The Iris*. She was operated by Mano until 2010 when she was sold to Kristina Cruises.

In 2009 the 12,637-GRT 1975-built vessel *Palmira* was re-named *The Jasmine*. She sailed for Mano briefly and, at the time of writing, is out of service at Piraeus, Greece, under the name *EasyCruise Life*.

Currently Mano operate two cruise ships with Golden Cruises Ltd as the registered owners; the 14,717-GRT, 1971 French-built *Royal Iris*, the former *Eagle*, obtained in 2005, and the 17,496-GRT, 1975 Danish-built, *Golden Iris*, operated since 2009. Both vessels are described as 'floating hotels' and are aimed exclusively at the Israeli home market with catering, entertainment and services tailored accordingly. The spectrum of cruises on offer ranges from three days to one or two weeks and calling at destinations in the Black Sea, Europe as well as the Mediterranean.

With its HQ at Haifa, Mano is a conglomerate that includes both cargo and passenger vessels and associated services, being both directly owned and operated or operated by the group. Its other extensions include container ships, bulk cargo and dry cargo, colliers and agencies aboard. The current President and group Chairman is Moshe Mano with Moran Mano as Business Development and Board member, while Moshe Ben-Hemo is Vice President for Liner and Cargo areas and is Mano Tourism Division Manager. The cruising arm is under the care of Mano Maritime Cruises while Mano Holidays provides tourist services.

Murmansk Shipping Company/Rosatomflot

The Murmansk Shipping Company (MSC) was originally established on 22 September 1939 as the Murmansk State Sea Dry-cargo and Passenger Shipping Company, which was mercifully abbreviated to its modern title in 1967. As such it was, as indicated, a Communist state-run operation of the Soviet Union specializing in opening up the Arctic sea routes. From the beginning of nuclear development at sea, MSC held the monopoly of nuclear icebreakers for decades, in addition to its many other maritime supply and maintenance fields supporting oil and mining companies in the Arctic area and shipping vital supplies to northern cities along Russia's 13,000-km northern coast. MSC also runs regular passenger services from Murmansk to Rotterdam (an eight-day voyage) and Dudinka (thirteen days) and has trucking and warehousing capacity. Nowadays MSC has three main strands, Murmansk Shipping Company itself, Northern Shipping Company and Northern River Shipping Lines and currently runs twenty-nine ships.

The company started operating nuclear icebreakers from as long ago as 1959, when the Soviet Union's first such vessel, *Lenin*, was commissioned. By 1977 the *Arktika had* become the first nuclear icebreaker to reach the North Pole, which proved highly significant to the tourist industry. By 1993 a regular series of internationally organized North Pole tours was inaugurated and proved very popular. With re-organization, from 1998 these nuclear vessels were transferred under the trust management of the MSC. Increasingly since the fall of the Soviet Union and the establishment of normal commercial trading arrangements, MSC sought to raise extra income by further increasing the leasing of its nuclear fleet to foreign tourist groups and opening up the northern seas to visitors. This proved a success in itself but proved sensitive to a Kremlin that was becoming increasingly hostile to Western intervention in any form in this region once more. At the same time these ships were still expected to continue to provide facilities for Arctic research, global warming studies, rescue missions and normal icebreaking duties.

After being managed from 1994 by the Murmansk Shipping Company, Rosatom, on the orders of federal authorities in Moscow, took over Russia's nuclear-powered fleet of eight icebreakers in August 2008 after a long debate lasting many years. Rosatom, first established on 29 January 1992, was given the task after allegations that MSC had run the 'strategically important fleet inefficiently and to the disadvantage of Russian state interests' even though more than a quarter of MSC was already owned by the State, with the rest owned by Arctic Technologies). It was claimed that the transfer of the icebreakers to MSC in 1998 was 'illegal' and that MSC had failed to pay rental on them, while at the same time chartering the nuclear icebreakers out to foreign tourism companies. However, MSC claimed in turn that in 2003 alone net profit from these tourist operations raised $6.5 million and $5 million in 2004. But some sources linked the decision to the development of the Shtokman oil field on the Arctic shelf and the opening up of northern sea routes. MSC bitterly disputed the decision at the time, saying that it had forty years' experience of running nuclear powered ships, and also that the Federal Government had failed to invest properly in the fleet and its maintenance. MSC claimed that it was only by running the tourist trips in ships like the *Yamal* that it raised sufficient income to keep the fleet in commission.

Nonetheless, along with the icebreakers themselves their service base, Atomflot, was duly absorbed by Rosatom on 28 August 2008.

Rosatom (officially Rosatom Nuclear Energy State Corporation) itself is now headed up by Sergei Vladilenovich Kiriyenko, a former Prime Minister, who replaced Alexander Rumyantsev, the latter having been appointed by President Putin to replace Yevgeny Adamov. The rest of the management team is Nikolai Solomn, Chief Financial Officer; Petr Shchedrovitskiy, Vice-Chairman, Scientific & Technical Board, Mamara Vorobyova, Head of Economics and Victor Pietel, Head Nuclear Materials Office. The Atomflot section, a Federal State Unitary Enterprise (FSUE) that runs the Icebreakers is but a small part of this vast organization and it designs, constructs, owns and operates the whole nuclear icebreaker fleet. The fleet currently includes four 75,000-hp nuclear reactor powered ships, *Rossiya* (23,000 tonnes, 1985), *Sovetsky Soyuz* (23,000 tonnes, 1989), *Yamal* (23,445 tonnes, 1992) and *50 Let Pobedy* (25,165 tonnes, 1993); two 40,000-hp nuclear reactor powered vessels, *Taymir* (21,000 tonnes, 1988) and *Vaygach* (21,000 tonnes, 1990) and the atomic lighter *Sevmorput* (61,000 tonnes, 1988). The base is located some 2 km north of Murmansk itself.

Despite the problems of an ageing fleet that requires de-commissioning and what to do with the mass of radioactive contaminated materials that results, Atomflot announced in 2012 the launch of Project 2220, under which the first of several new 33,540-tonne mega-ton generator atomic icebreakers will be built. The first vessel was laid down at the St Petersburg Baltisky Zavod shipyard in 2013 and has the capacity to force her way through ice of 4m+ thickness. Whether tourism will still have a place aboard such strategically important vessels is problematical. Some even question if indeed such ships are really necessary at all, as global warming is clearing the Arctic seaways at a far greater rate than any icebreaker could ever do.

New Century Tours Corporation Pte Ltd

Headquartered at 51 Ubi Avenue, on the Paya Ubi Industrial Park in Singapore, New Century Tours Corporation Pte is a limited company that was first established in 1977. The group has steadily grown and now includes a travel agency, ferry services, property, travel insurance and a tour/cruise operator in its portfolio. The Operations Executive is Son Nyek Yuen and the Director is NG Eng Leng and there are also offices at Tanah Merah Ferry Road Terminal and Maritime Square, Harbourfront Centre.

The company runs two gambling ships, the *Leisure World* from Singapore and the *Amusement World*, which is accessed from the Swettenham Pier Cruise Terminal at George Town, the capital of Penang. The *Leisure World* was originally the Norwegian Cruise Line's *Skyward*, one of a quartet of innovative ships introduced in the late 1960s and which served for twenty-two years before being run from Singapore by Johnson Sembawang Shipmanagement between 1991 and 1995 under the names *Shangri-La World*, *Asean World*, *Fantasy World* and *Leisure World* respectively. She was rebuilt in Jacksonville, Florida and sold to Queenstown Investment Ltd in 1995 who in turn sold her to New Century Cruise Line in 2000.

Access to the *Leisure World* is via the Pasir Gudanag Ferry Terminal, Johor, with up to four services a day connecting with the ship when in harbour, which takes one-and-a-half hours' travelling time. The same ferry conveys passengers from Pasir Gudang to Batam and other Indonesian destinations. Most go for the casino facilities rather than the actual cruise itself, which is overnight. The ship also holds its own poker events, which are attended by many of the leading players. There is, however, a restaurant, stage show, bars, the Tropicana Karaoke Lounge, a sauna, basketball and badminton court and table tennis facility, a pub and a lounge, fitness spa, hairdressing salon, and gift shop for those who prefer not to gamble the night away. There are no no-smoking areas.

The *Amusement World* is similarly equipped and has a sun deck with a mini golf driving range, the sports bar, Patricia's Restaurant with 250 seats, the Lion Bar with magic shows and a video arcade. But the centre of events is, of course, is the main gaming hall. She was one of a trio of Ro-Ro ferries built for Swedish Lloyd in 1967 and operated on the Southampton to Bilbao route as the *Patricia*. In 1978 she was sold to Stena Line becoming the *Stena Saga* (and, briefly, the *Stena Oceanica*) before being sold on in 1988 to Lion as the *Lion Queen*. After a similar conversion she is now a regular feature of the Penang seascape.

Noble Caledonia

Noble Caledonia, incorporated on 1 August 1991, is headquartered in Belgravia, London, and operates river cruises, expedition cruises, small ship cruises and land tours in some fifteen areas of the globe, including Antarctica and the Arctic, South America and the Caribbean. The company currently has seven cruise ships and vessels with capacities ranging from 50 to 160 passengers. Noble Caledonia owns two vessels and operates the others on long-term charters. The company has a wide range of cruises and markets its holidays with the philosophy of providing the discerning fifty-plus customer base with high-quality, high-comfort, a small group, fully inclusive pricing and professionally escorted travel experiences. Noble Caledonia operates independently under the long-term direction of London-based Managing Director

Andrew Gordon Cochrane and with Anna Katarina Viktoria Salen from the Swedish Salen family who have a long pedigree in ship ownership and operation, as a Director since 2003. Other CEOs include Per-Magnus Sander Tolf, Barry John Matters and Pradip Kumar Mahendra Patel as Company Secretary.

The cruise ships that have been utilized by Nobel Caledonia, which are chartered from various cruise operators, some of which are featured in these pages, are as follows:

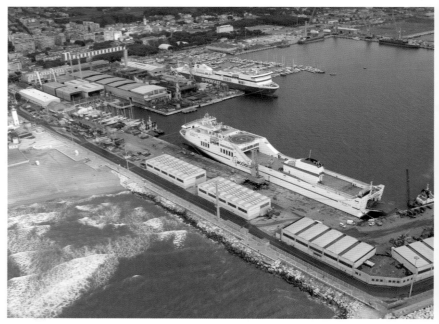

The *Nuovi Cantieri* at Carrara, Italy, as it is today. (*Nuovi Cantieri Apuania SpA*)

The 11,563-GT *Aegean Odyssey*, was originally a Ro-Ro ferry built in 1974 for Romania shipping company Zim and named *Narcis*. She was purchased by Dolphin Hellas Cruises in 1986 and converted to a cruise ship as *Aegean Dolphin* and chartered out to Epidotic Line, Renaissance Cruises (as *Aegean I*) and Golden Sun Cruises respectively. The sale to Louis Cruises in 2005 was aborted and she was laid up. She was refitted at Ermoupoli, Syros, and renamed *Aegean Odyssey* with the reduced capacity of 380 passengers and new balcony class staterooms. She is now owned by Samos (Island) Maritime Co. Ltd, Piraeus, and has been operated since May 2010 by Voyages to Antiquity and registered at Malta.

The 4,200-GT *Caledonian Sky* was built in 1991 for Renaissance as *Renaissance VI* at Nuovi Cantieri Apuania shipyards in Carrara, Italy. After two years' service she was chartered out to various companies and thus had frequent changes of ownership and name, *Sun Viva 2*, *Megastar Capricorn*, *Hebridean Spirit* and *Sunrise* until Caledonian Sky Shipping Inc. took her over in 2012 and refitted her, with management by Salen Ship Management AB, and bestowed her current name. She is registered in the Bahamas. She cruises South America, Asia and the Pacific Rim.

The 4,077-GT *Corinthian II* was built in 1992 by Nuovi Cantieri at Apuania, Italy, for Renaissance as *Renaissance IV* and later chartered out as *Island Sun*. She was refurbished in 2004 at Drammen, Norway. Her current owner is Corinthian II Owner Ltd and she is operated by International Shipping Partners and registered in the Marshall Islands. She has a 116-passenger capacity, with a crew of 72. At the time of writing she is working for Polar Latitudes as the *Sea Explorer*.

Hanseatic (8,375 GT) was built in 1993 Rauma Repola Yards, Finland, for Society Cruises. She was to have been named *Society Adventurer* but the company went bankrupt before completion and she never used this name in service. Her design was tailored toward Arctic cruising and she is an Ice E4 listed vessel. The current registered owner in Bunnys Adventure and Cruise Shipping Co. Ltd and she is operated by the German Hapag-Lloyd, which is a TUI subsidiary. She recently underwent a comprehensive refit at the Blohm und Voss shipyard, Hamburg, emerging with a new colour scheme and renovated cabin decks plus a pool and sauna facility and a buffet restaurant. Passenger capacity is 184 with six passenger decks. She is registered in the Bahamas.

The 1,025-GT *Isabela II* is a luxury motor yacht built in 1979 at Pensacola, Florida, and she was totally refurbished at Panama in March 2000. She can carry forty passengers accommodated in nineteen outside air-conditioned cabins, each with their own private bathrooms, plus an owner's suite. She has a crew of twenty-four plus a resident physician and three naturalist guides. She carries eight two-person ocean kayaks, three Zodiacs and a glass-bottom boat as well as wetsuits. There are three passenger decks, Sun, Cabin and Main. There is a bar-salon, dining room and library, jacuzzi and solarium, gift shop and boutique. She also conducts tours in the Galápagos Islands with Ladatco Tours.

Another of the former Renaissance fleet, the 4,280-GT *Island Sky*, built in 1992, was originally the *Renaissance VIII* and was built to a very high standard in France. She was totally refitted in 2003 and can now accommodate 118 passengers in a total of 60 cabins, 13 of them with balconies and 47 with ocean views; with two singles. She has a crew of 72. Facilities aboard include a pool, a teak promenade deck, a spa, gym and dining room. There is a lounge with a stage and dance area, a club lounge and library. She carries Zodiacs and other water-sport equipment.

The truly luxurious 10,700-GT *Le Boreál* was built in 2009 by the Fincantieri shipyard in Italy for the Compagnie du Ponant and is owned by CMA CGM. She entered service in May 2010, immediately winning the European Cruiser Association (EUCRAS) 'Best Newcomer of the Year – GOLD' award. She can carry 264 passengers and has six passenger decks. In the French tradition of excellent food there are two restaurants, the Gastronomic Restaurant, which can seat 268, on Le Liberté deck with French and international menus and the Grill Restaurant for a choice of themed dining or a buffet. She has a theatre, beauty salon, games area, library, a Carita (TM) spa, games area, internet zone and excellent health and fitness facilities with a Kinesis Wall.

The 2118-GT *Ocean Nova* was built by Orskov Christensens, Denmark, as a Greenland ferry in 1992 and named *Sarpik Ittuk*, one of three identical ships built for Arctic Umiaq Line A/S, a subsidiary of Air Greenland, to ply the Uummannaq Fjord and Upernavik areas of the island. Following thirteen years of service, she was extensively refitted between 2002 and 2006 when she sold to US company Quark Expeditions, whose subsidiary Nova Cruising concluded the deal that November and registered her in the Bahamas. She can carry up to ninety-six passengers in forty-five ocean-view cabins and one single cabin, with thirty-four crew. She has a glass-enclosed forward observation lounge with bar, a fitness centre, library, lecture room, exercise room and a sauna. There are two main dining-rooms, which are non-smoking. There is a clinic with a licensed doctor in attendance. She carries Zodiacs for land exploration and two fully equipped life-boats. She had the misfortune to run aground in Marguerite Bay, west of Debenham Island, Antarctica, in February 2009 with sixty-four passengers embarked.

The *Quest*, also built in 1992 is the *Ocean Nova's* sister ship, formerly the *Saqqit Ittuk*. She was later converted into an expedition ship for the Norwegian Hurtigruten line and named *Disko II* and, in 2007, was in turn sold to the *Quest* owners. She was refitted in 2008 and given her present name; she is currently under long-term charter to Noble Caledonia for tours, which include Spitsbergen, Greenland, Norway and the Scottish Isles. She has the capacity for fifty guests on two decks, plus an owner's cabin. There is the panorama lounge on the top deck, where lectures are given and expeditions planned and she has a bar and a library.

Sea Bird (95 GT) was built in 1981 by Nichols Brothers Boat Builders, Freeland, Washington, especially for cruising the waters of Baja and the Sea of Cortez, which larger ships cannot penetrate. She is equipped with comprehensive exploration equipment for those waters, including Zodiacs and sea kayaks, splash-cam, underwater video cameras, video microscopes and hydrophone snorkelling gear. In 2009 she adopted the name *National Geographic Sea Bird*. She can carry sixty-two passengers in thirty-one outside cabins, six on the main deck between the dining room and the lounge/bar, seven on the bridge deck, with the captain's cabin between the bridge and sun deck and Lex Spa, and the rest on the upper deck, abaft the observation deck. She is based at Seattle and has three cruises scheduled for 2013 entitled 'Among the Great Whales'.

The company also chartered the *Sea Cloud*, *Sea Cloud II*, owned by Sea Cloud Cruises GmbH of Hamburg, whose histories are recorded elsewhere here.

The 2,632-GT *Serenissma* was originally built in1960 as the *Harald Jarl* by Mekkaniske Verkstedt at Trondheim for the Norwegian Hurtigruten company with whom she remained in service until 2002. She was given a £20 million refit in Sweden in 2003 and became the *Andrea*, owned by the US-based Elegant Cruises who chartered her out for cruises around the UK, Baltic, Mediterranean and Arctic until the financial meltdown of 2008 led to the closure of the company. After being interned at Spit, Croatia, from March 2009 a new owner was found on 21 February 2012 in Vladimir Esakov, owner of the Russian Volga Dram river cruiser company, who, after a major refit operated her as Premier Cruises working from Mariehamn, Finland, from the spring of 2013. She is registered in Liberia.

Variety Voyager is a mega yacht of 1,593-GT built in 2012 at the Psarros Shipyard in Athens for Touristiki Maritime of Pleasure Yachts. She is registered at Valletta, Malta, and is a 156-ton single hull vessel powered by two Caterpillar 1,800 bhp engines, which give her a speed of 14 knots. She can carry seventy-two passengers in thirty-six cabins, has a crew of twenty-eight and is based at Piraeus. Sumptuous interior decoration with wooden panelling, marble, and deep Axminster carpets make her a true luxury vessel. Her facilities include a seventy-five-guest lounge area on the main deck, a reception area and bar with audiovisual equipment, a library, internet corner, mini spa with massage room, sauna, hair and beauty salon; both indoor and outdoor dining areas and a sun deck.

In addition to these vessels there is a fleet of river cruising craft, which are: *Bengal Ganges, Charaidew, Douro Prince, Fidelio, Florentina, Grande Caribe, Grande Mariner, Johann Strauss, Johannes Brahms, Katha Pandaw, Litvinov, Michelangelo, Misr, Pandaw II, Rembrandt, River Cloud II, Royal Crown, Thurgau Exotic, Thurgau Exotic II, Victor Hugo* and *Volga Dream.*

The APT Group, a long-established (eight-five years) and third-generation family-run Australian travel agency based in Cheltenham, Melbourne, with a very similar policy and agenda, was first established by Bill McGeary in the 1920s. In June 2012 APT's owner, Geoffrey William McGeary, who became a Noble Director on 20 April 2012, decided to take a strategic interest in Noble Caledonia for an undisclosed sum, claiming the deal would mean 'business as usual' for Noble Caledonia. He claimed that the resulting partnership would bring two-way benefits by strengthening Noble Caledonia's Australian distribution and APT's UK distribution from Noble's strong customer base.

Oceania Cruises

This American company is a relative newcomer on the scene, but was established in 2002 by two very experienced men, Frank Del Rio of Renaissance Cruises and Joseph A. Watters, who has the impeccable Crystal, Royal Viking and Princess Cruise Lines on his impressive list of former companies. This pair soon recruited an equally capable team of top-level managers. The company has marketed itself as 'the world's only upper-premium cruise line' and outfitted ships accordingly. Oceania Cruises espouses fine cuisine and extra attention to passenger comfort in all its aspects.

The fleet was first established in October 2002 with the chartering from Cruisinvest LLC (a Jersey-based charitable company set up after the collapse of Renaissance after the 9/11 Islamic terrorist attacks to administer the forty-two ships of that fleet), of the 30,277-ton *R Two*, a former Renaissance ship built in the Aker Yards at St Nazaire in 1998. Renamed as *Insignia*, given a US$10 million refit, and marketed under the temporary name *Vaisseau Renaissance*, this ship was then sub-chartered to TRM (Tourism & Recreational Management) of France for a short period in 2003. On return this ship was given another new name, becoming the *Regatta*. A sister ship, the former Renaissance *R One*, was chartered and, confusingly, became another *Insignia*. She was finally purchased outright by the line in 2006. This pair operated for two years before being joined by the *R-Five*, of the same class built in 2000, also under charter from Cruisinvest, and she was given the new name *Nautica*. They are majestically decorated in the art deco styling of old ocean liners from the 'between-the-wars' era of the twentieth century, and have 323 cabins, a maximum passenger accommodation of 824 and a crew of 386. Del Rio's announcement of plans for a fourth ship, to be named *Marina*, proved premature and the fleet continued operating with this trio, known as the *Regatta* class, for a number of years. Oceania, true to its name, boasts a 300-destination spread over a worldwide canvas. All three have been refurbished between 2007 and 2009 to maintain the highest standards of comfort. This planned customer targeting would appear to have worked most successfully, with Oceania reporting record bookings.

In February 2007 Apollo Global Management in New York, a well-known Wall Street Private Equity Investment Partnership, who already owned Norwegian Cruise Line, assumed control of Oceania and Del Rio was appointment Chairman and CEO of Prestige Cruise Holdings set up to the parent company for both Oceania and Regent Seven Seas Cruises, itself well-established at the luxury end of cruise ship operations. PCH's first major development was to order two new 66,000-ton liners each with a top-end passenger capacity of 1,260 from Fincantieri's Sestri Ponente shipyard at Genoa, with the stated aim of increasing their 4,000 existing berths to 6,500 by 2011. Luxurious in their concept, 580 of the planned 626 cabins and suites, including the veranda staterooms and penthouse suites, have private balconies. The interior design was provided by the Norwegian Y&S Architecture and Interior Design Company. Catering standards are very high, with Master Chef Jacques Pèpin having his bistro aboard; the first-ever Culinary Studio at Sea, and with chefs provided by *Bon Appétit* magazine and Red Ginger Asian-fusion fare on offer. For the new ships *Marina and Riviera*, Oceania provided a total of six open-seating restaurants, named the Grand Dining Room with Continental cuisine, the Polo Grill Steak House, a gourmet Italian restaurant, Toscana, a French bistro, an Asian restaurant and the Terrace Café. Del Rio's intention remains to have 'the most beautiful ships to sail the seven seas'.

Currently Oceania, under control of Prestige Cruise Holdings, is the market leader in the upper premium and luxury portions of the industry, and continues to run both the *Regatta* and *Nautica*, under the tag line, 'Your World, Your Way', while the *Insignia* is chartered out to Hapag-Lloyd as *Columbus 2*. Oceania Cruise's tenth anniversary was marked on 7 January 2013, which triggered a series of special events, designated 'Anniversary Sailings' hosted by company executives and founders Frank Del Rio, Joe Watters, Bob Binder (Vice-Chairman of Prestige) and Kunal S. Kamlani, President of Oceania, to a series of special destinations with cocktail receptions, caviar brunches and gala dinners with complimentary private label Tenth Anniversary wines.

Oceanic Group (International Ltd/ Capital Dragon Global Holdings Ltd)

The Oceanic Group is a holding company, which from 2009 has focussed on the cruise and leisure industry, with emphasis on cruise ship management, sales and purchase, chartering and crewing. It has offices at the MG Tower, Kwun Tong, Kowloon, Hong Kong and at Maritime Square, Harbourfront Centre, Singapore as well as in China. The Managing Director is Daniel Chui, formerly with V-Ships Asia, and the Deputy Managing Director is Winni Ip, with Jessica Wong as Chief Financial Officer. Capital Dragon Holdings Ltd is based in the Bank of America Tower, Harcourt Road, Hong Kong, and owns the *Oriental Dragon*. Jenkin Luk is the CEO of Capital Dragon Global (HK) Limited and Aaron Wu is the Ship Manager.

The 18,455-GT *Ocean Dragon* is the former Royal Caribbean Cruise Line vessel, *Sun Viking*, built in 1972 by Oy Wärtsilä AB at Helsinki. She was especially constructed for the job and spent her early days in the Caribbean, but from the 1990s moved over to Los Angeles and cruised down to the Mexican Riviera. In January 1998 she was sold to Star Cruises who renamed her as *Superstar Sagittarius* and, after a refit, she operated in the Far East. In 2003 the Hyundai Merchant Marine Company acquired her and she was refitted once more and renamed as

Oriental Dragon suite room. (*Daniel Chui, Oceanic Group*)

Oriental Dragon 24-hour café. (*Daniel Chui, Oceanic Group*)

Hyundai Pongnae in February and then just as *Pongnae* owned by Kong Way from May before being transferred to Asia Cruises, owned by Real Win Ltd and managed by Sanyang Marine Pte Ltd, when she became the *Omar III*. In June 2007 she was again renamed, this time as *Long Jie*, serving thus until March 2011 when she was put up for sale once more.

She became the *Oriental Dragon* at a cost of $15 million and was dry-docked at Singapore before sailing to Guangzhou, China, for a complete refit during which a new reception area, restaurant karaoke room and more suites were added. Her maiden voyage was on 18 June 2011 from Shanghai International Cruise Terminal at Pier One and she was met at Geju's Port No. 7 by many dignitaries. Initially she operated for six months on twice-weekly voyages between Shanghai and Cheju and during the winter months she operated short cruises to Xiamen (Amoy), Fujian on the Taiwan Straits and to St Vincente from Hong Kong. However, by April 2012 she was acting as a Casino ship at Hong Kong.

As a cruise vessel the *Oriental Dragon* can accommodate 450–500 guests. She is registered in Panama City, Panama.

Oceanwide Expeditions

This organization runs three cruise vessels, the *Expedition, Ortelius* and *Plancius*, whose details are described elsewhere here and marketed in tours under the slogan 'A passion for Polar Regions!' The company had its origins in the Netherlands Plancius Foundation, founded in 1981, which two years later was the first cruise company to run annual expeditions in the Spitzbergen area with the *Plancius*. When the foundation was terminated in 1996 Oceanwide Expeditions took its place and has sailed the Arctic and Antarctic routes for over a quarter of a century ever since, combining cruising with dedicated shore explorations led by experienced guides and educational lectures to round off the full picture of both these regions and their unique wildlife. The destinations are varied and in the summer season they visit Greenland, Jan Mayen Island, the Lofoten Islands and Iceland, the Faroes and Britain's remote Hebrides, Orkney and Shetland Islands. In the winter months the focus is on the south with Ushuala being the starting point for such remote specks at Tristan da Cunha, St Helena, Ascension Island and Cape Verde islands and the Antarctica Peninsula and the South Atlantic with the Falkland Islands, South Georgia and South Orkney islands.

The Managing Director is Michel van Gessel with Rima Deeb-Granado as Director of Sales. There is a large specialist management team while the expedition team of guides and lecturers is equally impressive and led by Rinie van Meurs with an international group of experts who have wide experience of both the area visited and the needs and safety of their customers. The organization has won the World's Leading Polar Expedition four times up to 2011.

Oceanwide has four vessels, two sailing craft and two cruise ships.

The *Noorderlicht,* was a 300-tonne three-masted vessel built as the *Kalkgrund* at Flensburg, Germany, over a century ago as a Baltic Light Vessel. From 1910 she served on this duty, her name being changed to *Flensburg* in 1925. The middle mast was replaced by a deckhouse in 1940. She remained in service until June 1963 and was laid up at Kiel. She was acquired by the Möltener Segelkameradschaft Yacht Club in 1991 as a prospective club house but instead was sold to Ted van Broeckhuysen and Gert Ritzema. The Dutchmen renovated her as a two-masted schooner and gave her a strengthened bow. She sailed to Spitzbergen in the summer and the Canary Islands and Azores in the winter, working from Enkhuizen.

She has an auxiliary engine and carries twenty guests in twin cabins. They are cared for by a three-man crew, a cook and an expedition leader and the passengers often have to assist the crew so excellent health is vital. She carries Zodiacs but comfort is not her main attribute.

The *Rembrandt van Rijn* is not quite as old, being built in 1924 by Gebr Boot at Leiderdorp, Netherlands, and christened *Anna Marta*. She later became the *Minde* and then the *Klaus D*. She was rebuilt as a 451-tonne three-masted schooner in Holland in 1994 and ventured as far afield as Spitzbergen up to 1996 and the Galápagos between 1998 and 2001. She was then withdrawn and underwent a long refurbishment, which was completed in 2011 to bring her up to SOLAS standards. Now she carries thirty-four guests in seventeen twin cabins, a fifteen-man crew, a cook and two guides. She also has a reinforced bow, a bow thruster and carries Zodiacs. She has a restaurant for buffet meals and a separate bar. Again, passengers help the crew in certain conditions. She is registered in Panama City and works out of San Cristobal, Nicaragua.

One of the two larger ships is the *Ortelius* (*Ship of Fortune*), which was originally built at Gdynia, Poland, in 1989 as *Marina Svetaeva* for the Russian Academy of Science. She carries the highest Ice-class notation – UL1 (= 1A) – and can carry 106 guests, in one suite and thirty-nine cabins of various types, with a crew of thirty-four Russian seamen, an international catering staff of fifteen, an expedition leader and five guides and a doctor. She has two restaurants, a bar/lecture room and a sauna. There are eleven Yamaha-powered Zodiacs embarked, including two reserves. She is registered in Cyprus.

The other vessel is the *Plancius*, which was built in 1976 as a Dutch Navy hydrographic research ship and christened as *Hr. Ms. Tydeman*. She served in that capacity until June 2004 when she was retired from active duty. A total conversion and re-building followed and she emerged five years later as a fully-to-date polar expedition vessel for Polar Cruises of Bend, Oregon, and trading as *Polar Latitude*. She had the capacity for 112 guests housed in 53 cabins and has an international crew of thirty, including expedition leader and five guides and lecturers. She has a dining room, with buffet services, an observation lounge, with bar and library, and the Leica Akademie photo workshop courses on some cruises. The ship cruises the Arctic and Antarctic under a programme defined as 'exploratory educational travel'. Unfortunately, while operating for the Dutch Oceanwide Expeditions, she had the misfortune to become stranded in the South Atlantic on 9 April 2012 due to 'mechanical dysfunction of the main propulsion system' and eventually made Cumberland East Bay, South Georgia, with seventy-three passengers and forty-two crew aboard, all reportedly unharmed, and they had to be repatriated via Argentina.

Orient Queen Shipping

The Orient Queen Shipping Company Ltd is registered at Valletta, Malta, with offices at 18/2 South Street and has Russian input. The company acquired the *Vistamar*, which was operated by the German company Plantours, and which had been refitted in 2011, from Elle Via Shipping Srl, Milan, Italy, on 14 July 2012 and renamed her *Orient Queen II*. She is operated by Lebanon-based Abou Merhi Cruises, part of the Abou Merhi Lines (AML) Group. Founded in 1992 by Merhi Abou Merhi, this privately owned shipping and ferry company has its headquarters on Weygand Street, Port Beirut, Beirut, in the Atrium Building. Initially it had services to Africa and Europe from Beirut and extended these to Libya from 1998. From 2000 it moved into the transport of second-hand motor vehicles worldwide, currently carrying 120,000 cars per annum on seventeen specialist charter ships.

Abou Merhi Cruises was first established in 2001. It purchased the original *Orient Queen* in 2004 and took delivery of her in Gibraltar in November that year. She was originally built as the Pax/Ro-Ro *Starward* for Norwegian Caribbean Line, a subsidiary of Kloster, later to become

Orient Queen Mermaid restaurant. (*Lous Cruise Lines*)

Norwegian Cruise Line. She was converted to a passenger cruise ship in 1977 and based at Miami cruising to Caribbean destinations until sold to Festival Cruises in 1994, which renamed her *Bolero* and chartered out to First Choice Cruises. On the collapse of Festival Cruises she was bought by Cruises Elysia who sold her on to Abou Merhi Cruises and she subsequently sailed to Beirut as *Orient Queen* to be totally refitted the following year at a cost of $9.5 million. A helicopter pad was added and managed by Oesterreichischer Lloyd Ship Management (Cyprus) with a further docking at Piraeus and was Panama registered. She then operated from Beirut for six months with seven-day cruises to Cyprus, Egypt, Greece and Turkey, and from the Dubai Cruise Terminal for the other six in conjunction with Alpha Tours Dubai cruising the Arabian Gulf, but this was a failure and she returned to Beirut to cruise the Mediterranean. In August 2006, Louis Cruises of Cyprus entered a five-year deal, with the option to purchase, which they did in 2006 and operate her under their Teal Shipping S A brand.

On 14 July 2012, the Elle Via Shipping SRL again sold a cruise ship to Orient Queen Shipping at Valetta, the *Vistimar*, and she became the *Orient Queen II* to again be operated by Abou Merhi Cruises. She had been built in 1989 by Union Navale de Levante, Spain, and was operated by the German company Plantours. They had refitted her in 2007/2008 and again in 2011 when they chartered her out to the French company Plein Cap during 2011–2012 to replace their *Adriana* but, when the period was up, she was sold. She has the capacity to carry 330 guests in 152 cabins and is Panama registered. Currently the Abou Merhi Cruises Company Manager is Popescu Tania with Linda Zarif as Marketing Manager. The *Orient Queen II* conducts cruises in the Eastern Mediterranean and Black Sea during July to October under the slogan 'Own your own Dreams'.

P&O Cruises

This major cruise line, the principal one still catering for mainly British customers, was formed in 1977 from P&O Passenger Division, itself formed only five years previously, as part of the long-established legendary Peninsular & Orient Shipping Company, and thus this renowned company has a lineage second to none. One of the very first companies to adopt the cruise concept as a major part of its portfolio, as far back as 1840, the current fleet is modern and specializes in the two-week tour out of Southampton to Caribbean, South American and Mediterranean destinations, interspersed with longer duration holidays of 80–100 days, of which a few circumnavigate the globe as true world cruises. For many years the company adopted an 'adults-only' policy for some of its more famous vessels and over the last decade or so new and bigger ships have been added at regular intervals as the older, famous-named stalwarts, became obsolete.

In modern times the 69,153-ton *Oriana* first appeared in 1995 and she has been followed by the circa-70,000-tonners, *Aurora* and *Oceana*, in 2000 and 2002, the 86,799-ton *Arcadia* (original designed and laid down as a Cunard vessel to be named *Queen Victoria* but transferred while still on the stocks) and the more modest dimensioned 44,348-ton *Artemis*, the former *Royal Princess*. A more significant quantum leap has been the magnificent 113,000-ton *Ventura*, which arrived in 2008. A half-sister, the 116,000-ton *Azura*, entered service in 2010 and a new 144,000-GT ship is being built in Italy.

These splendid giants of the oceans are a far cry from the rather more humble origins to which they can claim to be chronologically descended from a century-and-a-half earlier, although all have carried the same famous diagonally-quartered house flag, which combines the colours of the Portuguese and Spanish royal families, an indication of the market it originally came to serve during those nations' respective Civil Wars in the early nineteenth century. However, the conveying of guns, supplies and volunteers from the British Legion and its ships acting as chartered makeshift warships helped to establish the young company earlier in its life, was not the prime motive behind its formation almost a decade earlier. In 1822 a London shipbroker, one Brodie McGhie Wilcox, went into business partnership with a former Royal Navy clerk named Arthur Anderson who hailed from Lerwick, Shetland Islands. They were originally concerned with sailing ships to convey diverse other cargoes to and from the Iberian Peninsula throughout the early 1830s. Even then Anderson was visionary enough to forecast that cruising for pleasure would one day become popular, putting an advertisement in his own local newspaper in 1835 for a Scottish island cruise.

The line flourished and, in 1835, the two London-based Scots joined forces with an Irish sea captain, one Richard Bourne, who had his own company based in Dublin, to initiate a regular and reliable mail service between the Empire capitals Portugal and Spain and further afield to the Eastern Mediterranean. The new company title reflected their growing horizons being named the Peninsular Steam Navigation Company. A regular contract was secured that gave the young company the right to convey mail and packages from London via the 'packet' port of Falmouth, Cornwall, to the southern equivalents at Vigo, Oporto, Lisbon, Cadiz and Gibraltar.

The title also announced that they intended to utilize the new-found potential of the steam-powered paddle steamer and the first such vessel to join the fleet was the 800-ton *Don Juan*, named after the claimant to the Spanish Crown. Her debut in September 1837 was not auspicious. She embarked passengers, including Anderson himself, and cargo and sailed from London and picked up her mail from Falmouth, duly taking them south, but was wrecked on the way back to England, fortunately without loss of life or, from the company's reputation viewpoint, any of the mail.

A merger with the Liverpool-based Transatlantic Steamship Company two years later gave P&O the necessary vessels to extend its activities throughout the Mediterranean, via Gibraltar to Malta, Greece, Turkey and Alexandria in Egypt from 1840 onward at monthly intervals. In order to raise the necessary £1 million to secure the wherewithal to finance the new expansion the company was re-launched under Royal Charter as a limited company named the Peninsular and Oriental Steam Navigation Company, soon to be known worldwide simply as P&O. Soon larger ships were demanded as the routes to India, Singapore, Hong Kong and Australia also opened up for mail, passengers and the import of high-quality products of the east. By the 1860s P&O was the imperial carrier, conveying the governmental administrators, diplomats, military officers, colonizers and the vital communications that connected the far-flung imperial dominions and colonies to the hub of the Empire in London.

P&O can claim to have initiated tourist cruising when, on 14 March 1843, it advertised in the prestigious London *Times* newspaper round-trip passenger 'excursions' on routes from Southampton to various Mediterranean destinations: Gibraltar, Malta, Athens, Syria, Smyrna, Mytilene and the Dardenelles. With the popular writer William Makepeace Thackeray among the first to avail themselves of it as the company's 'special guest' one of the first pieces of tour 'PR' occurred with the voyage duly celebrated in his subsequent book *From Cornhill to Cairo*. As yet only within the means of the wealthy, the precedent had been set. In 1904 the 5,500-ton *Vectis* (ex-*Rome*) cruised to the Norwegian fiords with accommodation for 150 upper class passengers only, and continued to do so for the next eight years. Explorations ashore at various ports of call were arranged by Thomas Cook, perhaps the first complete 'package deal'. Despite the losses suffered during the Great War the company continued to expand, absorbing its rivals as it went, including the British India Steam Navigation Company, the Orient Steam Navigation Company and the New Zealand Shipping Company among others. Despite the Great Depression of the 1930s and enormous losses during World War II, P&O emerged stronger than ever.

Immortalized in verse and legend, the reputation of P&O was an established institution of Britain's power and reach. This reputation only grew in the century that followed, and the fleet grew both in size and number. As just one small illustration of P&O's 'permanence' as part of the British way of life, during the bombardment of Genoa by the Royal Navy's famous Force 'H' in 1941, the British Admiral, James Somerville, signalled to the battleship *Malaya* as her 15-inch guns roared out salvo after salvo into Mussolini's 'secure' northern port, 'You look like an enraged P&O.' Everyone present got the joke for so famous was P&O as a shipping line, that all instantly knew what he mean. Today, of course, it must be explained to most that the *Malaya*, originally a gift from the people of the Malay States to the Mother Country, was traditionally flying the Malaysian flag at her jack, and, at a distance, the two ensigns in those days were similar.

The post-war period saw an expansion by the company into cargo carrying, with tankers and other specialized vessels largely replacing the conventional passenger liner, and the arrival of the container ship was also pioneered by P&O with the establishment of Overseas Containers Ltd, which completely revolutionized sea haulage. A lingering confidence in the continuation of the long-established passenger service was epitomized by the construction of the famous *Canberra* in the early 1960s, but the Empire had by then largely been demolished, air travel was burgeoning and the old ways were really on their last legs. By the 1970s many famous liners had gone to the breakers until only a few stalwarts remained. Facing these hard facts the company diversified into many other fields ashore but at sea the biggest re-organization was the re-branding of the company passenger division as P&O Cruises in 1977.

This quantum shift merely acknowledged the inevitable and the new way ahead. In 2000 came talk of further change with P&O Princess as the new independent line and the following year Carnival absorbed both companies, retaining their separate identities. P&O Cruises thus remains the largest British-customer based line, being Southampton-based and Bermuda-flagged. Oddly enough, P&O's most recent addition has been one of the oldest cruise ships, for she had started life as one of last of the R type vessels in the Renaissance Cruises fleet, being completed in 2001 only for the company itself to declare bankruptcy the same year and this brand-new ship was decommissioned at Marseille for two years seeking a new owner. The Swan Hellenic organization, a single-ship cruise company, took the ship onto their books and they gave her a new name, *Minerva II*, as she was to replace their previous cruise ship, *Minerva*. She served for over three years and was then transferred over to Princess Cruises in April 2007 by the parent company Carnival Corporation plc. However, in December 2008 after less than two years of services with Princess Cruises as the *Royal Princess*, a period which terminated in a serious engine room fire, Carnival again decided to transfer this vessel, this time to P&O after undergoing a renovation to repair the damage and bring her up to modern standards. This took place on 21 May 2011, the ship being renamed *Adonia* by singer Shirley Bassey in a new ceremony to mark the occasion. She is the smallest of the P&O fleet, with a total capacity of just 710 guests in 355 cabins and a crew of 373. She fills an important niche market in that she is an 'adults-only' vessel working out of Southampton to global destinations. No less than 75 per cent of her staterooms have balconies and her new interior is stunning and tasteful in the uniquely understated British style. Among her myriad facilities are a central atrium with its grand staircase, Curzon Lounge, a theatre, the Sorrento restaurant, Ocean Grill, Anderson's the Crow's Nest among eight bars, and the six-star Pacific Ocean dining room. There is a library, boutique shopping, the oasis spa and health club, two swimming pools and two whirlpools. She should have a good future in her new role.

Paul Gauguin Cruises

Since August 2009 this company is now owned by Beachcomber Croisieres Ltd, Bellevue, Washington, which specializes in luxury destination resorts in French Polynesia of the highest standards. Operating in the South Pacific for many decades as Pacific Beachcomber SC, the group has operated to the highest standards for more than a quarter of a century. PBSC was bought by Richard Bailey in 1998 and in 2001 the hotels were rebranded under the five-star InterContinental banner. The company now owns six high-standard hotels on Tahiti and is developing a luxury eco-resort of forty-seven deluxe bungalow villas named The Brando, built on Marlon Brando's own former private island, which is totally self-sustaining from renewable energy sources to LEED Platinum certification status. The resorts are Green Globe-EARTHCHECK certified. Paul Gauguin Cruises owns two small but luxurious cruise ships, the *Paul Gauguin* herself and the *Tere Moana*, which joined the company in December 2012.

The *Paul Gauguin* was specially built for the job she does, being launched by Chantiers de l'Atlantique in 1997 and operated by Radisson Seven Seas Cruises, later (Regent Seven Seas Cruise from 1998). She takes her name from the famous French artist who made his home and fame on Tahiti and she is the longest-serving cruise ship to serve these exotic destinations and unique ports-of-call. Since commencing service she has undertaken in excess of 570 such cruises and entertained over 155,000 guests, among them 14,000 honeymoon couples, and earned an enviable reputation for sheer luxury and elegance. In 2010–2011 the ship hosted Jean-Michel Cousteau, the renowned explorer and environmentalist on a sixteen-day cruise to Fiji, Tonga, the Cook and Society Islands and Tuamotus, during which he conducted a series of lectures, and this resulted in the Ambassadors of the Environment Youth Program. A series of renowned chefs, including Dean Max and Jean-Pierre Vigato, have also sailed with her demonstrating and giving classes to impart their skills, likewise equally famous photographers such as Roger Paperno and Jesse Kalisher have sailed on photography-themed voyages during the same period. New Zealand featured on her itinerary for the first time in 2012.

Among her facilities is a retractable water sports marina. Her voyages can also include a complimentary day on Motu Mahana, a private islet off Taha'a and use of a similar beach on Bora Bora. The *Paul Gauguin* underwent a multi-million dollar refit, which increased the number of staterooms to 166, and incorporated new interior décor. She now carries 332 guests with a crew of 215 and is registered in the Bahamas.

The *Tere Moana* is a smaller vessel, again designed for global operations and able to penetrate the smaller and less frequented islands and harbours of the Caribbean, Latin America and European destinations in the summer period. She was originally built in November 1998 for French company Compagnie des Iles du Ponant, Nantes, by Alsthom Leroux Navale at a cost of $36.5 million. She had an ice-strengthened hull and very shallow draught enabling her to penetrate close inshore and was also fitted with stabilizers. She had five decks and featured a ninety-five-seat panoramic restaurant, and a gastronomic restaurant, a library, two bars, a hairdressing salon, sauna, swimming pool and boutique. She worked from Martinique to Guyana, up the Amazon to Peru and in the Great Lakes and later worked the Dalmatian Coast and Eastern Mediterranean to the Black Sea. On being taken over by Paul Gauguin Cruises in 2012 she was given a massive multifaceted refurbishment and can now carry ninety guests accommodated in forty-five ocean-view staterooms, eight having balconies, with a crew of fifty-four. She has a water sports marina, Wi-Fi hotspots and a spa and has the L'Etoile restaurant. She sails to Caribbean, Latin American and European destinations.

Richard Bailey remains Chairman and Chief Executive Officer of the company, with Diane Moore, President, Florence Courbiere, Chief Operating Officer, Oscar Abello, Vice President, Product Planning and

Revenue Management, Sandy Stevens Vice President, Sales and Vanessa Bloy, Director of Public Relations for both Paul Gauguin Cruises and Pacific Beachcomber.

Peace Boat

Pīsu Bōto was a non-government and non-profit organization founded in 1983 by a Waseda, Japan, university student named Kiyomi Tsujimoto with input from fellow students around the world. It is now a recognized worldwide movement using a former cruise ship to visit sensitive destinations to spread and foster its ideals of universal peace, advancement of human rights, protection of the environment and eco-friendly development. Now headquartered at Shinjuku, Tokyo, the organization has made some twenty-five voyages with crews and teacher volunteers from around the planet with like-minded ideas. Lecturers are embarked for forums, courses and conferences are hosted and the dispensing of aid to victims of natural or other disasters is also part of the self-ordained remit as well as the P-MAC (Peace Boat Mine Abolition Campaign) to do away with land mines and provide support for victims of Agent Orange and atomic bombs. The United Nations has since granted Peace Boat 'Special Consultative Status' ensuring its findings, reports and recommendations get a worldwide hearing. Unfortunately, their noble ideals ('the ship as a neutral and mobile meeting space') proved no protection against Somali pirates who attacked their ship on two occasions in 2010 and they had to be rescued by NATO warships, which represented the real, rather the idealistic world.

A variety of chartered vessels was used by Peace Boat, including between 2002 and 2008 the *Topaz* (built as long ago as 1956 as the Canadian Pacific Railway's *Empress of Britain*). She had clearly had her day and a replacement was sought and found. The present Peace Boat is the *Ocean Dream* (named despite the fact that there is also a cruise ship sailing of the same name). She was built back in 1981 by Aalborg Vaerft, Denmark, for AVL Marine Inc. and christened *Tropicale*. She was operated on Caribbean cruises by Carnival Cruise Lines between 1982 and 2000 surviving an engine-room fire and a hurricane. The parent company refitted her and then transferred her to its Costa subsidiary in 2000. She became the *Costa Tropicale* and served for a further four years before once more being given a makeover and transferred over, this to the Australian P&O Cruises who renamed her as *Pacific Star* in December 2005. She mainly cruised the South Pacific, Australian littoral and New Zealand. She was retired in March 2008 and purchased by Pullmantur Cruises who gave her a major refit at Singapore and yet another new name. From April 2012 she has been chartered out to Pīsu Bōto.

The ship has been fitted out with lecture halls, classrooms, offices, workshop rooms and rehearsal areas. Students from the Global University, International Student and Global English and Espanol Training programs all make use of these facilities while the former ballroom and lounges now act as both lecture halls and stage spaces. The Peace Centre or 'P-Cen' is used by both staff and participants to coordinate on-board events, edit videos, produce posters, plan campaigns and publish the *Peace Boat* newssheet. Leisure facilities include a sports deck, gym, library, cinema, swimming pools, coffee shops, bars and a sun deck. The Director of Peace Boat is Yoshioka Tatsuya with an executive committee of 120 'Responsible Members', and the cruises are managed under an arrangement with the Japan Grace Company Ltd.

Pearl Seas Cruises

Pearl Seas Cruises (PSC) is a Limited Liability Company (LLC) established in Guildford, Connecticut, and registered in the Marshall

Islands. It was set up in 2006 by the team behind American Cruise Lines for the purpose of owning and operating a cruise ship to be built by Irving Shipbuilding Inc. (ISI) based at Halifax, Nova Scotia. The PSC President is Charles Robertson, with Vice-Presidents Timothy Beebe and Anthony Severn. In March 2006 PSC first contacted ISI to discuss building the vessel and following discussions signed a contract on 20 September that year valued at $43.5 million for delivery of the ship by 29 May 2008.

The vision of PSC is a grand one. Under the slogan 'The intimacy of a Yacht. The safety and comfort of a Ship' it promises future guests 'a new style of Luxury Adventure Small Ship Sailing' with a fleet of such vessels, equipped with the latest navigation, communication, stabilization. Certainly the *Pearl Mist*, as the the first ship of the proposed class of four, seemed to fulfil its promises. Of 4,985-GT, she was designed to accommodate 216 passengers in 108 double-occupancy staterooms with private balconies, with six passenger decks attended by sixty-five crew and be fully compliant with international safety standards. Each suite was equipped with a flat-screen satellite television, DVD player, individual climate control and internet access. Among the ship's facilities are a panoramic view dining salon, several lounges, a library, and three observation decks, a games room, fitness centre and gym and a wellness spa, a range of boutiques and a medical centre. She is also fully stabilized.

Work commenced on the ship in March 2007 but progress was marred by a series of disputes and arguments between the two companies, and by 2008 she was still not complete. Meanwhile ,the global financial picture had darkened with the sub-prime meltdown in the USA leading to worldwide recession. It was not until a year later, in April 2009, that the vessel was completed and undertook dock and sea trials and on 6 May she completed her trial run. However, three days later the ship was rejected by PSC who claimed some deficiencies had been found that would entail the cancellation of the planned inauguration. Therefore, on 25 June, Lloyd's Registered informed them that they were unable to issue certification for the ship due to incomplete inspections and trials. Moreover, the Marshall Islands said they could not register her under their flag because of material safety concerns and the US Coast Guard has expressed reservations about her compliance with SOLAS regulations. Since then the beautiful *Pearl Mist*, as she had been named, has lain idle at the Woodside Dock, Shelbourne shipyard, mired in legal challenge and counter-challenge, a terrible waste of a wonderful vessel. The legal complications are enormous; PSC sued Irving for $60 million, half for the return of its initial investment and half for damages resulting from loss of service, and that the contract be cancelled.

Despite this seeming impossible situation American Cruise Lines appeared confident that Pearl Seas Cruises would finally go ahead with the much-delayed launch. They advertised a full *Pearl Mist* sailing schedule for 2012 that included the Bahamas, Canada/New England and the Caribbean with the motto 'Cruising. It's all about you.' Future ships of the class are planned to be built by ACL's shipbuilding subsidiary, Chesapeake Shipbuilding, Maryland. However, at the time of writing that had not happened.

Peter Deilmann Reederei GmbH

This company is a German cruise firm that owns and operates touring services. The company is based at Neustadt, Holstein, and was first established in January 2010 following the insolvency of Peter Deilmann Reederei GmbH & Co. KF (which had run river tours since 1976 with day trips along the Baltic coast) the year before. This company had been badly affected by the crash of the Air France Concorde at Gonesse, France, in July 2000, with the loss of everyone aboard, which had been chartered by the company to fly passengers to New York City to board the *Deutschland*. That same October the new company was acquired by Industrial Holding Company Aurelius AG and now has a staff of 325. The Managing Director is Konstantin Bissias, and other executives include Andreas Demel, Marcus Mayr, Gisa Deilmann and Hedda Deilmann. The river cruise fleet inherited from its predecessor was disposed of due to adverse trading conditions.

The *Deutschland* herself was completed in 1998 for the company at Howaldtswerke-Deutsch Werft, Kiel shipyard, the first such vessel built there since 1987, after being built by 130 different sub-contractors in sections at four yards before being finally assembled and floated out. She made her delivery voyage on 11 May. She can carry 513 guests in high comfort. Her interior décor is based on the 1920s art deco style featuring brass, marble, teak and crystal chandeliers, Tiffany ceiling lights, roof paintings in the Kaiseraals, potted palms and original works of art to symbolize that grand era.

Accommodation on board is varied, there is a 382 sq ft owner's suite with private balcony, a 312 sq ft honeymoon suite, 309 sq ft grand suite, a 232 sq ft suite on deck 8 and luxury 195 sq ft double and single staterooms of various sizes. For on-board recreation there is one outdoor and one indoor swimming pool, a library, table tennis and skeet shooting; health is well catered for with a sauna, a wellness spa and fitness centre, steam room, massage parlour and sun lounges. There is also the Empress Ballroom with resident orchestra; while for sumptuous eating there is the choice of the Berlin Restaurant, the Four Seasons à la carte restaurant for dinners with candle-lit tables and the lido buffet.

She suffered an engine-room fire while docked at Eidfjord, Norway, in May 2010, fortunately with no loss of life. She was subsequently repaired at Blohm und Voss shipyard between June and July and re-entered service. In 2012 she was employed during the London Olympics as a hospitality ship by the German Olympic Committee. She also served as the backdrop for a German TV soap opera, *The Dream Ship (Das Traumschiff)* set aboard a mythical cruise ship. A rather misguided attempt to register her in Malta encountered fierce protests in Germany and the idea was hastily dropped and she retains the German flag.

Phoenix Reisen GmbH

Phoenix Reisen GmbH based in Bonn, is a well-established German travel agency that first entered the cruise market in 1988 and has since chartered a small number of select vessels. Its targeted audience is elderly Germans in the main and the occasional world cruise is supplemented by Baltic, Caribbean, Mediterranean and South American excursions. The company's first vessel was the *Sovcomflot* Black Sea Shipping Company's *Maxim Gorkiy*, a 25,000-GT ship built in 1969, which it leased under a twenty-year agreement. She was originally built as the Deutsche Atlantik Line *Hamburg*, and had been briefly named *Hanseatic* in 1973. She served their needs alone for over five years before being joined by a second, the Vlasov (V-ships) vessel *Albatros*, which was the former Cunarder *Sylvania*, which had been rebuilt as the *Fairwind* in 1968 and which had become the *Sitmar Fairwind* twenty years later and then Princess Cruise ship *Dawn Princess*. This new acquisition became the first Phoenix charter to be repainted in the new company colours and logo from the start. However, she eventually proved unreliable in service and after several breakdowns she was discarded in December 2003 and she went to the breakers yard at Alang, India, in 2004. Her replacement, in January 2004, was the 21,800-GT Actinol Shipping vessel *Crown*, which herself was promptly renamed *Albatros*. She had first seen life as the Royal Viking Line's *Royal Viking Sea*, before moving to Royal Cruise Line as the *Royal Odyssey* in 1990, back to NCL in 1996 as the *Norwegian Star* and, briefly the Spanish Cruise Line's *Crown Mare Nostrum*.

Several other ships were chartered briefly by Phoenix in the 1990s. The *Akdeniz* was a Turkish ferry/cruise ship built for Turkish Maritime Lines in 1955 in the German shipyard AG Weser. She was of 8,800-GT and could carry 1,056 passengers until refitted in 1980 and again in 1989, which reduced her capacity to 561 then 314. Air conditioning, a gym, disco and sauna were all installed and she was leased to Phoenix for several seasons before becoming the Istanbul Technical University accommodation and training unit in 1997.

The *Carina* was a similar vessel, a 7,662-GT vessel built as the *Ayvazovskiy* in 1977 by Chantiers Dubigeon Normandie at Nantes, St Nazaire, France. She was renamed *Karina* in 1996, then *Primexpress Island* in 2000 before becoming the Ukrainian *Carina* in November 2003 when Phoenix chartered her for a period.

The *Jason* belonged to Epirotiki Lines and was a 4,561-GT passenger ship built by Fincantieri Monfalcone in Monfalcone, Italy, in 1965. She became the *Ocean Odyssey* registered in Panama in November 2005. Finally the *Regina Maris* was a pretty little 5,933-GT vessel built for Sete Yacht Management, Athens, by Flender Werft at Lübeck, Germany, in 1966. She still survives as the *Alexander* hotel ship.

Another former V-ships cruise ship, the *Alexander von Humboldt* was chartered in 2005 but only remained for three years before being replaced by the Club Cruise vessel with the same name (serving briefly as *Alexander von Humboldt II* but soon reverting). She sailed with Phoenix until 2008 before becoming the Voyages of Discovery ship *Voyager*. The following year the *Amadea* joined the Phoenix fleet being originally built in Japan by Mitsubishi Heavy Industry as the *Asuka*. By 2008 the *Maxim Gorkiy* was discarded as uneconomical to run and was also scrapped in India the following year. She was replaced by Nina SpA's 1948-built

veteran, the 16,400-GT *Athena* under short term charter, before she joined Classic International Cruises the same year. Finally, in 2001 the P&O ship *Artemis* was taken into the company as the *Artania*. This ship had been built as the *Royal Princess* for Princess Cruises and transferred to P&O in 2005. At the time of writing the *Albatros*, *Amadea* and *Artania* are still serving.

Phoenix Reisen itself continues to prosper and is at the forefront of German cruising. In 2012 the company was awarded the Atlantic Alliance 'Triple A' award, which was received by Cruise Director Michael Schultze. In November the Enterprise Director, Johannes Zurnieden, signed the Private Sector Commitment to the Global Code of Ethics for Tourism on behalf of the company at Budva, Montenegro.

Plantours & Partners GmbH

This German company is based in Upper Road, Old Town, Bremen, and has been operating for twenty-two years. The company runs several river cruisers as well as having taken over the operation of the cruise ship *Hamburg*. The CEO is Oliver Steuber and the Managing Directors are Ilatio Di Vita and Riccardo Polito.

The river cruise fleet includes *Swiss Coral*, *Swiss Crystal Flusskreuzfahrten*, *Kreuzfahrten*, *Nicolay Bauman* and four others.

The *Hamburg* was built for Conti Reederei and chartered by Hapag-Lloyd's cruise arm MTW Schiffswerft GmbH, at Wismar since 2007 having been completed as the *C. Columbus* in June 1997. She was delivered to Plantours in April 2012. She can carry 423 guests accommodated in 205 cabins and has a crew of 170. *Hamburg* has an ice-hardened hull and folding bridge wings, which gives her access to narrow waterways as she was built with cruising the St Lawrence Seaway in mind. She is Bahamas registered.

She specializes in destinations away from the usual areas and her size makes this possible. Her itinerary includes the North Cape, the Baltic, the Black Sea, Antarctica, South America and the Caribbean. She hosted the Ocean Liner Society's 2013 Annual Cruise from Hamburg to Kiel in May.

Polaris Shipping/Club Harmony

Polaris Shipping is a South Korean company with head offices located at Daechang-dong Busan Busan (formerly known as Pusan) in the south-eastern province of Yeongnam and Hwang SeongHo is the main contact. They are investors into Korea Harmony Cruises having purchased the former *Costa Marina*, which was refitted as the *Harmony Princess*, in 2011 and then renamed her *Club Harmony*, re-launching the brand in the Far East as an operational concern by Harmony Cruise, South Korea. The vessel was original built as a container ship for the Swedish company Rederi AB Nordstjernan by Wärtsilä Turku Shipyard in Finland being launched in January 1969 as the *Axel Johnson*. She was purchased by Regency Cruises who planned to rebuild her as a cruise ship, which they were to name *Regent Sun*, but this did not happen. She was still out of service when re-sold and named *Italia* in 1987 and was not taken over by Costa Crociere until 1988. Finally the conversion was undertaken at Mariotti shipbuilders, Genoa, and she emerged in her new guise and re-styled in the Costa traditional Italian branding decor. From 1990 on she served in the Mediterranean and the Red Sea, and another refit took place in 2002, with the emerging German market in mind until 2011.

The vessel can now accommodate about 1,000 guests and has a crew of 356 and the official on-board language is English, although the crew are of thirteen different nationalities. The ship is registered in the Marshall Islands.

Club Harmony operates a range of three-day cruises, with four- tofive-day voyages to Fukuoka and Nagasaki, on Kyushu, Beppu, Kagoshima, and Osaka, Japan, at economical prices. Currently eight cruises a month is the schedule. Among the amenities on board are the Cristallo Restaurant, which features fusion-Korean dining, and there is also a buffet for all-Korean fare. The Marina Ballroom has a resident band, with a disco provided by the Laguna Club with Harry's Bar for late-night drinkers. There is the Elemis Spa with jacuzzi for health fanatics and the kids' club for junior guests.

Polar Latitudes

This company was founded by Shanchen Ting and has headquarters in America and offices on both east and west coasts as well as Canada and Austria. The President is John McKeon, who has many years' experience of polar travel. His management team includes Chris Dunham for Sales and Client Services, Ian Michael Shaw for Expedition Operations, John Svidro, Accounts, and Erich Graf in Austria overseeing the partnership Signum Hotels. Itineraries include Antarctica, Falklands, South Georgia, with departures via Buenos Aires and the Weddell Sea.

This company operates the *Sea Explorer*, formerly the *Corinthian II*, which is 4,077 GT, built in 1992 by Nuovi Cantieri at Apuania, Italy, for Renaissance as *Renaissance IV* and later chartered out as *Island Sun*. After a full refit in 2004/5 at Drammen, Norway, she was acquired by Corinthian II Owners Ltd and is operated by International Shipping Partners and registered in the Marshall Islands. She has a 114-passenger capacity, with a crew of 72. Her suites each feature ocean views, queen-sized beds, a sitting area, satellite TV/ DVD/CG players, telephones, mini-fridges, marble-appointed bathrooms, and the penthouse and veranda suites have private balconies and a butler service. The ship carries international chefs for the restaurant. Other amenities include

Sea Explorer jacuzzi. (*Polar Latitudes Official*)

Sea Explorer library. (*Polar Latitudes Official*)

Sea Explorer dining.

a library with internet access, a lounge with audiovisual capability, a wraparound sun deck with jacuzzi, an exercise room, eight Zodiacs and a Zodiac platform that can be used for swimming. She is registered in the Marshall Islands.

Poseidon Arctic Voyages Ltd

This group was founded in 1999 and has its head office located at Perseverance Works, on the Kingsland Road, Bethnal Green, London. The Sales and Marketing Director is Maxim Chernyshev.

The company markets a range of environmentally-sensitive tours to the polar regions with destinations including the North Pole, the Arctic, Antarctica, and the Russian Far East under the banner title 'The Snow Collection'. Tours include land exploration in Franz Joseph Land Archipelago and cruises along the Northeast Passage under the title 'Pearls of the Russian Arctic'. The natural wildlife of these areas can include polar bears, polar foxes, penguins, whales, walruses, seals, and huge numbers of sea birds which are enormous attractions.

Poseidon has down the years used an equally wide range of specialist ships ice-breaking vessels, starting in 1999 with the *Yamal*, under charter to carry their guests there and back safely. Their fleet has also included the giant Russian nuclear-powered ice-breaker *50 years of Victory*, and the following smaller ships.

The 1,385-GT *Sea Explorer* was built in 1976 as the *Marjata* by Mjellem & Karlsen Verft at Bergen, Norway, as a research and survey ship. She was lengthened in 1983 during a major refit and renamed *Marjata II* in 1994 before being sold to Gardline Geosurvay Ltd in July 1995. She is owned and managed by Gardline Marine Sciences, Great Yarmouth, Norfolk, and works out of Bergen, Norway, being currently chartered by Polar Cruises. She underwent a major refurbishment in 2004 and now has fifty-seven ocean-view suites, including the veranda and penthouse suites with a butler service. Her facilities include a lounge, The Club, a restaurant, an outdoor café and bar, a gym, beauty salon, and sun deck with jacuzzi. She carries a fleet of Zodiacs and is ice-strengthened. She has a crew of seventy and is registered in the Bahamas

The 4,077-GT *Corinthian* was originally built in 1990 as the *Renaissance IV* for Renaissance Cruises, a Florida-based firm that closed in 2001. She became the *Clelia II* and was then chartered to Travel Dynamics. She was involved in two incidents, the latter at Petermann Island, Penola Strait, in Antarctica on Boxing Day 2009 where she had to be towed to Ushuaia

by the *Corinthian II*. She was also chartered to Orion Expeditions as *Orion II* for a period. She was later declared to be unsatisfactory by the tour operator but was chartered by the Smithsonian Institute in February 2011 for an Antarctic voyage with no problems. Since November 2012 she has become the *Corinthian* and operated by Travel Dynamics International having undergone an extensive refit and redecoration in 2009. She carries one hundred guests in fifty ocean-view suites, each of which is lavishly equipped with a satellite TV, DVD/CD player, telephone, mini-refrigerator and marble bathroom. Her amenities include a large dining room, two lounges with audiovisual equipment, two sun decks, a library, a gym/spa, jacuzzi, swimming platform, a beauty salon, boutique, and hospital. She has a crew of sixty, carries Zodiacs for shore exploration, has an ice-strengthened hull and is fitted with stabilizers.

The *Expedition* is a 6,334-GT vessel, built in 1972 by Helsingor Skibsvaerft & Maskinbyggeri at Helsingor, Denmark, as the *Kattegat*. In 1978 she became the *N. F. Tiger* and in January 1985 was renamed as *Tiger*. Sold again in June 2008, she was renamed the *Alandsarian*. She is currently owned by Expedition Shipping of Bridgetown, Barbados, and managed by G Adventures, Toronto, becoming *Expedition* and works from heritage Expeditions New Zealand Ltd, based at Antarctic House, Christchurch, when touring Antarctica. She is registered in Monrovia, Liberia.

The 4,575-GT *Ortelius* was built for the Russian Academy of Science as a special purpose ship by Stocznia Gdynia, at Gdynia, Poland, in 1989 under the name *Marina Svetaeva*. She served until 2006 alternately as a supply ship, passenger vessel and oil-rig support ship in the northern Pacific area. In December 2007 she was taken under charter for cruising by the Australian-based Aurora Expeditions, Sydney, NSW. After four years she was sold to the Netherlands operator Oceanwide Expeditions, Vlissingen, and renamed *Ortelius*.

The details of *Plancius*, built in Holland, are covered elsewhere.

The *Professor Khromov* is of 1,759 GT and was one of a trio built with ice-strengthened hulls for polar and oceanographic research in Russia in 1983 by STX Finland Turku, at Turku shipyard for Far Eastern research at Vladivostok, Russia.

In 2004 she was given a large refit and renamed as *Spirit of Enderby* and operated cruises for Aurora Expeditions in 2012 working mainly with Aurora Expeditions and Heritage Expeditions, New Zealand, when in the Antarctic. She can accommodate fifty passengers in twenty-five ocean-view cabins and has a crew of twenty. She carries Zodiac craft for beach exploration. She has two main dining rooms and is non-smoking throughout. There is a library and a lounge used by the expedition team as a cinema and lecture hall.

Princess Cruises

This Anglo-American company has a long and successful history. A pioneer in the early days of cruise holidays and always an innovator, it is based at Town Center Drive, Santa Clarita, California, and is part of the Carnival Corporations extensive range of cruise brandings. The President and Chief Executive Officer is Andrew Buckelew.

There are many claimants to the title of pioneer of the modern cruise line industry, but few can have a better right to the title than Canadian-born Stanley B. McDonald, the founder of Princess Cruises. After wartime service with the US Navy McDonald established a material handling company, AirMac, and during the Century 21 Exposition (or World's Fair) held at the West Coast city of Seattle in 1962 this company landed the contract to supply the entire ground transportation for that event. As McDonald himself tells it, during the planning of the Fair it was found that there was insufficient hotel accommodation to house all those expected to attend and the decision was made to bring in floating hotels by chartering in passenger ships including the *Catala*, *Dnieper* and *Dominion Monarch*. McDonald recalled how:

We bought a ship and brought it out to the west coast from the Caribbean and it sailed from San Francisco to Victoria BC then down to the Seattle World Fair for a 10-day cruise. For four days of the cruise the ship was used as a hotel while our people onboard visited the fair. This was a howling success and it continued operations during the entire fair. From that we got the idea of a cruise ship. I saw people loved to cruise.

As a result of this experience, in 1965 a suitable vessel was found, the fourteen-year old, 6,062-ton Canadian Pacific Railway ferry *Princess Patricia*. She had accommodation for 318 passengers and she operated out of Seattle and Los Angeles down to Acapulco, which Princess first dubbed 'the Mexican Riviera' under charter during the off-season winter months for two years. Unfortunately, '*Princess Pat*', as she was affectionately known, had been designed for work in the northern climes of Vancouver and Alaska and was hardly the most suitable or comfortable vessel for the job. Nonetheless her name had a regal ring with pleasing connotations and McDonald got permission to adopt it as the name for his new company. It was soon obvious that a more suitable vessel was desirable and it was found in the ideal form of a new cruise ship built in Italy.

The lovely little *Italia* was a 12,219-ton motor vessel built to the latest designs by the Sunsarda SpA, a subsidiary of the Giacomelli Group at the Felszegi shipyard, Muggia (Trieste). She had been launched as *Italia* in April 1965 but lay unfinished as her owners went bankrupt, and was possessed by the creditors, the Banca Nazionale del Lavoro, who arranged to have her completed to the highest standards through an operating company, Crociere d'Oltremare, Cagliari, Sardinia.

With stylish raking flared lines and an interior designed by the very experienced team of Finali and Boico, *Italia* could accommodate 525 single-class passengers in some style, with 213 sumptuously-equipped cabins, serviced by a 252-strong crew. She made three voyages around various western Mediterranean ports in 1967 before Princess Cruises negotiated her sub-charter and she sailed from Trieste to Los Angeles in November of that year.

Marketed as '*Princess Italia*' by McDonald, the *Italia* actually retained her own name during the whole of the two-year charter period, carrying it on her hull for her entire lifetime, and initially she still sported the Crociere d'Oltremare yellow and red triangles on a white background on the shark-fin sweep of her funnel as well. She was initially employed on the Acapulco run but later made the company's first transatlantic crossing from Nassau, Bahamas, to Genoa, and subsequently moved her base up to San Francisco where she began one of the very first Alaskan cruise schedules in June 1969 and continued thus until 1973 when she was taken over by Costa Cruises.

A third ship taken under charter, strangely-enough *from* Costa, was the 20,460-ton *Carla C* (the formerly Compagnie Generale Transatlantique ship *Flandre*), which was once more styled '*Princess Carla*' without the trappings of an actual name-change. She was to prove a significant arrival in a most unexpected and oblique way, and was to achieve a publicity boost for the young company beyond any expectation. She and a sister, *Antilles*, had been constructed by Ateliers et Chantiers de France at Dunkirk originally for service in the French West Indies, although later adapted for the Le Havre-New York service, being completed in July 1952. A series of embarrassing engine and machinery failures blighted her first decade of service, which covered transatlantic, Caribbean and Canadian waters, and she was refitted and re-quipped several times before being taken over by Costa Crociere in 1968. She was refitted once

more by Officine Allestimento e Riparazione Navi at Genoa, this time a major re-construction and she was redesigned internally to the highest Italian standards at considerable cost. She re-emerged with enhanced single-class accommodation for 740 passengers and 370 crew. Despite this, on completion of this transformation in November 1968, the Naples-registered vessel was immediately leased out to Princess.

The service of *Costa C* with her new operators was immeasurably more successful than her previous career had been, and she served until August 1970 conducting voyages to the traditional Princess Mexican destinations and into the Caribbean via the Panama Canal. It was on one such cruise that Jeraldine Saunders, then a Princess cruise director, the first female to hold this position, conceived and wrote her book about the cruise industry from insider knowledge, *Love Boats*. This often funny and revealing book became a bestseller, and has been claimed to have increased American interest in cruising 'by 3,000%'. Whether this was the case, the book spawned an equally popular 20th Century Fox Television show, produced by Aaron Spelling, *The Love Boat*, which ran for three series between 1976 and 1998. Filming for some of these shows was actually conducted aboard later Princess ships, the *Island Princess* and *Pacific Princess*. McDonald himself, although delighted by the enormous publicity it generated, was not over-enamoured by having a television production team aboard his ships. He recalled:

Looking back it was a very difficult decision to make. Before The Love Boat *we had various movie companies using our ship from time to time. Remember* Colombo? *[This refers to the episode of that famous series entitled* Troubled Waters *filmed aboard* Sun Princess, *which had also been the venue for the movie* Herbie Goes Bananas.] *We had various ones like that. It was fine, but they took up passenger cabins, which was bad because we were sold out. It gave us exposure, but they were somewhat of a nuisance from the viewpoint of the passengers who could be irritated because they were out on the deck. It didn't turn out to be too big of a problem but it was costly.*

He recounted that, 'It was a big commitment for us, the small company that we were,' adding 'And the show made the cruise industry jump way ahead, years and years with that one program.'

Meanwhile, with the arrival of the *Costa C* and to reflect the wider horizons of the company in its third year of trading the corporate brand was modernized. Out went the old localized logo of a Mexican sombrero and it was replaced by a designer–created stylized 'Seawitch' with the head of princess with hair flowing in the wind, which has remained to this day. Princess was also one of the first cruise companies to develop its own ports-of-call, another move that has been copied by most other major organizations but which was then, unique. One such was Puerto Vallarta where the company helped by the local community built and then re-built the landing pier especially for their ships. All this pioneering was well done. In 1972 two former Flagship Cruise vessels, the 19,910-ton *Island Venture* and *Sea Venture*, joined the fleet, serving as *Island Princess* and *Pacific Princess* until 1999.

Initially, competition had been scarce, with only the US-flagged Matson Line running ships out to Hawaii and a few transitory cruise ships, but as Princess opened up the area to cruising, more serious contenders arrived on the scene, particularly Società Italiana Trasporti Marittimi's Sitmar Cruises with their 'Fair' series of ships. There was obviously a need for Princess to expand to meet both the growing market and the incursion of such rivals and McDonald sought a way to ensure not only that growth was sustained but the essential 'American' feel that Princess had cultivated, would be maintained. He found what he sought, bizarrely enough, in a traditional British shipping company.

In 1974 Princess was sold to the then Peninsular & Orient Steam Navigation Company, which at the time was one the largest fleets in the world with the assets and will to match. McDonald remained the Chairman and President of P&O North America until 1980. For Princess Cruises the first obvious benefit from P&O was the transference of its *Spirit of London* (formerly NCL's *Seaward*) which became *Sun Princess*. As in previous deals made by Princess, the new vessel was available as a result of financial difficulties, the privatization of Italian shipyard leading to a rise in construction cost, which meant that NCL withdrew from the contract with the ship incomplete. P&O had taken over, renamed her in 1972 and two years later Princess became the recipient of this 17,042-ton vessel, which had a crew of 300 and could carry 700 passengers. In 1979 Princess absorbed the Canadian travel company Johansen Royal Tours to consolidate its Alaskan market ashore as well as afloat and in a similar move developed Palm Island in the Grenadines as a new stopover, although this venue was later superseded by nearby Mayreau a few years later and in 1992 the Princess Cays in Eleuthera was added to the real estate portfolio. Another new Princess destination in 1985 was the Mediterranean and the same year *Pacific Princess* started operating out of San Diego, while *Sea Princess* inaugurated the 'Voyage of the Glaciers' tour from Vancouver to Whittier. In 1987 the itineraries included the first to the Baltic, Asian and Caribbean ports, while the next year Princess swallowed Sitmar and renamed its three ships *Fairwind*, *Fairsea* and *Fairsky* as *Dawn Princess*, *Fair Princess* and *Sky Princess*.

By the 1990s fleet expansion was unbridled with the first ships named *Crown Princess* and *Regal Princess* joining between 1990 and 1993, while two years later saw what was then the world's largest cruise ship, the 77,000-ton *Sun Princess* commissioned. *Dawn Princess* followed in 1996 and a new 'world's largest' appeared with the 109,000-ton *Grand Princes* in 1998 along with *Sea Princes*, a year which also witnessed Princess

Cruises undertake its first 64-day World Cruise. New additions continued apace, with *Ocean Princess* in 2000, *Golden Princess* in 2001, *Star Princess* in 2002 and the new *Pacific Princess* and 92,000-ton *Coral Princess* and *Island Princess* in 2003; as these new giants arrived on the scene many of the older, smaller ships were discarded and transferred out. The new ships also included the smaller 30,200-ton *Explorer* class *Pacific Princess*, *Royal Princess* and *Tahitian Princess*.

In 2000 P&O Princess had become 'demerged' from P&O and another innovation saw the transferring of the company registration to Bermuda and a cruise programme to that island initiated. Similar upheaval followed in 2002 as the corporate headquarters was shifted to Santa Clarita, California. Environmental concerns had seen the introduction of the 'Shore Power' programme at Juneau, Alaska, in 2001. The very first Princess cruise to Antarctica occurred two years later. On 17 April 2003 the giant Carnival Corporation fused with P&O Princess Cruises in a US$5.4 billion deal and the following year Cunard, the British North Atlantic carrier, was integrated into the Princess operation.

New ships continued to be built in numbers, the 116,000-ton *Diamond Princess*, first of the *Gem* class, the 113,000-ton *Grand* class *Caribbean Princess* and *Sapphire Princess* in 2004, *Crown Princess* in 2006, with *Emerald Princess* and *Royal Princess* in 2007 and *Ruby Princess* the following year. Currently two brand-new mega-liners, the 141,000-GT sisters *Royal Princess* and *Regal Princess* built at the Fincantieri shipyard are the pride of the Princess fleet.

However, although the current fleet mainly comprises super-large vessels, most of which were detailed in volume one of *Cruise Ships*, the company still retained two smaller vessels in its listings, the two sister ships *Ocean Princess* and *Pacific Princess*. However, *Pacific Princess* was finally sold for us$3.3 million to Izmir Ship Recycling Company in August 2012. They were the former Renaissance ships *R-4* and *R-3* respectively.

Of 30,277 GT, they were built by Chantiers de l'Atlantique in 1999 and served until Renaissance went under in 2002 when they were acquired by Princess and entered service in 2002/2003. The *R-4* was named as the *Tahitian Princess* from 2002 to December 2009 when she underwent a major refit at Singapore and emerged as the *Ocean Princess*. They had accommodation for 826 guests over nine passenger decks (3 to 11). Both had the following selections of accommodation – suites with balconies, mini suites, balcony staterooms, ocean-view double staterooms and interior double staterooms and ocean-view staterooms.

Their facilities were similar, with the cabaret lounge, club restaurant and bar, Lotus Spa, main pool, panorama buffet, Princess casino and bar, Sabatini's, Sterling Steakhouse, casino and bar and pool bar. The *Pacific Princess* also had the Pacific Lounge while the *Ocean Princess* had the Tahitian Lounge and bar featuring ultimate balcony dining.

Both ships were registered in Hamilton, Bermuda.

Profit Summit Deluxe Cruise/Shanghai Sail Shipment

This Chinese company was established in Shanghai and was granted an International Liner Shipping Qualification Registration Certificate by the People's Republic of China's Ministry of Communication. It was planned to fill the gap left by Star Cruises, which abandoned that market in 2002 and meet the demands of the new and rapidly-increasing affluent young Chinese. The company has offices at Chevalier House, Tsim Sha Tsui, Kowloon, Hong Kong. It operates in conjunction with the Thai-based Easttime Shipping Limited of Tugsukla, Sriracha, Chonburi, Thailand, as a joint venture to operate the *Ocean Dream*, which was rescued from the Indian ship-breakers blow-torches and refitted. Cruises are managed by Hanzhou Global Sailing Shipping Company Ltd, with an office at Mei Road, Shanghai, managed by Ms Karl Yang and Ms Hoya Ren.

The 17,042-GT *Ocean Dream* (IMO 7211517) was designed by Danish naval architect Knud E. Hansen, and built in 1972 at Cantieri Navali del Tirreno and Riuniti SpA, Italy, as the *Seaward*. She had been ordered for the Norwegian Caribbean Line by Kloster Rederi A/S. However, the Italian shipyard went into administration and the quasi-Government regeneration organization that took it over, Istituto per la Ricostruzione Industriale (IRI), refused to complete the vessel for fear of compounding existing losses and terminated the contract. The Norwegian Government stepped in and work proceeded slowly until she was completed sufficiently for the hull to be sold off. In that condition she was purchased by P&O in 1971 and work proceeded to completion in the autumn of the following year. Under a new name, *Spirit of London* she commenced operations in October 1972. She initially cruised to Alaska and Canada in the summer season and to Mexico in the winter season, and was also chartered out to West Line in 1974. When P&O took over Princess Cruises she was transferred to their fleet and renamed as *Sun Princess* and served thus for fourteen years. She 'starred' in an episode of the US Detective series *Colombo* in 1975 with Peter Falk and Robert Vaughn. She also featured in the TV series *The Love Boat* and in the movie *Herbie Goes Bananas* in 1980. During that long period her destinations included the Caribbean and Mexico and also Alaska. P&O then bought the Sitmar Group and consequently the *Sun Princess* became redundant.

In September 1988 she was sold to Premier Cruise Line's subsidiary Noel Shipping in the Bahamas for $6 million, and was renamed *Majestic*. She was refitted at the Lloyd Werft shipyard and again renamed, this time as *Starship Majestic* and began operating out of Port Canaveral, Florida and to the Bahamas. In July 1994 the CTC Cruises (formerly Charter Travel Club) and now Ukrainian-owned, agreed with Premier to charter her from 1995. She was accordingly refitted by Coast Line at Birkenhead, UK, and renamed by Gloria Hunniford at Tilbury as *Southern Cross* in March. From there she cruised to the Caribbean and then left for Australia and back. The CTC organization failed to maintain her very well and that same year went out of business with the fall of the Soviet Union. Premier Cruises then sold her to Bowyers Maritime Corporation in December 1996, who almost immediately sold her the following January 1997 to Greek-based Festival Cruises (the American First European Cruises) for $25 million. They named her *Flamenco*. She underwent a $9 million refit at Genoa from October 1997 and commenced operating from Savona to Santo Domingo. Subsequently she was under charter to Regent Holidays of Canada and then resumed working to the Mediterranean with Festival and, after operated out of Kiel to Baltic and Norwegian ports. Festival went bankrupt shortly afterwards and the ship was put up for sale at auction, being purchased by the Ravenscroft Shipmanagement subsidiaries Fulton Shipping Inc and Elysian Cruises, both based at Coral Gables, Miami, on 1 February 2004 for $12.25 million. She became a Cruise Elysia Line ship and was promptly dubbed *Elysian Flamenco*, changing that name just a month later to *New Flamenco*. She was placed under joint charter to the Spanish travel agency Travelplan and Globalia Cruises, both parts of the Grupo Globalia.

In November 2007 she was purchased for $28 million from Fulton Shipping by the Netherlands-based arm of Club Cruises of Rotterdam and, in June, 2008 they renamed her once more as *Flamenco 1*, operating her as a floating hotel at Nouméa, New Caledonia, for the rest of that year, before the company went bankrupt and the ship was seized at Singapore. In February 2009 she was put up for auction yet again and acquired by Singapore Star Shipping for $3.2 million, but remained laid up inactive until sold for scrapping in India. Saved at the last minute from the Alang breakers she was obtained by the Chinese company and moved to Port Clang (Port Swettenham) Pelabuhan Klang on Malaysia's west coast, but still not in use. Instead she was used as a Casino ship under Macau Casino regulators, off Pattaya, operating three- or four-night cruises in the Gulf of Thailand until abandoned by her owners. She was to have become a Run Feng Ocean Deluxe Cruises, Kowloon, Hong Kong, vessel managed by Sail Ship Management of Shanghai, but this did not occur. Run Feng was dissolved by de-registration in December 2011. The ownership changed to Profit Summit Deluxe Cruise, still at Shanghai, with management by Shanghai Sail Management. In August 2011 she commenced a full refit ready for service with a schedule to begin cruising in July 2012.

She has a variety of accommodation, VIP suites, ocean-view honeymoon, ocean-view executive, ocean-view business, family and standard. Facilities aboard include a choice of either international or Chinese/Thai restaurants, clubs, a swimming pool, a 'mini' casino, movie theatre, pub, discotheque, theatre, basketball courts, sport deck, shopping galleria and internet access.

She finally commenced operations, still as *Ocean Dream*, with twice-weekly, three or four-day cruises from the Laem Chabang Terminal at Pattaya, Thailand, to Koh Samui and Sihanouk, Cambodia, in a combination with Easttime Shipping and Profit Summit Deluxe Cruise's Hong Kong office. The *Ocean Dream* is registered in Freetown, Sierra Leone.

Quark Expeditions

Quark Expeditions, Norwalk, Connecticut, has its headquarters at Suite 1, Pilgrim Park, Waterbury, Vermont. The company was first established in 1991 by Lars Wikander and Mike McDowel after they had visited the North Pole for the first time. Their ethos was a specialist cruise line to explore the polar regions with specially equipped with outfitted ships

that were either icebreakers or ice strengthened. The current President and CEO is Hans Lagerweij with Andrew White as Vice-President, Sales, Bill Davis as Vice-President Expedition Operations, Eric Stangelany, Executive Vice-President, Operations, Petr Golikov as Vice-President, Logistics and Tim Post as Director Sales and Client Services. The first voyage from Murmansk, Russia, was the Transpolar Bridge cruise, which commenced in July 1991 aboard the icebreaker *Sovetskiy Soyuz* and a second followed a month later.

Among the groundbreaking feats achieved by Quark were being the first to carry guests via the North-East Passage; the first to carry visitors to the distant regions of Antarctica, and the first to have circumnavigated Antarctica. They also made the most southerly penetration of southern latitudes when they crossed the Bay of Whales in 2006 and in 2012 transited the North Pole in a hot air balloon. They have received National Geographic Traveller's Fifty Tours of a Lifetime award in both 2006 and 2007. Also since 2007 the company has been a subsidiary of the German TUI Travel.

The company has recently employed four vessels for their cruising to the polar regions, outlined below.

The 23,439-GT *50 Years of Victory* first entered service in 2007 as the Nuclear Ship (NS) *Ural* and was the world's most powerful icebreaker at that time. She was built by Baltiiskiy Zavod, St Petersburg, Russia, and is of the *Artika* class and is owned by the Rosatom State Nuclear Energy Group, Russia, and chartered by Quark Expeditions. Although initially laid down in 1989 the construction was complicated by lack of funding from the Government and much delayed and all work was totally stopped in 1994. Not until 2003 did things get underway once more and it took another four years to complete her.

With two nuclear reactors generating 74,000 hp she had the power to penetrate polar regions difficult or denied to most other vessels. She has a 5-m wide stainless-steel ice protective belt and can penetrate up to 3 m (10 ft) of ice. Thus she has the attraction of being able to transport tourists to the North Pole on occasion. She can accommodate 128 guests in a variety of suites, mini-suites and cabins of various types and sizes, all with ocean views. She has a helicopter embarked for aerial viewing; four fully enclosed lifeboats; a fleet of Zodiac inflatables for close-in exploration; there is a dining room, a saloon, a bar, an on-board gym, two saunas, a swimming pool and a library. She has a crew of 140.

She is registered at St Petersburg, Russia. *Ocean Diamond* is advertised as a 'super-yacht 'adapted for polar exploration. She was built by Kristiansandund N/V (KMV), Kristiansund, Norway, as the *Femhill in* 1974 as a container ship and was shortly after renamed as *Begonia*. In 1986 she was totally converted to a cruise ship at Lloyd Weft's German shipyard as the *Explorer Starship* and then from May 1997 as *Song of Flower* with Radisson Seven Seas. She was purchased by Ponant Cruises and in 1989 her name was to changed *Le Diamant* and she was again fully refurbished in 2004 in Norway to accommodate 226 guests in 113 cabins and with a crew of 120. On 22 November 2011 International Shipping Partners (ISP) became the administrative, commercial and technical manager of *Le Diamant*. Delivery took place in December 2011 and she was under charter to CMA CGM subsidiary Explorer Partners Ltd of Miami and registered in the Bahamas for a season. She resumed service with Compagnie du Ponant in the summer of 2012 and has been chartered out for repeat winter season cruising with Quark Expeditions as the *Ocean Diamond*, with the summer season of 2013 spent under charter. *Le Diamant* has been chartered for multiple winter seasons to Quark Expeditions as the *Ocean Diamond*. The vessel is available for charter for the summer season from 2013.

Her registered owner is listed in Bureau Veritas as Explorer Partner Ltd, Port Everglades Center, Miami. She carries just 114 guests and

apart from this exclusivity, her attributes include contribution to and enrolment into the Scott Polar Research Institute, Cambridge. Also Quark offsets emissions of the ship thus claiming to provide the first 'carbon-neutral' voyaging in polar history. Her facilities and amenities include massage and wellness rooms, a photography program, optional camping, kayaking, snowshoeing, skiing and mountaineering, a polar Library and resident experts on board.

She is registered at Nassau, Bahamas

The *Sea Spirit* (4,200 GT) was built as the *Hanseatic Renaissance* and served as such until June 1992. She was one of the famous Renaissance class vessels modelled on the Sea Goddess vessels and was built for Renaissance Cruises (Antigua) Ltd, but based at Fort Lauderdale, Florida, and Liberia-registered. In 1991 she was chartered to Hanseatic Kreuzfahrten, Hamburg, Germany. She then was renamed as *Renaissance V in* 1992 and served as such up to November 1997. In 1997 she was sold to Metro Holdings, Singapore, who renamed her as *Sun Viva* from then until March 2000. She was sold again, this time to Star Cruises, Hong Kong, and became the *Megastar Sagittarius* but in April 2001 Cruise West, Seattle, Washington, purchased her and she was renamed as *Spirit of Oceanus*. In September 2010, following the collapse of Cruise West, she was sold for $10 million yet again, to ISP, and renamed, this time becoming the *Sea Spirit*. A contract was signed with Quark Expeditions, Toronto, and in June 2012 she was chartered out to Oceanwide Expeditions, the Netherlands, for a summer cruising season to Greenland, Iceland and Spitsbergen. In November 2010 she was dry-docked at Grand Bahama Shipyard, Freeport, Bahamas, and upgraded and strengthened for ice certification. The contract for Quark Expeditions to operate her now extends to 2014. She is registered to TN Cruises Kommanditsekab (K/S), Clipper House, Sundkrogsgade, Copenhagen, Denmark, and operated by US-based International Shipping Partners.

She is registered at Nassau, Bahamas.

The 4,376-GT *Sea Adventurer* was built as a coastal ferry of the *Mariya* class at the Titopvo Brod shipyard at Kraljevica, Croatia, in 1974. Originally named *AllaTarasova* she was fully stabilized and was one of a class of such ferries built for the Soviet Union. She was operated by the Murmansk Shipping Company and she was based at Murmansk where she was registered between completion in 1975 and June 1997. On 28 June 1996 she suffered an engine breakdown and electrical failure, taking water into her engine room. Engineers and pumps were transferred to the ship and water pumped out and she had to be assisted into Peterhead before sailing to Reykjavik on 6 July.

In June 1997 she was acquired by Clipper Cruise Line, St Louis, Missouri, and became their *Clipper Adventurer*. In 1998 she underwent a $13 million refit. The ship has been involved in a number of mishaps down the years. On 26 March 2012 she was stranded on a sandbank in the Essequibo River and refloated with assistance of a tug. She grounded again on 24 November, this time near Deception Island, Antarctica. On 11 August 2005 she hit ice south-east of Greenland and damaged a propeller. She had to be dry-docked at Belfast. Finally, on 27 August 2010 she struck a rock in Coronation Gulf, east of Kugluktuk, and took water in. She transferred 110 guests to the icebreaker *Amundsen* and needed four tugs from the Resolve Marine Group to get her into Port Epworth; she was later repaired at Gdansk.

In October 2012 she was renamed as *Sea Adventurer*.

Her facilities and amenities are modest due to her size but she operates as an all-suite ship including a 550 sq ft owner's suite, deluxe and premium suites, all of which have flat screen TVs and DVD players and exterior views, and fifteen of which have balconies. There is a dining room with unreserved seating, multi-purpose lounge and presentation room, club room, observation deck, a library, hair salon, hot tubs, open bar, gift, shop, infirmary, laundry, workout room and e-mail access. She also carries four partially-enclosed lifeboats and a flotilla of Zodiac inflatables for close-in expeditions as well as kayaks. Her cruise itinerary includes Antarctica, Artic, the Falklands and South Georgia. She is registered at Nassau, Bahamas.

Regent Seven Seas Cruises

Regent Seven Seas Cruises was founded in 1990 and since February 2008 is a subsidiary of the global Apollo Management L P Investment Group. The company is based at Suite 100, 334rd Street, Miami, Florida. It was original titled Radisson Seven Seas Cruises, which had come about when Radisson Diamond Cruises and Seven Seas Cruise Line merged in 1994. On rebranding in 2006 the company became part of Prestige Cruise Holdings, Doral, Florida. Apollo purchased Regent Seven Seas Cruises from the British Carlson Group (which owned luxury Radisson Hotel chain), at a price of $1 billion and they also own Oceania Cruises plus 50 per cent of Norwegian Cruise Line (NCL). The registered owner is Celtic Pacific II, part of Celtic Pacific (UK) Ltd, sharing an address at Beresford House, Town Quay, Southampton, with Regent Seven Sea Cruises UK base.

The company positions itself at the top end of the luxury cruise market with the added kudos of its 'all-inclusive' policy whereby alcohol, shore excursions, air fare to and from ports and gratuities are mostly included in the guests holiday price to give what is claimed as an upper premium or six-star service.

The Regent Seven Seas Cruises executive leadership team comprises – Frank Del Rio, Chairman & Chief Executive Officer, Prestige Cruise Holdings; Kunal S. Kamlani, President and Chief Operating Officer, Prestige Cruise Holdings; Mark S. Conroy, Executive Advisor, Prestige Cruise Holdings; Robin Lindsay, Executive Vice President, Vessel

Operations; Jason Montague, Executive Vice President and Chief Financial Officer; Randall Soy, Executive Vice President, Sales and Marketing and Franco Semeraro, Senior Vice President, Hotel Operations.

Between 1990 and 2003 the company utilized the former Seven Seas ship *Song of Flower*, which it was later to sell to Cie des Iles du Ponant. Between 1992 and 2005 the company utilized the Diamond Cruises ship Radisson *Diamond* which has since become the Casino Cruise Ship *Asia Star*. Other vessels that served in the Regent fleet included two which are also still cruising to this day, and which are described in detail elsewhere in this section, the *Paul Gauguin* and *Minerva*.

Currently Regent Seven Seas cruises has three operational ships, the large *Seven Seas Mariner* and *Seven Seas Voyager* (both of which featured in volume one), and the smaller, but equally sumptuous *Seven Seas Navigator*.

The 28,550-GT *Seven Seas Navigator* had a complex birth. She was laid down in 1991 as the ice-strengthened *Akademik Nikolay Pilyugin* in the Sudostroitelnyy Zavod, Rybinsk (Admiralty Wharves) shipyard at Leningrad (now St Petersburg) shipyard as a 'research vessel', which was Soviet-speak for a communications spy ship. With a change of policy at the Kremlin the concept was abandoned as post-Cold War redundancy in 1993 and the almost complete hull lay on the slipway with work at a standstill through lack of funding. In 1996 this hull was purchased by V-Ships of Monaco / Carlson Company on an equal basis and was towed away to be completed to a different scenario at the Italian shipyard of T Mariotti in Genoa with the assigned, but never conferred, names of *Blue Nun* and later *Blue Sea*. Using the luxury hotel concept only applying it afloat resulted in the emergence of a top-class and stylish cruise vessel. She was renamed in August 1999 as the *Seven Seas Navigator* and was registered in Panama on entering service. From February 2005 she was chartered out as a floating hotel or accommodation ship at Jacksonville,

Florida, for the Super Bowl final. She retained her existing name when Radisson became Regent and was refurbished in December 2009 when the ship's stern was radically altered adding much-need stability to reduced her notorious vibration problems, along with the fitting of new propellers and rudders. Considerable internal modifications were also carried out at this time.

Her facilities across decks 5 to12 include many dining outlets – Prime 7 Steakhouse, the Signatures, Terrace, Compass Rose Restaurants, Pool Grill, La Veranda, Galileo's. There is a Casino, the Horizon, Stars, Seven Seas and Navigator Lounges, the Connoisseur Club, card room, library, two boutiques, beauty salon and Wi-Fi access. For fitness there is the gym, aerobics hall, swimming pool, jacuzzis and a relaxation room. Most cruises include guest speakers such as a range of historians, anthropologists, historians and naturalists.

She is registered at Hamilton, Bermuda.

A new Regent cruise ship is planned, similar in style to the larger *Mariner* and *Voyager*.

Saga Cruises

Saga Cruises, aka Saga Holidays, is a British Cruise Line and a division of the Saga Group. Saga Holidays is a trading name of Acromas Holidays Ltd and Saga Shipping is a trading name of Acromas Shipping Ltd. Both companies are subsidiaries of Acromas Travel Ltd. All three companies are registered in the UK and their offices are at Enbrook Park, Sandgate, Folkestone, Kent. The CEO of Saga Cruises is Robin Shaw and his team includes Cruise Directors Jo Boase, Tanya Whitehurst and Jonathan Neal. The make-up of Saga means that there is a minimum age of fifty for passengers; the company also recognized the demand from younger passengers and, in 2005, introduced a subsidiary company, Spirit of Adventure Cruises, to cater for these guests aged over 21.

The first cruise ship operated by Saga Cruise in 1996 was the 24,474-GT *Saga Rose*, built in 1965, which was acquired from Norwegian American Line. She was the former *Orange Melody*. She served until 2010 then was laid up at Gibraltar for a period and finally scrapped in China. In 2003 she was joined for a short summer season by a chartered vessel, the 12,500-GT *Saga Pearl*, built in 1989. The *Spirit of Adventure* was the former Deilman Cruises, Neustadt/Holstein, consortium's ship *Berlin*, ordered by Peter Deilman and partners. She was chartered out between October 1982 and January 1985 to Blue Funnel Line Cruises Singapore and then laid up in 2004. Again chartered out, this time to the Russian Metropolis company as *Orange Melody*, she was later sold to Saga and was to have become the *Saga Opal*, but instead became the *Spirit of Adventure*, serving from 2006 to 2012 before becoming the *FTI Berlin*. Between 2010 and 2012 a former Transocean Tours vessel, the 18,591-GT *Astoria*, built in 1981, served as the *Saga Pearl II*. In 2013 she became the new *Spirit of Adventure*. The 24,292-GT *Saga Ruby* was the former Cunard ship *Caronia* and later the Norwegian American *Vistafjord*. She was built in 1973 and is due to be retired in 2014. The 37,301-GT *Saga Sapphire* was the former CDF Crosières de France vessel *Bleu de France* built originally in1981 and acquired by Saga in 2012. Finally, the 18,591-GT *Quest for Adventure* was a second ship for the over 21s and was original built in 1981. She is the former Transocean Tours ship *Astoria*; she operated originally as *Saga Pearl II* as noted above, and it is planned she will resume this name with Saga once more in 2014.

The *Saga Ruby* started life as the *Vistafjord* built by Swan Hunters shipyard, Tyne and Wear, in 1973 built for the Norwegian American Line (NAL). She alternately acted as a transatlantic liner with 830 passengers or as a cruise ship embarking just 550. In 1990 she was transferred to Norwegian American Cruises (NAC), a subsidiary of NAL, and acted solely as a cruise vessel. Trafalgar House, parent company of Cunard at that time, acquired NAC but she kept her existing name until December 1999 when she was renamed as *Caronia* in the Cunard fleet and had additional cabins added to accommodate a total of 736 guests. She was sold to Saga and in November 2004 she became the *Saga Ruby*. She underwent a major refit at Malta Drydock in 2005 and it is expected she will soldier on until 2014.

The *Saga Ruby*'s amenities and facilities include: on the veranda deck – Britannia Lounge, South Cape bar, library, card room, veranda shop, ballroom, lido, outside pool and photo gallery. On the panorama deck is the view bar. On the sun deck is the View Restaurant. On the bridge deck is to be found the Concerto Suite and the Symphony Suite. The upper deck contains the dining room while the main deck houses the computer centre, the board room and the launderette. Finally on C deck is the Aquarius spa, with plunge pool, treatment room and sauna and the hair salon.

She is registered at Valletta, Malta.

The *Saga Sapphire* was built for Hapag-Lloyd as *Europa* at Bremen Vulkan shipyard, Bremen, Germany, and entered service in 1981. She became Star Cruises' vessel *SuperStar Europe* and subsequently the *SuperStar Aries*. She was acquired by Pullmantur in 2004 and renamed as *Holiday Dream*. She was refitted in 2004 and again in 2008 when she was leased to Croisières de France (Royal Caribbean Cruises) as the *Bleu De France*. She was sold to Saga Cruises in November 2010 and owned by Acromas Shipping Limited. She was refitted again at the Palermo shipyard of Fincantieri from November 2011 to March 2012; full refurbishment took place from November 2011 with a design by RPW Design described as 'contemporary and eclectic, with a British twist'. A new balcony deck was added and all public spaces were re-designed to give a 'British seaside' feel with fish and chips and an ice cream parlour at the Pier and Cooper's Bar, a tribute to endearing comedian the late

Tommy Cooper. Other dining areas included Pole to Pole and The Grill. Venues included The Clubhouse, and Britannia Show Lounge. An open-air cinema and hot tubs were added along with iPads and Wi-Fi. Modifications included fitting six Juliet balconies, and nineteen new suites with balconies; all cabins were also refurbished and most internal public spaces renewed. The observation lounge became the drawing room; an Asian fusion Restaurant (East to West Restaurant) was added as well as a cinema. Thus embellished she commenced operations for Saga in April 2012.

She is registered at Valletta, Malta.

Quest for Adventure (Saga Pearl II again from 2014). The ship was originally built in 1981 at the German shipyard Howaldtwerke-Deutsche Werft AG, Werk Ross, Hamburg, as the *Astor* for Hadag Cruise Line. In 1985 she was transferred to the South African company Safmarine working from Cape Town. She then became the *Arkona f*or Deutsche Seereederei. She served thus until 2002 when Transocean Tours acquired her as their *Astoria*. She started a refit in Barcelona in 2008 and then was towed to Gibraltar and auctioned off when Transocean went bankrupt. She was sold by auction and she joined Saga in August 2009 as the *Saga Pearl II,* being refitted at a cost of £20 million in Swansea Drydocks and emerging in March 2010. Then, in May 2012, she became their Spirit of Adventure Holiday ship *Quest for Adventure* and is due to return to Saga as *Saga Pearl II* once more in 2014.

The *Quest for Adventure* has seven passenger decks, Sun, Bridge, Boat, Promenade, A, B and C. She accommodates her guests in a variety of accommodation, owner's suites with terrace, suites with balconies, deluxe, superior and standard; double/single, outside/inside cabins. The *Quest's* amenities and facilities include: sports deck with a short tennis court; sun deck and BBQ; The Sundowner Bar; the veranda; swimming pool; the Discovery Lounge; briefing room; shop;

Shackleton's; chart room; ward room; library; card room; dining room; hair/beauty salon; cinema; treatment rooms and pool, gym, sauna and medical centre.

She is registered in Nassau, Bahamas.

Saimaan Matkaverkko Oy

Saimaan Matkaverkoo Oy is a Finnish travel company that was established in 1996 by Kirsti Laine. The company now specializes in Russian and Baltic travel. It is based at Valtakatu 49 FI-53100 Lappeenranta, Finland. The company has a cruise ship line with Jussi Laine as Manager and Hulkkonen Lauri as Technical Security Manager and runs two small cruise ships, the *Brahe* and the *Carelia*.

The *Brahe* has the capacity for two guests in forty-five well-appointed cabins of five different classes. She has five passenger decks and her staff is principally Finnish. She was constructed by the Pullman Standard Car Company of Chicago, Illinois, during World War II as the US Navy hospital ship *Solace* (PCE 830) but under the Lend-Lease scheme later served as the Royal Navy vessel HMS *Kilchernan* (Z 04). She was based at Gibraltar as a convoy rescue ship and escorted convoys from there down the West African coast. Post-war she was returned to the US Navy and decommissioned in 1947. As war surplus in 1948 she was sold out of service. She was purchased by a Norwegian company who utilized her as a mail steamer for their Kotka Line between Bergen and Stavanger and renamed her *Sunnhordland* until 1973. She was purchased by the Partanen family for their Kotica-based Kristina Cruises, Finland, who converted her to a cruise ship and renamed her as *Kristina Brahe*. She was then based at the port of Ristiina in eastern Finland, cruising to Lake Saimaa, along the Saimaa Canal to Tallinn, Estonia and to St Petersburg. In 2010 she was purchased by Saimann Matkaverkko Oy. Her newly renovated cabins are of five classes, Kristina, Brahe, Saint Petersburg, Lake Saimaa and Seal. She has four passenger decks, a fully licensed restaurant, a dance lounge and a sun deck. Her itinerary in the summer months are from Helsinki and Hamina to Lake Saimaa and onward. She also operates specialist themed cruises, birdwatching to the Gulf of Finland, and war history to the Gulf of Finland, both in May.

The 393-GT *Carelia* was the former German passenger ship *Ostee*, built at Husum, Schleswig-Holstein in 1969. In 1985 she was acquired by Lappeenranta Ships Ltd and in 1986 she was given a full refit and renamed after which she was chartered to Saimaan Matkaverkko Oy for cruising along the Vyborg Saimaa Canal and Lake Saimaa between May and September; guests can then disembark and continue to St Petersburg by coach. She is also chartered out to various companies as listed elsewhere. She underwent another renovation in 2004 and a third in 2011.

She now has capacity for two hundred guests, and has three passenger decks, with two restaurants – the Môn Repos Music restaurant and the Knut Posse, plus a sun deck and a duty-free shop for perfume, cosmetics and souvenirs. Her staff is mainly English.

Salamis Cruises

Salamis Cruises Lines is part of the Salamis Organization, whose President is Vassos G. Hadjitheodosiou, with Dimitris P. Ioannou, Antonis S. Loupis, Elena V. Hadjitheodosiu and Secretary Voastas Tserides. Salamis Cruise Lines is the manager of the *Salamis Filoxenia* and the registered owner is Messaoria Shipping Company Limited with Mana Shipping Company Ltd, Cyprus. The Salamis Group offices are at Salamis House, Georgiu Katsounotou Street, Limassol, Cyprus, and there is an office at Commercial Bank Building, Bayuquan Quarter, Yinkou, Liaoning, China.

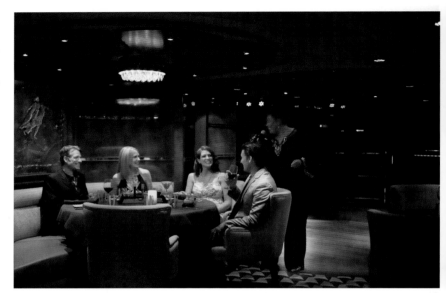

The Stars supper club at Silverseas. (*Silverseas Cruises*)

The 10,392-GT *Salamis Glory* was the first ship operated by the company and she cruised for them for thirteen years. She was built by Brodogradiliste Uljanik, Yugoslavia, in 1962 for the Brazilian Companhia de Navegacao Coseiraas the *Anna Nery*. She was delivered to Santos in October 1962 but was damaged by a boiler explosion. The following year she collided off Haifa, Israel, with a Brazilian tanker, *Presidente Deodoro*, and was badly damaged. Repaired, she sailed between Rio de Janeiro and Santos for three years. In 1968 she conducted transatlantic crossings interspersed with coastal cruises. In 1978 she was decommissioned until she was sold to Greek

Floor show aboard *Salamis Filoxenia*. (*Salamis Cruises*)

The casino aboard *Salamis Filoxenia*. (*Salamis Cruises*)

Hellenic Cruises in 1978 when she was renamed *Danaos*. After another idle period she underwent a refit in 1982 and sailed for the Greek subsidiary of the Japanese Kawasaki Kisen Kaisha Ltd (K-Line) for five years, becoming the *Constellation*. When her owners were made bankrupt she was again paid off until 1992, when Antonios Lelakis purchased her, refitted her and renamed her *Morning Star* for Pacific voyaging. She was acquired by the New York-based Lelakis Group's Regency Cruises who gave her another makeover, changing her name yet again, to *Regent Spirit*, and she sailed for them in the Mediterranean in the summer season and Mexico during the winter period. Regency

in their turn went bankrupt in 1995, and the ship was arrested and held in October at Nice before being auctioned off. Salamis bought her for $3.5 million in 1996 and gave her the name *Salamis Glory*. Her past caught up with her again when, on 30 August 2007, with 474 passengers embarked and 178 crew, she was once more in collision off Haifa, this time with the cargo vessel *Shelly*, which went down with the loss of two of her crew.

She retired in 2009 and was sold for scrap in November. She was renamed *Glory* and registered at St Kitts and Nevis in December, arriving at Alang, India, on 22 December for scrapping.

Her place was taken by the present *Salamis Filoxenia*, which was a Ro-Pax built by Oy Wärtsilä AB at Turku, Finland, in 1975 for the Soviet Black Sea Shipping Company (Blasco) and named *Gruziya*. She sailed between 1975 and 1995 as *Gruziya*, even when, in 1991, she passed to Ukraine registration upon the collapse of the old Soviet Union. Between 1995 and 1996 her main operator was Blasco UK and she sailed between 1995 and 1999 as *Odessa Sky*. She went in for an engine refit at Wilhelmshaven, but the ship and crew were impounded due to claimed non-payment of bills. As a result, in 1998 she was auctioned off and purchased by Gerard van Leest from the Netherlands. She was refitted in Bremerhaven to be rebuilt as a cruise liner, *Club 1*, and based at Rotterdam. Between 1998 and 2009 her owner remained Club Cruise but she was chartered out frequently after being laid up in September 1999 due to lack of customers for the Club idea, the concept being very popular in France but not taking off in Holland.

By 1999 she was under a charter operator with the French-based Nouvelles Frontières, Nantes, France, for a period. In 2002 she was placed under charter to UK Company Travelscope. While working for them she was in a collision off Gibraltar in thick fog with tanker *Spetses*, and was badly damaged. An inquiry found *Van Gogh* at fault and Travelscope was later declared bankrupt in December 2007. After she was repaired Club Cruises established a new operator, Van Gogh Cruises, and she sailed under the name *Van Gogh* for Caribbean and Mediterranean cruising. In 2008 her charter operator was Russian Metropolis Tur LLC, Ansalta, Dagestan, for Baltic and Arctic cruising. In July 2009 Club Cruise became bankrupt and the Van Gogh was auctioned off at Eleusis, Greece, being sold for $6.5 million to Salamis and thus becoming *Salamis Filoxenia*.

The *Salamis Filoxena* has eight passenger-accessible decks: Bridge, Olympus, Poseidon, Dionysus, Venus, Minerva, Arion and Atlas.

She has a variety of accommodation – the grand deluxe and junior suites and a host of two to four berth cabins. Her amenities include the Symposium restaurant, a buffet for self-service, Casino, night club, sky and pool bars, cinema, library, two swimming pools, fitness room, sauna, internet centre, beauty salon, playroom, photo centre, travel shop, video arcade, Captain's Club, Salaminia Club Live for shows, a kids' club, and a teens' club .She conducts two or three-day cruises from Piraeus to the Holy Land, Santorin, Rhodes, Kos and other Aegean destinations.

She is registered at Limassol, Cyprus.

Seabourn Cruise Line

Also marketed as 'The Yachts of Seabourn', this top-end luxury cruise company was first founded by entrepreneur Ate Brynerstad, a Norwegian business leader, as Signet Cruise Lines in 1986. The company was forced to change its name to Seabourn following objections from another organization, Signet Oy (Signet Maritime). However, since 2002 Seabourn Cruise has been a fully owned subsidiary of the huge Carnival Corporation which also owns the AIDA Cruises, Azamara Cruises, Carnival Cruises, Cunard Line, Costa Cruises, Holland America Line, P&O Cruises and Princess Cruises.

The first vessel built for the fleet was the *Seabourn Pride*, which was launched in July 1988 and her sister, *Seabourn Spirit*, entered service a year later. A third sister was part of Seabourn's expansion plans, but only joined the fleet after a rather torturous route. In 1991 the Carnival Corporation bought a 25 per cent share of Seabourn, but even so approval to proceed with the third ship was withheld by some of Seabourn's investors who got cold feet, and she was acquired while still on the stocks, by the rival Royal Viking Line (which had been founded in 1972 by Warren Titus at San Francisco but who were then owned by Kloster Cruises, Nassau) who commissioned her as their *Royal Viking Queen* in 1992. Within two years she had been transferred from Royal Viking to another Kloster Cruise subsidiary, Royal Cruise Line and she was renamed as *Queen Odyssey* from 1994 onward. Two years later Carnival increased its holdings in Seabourn to 50 per cent and this influx of cash enabled Seabourn to buy back the *Queen Odyssey* in January 1996 and she duly received her originally planned name of *Seabourn Legend*. Another two years passed and *Carnival*, in partnership with a group of Norwegian speculators, acquired Seabourn totally and also took over the British-orientated Cunard Line brand, at that time owned by Kvaerner ASA by its acquisition of Trafalgar House. Three ships of the Cunard stable, *Royal Viking*, *Sea Goddess I* and *Sea Goddess II* (which had been built in Akers Finnyard, Helsinki in 1984/85 for the Norwegian Sea Goddess Cruises, marketed as 'Boutique Mega Yachts' and which in 1986 had been chartered to Cunard for twelve years) were absorbed into the Seabourn brand as *Seabourn Goddess I* and *Seabourn Goddess II*. Also, the 37,983-GT *Royal Viking Sun* was similarly transferred, to become the *Seabourn Sun* in 1999, but in 2002 she became the HAL *Prisendam*. The final stages in this long-drawn out take-over were equally protracted. In 2001 Carnival bought out the Norwegian group entirely and sold the two *Goddess* vessels to Atle Brynestad for his new Miami-based company, the SeaDream Yacht Club, which he founded in September 2001, where they were renamed as *Sea Dream I* and *Sea Dream II*. Subsequently, the third of this trio, the *Seabourn Sun*, was switched to Carnival's Holland America Line, and, in 2002, Seabourn was removed completely from its new Cunard set-up and the company was established as a separate subsidiary of Carnival

It now has its headquarters at Elliott Avenue W, Seattle, Washington, in the same block as Holland America Line. The CEO is Richard D. Meadows. Other Seabourn executives include Stein Kruse, the Seabourn Chairman, and President and CEO of Holland America Line Inc., Dan Grausz, Executive President, Fleet Operations, Pat Riley, Executive Vice President Sales, Larry D. Calkins, Senior Vice President, Information Technology, Paul Goodwin, Executive Vice President, Onboard Revenue, Planning, Port Operations and Tours, John Delany, Senior Vice President, Marketing and Sales, Kelly P. W. Clark, Vice President, General Counsel and Ethics Officer and Brendan J. Vierra, Vice President, Human Resources.

The company currently operates three high-quality cruise ships on a worldwide basis. Its attractions included top-class amenities, attention to detail, its range of fine cuisine and the ability of its smaller vessels to penetrate ports and harbours little visited by its rivals.

The Seabourn Company has received numerous prestigious awards down the years, including being voted 'Best Small-Ship Cruise Line by Conde Nast Traveler Readers' Choice Poll in 2008 and again in 2010. It was also voted 'World's Best Small-Ship Cruise Line' by *Travel & Leisure* magazine in 2007, 2009, 2010, 2011 and 2012. It also won *Condé Nast Traveler*'s 'Gold List' of top hospitality venues for no fewer than seventeen consecutive years.

The *Seabourn Odyssey* (32,346 GT) was built at the Cimolai-Maritoti Yard, in Genoa, Italy, in 2009 as one of the new, larger class of Seabourn cruise ship. Her guest accommodation increased to 405 with a crew of 330.

Her range of suites comprise the Wintergarden, Signature, Owner's, Penthouse, Veranda and Oceanview.

Her main public features are the sun terrace with three-dozen double sunbeds, the retreat, a multi-use plaza with shuffleboard courts and nine-hole contoured golf putting green, atrium, boutique, the casino, and a club with live music, drinks and a disco in the evening. Other facilities include a card room, the colonnade for buffet dining, the grand

The main ships galley of *Seabourne Odyssey*. (*Colin and Maureen Butterworth*)

Bridge of *Seabourne Odyssey*. (*Colin and Maureen Butterworth*)

salon for lectures, demonstrations, films and meetings, with live dance music and cabaret, a gym/fitness studio, and the marina for water sports when applicable, with kayaks, banana-boats, pedal boats and steel-mesh enclosure for sea swimming. There is also the observation bar with panoramic views and a patio bar/grill, pool. The Restaurant is the main dining room with open-seating, whereas Restaurant 2 is a reservation-only venue. Seabourn Square combines reception area facilities with a reference library, workstations, a Konditorei-style coffee bar, shop, the Sky Bar and two launderettes. The spa houses six treatment rooms, a thermal area, sauna and steam rooms, Kinesis Wall, Thai massage, the spa pool, and the spa terrace with spa villa and whirlpools.

She is registered at Nassau, Bahamas.

The 32,346-GT *Seabourn Quest* was built at the Cimolai-Maritoti Yard, in Genoa, Italy, in 2011. She has a selection of suites – Wintergarden, Signature, Owner's, Penthouse, Veranda and Oceanview. Her range of public rooms include the atrium, a boutique, casino, the colonnade, grand salon, gym/fitness studio, marina, observation bar, patio bar/grill, pool, The Restaurant, Restaurant 2, Seabourn Square, Sky Bar, spa, spa pool, spa terrace, spa villas and whirlpools.

She is registered at Nassau, Bahamas.

The *Seabourn Sojourn* (32,345 GT) was built at the Cimolai-Maritoti Yard, in Genoa, Italy, in 2009. She carries 450 guests in an all-suite selection of Wintergarden, Signature, Owner's, Penthouse, Veranda and Oceanview. Her public rooms include the atrium, boutique, casino, club, the colonnade, grand salon, gym/fitness studio, marina, observation bar, patio bar/grill, pool, The Restaurant, Restaurant 2, Seabourn Square, the Sky Bar, spa, spa pool, spa terrace, spa villa and whirlpools.

She has a crew of 335 and is registered at Nassau, Bahamas.

Windstar purchased Seabourn Cruise Line's *Seabourn Pride, Seabourn Legend* and *Seabourn Spirit* on 19 February 2013. They have now become Windstar ships and have received new names commencing with *Star*.

Seacloud Cruises GmbH/ Hansa Shipping (Hansa Treuhand Holding AG, Hamburg)/Schiffahrts-Gesellschaft *Sea Cloud* MbH & Co KG.

The Hansa Treuhand, based at Hamburg, Germany, was established in 1979, to own, operate and charter out the *Sea Cloud* and *Sea Cloud II* sailing cruising vessels. It also operates river cruises. The consortium is active in ship management, construction and naval engineering. Sea Cloud Cruises expressed philosophy was YACHT: **Y**achting – **A**mbience – **C**haracter – **H**ospitality – **T**radition. The Chairman and Owner is Hermann Ebel, the President is Konstantin Bissias, with Cathrin Meyer as Ship Operations Manager and Petra Quasdorf and Vice-President and Product Management. In 2008 the company won the accolade 'World's Leading Green cruise Line'.

A most famous vessel, the 2,532-GT four-masted barque *Sea Cloud* has a long and turbulent history. She was originally launched as the *Hussar*, a private yacht, at the end of April, 1931, by the Krupp

Shipyard at Kiel to the plans of American company Gibb and Cox for one of American's richest men, Edward F. Hutton, to the design of his wife, Marjorie Merriweather Post. Upon their divorce four years later Marjorie inherited the yacht and renamed her *Sea Cloud*. She married the US ambassador to Moscow, Joseph Davies, and took the *Sea Cloud* to Leningrad to entertain and later put her on sale, without any offers. On America's entry into World War II she was inducted into the US Coast Guard, dismasted, armed and served as the patrol boat *IX-99* on active service. Between 1946 and 1949 she was slowly re-furbished piece by piece once more and used by the family until finally sold to President Rafael Trujillo Montinas, dictator of the Dominican Republic, who renamed her *Angelita*. On his assassination in May 1961, renamed *Patria*, she was sold in 1966 to Operation Sea Cruises Inc., a Panama-based American company, and received the name *Antarna*. She was laid up for eight years at Colón, Panama, after a brief period with Stephanie Gallagher's Oceanic Schools.

She was finally bought in 1978 by German Hartmut Paschburg with a Hamburg-based consortium who restored her name to *Sea Cloud* once more. From February 1979 she was docked at the Howaldtswerke-Deutsche Werft AG, the same dock where she had been built and underwent an eight-month restoration to her former glory. Another refit took place at Motorenwerke Bremerhaven (MWB) between November 2010 and April 2011 to bring the eighty-year-old lady up to the new SOLAS standards. Owned by Schiffahrtsgesellschaft Sea Cloud GmbH, Hamburg, and operated by Sea Cloud Cruises GmbH, she is registered at Valletta, Malta.

Sea Cloud II is a 3,849-GT modern three-master barque. The enormous popularity of the original *Sea Cloud* once she had been restored encouraged Pachburg and the company to build a similar square-rig vessel from new specifically as a cruise ship but with every modern convenience put into her. She is totally SOLAS compliant. Reference was made to the classic German 1908 book on such vessels by Mittendorf and the contract was awarded to Spanish shipbuilders Astilleros Gondán SA, at Figueras, Spain, in 1998, with Navicom Company at Wolgast, Mecklenburg-Vorpommern, Germany, making the specialized rigging. Her twenty-three sails of 3,000 square metres extent were manufactured in Poland. There was a one-year delay due to the complexity and high standard of the interior outfittings but she was finally christened in February 2001 at Las Palmas, Canary Islands. She is a lovely ship but was disappointingly given her rather unimaginative name even though in no way a sister to the original vessel. She can carry ninety-six guests in her twenty-seven fully air-conditioned outside cabins and sixteen junior suites, and has a crew of sixty-three. Her facilities include a restaurant, boutique, lounge bar, library fitness room, sauna and medical room. She currently works a schedule that incorporates Mediterranean cruises in the summer months and the Caribbean in the winter.

The 4,228-GT *Sea Cloud Hussar* (IMO 9483712) was being built at Factoria Naval de Marin, Marin, Vigo, Spain, for Hansa Treuhand Holding, Hamburg, Germany, and managed by Hansa Shipping. She is a three-masted vessel, with a length of 135.70 m, a beam of 17.2 m and a 5.65 m draught, and carrying twenty-seven sails with a total sail area of 3,975 m². She also had a 4,920 kW diesel-electric engine. Capacity is 136 guests in 69 luxury cabins. There was to be a crew of ninety. The cabins are divided between forty-three deluxe, twenty-three junior and three owner's suites. Facilities include the lido bar and bistro, a restaurant, a lounge/bar, library, boutique, spa area with sauna, steam bath and relaxation area, hydro-massage shower, hairdresser, sun deck, gym and hospital. She was scheduled for completion in September 2009; however, the company went bankrupt in 2010 and she was left on the stocks in an incomplete state. She was still *in situ* thus in November 2012. She is registered at Valletta, Malta.

There are also the 1,300-ton river cruising yachts *River Cloud* and *River Cloud II*, which sail the rivers Rhine, Main, Danube and in the Black Sea. The theme is 1930s-style luxury. The *River Cloud II* has three passenger decks and accommodation totalling forty-four external cabins. There is a restaurant, lounge, boutique/hair salon, games area, promenade and sun decks.

Silversea Cruises

Among the most luxurious of cruise lines and winner of many prestigious awards, the Italian Silversea Cruises is owned by the Lefebvre Family Trusts in Rome, who owned Sitmar Cruises. The company operates from Monaco, where it has offices at 7 Rue Du Gabian. There is also the USA office at East Broward Boulevard, Fort Lauderdale, Florida, and the London office at the Asticus Building, Palmer Street, SW1. The Company Board comprises Manfredi Lefebvre d'Ovidio, Chairman, Enzo Visone, Executive Chairman, Giorgio Sceisi, Jay Witzel in the States and Robert Martinoli. The company was founded in April 1994 with the *Silver Cloud*. Aimed at the high-end market, a sister ship, the *Silver Wind,* was completed in January 1995, the combination of luxurious, all-suite surroundings, impeccable service and outstanding culinary offerings proved a winner and the pair thrived despite fierce competition. Expansion followed in the new millennium with two further vessels of the same standard but with increased dimensions, the *Silver Shadow* and *Silver Whisper*. During the next decade the quartet was joined by the expedition ship *Prince Albert II* in June 2008 (she was later renamed as the *Silver Explorer* in April 2011) and a new concept, Silversea Expeditions, was launched. The new *Silver Spirit* arrived in December 2009. In June 2012 Silversea took over the Ecuadorian tour company Canodros SA based at Guayaquil. Its specialist ship, the *Galápagos Explorer II*, was already of the Silversea quality being one of the famous former Renaissance vessels and she was renamed as *Silver Galápagos*, although her Ecuadorian crews and the expertise of Canodros effectively continued in service under the new banner. With these expedition ships Silversea cruise itineraries now reach every corner of the world and all seven continents. The company also has a

A happy group of diners with their chef at Silverseas, the restaurant. (*Silverseas Cruises*)

'Personalized Voyages' option whereby guests can select which ports they embark and disembark at for a minimum of five nights aboard.

Accolades have been numerous, Silversea being voted 'World's Best' by *Condé Nast Traveler* on nine occasions, and by *Travel & Leisure* seven times, as well as winning the 'Best Cruise Line for Luxury Small Ships' award from *Luxury Travel Advisor* in 2011. The company also introduced its 'Partners in Culinary Excellence' concept in collaboration with Relais & Châteaux and launched the La Collection du Monde range of signature dishes prepared and presented to the highest standard. The company hosts Culinary Arts Voyages where world-renowned guest chefs such as Anne Desjardins, Eyvind Hellstrøm and Jacques Thorel feature their skills and artistry and Silversea Executive Chef David Bilsland hosts the L' École des Chefs range of workshops.

The 16,927-GT *Silver Cloud* was built in 1994 by Cantieri Navali Visentini, Trieste, with her final outfitting done by the Mariotti Shipyard, Genoa. She underwent a refit in 2004 and in 2012 a second three-week refurbishment was carried out at Fincantieri, Palermo, under the direction of Giacomo Mortola, during which her entire interior decor was totally revamped and upgraded.

She now accommodates 296 guests in 146 suites, ranging through vista, veranda, silver, royal, grand and owner's suites. Her facilities include: The Restaurant, with seating for 324 guests, La Terrazza, for à la carte dining, Le Champagne Wine Restaurant by Relais & Châteaux, the Venetian Show Lounge, the panorama lounge, Connoisseur's Corner, the Casino, the bar, the pool grill, the pool bar, the card and conference room, internet café, two boutiques, the spa with two massage rooms, two sauna/steam room and relaxation room, a beauty salon, fitness centre, library, an outdoor swimming pool, two whirlpools and a launderette.

She is registered at Nassau, Bahamas.

The 17,400-GT *Silver Wind* entered service in 1995 making her maiden voyage on 29 January. She was refitted at San Giorgio Shipyard, Genoa, in 2008. A major renovation took place during which they installed a sixty-seat observation lounge, a spa and fitness centre and a two-floor glass lifts between decks 8 and 9. Extra accommodation was added by adding an owner's suite, a medallion suite, a vista suite and four silver suites. She now accommodates 298 guests in a total of 149 outside suites: vista, veranda, medallion, silver, royal, grand and owner's.

Her amenities and facilities include, for dining, the 324-guest Restaurant, Le Terrazza, for à la carte dining, Le Champagne Wine Restaurant, the Parisian Show Lounge, the Observation lounge, the Panorama lounge, Connoisseur's Corner, the Casino, the bar, the pool grill, the pool bar, card and conference room, internet café, two boutiques, the spa with five massage rooms and two sauna/steam rooms, a beauty salon, fitness centre, library, an outdoor swimming pool, two whirlpools and a launderette.

She has a crew of 212 and is registered at Nassau, Bahamas

The 28,258-GT *Silver Shadow* entered service in 2000, making her maiden voyage on 15 September. She accommodates 382 guests in 194 ocean-view suites: vista, terrace, veranda, medallion, silver, royal, grand and owner's. Her facilities and amenities include The Restaurant for 424 guests, La Terrazza for à la carte dining, Le Champagne Wine Restaurant, the show lounge, the Observation lounge, the Panorama lounge, Connoisseur's Club, the Casino, the Casino bar, the bar, the pool grill, the grill, the pool bar, a conference room, the card room, an internet café, two boutiques, the spa with four massage rooms and two sauna/steam rooms, the beauty salon, fitness centre, library, an outdoor swimming pool, two whirlpools and three launderettes.

She was refitted in 2011. She accommodates 423 guests.

She is registered at Nassau, Bahamas.

The 28,200-GT *Silver Whisper* entered service in 2001 and was refitted in 2010 and made her maiden voyage on 2 July. She accommodates 382 guests in 194 ocean-view suites in the range vista, terrace, veranda, medallion, silver, royal, grand and owner's. Her facilities and amenities include The Restaurant for 424 guests, La Terrazza for à la carte dining, Le Champagne Wine Restaurant, the show lounge, the Observation lounge, the Panorama lounge, Connoisseur's Club, the Casino, the Casino bar, the bar, the pool grill, the grill, the pool bar, a conference room, a card room, an internet café, two boutiques, the spa with four massage rooms and two sauna/steam rooms, the beauty salon, fitness centre, library, an outdoor swimming pool, two whirlpools and three launderettes.

The fitness club aboard the Silverseas *Silver Spirit*. (*Silverseas Cruises*)

She is registered in Nassau, Bahamas.

The 36,009-GT *Silver Spirit* entered service on 23 December 2009 and made her maiden voyage from Barcelona to Lisbon. She accommodates 540 guests in accommodation that includes the largest suites in the fleet, almost all of them with a private veranda and ranging between vista, veranda, silver, royal, grand and owner's. The interior decor is 1930s art deco throughout.

For dining there is the choice of six venues: The Restaurant with seating for 456 guests, La Terrazza for à la carte meals, Le Champagne, a wine restaurant by Relais & Châteaux, the Seishin, which has Asian-fusion cuisine, and the Stars Supper club with all-night entertainment. There is also the Pool Grill. For entertainment there is the choice of the show lounge, the Observation lounge, the Panorama lounge, Connoisseur's Corner, the Casino, the bar, the pool bar, three boutiques and a fitness centre. She also has a conference room, a library and card room, an internet café, a 770 m² (8,300 ft) indoor/outdoor spa, a resort-style swimming pool, four whirlpools and a seven launderettes.

A sister ship is under option. She is registered at Nassau, Bahamas.

The 6,072-GT *Silver Explorer* has led a very varied existence since she was first built in Finland at the Rauma-Repola shipyard as the *Delfin Clipper* for Delphin Risteilyt Oy, Helsinki, and delivered to them on 1 June 1989. She was described at the time as 'the Deluxe *Delphin Clipper*, with three hundred berths, on which only round-trip voyages can be booked' and was considered the ultimate in small cruise-ferry (USPH) luxury. She was equipped with the Kantautunut night club, the Sigyn Sauna and whirlpool, the Pequod piano bar, the Cutty Sark Disco and a swimming pool. She had a crew of 130. Her main route in the years 1989–1990 was between Turku and Visby, Sweden, although she also visited Gotland in Sweden, Bornholm in Denmark, Tallinn in Estonia and the Aura River in Finland. From 26 January 1990 she was chartered

to Rederi Ab Sally, Helsinki, as the *Sally Clipper* until 17 June 1992 when Sally was terminated and merged into the Silja Line. Between 1990 and 1996 she was registered as being owned by Rauma-Repola Marine Oy, who chartered her briefly to Baltic Link, Karlskrona, as the *Baltic Clipper* in 1992 and then to Ocean Trade Chartering, Singapore, as the *Delfin Star* until 1997. She was acquired by the Phoenix Maritime Shipping Company, a Panamanian company, in 1996 serving with them after another refit until 2001 as the *Dream 21*. From 2001 until 2003 she was the expedition ship for Discoverer Reederei, the Bremen-based Germany travel company, after their existing vessel had been wrecked and the replacement had not appeared. She served as the *World Discoverer* from 2001 to 2004, when the German-based Society Expeditions went bankrupt in June 2004. She was then laid up idle at Singapore as *World Adventurer* between 2004 and 2005 and again as *World Discoverer* II from 2005 to 2008, being under the ownership of Delta Steamship between 2003 and 2007. She was laid up at Singapore as the *World Discoverer II* (2004) and *World Adventurer* (2004–2007) and *World Explorer* respectively until she was bought by Silversea in September 2007 and, after a major refit and conversion at Fincantieri's Trieste yard, made her maiden voyage on 12 June 2008. She served as the *Prince Albert II* between June 2007 and April 2011 when she was again renamed, this time as the *Silver Explorer*.

The *Silver Explorer* carries 132 guest in 66 suites, which range through adventurer, explorer, view, vista, veranda, expedition, medallion, silver, grand and owner's. Her public areas include the restaurant for buffet breakfast, lunch and à la carte dinner, the theatre with seating for 110 guests, the Observation lounge, the Panorama lounge, Connoisseur's Corner, outdoor grill, library/internet café, a boutique, the spa with massage room and sauna/steam room, a beauty salon, fitness centre, two whirlpools and a launderette.

She carries eight Zodiac inflatables for in-shore exploration.

She now accommodates 132 guests and she is registered at Nassau, Bahamas.

The 4,077-GT *Silver Galápagos* was built as *Renaissance Three* for Renaissance Cruises and entered service in August 1990. She became the *Galápagos Explorer II*. She served as such until 15 January 1998 when she was acquired by Canodros SA, the Ecuadorian Tourist Company. She was extensively refitted in 1998. The former *Galápagos Explorer II* was acquired in 2012 when Silversea took over Canodros SA and was renamed. A refit lasted until late September 2013 and the maiden voyage with Silversea took place on 28 September. She is based at Baltra Island. She now accommodates 132 guests in sixty-six ocean-view, silver, veranda, terrace, deluxe veranda, and explorer 1 and 2 suites. Her facilities include, for dining, The Restaurant and The Grill, and, for relaxation, the Explorer Area, the lounge, the grill bar, the piano bar, the stargazing area, snorkelling area and jacuzzi. She has Wi-Fi access, a boutique, beauty salon and a medical centre.

She is registered at Nassau, Bahamas.

Star Clippers

The Swedish company Star Clippers was founded by the present Swedish-born owner and President, Mikael Krafft, in 1990. He was a successful entrepreneur and founder of the Belgian White Star Property development group, but had always hankered after the concept of the old clipper-time ships but with every modern convenience and material. The final idea to form a company with a pair of modern equivalents was said to have come to him during a Caribbean cruise on his private yacht *Gloria*. A limited company was duly formed and the first vessel was commenced at Belgium Shipbuilders Corporation, Ghent, after three years of intense research into the practicalities of such a scheme.

This vessel was the 360-ft, four-masted *Star Flyer*, launched in 1991, and claimed to be the first clipper ship constructed from scratch for ninety years. Her sister, *Star Clipper*, followed in 1992. The concept, and the ships, caught the public imagination and the company thrived. As a result an even larger vessel followed in July 2000, the five-masted *Royal Clipper*, the largest such vessel afloat.

The company headquarters is at Clipper Palace, Rue de la Turbie, Monaco, where Mikael's wife, Ann, his son Eric and his daughter Marie are respectively Overseer of Quality Control Hotel and Shipboard Entertainment, Vice-President Finance and Director of Sales; while the Marketing and Sales office is at Suite 100, 107th Avenue, Miami, Florida, headed up by Vice President Sales, Larry G. Haugh. The ships operate worldwide, but usually spend the summer months based in Europe operating either from Monaco or Cannes, with winters spent in the Caribbean, working from Barbados or St Maarten, or in the Pacific from Tahiti.

The 4,425-GT steel-hulled *Royal Clipper* had her hull constructed at the Polish shipyard of Stocznia Gdańska and was finished off at the Dutch shipyard of IHC-de-Merwede. Her five 63-m (197-ft) masts spread forty-two sails (twenty-six squaresails, eleven staysails, four jibs, one gaff-rigged-spanker) manufactured from Dacron by Doyle Ploch Sailmakers, Clearwater, Florida. They have a total of 5,204 m² (56,000 ft²) sail area and are handled by powered controls. Her mainmast has a hinged top section. Her design is based upon the old preserved clipper *Preussen*, of 1902, Krafftin's boyhood inspiration. She has four decks, Sun, Main, Clipper and Commodore. Her 227-guest accommodation consists of two owner's suites, two deck cabins, deluxe outside staterooms, super deluxe outside suites, deluxe outside suites, superior outside staterooms, all with marble fitments, some with whirlpool baths. Her facilities include three pools, a three-level atrium, library, observation lounge, clipper dining room, tropical bar, piano bar lounge, Captain Nemo underwater spa and lounge, and a marina. She also has a fitness centre, unisex hair salon, massage room and skin and body treatment centre. There is a staff of 106 of which twenty handle the sails. She chiefly alternates between the Mediterranean and Caribbean.

She is registered in Luxembourg to Luxembourg Shipping Services with Star Clippers as the operator.

The almost identical sisters *Star Flyer* and *Star Clipper* are smaller vessels, but equally as well-appointed. Rigged as barquentine schooners, they are four-masted vessels carrying sixteen sails with a 36,000 ft² sail area. Both have Caterpillar diesels for auxiliary power, developing 1,030 kW for 12 knots under power and 17 knots under sail. They were both built by Scheepswerven van Langerbrugge, Ghent, Belgium. Both have four decks, Sun, Main, Clipper and Commodore, and can accommodate 180 guests in considerable comfort with a combination of deluxe, luxurious or larger outside or inside deck staterooms with marble baths and whirlpools. Facilities include two pools, the tropical bar, piano lounge, library featuring a Belle Époque fireplace and relaxing Edwardian styling and fine art prints throughout. They have crews of 75 and carry four semi-enclosed launches.

Both *Star Flyer* and *Star Clipper* are owned by Star Clippers Ltd, Monaco, and registered in Luxembourg.

Star Cruises (Genting)

Marketed as 'The First Global Line', Star Cruises was established in September 1993. As a major part of the Malaysian-based Genting Berhad, an investment and management holding company, Star Cruises forms part of Genting Hong Kong, which has its headquarters at the Ocean Centre, Canton Road, Tsimshatsui, Hong Kong, and the Chairman is Tan Sri Lim Kok Thay with David Chua Ming Huat as President,

Blondel So King Tak as Chief Operating Officer, William Ng Ko Seng as Chief Operating Officer, Cruise and Tan Wei Tze as Chief Financial Officer. The Directors are Alan Howard Smith, Deputy Chairman, Lim Lay Leng, Au Fook Yew and Heah Sieu Lay, all non-executive Directors.

It has rapidly grown to become the third largest cruise company in the world and absorbed both the Norwegian Cruise Line (NCL) and the Orient Lines shipping companies in the process, although these were then subsequently discarded in 2008. Star has tapped into the lucrative Asian market ahead of all its rivals. It was awarded the accolade of 'Favourite Cruise Company' at the Outlook Traveller Awards, Mumbai, in 2013.

Ranking only behind the giant Carnival Corporation and Royal Caribbean Cruise Line, Star Cruises is one of the major players in the cruise industry, which between them own and operate 77 per cent of the market. This ranking is achieved despite Star being a relative newcomer on the scene, having been established as an associate of the Malaysian Genting Group as recently as 10 November 1993. The company has extended its field of operations by its acquisition of NCL and is currently one of the leading cruise line operators.

The tourist industry of Malaysia owes much to the visionary concept of Tan Sri Lim Goh Tong in establishing a first-class hotel and tourist resort at Gunung Ulu Kali, in the cool mountains of the Cameron Highlands in the difficult and then remote jungle, not too distant from Kuala Lumpur, in 1964. From this start the group has grown consistently over more than four decades to five top hotels, two apartment blocks and a cable car system, as well as expanding into palm oil production, with three plantations, electric power generation and supply, and paper manufacture as well as oil and gas exploration.

Star Cruises itself was incorporated in Bermuda and has its corporate headquarters in Hong Kong, and its fleet began with the purchase of two sister ships, the former large cruise ferry sisters, the 40,039-GT *Athena* (IMO 8701674) and the 40,054-GT *Kalypso* (IMO 8710857), built at STX Finland yard in Helsinki in 1989 and 1900 respectively for the Swedish Rederi AB Slite's Viking Line, when their parent company Rederi AB Slite had become bankrupt in April 1993. These vessels were reflagged in Panama as *Langkapuri Star Aquarius* and *Star Pisces* respectively (the *Langkapuri* frequently being omitted both on the ships themselves and in promotional material) and converted at Sembawang dock, Singapore, into fully fledged cruise ships, the former car decks incorporating cabins and a casino, with design by Per Dockson. The former Viking funnel livery was altered to become the new company's logo, blue base, red top with a combining yellow star and eventually, white hull. Originally based at Singapore, the ships soon changed to the present Hong Kong base of operations. The *Langkapuri Star Aquarius* subsequently became the *Aquarius* up to May 2001, then the *Athena* until September 1993, then was sold to DFDS Seaways in 2001 who renamed her *Pearl of Scandinavia* until January 2011 when she was renamed again as the *Pearl Seaways*. However, the *Star Pisces* is still in service with Star at the time of writing but since 2009 has been laid up at Port Klang, Malaysia.

Further purchases and conversions followed as the line prospered, *SuperStar Gemini* in 1995, *SuperStar Capricorn* in 1997, *SuperStar Sagittarius* in 1998 and *SuperStar Europe* (later Aries) in 1999. The flourishing of Star Cruises was emphasized in 1998/9 with the delivery of the first new build vessels, the *SuperStar Leo* and *SuperStar Virgo*. Further large hulls were ordered and in the pipeline, when, in 2000, the company became a global player with the total acquisition of the Norwegian Cruise Line along with Norwegian Capricorn Line (merged into NCL) and Orient Lines (which continued trading until ceasing operations in 2008). While NCL continued to trade very successfully, as described

elsewhere) and later 50 per cent was sold to Apollo Management for US $1 billion in 2007, Star continued its operations with five major ships, *SuperStar Virgo*, *SuperStar Aquarius*, *SuperStar Libra*, *Star Pisces* and *MegaStar Aries* as the premier Far Eastern cruise line, albeit at more modest rate with Asian-Pacific custom as its almost exclusive power house. With fly-cruise hubs at both Singapore and Hong Kong, under the presidency of CEO Tan Sri Lim Kok Thay, the son of Genting's founder, Star Cruises is a consistent winner of the 'Asia-Pacific 'Best Cruise Award', and entered the 'Top 50 Asian Brands' in 1999, which is perhaps a reflection of its 1:2 crew-to-passenger ratio, one of the highest in the world. Crew training is conducted at the company's own facility at the terminal complex at Port Klang, which houses the Star Cruises' Simulator Centre for officers.

Currently Star Cruises has on its list the 42,275-GT *SuperStar Libra* (IMO 8612134), built in 1988 as the *Norwegian Sea*; 40,012-GT *Star Pisces* (IMO 8710857), built in 1990 as the *Kalypso*; the 50,764-GT *SuperStar Gemini* (IMO 9008419) built in 1992 as the *Norwegian Dream*; the 51,309-GT *SuperStar Aquarius* (IMO 9008421) built in 1993 as the *Norwegian Wind*; and the 75,338-GT *SuperStar Virgo* (IMO 9141077), built in 1999 as Star's first new-build vessel. Two other new-builds were the planned 91,740-GT *SuperStar Libra* (IMO 8612134) and the 92,250-GT *SuperStar Scorpio* (IMO 9195169) but they never entered service with Star and were put into operation with the Norwegian Cruise Line brand as *Norwegian Star* and *Norwegian Dawn* respectively, and their tonnage rules them out of further detail in this volume. The same is the case with the 75,338 *SuperStar Leo*, built in 1998. She served until 1998 but was also transferred over to Norwegian Cruise Line to become their *Norwegian Spirit*.

In 1989 two vessels were taken under charter, these being the 1989-built, 3,341-GT sisters *MegaStar Aries* (IMO 8705278) and *MegaStar aurus* (IMO 8705266). Built by Flender Werft at Lübeck, Germany, as *Luxury Mega Yachts'* for the now defunct Windsor Line, this pair were originally named as *Lady Diana* and *Lady Sarah* respectively, becoming the *Aurora* and *Aurora II* in 1991 and the former being renamed as *Aurora I* in 1994. They were acquired by Star, initially on charter, and later served between 1994 and December 2012, but are now for disposal. Other vessels that served with Star are outlined below.

The 40,012-GT Ro-Ro ship *Star Aquarius* (IMO 8701674), was built by STX Finland at Helsinki in 1988 as the *Athena* until September 1993 and served with Star as the *Langkapuri Star Aquarius* between 1993 and March 2001 and then *Aquarius* to May 2001 before becoming the *Pearl of Scandinavia* for the Copenhagen-based DFDS until January 2011 and is now the *Pearl Seaways*. The 19,093-GT *SuperStar Gemini* (IMO 9000687) was built by Union Navale de Levante, Spain, as the *Crown Jewel* in 1992 and then became the Cunard vessel *Cunard Crown Jewel* from 1992 to 1995. She served for Star Cruises as the *SuperStar Gemini* between 1995 and 2009 before becoming the *Clipper Jewel* in 2009, then the *Vision Star* later the same year and finally just the plain *Gemini* since 2009, and is currently laid up at Port Klang awaiting disposal. The 21,891-GT *SuperStar Capricorn* (IMO 7218395) was built in 1973 by Oy Wärtsilä, Helsinki, as the *Royal Viking Sun* until 1990 when she carried a succession of names: *Sunward* from 1990 to 1992, *Birka Queen* in 1992, *Sunward* again from 1992 to 1997, *Golden Princess* from 1993 to 1996, and *Hyundai Kunigang* between 1998 and 2001. She was in service with Star for the 1997 to 1998 and the 2001 to 2004 seasons as the *SuperStar Capricorn*. She received the name *Grand Latino* from 2004 to 2005 and she is now serving as the *Boudicca* with Fred Olsen Cruise Lines.

The 16,607-GT *SuperStar Sagittarius* (IMO 7125861) was also built by Oy Wärtsilä, Helsinki, in 1972 as the *Sun Viking* before serving briefly in 1998 for Star. She subsequently enjoyed the titles *Hyundai Pongnae*, *Omar II* and *Long Tie* and is currently the *Oriental Dragon*.

The 37,301-GT *SuperStar Europe* (IMO 7822457) built in 1980, served with Star Cruises between 1998 and 2004, and served again, but as the *SuperStar Aries*, from 2000 to 2004. She is now the Saga Cruises ship *Saga Sapphire*. The 15,179-GT *SuperStar Taurus* (IMO 7827213) built in 1980 by Oy Wärtsilä, Turku, as the *Viking Saga*, which name she bore until 1986 when she was redubbed as *Sally Albatross* from 1986 to 1990 then *Sally Albatross II* from 1990 to 1995. She was next renamed as *Leeward* until 1999. She served with Star as *SuperStar Taurus* from 2000 to 2001 and was then the *Sija Opera* between 2002 and 2006, and then just *Opera*

Louis Cristal sun deck. (*Louis Cristal Line*)

between 2006 and 2007 when she became the Louis Cruise Lines' *Cristal*. The 4,200-GT *MegaStar Sagittarius* (IMO 8802870) was built as *Renaissance Six* for Renaissance Cruises by Nuovi Cantieri Apuania, Italy. In November 1997 she was renamed as *Sun Viva II* and carried that name until April 2000 becoming the *Megastar Capricorn* until March 2001. She was briefly given the name *Capri* but in May 2001 this was changed to *Hebridean Spirit*. In April 2006 she took the name *Sunrise* for six years before, in September 2012, becoming the *Caledonian Sky*. She is managed by Salen Ship Management AB, Gothenburg, Sweden. The 4,280-GT *MegaStar Capricorn* (IMO 8802868) was built in 1991 for Renaissance Cruises by Nuovi Cantieri Apunana SpA as *Renaissance Five*. She later became the *SunViva* and then served briefly in 2000 for Star as *MegaStar Sagittarius*. She was renamed as Cruise West's *Spirit of Oceanus* from 2001 to 2010, before becoming the *Sea Spirit* and she is currently owned by TN Cruise K/S, Denmark, and managed by ISP.

Swan Hellenic Cruises

Now part of All Leisure Holidays of Burgess Hill, West Sussex, Swan Hellenic originated from the UK-based Swan Travel Agency and has always maintained a strong tie with educational tourism based on their particular connections with Greek culture dating back to the 1950s. Starting with famous archaeologist Sir Mortimer Wheeler, who enjoyed enormous status fame at the time, the policy of having experts in their field embarked on their ships to lecture and enlighten guests and lead shore expeditions to fabulous sites around the Eastern Mediterranean, and now globally, has ensured a dedicated and educated clientele ever since. The Swan Founder brothers, W. F. Swan and R. K. Swan, eventually sold the company to P&O in 1983 and that, in turn was assimilated into the Carnival conglomerate with a totally different ethos. The introduction of a much larger ship reflected this, and they

did not seem to understand that it was in the very intimacy and elite nature of the original *Minerva* that much of her appeal lay. They did not appear to understand this unique (principally) British-cultural concept and shed the Swan Hellenic brand in 2007, transferring the existing ship to their Princess subsidiary. To the rescue rode Lord Geoffrey Sterling a previous P&O Chairman, and he purchased the brand, saving it from oblivion. The company was re-launched in 2008 and was again successful in capturing this top-end niche market once more.

The ships utilized by Swan Hellenic over their decades of operation are:

Miaoulis (1,714-GT) was a passenger cargo ship built by Cantieri Riuniti dell'Adriatico, Monfalcone, Italy in 1952 for the Greek Nomiko Line, Piraeus. She was chartered by Swan in August 1954 for the first cruise. In 1988 she became the *Sadafi* and then *Junior 3* the same year but was scrapped in May 1988 at Gadani Beach.

When the educational cruises became the regular and principal rationale of the company a replacement vessel was found. This was the 6,178-GT ship *Ankara*, which dated back to 1927. She had originally been constructed by Newport News Shipbuilding and Drydock Corporation, Virginia, as the *Iroquois* for the New York and Miami Steamship Company, and later became a Clyde Mallory Lines vessel. She was taken over by the US Navy in July 1940 as a hospital ship and renamed *Solace* (AH5) She survived the Japanese surprise attack on Pearl Harbor and served throughout World War II. She had been sold to the Turkish Maritime Line in 1948 and was acquired by Swan Hellenic Despite her own antiquity she served until 1974 before being laid up in 1977 and finally scrapped at Kaliç Cove, Turkey, in 1981.

The 4,145-GT *Orpheus* took her place. She started life in 1948, being built at Belfast by Harland & Wolf for the British and Irish Steam Packet Company (B+I). She served as the *Munster IV* on the Liverpool to Dublin ferry route across the Irish Sea for two decades. In 1968 she became the Epirotiki Lines vessel, provisionally named *Theseus*, and was rebuilt over two years as a cruise ship. With Epirotiki (later Sun Line and then Royal Olympic Cruises) she was chartered to Swan Hellenic many times from 1974 onward and served for over twenty years. She was finally disposed of in 1996, being laid up in 1998 and finally scrapped in 2001.

The 12,500-GT *Minerva* was the next ship to fly the Swan Hellenic flag. She has carried many names in her life, but had been originally ordered as the Soviet Union 'research ship' (the Soviet euphemism for an electronic spy ship) *Okean* in 1990 and was built by Okean Shipyard at Nikolayev, Ukraine. However, while still incomplete, the Soviet Navy terminated its interested and she was purchased by V-Ships and after undergoing a complete conversion at Mariotti shipyard in Italy, commenced service in April 1996 for Swan Hellenic as *Minerva*. She cruised for them until 2003. She next served with Saga Cruises and Abercrombie & Kent, and became alternately the *Saga Pearl* or *Explorer II* depending on the season. Saga's place in this dual operating arrangement was then taken over by the Bonn-based Phoenix Reisen who named her *Alexander von Humboldt* until 2007.

Meanwhile, her replacement with Swan Hellenic was the 12,500-GT *Minerva II*, built in 2001 as the Renaissance vessel *R-8*, which had been owned by Cruiseinvest but had been inoperational up until then. Under charter, she replaced *Minerva* in 2006, officially with the Princess Cruises arm of Carnival, but in practice, still serving with Swan Hellenic up to April 2007, when, with the ditching of Swan Hellenic, she finally *did* become the *Royal Princess* and served with Princess Cruises up to May 2011 when P&O took her over and renamed her as *Adonia*.

The re-constituted Swan Hellenic company, being part of the same group, now had the *Explorer II* transferred over to them under a long-term lease as the *Minerva* once more and she recommenced operations in May 2008. In 2012 the ship underwent a big refit at Lloyd Werft shipyard, which, among other improvements, saw the Orpheus observation lounge and bar added to the her top deck with a walk-round promenade deck, the Shackleton bar enlarged, a new internet lounge built in, the removal of six cabins to make room for a beauty centre and fitness room, leaving her 181 cabins with en-suites, and added balcony upgrades to thirty-two of her cabins taking the total to forty-four. This increased her passenger capacity to 350. Refurbishment internally saw the adoption of what is termed 'British country elegance and style'. On the engineering side a new double crankshaft plant with new propellers was fitted along with a further Rolls-Royce Promas integrated propeller and rudder and new Voith stern thrusters.

TAC Cruise LLC

This is a limited liability company, established in January 2011, which has its registered officer at Wilmington, Delaware. It is owned by Xanterra Holding Corporation, a hospitality company established since 1876 with the Fred Harvey organization. Xanterra, whose CEO is Andrew N. Todd, is itself now an arm of the vast Philip Anschutz Empire, which runs Xanterra Parks & Resorts from Greenwich Village. It came into prominence on 25 May 2011 when it acquired the Windstar Cruises, Seattle, business with a $39 million bid, through the bankruptcy courts from Ambassadors International Inc. (AMIE) over the White Plains, New York-based Whippoorwill Associates, which was a rival bidder. Through this acquisition it gained the Windstar Sail Cruises fleet of three vessels, *Wind Spirit*, *Wind Star*, and *Wind Surf*. Windstar is now run as a wholly owned subsidiary of Xanterra.

TAC also brought under its control in the same deal the 1,650-ton stern-wheel paddle steamer *Delta Queen*, which was originally built in

Scotland by Denny Shipbuilding at Dumbarton in 1924 and assembled at Stockton, California, in 1926. She served on the West Coast pre-war, was requisitioned by the US Navy during World War II and served up the great river systems of the southern states under a variety of owners post-war. In June 2008 her then operators, Majestic American Line, laid her up due to the demands of SOLAS and she became a floating boutique hotel. She is listed as a national monument.

Thomson Cruises

Thomson Cruises is an arm of Thomson Holidays that charters cruise ships for principally, although not exclusively, European and Mediterranean destinations. Original set up in 1973, the subsequent worldwide oil-fuel crisis saw it abandoned three years later. Following the lead of rival company Airtours Thomson resurrected the line in 1995, and now operates with four major ship charters, *Thomson Celebration*, *Thomson Destiny*, *Thomson Spirit* and *Island Escape* and with a fifth, *Thomson Dream*. The company now operates as a division of TUI UK and is based at Travel House, Crawley Business Quarter, Fleming Way, Crawley, West Sussex. The CEO is David Borling, with Jeremy Ellis Marketing Director among the Board members and Fraser Ellacott as Managing Director.

The parent company was originally founded in 1965 as the Thomson Travel Group, the Canadian Thomson Corporation, but went public in May 1998. In 2000 the giant German Preussag AG conglomerate based in Hanover, which included steel production, shipbuilding and repair as well as transport interests among its interests, acquired it as part of their diversification and re-positioning policy following the slump in steel requirements. When Preussag became Touristik Union International (TUI AG), TUI's rapid selling off of old industrial assets and purchasing of new companies in Germany soon transformed it into one of the world's leading travel and transport organizations, with ten cruise liners on a portfolio that includes travel agencies, aircraft and hotels worldwide. In Germany TUI owns Hapag Loyd Kreuzfahrten and in 2009 launched TUI Cruises with a 50 per cent stake in the UK Thomson Cruises while a 50 per cent share in Island Cruises was achieved in 2008 via a purchase from Royal Caribbean. In July 2002, Thomson Travel had been rebranded as TUI UK. On 19 March 2007, TUI AG and First Choice Holidays plc agreed to merge the TUI Tourism and First Choice Holidays plc and form a new company, TUI Travel plc. This was completed in September of the same year when the company launched on the London Stock Exchange and by Christmas Eve had entered the FTSE 100 index, giving Thomson Cruises a strong base for continued operations in the charter ship field. The Thomson fleet now includes the following vessels:

The 37,773-ton ex-Airtours/MyTravel *Sunbird*, was the former RCCL *Song of America* built in 1982, and was the first cruise ship proper to carry all her passenger accommodation forward, away from the noise of the engines and propellers. She is also the only one of the transferred Royal Caribbean ships of that early era to retain the distinctive sky lounge, which encircles the funnel, while under new ownership. She has been chartered to the Thomson fleet from 2005 to 2011 as *Thomson Destiny*, as the largest ship in the fleet at that time, with an enhanced passenger capacity of 1,611 spread across eleven decks, and a crew of 540, but is owned and managed by Louis Cruise Lines based in Limassol, Cyprus. She mainly sails to ports in the Mediterranean, the eastern Atlantic from the Canary Islands down to Morocco, plus some excursions further afield, including the Caribbean.

Another Louis Cruise Line charter to Thomson is the 11,162-ton *Calypso*. This ship was originally one of three car ferries built for Traghetti Sari working out of Cagliari, Sardinia, to Genoa and other western Italian ports. This particular vessel, the *Canguro Verde* (*Green Kangaroo*) was built by the Italian shipyard Italcantieri SpA at Castellammare di Stabia for Navigazione Traghetti Sardi and worked to the Italian western Mediterranean ports until 1974. Further owners followed with the Società Linee Canguro of Cagliari, Sardinia, acquiring her in 1974, and the Saudi Arabian company Fayez Trading and Shipping using her in the Red Sea on the Jeddah-Suez-Jeddah circuit for a further eight years, renaming her as the *Durr*. Sold again in 1989

Much of the enjoyment of a cruise is the positive attitude of the crew. This ever-cheerful bunch from the *Thomson Celebration* on the 17th August 2006, made a Norwegian journey double pleasurable. (*Peter C. Smith*)

this much travelled warrior became the *Ionian Harmony*, running up and down the Adriatic for Strintzis Lines. Yet a further planned new name (*Sun Fiesta*) and change of operating venue (the US Caribbean islands) beckoned in 1990, but this fell through and instead she was purchased by Regency Cruises as the *Regency Jewel*. After a thorough refit it was planned for this veteran to work out of New York but the abrupt demise of her parent company terminated those operations almost before they had begun. Instead she was chartered to Transocean Tours, a German company, who bestowed her present name on her. In May 2006 she suffered a fierce fire off Beachy Head and had to be towed into Southampton to be refitted. After being out of service for two years Louis Cruise Lines obtained her in 2000, refitted her and retained the name *Calypso*. Thomson currently markets her as 'reserved exclusively for adults' and her 486 passengers in 243 cabins are given that select service by the crew of 220.

The 33,930-ton *Thomson Celebration* and 33,960-ton *Thomas Spirit* are sister ships constructed in 1984 at Chantiers de l'Atlantique, St Nazaire, being the former Holland America ships *Noordam* and *Niew Amsterdam*. *Nieuw Amsterdam* was sold to American Classic Voyages in 2000, being renamed *Patriot*, to found a new United States Line, for cruising the Hawaiian Islands, but the Islamic terror atrocities against New York's Twin Towers the following year caused a slump in bookings and the company ceased trading. She reverted to her old name and ownership in 2002. From 2003 the *Niew Amsterdam has* been chartered out to Louis Cruise Lines, who in turn sub-chartered her to Thomson, while the *Noordam* was originally directly chartered out to by HAL to Thomson in 2005.

Following the founding of Island Cruises by Royal Caribbean Cruises and First Choice Travel in 2001, the company began operations with 26,747-ton *Island Escape*, the line being operated by Sunshine Cruises Ltd. The *Island Escape* was the former cruise ferry Scandinavia, built by the Nantes, France Company, Dubigeon-Normandie SA, in 1982 and was the largest ship of this type on completion. She only served briefly under this name before being operated by DFDS Seaways until 1985 and then by Sundance, Admiral Cruises and Royal Admiral Cruises under the new name of *Sundancer* to 1990. Royal Caribbean took her over that year when she was renamed *Viking Serenade*, and placed her with the Norwegian Wilh. Wilhelmsen ASA at Lysaker. Before commencing operations she was sent for full conversion into a proper cruise ship, which involved stripping out the car decks, and which totally transformed her. She re-emerged as a 40,132-ton vessel, with a 1,741-passenger capacity over ten decks and a crew of 540. In 2002 a joint venture with First Choice Holidays was announced, marketing her for the already-identified breed of new young customer, popularized by AIDA in Germany, for whom informality was the key to new-style cruising. Again renamed, as *Island Escape*, she sailed with Royal Caribbean's new subsidiary, Island Cruises, until 2009. Of the two partners in Island, First Choice was taken over by TUI Travel and then in 2008, Royal Caribbean sold its half to TUI who also transferred her to Thomson, to become their only fully owned vessel. To date, *Island Escape* has retained her name and now operates with a mainly British clientele in the Mediterranean and Canary Islands.

In 2012 Thomson Cruises announced its new range of products designed to bring fresh impetus during difficult times, Platinum Cruises. With both *Thomson Dream* and *Thomson Celebration* receiving multi-million pound makeovers the opportunity was taken to equate these vessels with the scheme, which proved successful when applied to the Thomson Hotel group. The whole interior decor are refurbished and updated with iPod docking stations, treatment rooms adjacent to the spas, upgraded bars and lounges and a new range of all-inclusive cruise options.

Currently the Thomson fleet comprises five vessels, three of which are under 40,000 GT as follows:

The 33,393-GT *Thomson Celebration* was built by Chantiers de l'Atlantique, France, as the *Noordam in* 1984 for the old Holland America Line (HAL). She served as such until 2004 when she had a $10 million refit and, still under HAL-Antillen ownership, was in November, chartered to Thomson as *Thomson Celebration*. The registered owner from October 2011 has been TUI, UK, and she is managed by Columbia Ship Management, Cyprus.

The *Thomson Celebration* has eight decks open to passengers, Bridge, Eagle, Mariner, Broadway, Main, A, B and C. Her amenities include the Meridian Restaurant with waiter service, Mistral's for à la carte dining, which is by reservation, and there is a weekly Captain's cocktail party and gala dinner with early or late sittings. The Lido Restaurant is a self-service buffet with an international theme; the terrace grill has open-air service and there is the weekly Buffet Magnifique with ice sculptures, fruit carvings as well as treats. For entertainment the *Thomson Celebration* has the Broadway show lounge with revues and guest artists, Liberties has live bands, karaoke, disco and game shows, Horizons offers live music from jazz to the classics and there is also a cinema. There are lounges and bars a plenty – Horizons, Hemingway's Bar, the Explorers' Lounge, Mezzanine Bar, Liberties Bar and the Lido Bar. For health fanatics there is Ocean's Health Club with spa and gym and saunas; the sports deck offers a choice of basketball, badminton and table tennis. For more peaceful pursuits there is a reading room, a card room, gift shop, library with internet access and for the junior guests there is the Thomson Kid's Club.

She is registered at Valletta, Malta.

The 33,930-GT *Thomson Spirit* was built by Chantiers de l'Atlantique, France, as the *Nieuw Amsterdam* in 1983 for the Holland America Line (HAL), which was absorbed into the Carnival set-up in 1988. She served under that name until 2000 when she became the *Patriot* as previously noted when sold to the American Classic Voyages Corporation, which went bankrupt the following year. Thus, in 2001 she reverted to her original name briefly but in 2002 became *Thomson Spirit for* a season under bare boat charter from Carnival. In 2002 to 2003 she was named as just *Spirit* and in 2003 once more became the *Thomson Spirit* being under charter to Thomson from Wind Surf, a HAL subsidiary under a sub-leasing arrangement from Louis Cruises who in turn had her under a bare-boat charter from Carnival. In May 2008 she was bought outright by Louis Cruises who extended the period of the loan under charter until the end of 2014. She is now owned by Spirit Holding Ltd, Cyprus, a Louis Holdings company, with the ship on long-term charter to Thomson until 2014.

There are nine passenger decks aboard the *Thomson Spirit*: Eagle, Bridge, Mariner, Promenade, Broadway, Main, A, B and C. For eateries there is the Compass Rose restaurant with open seating and waiter service, Sirocco's for an à la carte choice with reservations and cover charge, the Lido Restaurant with self-service buffet and international theme nights, the terrace grill for BBQs and pizzas in the open air, and there is also the weekly Captain's cocktail party and gala dinner with two sittings. There is a choice of entertainments, including the Broadway show lounge for variety and guest acts, and High Spirits also has game shows, live music and a late-night disco. Raffles Casino has all the favourites for high-rollers and there is a cinema. Bars and lounges include Horizons with cabaret acts and classical music options, Raffles Piano Bar, the Lido Bar Explorer's Lounge with a nautical theme, the Mezzanine Bar and the High Spirits Bar in the Night Club. Fitness can be had at Ocean's Health Club, with spa, beauty salon and gym; there is a card and reading room, while the sports deck is given over to basketball, football and table tennis. There is a library, gift shop and the Thomson Kids' Club.

She is registered in Valletta, Malta.

The 26,747-GT *Island Escape* belongs to Island Cruises, UK, which is a totally-owned subsidiary of TUI UK. She was originally built in France by Dubigeon-Normandie SA, Nantes, as a cruise/ferry for DFDS subsidiary Scandinavian World Cruises and named *Scandinavia*. She only served for three years from 1982 before becoming the *Stardancer* in 1985 under which name she served for both Sundance Cruises and then Admiral Cruises. Royal Caribbean Cruises acquired her in 1990 and gave her a new name, *Viking Serenade* working under the Wilhelm Wilhemsen, Lysaker, Norway, management and then converted her wholly into a cruise ship. She served until 2002 when she moved over to the subsidiary Island Cruises as the *Island Escape* and then in April 2009 to Thomson Cruises still under her old name. She is registered to another TUI concern, Sunshine Cruises Ltd, Cyprus, having been fully purchased from Royal Caribbean Cruises in 2008. After being laid up for a while at Limassol, Cyprus, she was refurbished in 2011.

The whole ambience of the *Island Escape* is informality and there is an emphasis on entertainment. She has nine passenger accessible decks: Compass/Lookout, Sun, Flamingo, Emerald, Diamond, Coral, Aqua and Bronze. The on-board facilities and amenities are therefore very comprehensive and include three main dining establishments – the Oasis, with waiter service and chef's à la carte specials, the Island Restaurant with British and international buffets, and the Beachcomber Restaurant with 24-hour self-service buffets and theme nights. For entertainment *Island Escape* has the Ocean Theatre for shows, cabaret and comedy routines, the Bounty Lounge, with live music, game shows and late-night comedy acts and the Lookout Panoramic Lounge/Bar, which features a disco. The casino has blackjack, roulette and poker plus gaming machines. There is a wide variety of drinking venues with The Pub, in traditional 'local' style, Champions, with a sports theme, Café Brasil for coffee and beverages, the Mirage Bar by the pool, the Sailaway Bar and the Sundowner. There is also a cyber café, a hair and beauty salon, a fully-equipped gym , a video arcade, gift shop, and for the young ones Palmy's. *Island Escape* is registered in Nassau, Bahamas.

There is also the 54,763-GT *Thomson Dream*, the former *Homeric* built in 1986 by Meyer Werft in Germany. In 1988 she became the HAL vessel *Westerdam* and in 1988 transferred to Costa as the *Costa Europe* until 2009. In April 2010 her registered owner became TUI UK under a bare-boat charter as *Thomson Dream* and she is now managed by Columbia Ship Management, but her tonnage rules her out of further detail in this volume. Similarly, the 40,876-GT *Thomas Majesty* is just squeezed out of full details by her tonnage. She is the former *Royal Majesty*, built by Kvaerner Masa-Yards, Finland, in 1992 and purchased by NCL in 1997 to become *Norwegian Majesty* between 1997 and 2009. In 2008 she had become a Louis Cruises-owned vessel until 2012 after a $162 million purchase price when she was promptly leased back to Star Cruises/NCL until December 2009 when she became the *Louis Majesty* until 2012. Thomson and Louis Cruises arranged for the former *Thomas Destiny* to exchange with Louis Majesty from May 2012 when she was renamed as the *Thomson Majesty*. Her registered owners are Crew Navigation, Ltd, Greece.

Transocean Kreuzfahrten Gmbh & Co., KG

A wholly owned subsidiary, with headquarters at Bremen, of the Munich-based Premicon AG, Transocean was restructured from the original 1954-founded Transocean Tours Turistik, later Transocean Tours, absorbed in 2009 and re-branded as Transocean Kreuzfahrten GmbH. Premicon AG itself was founded in 1998 as an investment fund organization that specialized in Rhine, Main and Danube River cruises from 1999 onward and now has a fleet of twenty-five such vessels. They also branched out into ship management and tourism. Their motto became 'All services from a single source' and the acquisition of *Astor* was a prime example of this in practice. Transocean's portfolio ultimately included international, domestic and package tours, foreign exchange, travel insurance and corporate logistic services.

The Managing Directors are Michael Jost and Alexander Nothegger with Andrea Kruse, Director Marketing and Sales, Lucia Rowe, Regional Director UK/USA, and Regina Schudrowitz, Key Accounts and Foreign Markets.

Transocean had originated as Transocean Passagierdienst D. Ottmann & Co., the latter being a German ship broker who acted as the German agent of the then Leningrad-based Baltic Shipping Company (BLASCO). A long list of these chartered Soviet cruise ships extended from 1972 when they utilized the 1960-built *Estonia*, which had been re-built as a cruise ship at Marseilles. They continued to charter her for periods between 1972 and 1984. Ignoring the river boats, the following vessels featured in the Transocean fleet list down the decades that followed:

The 1974-built, 13,252-GT *Odessa* was operated between 1982 and 1995. She was later laid up for years at Naples and finally scrapped in 2007; the 1981-built *Lev Tolstoi* (9,878-GT) served between 1986 and 1988; and the 1990-built, 7,560-GT *Columbus Caravelle* served between 1992 and 1994 and this period culminated with the 22,080-GT ship *Alexsandr Pushkin*, a 1965-built ship that was chartered from Baltic Shipping and the Far Eastern Shipping Company in 1979 until 1984. They next obtained the 11,162-GT *Calypso* in 1994. She later became the Louis

Lines ship *The Calypso*. For the 1996/1997 season they chartered the 1965-built *Gripsholm* (24,528 GT) the former *Saga Fjord*, from Norwegian American Line, for a six-month period. She was sold to Saga Cruises and was renamed as *Saga Rose*, being discarded and broken up in 2009. The 1981-built, 18,853-GT *Astoria* was used for several tours between 2002 and 2009 on charter from Club Cruise before she too joined Saga Cruises as *Saga Pearl II*. Between 2006 and 2008 the Louis Cruises *Arielle*, a 23,149-GT ship, built as the *Nordic Prince* in 1970, was chartered. She returned to Louis Cruises and was discarded and sold out of service. Finally, the 22,080-GT *Marco Polo*, which had originally been the *Aleksandr Pushkin*, re-appeared in her new guise on charter from Global Maritime between 2008 and 2010. Both *Arielle* and *Marco Polo* were operated by the UK arm of the business working out of Tilbury. After Transocean went bankrupt a second time she was taken over by Cruise & Maritime Voyages.

The *Astor* was built in 1987 as a passenger ship/cruise ship for the Southampton to Cape Town route at Howaldtswerke/Deutsche Werft AG, Kiel, Germany, for South African Marine Corporation (Safmarine). She was transferred to Marlan Corporation and registered in Mauritius and chartered and operated by British Morgan Leisure as the *Astor*. She was not a success and was sold the following year to Sovcomflot, being managed by Black Sea Shipping Company, working from Odessa under the name *Fedor Dostoevskiy*. She was chartered to Bremen-based Transocean Tours and then another German company, Neckermann Seereisen, took her under long-term charter. Ownership changed with the collapse of the Soviet Union and in 1991 and she was acquired by the Monte Carlo-based Prestige Cruises, itself established by Sovcomflot and Costa Crociere and her registration changed to Nassau. The following year a new management structure was established as Fedor Dostoevskiy Ltd. She was taken under charter in December 1994

by AquaMarin Cruises, who reverted to her original name of *Astor*, and owned by Astor Shipping, Cyprus. AquaMarin Cruises folded in 1996 and Transocean Tours took out a ten-year charter and, after a major overhaul, operated her from Bremen exclusively for the German-speaking market. In 2006 the main company behind Transocean, Premicon AG, acquired her from Astor Shipping. Transocean itself was declared bankrupt in September 2009 upon which Premicon purchased it and the *Astor*. She was threatened by Somali pirates in 2008 but they were driven off by the German frigate *Mecklenburg-Vorpommern* and she suffered no casualties. Premicon gave her a large refit at the Lloyd Werft shipyard at Bremerhaven in 2010 and re-launched her on a worldwide cruise programme. In 2012 Transocean again filed for bankruptcy following bad publicity on a Norovirus outbreak aboard the *Marco Polo*. The statement at the time was that Transocean would continue to operate the ships while the company underwent 'a strategic realignment and restructuring'.

Astor has seven passenger decks, Caribic, Baltic, Atlantic, Promandaden, Boots, Brücken and Sonnen.

Currently the *Astor* cruises to the Caribbean, the Mediterranean, the Orient, India, Africa, the Seychelles and Cape Verde Islands, South America and Northern Europe.

Travel Dynamics International (TDI)

Founded by two Rhodes-born, Greek brothers in 1969, Travel Dynamics International has offices on East 70th Street, New York, NY. The company President is George Papagapitos and the Co-President is Vasos Papagapitos, with Javier Cortez as MIS Manager and Jose Fuentes as Company Secretary.

The company charters specialist cruise vessels such a the *Sea Explorer* for their 'Travel and Learn' themed tours during which guest lecturers who are experts in their field are embarked and there are local-led shore excursions to sites that concentrate on the art, archaeology, history and myth of the Mediterranean littoral. The company also operates exploration voyages to the Antarctic regions and was a founder member of International Association of Antarctic Tour Operators (IAATO), which ensures a respectful and environmentally aware approach to this sensitive area.

The company's fleet includes the following vessels:

Callisto (IMO 5416553, MMSI 239749000, callsign SV3536) was built in 1963 by Kremer Werft, Elmshorn, Germany as the *Marina*. She is of 499 GT with a length of 50 m and beam of 8 m and a 2.5 m draught. In 1985 she was renamed as *Illyria II* and recorded under the Russian Maritime Shipping Register. In May 2000 she became the *Callisto* and was managed and owned by Blue Sea Line Shipping, Piraeus. She was refitted in 2007 is also registered in Piraeus, Greece.

Her current capacity is thirty-four guests housed in seventeen ocean-view cabins, each of which has a satellite TV/ DVD/CD player, telephone, mini-refrigerator, marble-appointed bathroom, and 24-hour room service. Facilities include a dining room, a lounge with audiovisual facilities for lectures, two sun decks, a jacuzzi, and a swimming platform. She has a crew of sixty.

The 4,077-GT *Corinthian* (IMO 8708672, MMSI 249556000, callsign 9HUT9) was built as one of the beautiful and revolutionary Renaissance Mega Yachts by Cantieri Navali Baglietto La Spezia, at La Spezia, Italy, in 1990. She has a length of 88 m, a beam of 15.3 m and a draught of 4.5 m. Renaissance had been founded by the Oslo-based company Fearnley & Eger in 1989. She served as *Renaissance Four* until November 1996. The company was later acquired by Edward B. Roudner and the ship based at Fort Lauderdale, Florida, between 2000 and 2003, when she was registered in the Bahamas. Renaissance

went bankrupt in September 2011 in the turbulent aftermath of the 9/11 terrorist attacks in New York. She was then operated as *Clelia II* by the Great Lakes Cruise Company for a period, visiting some of the remoter ports and harbours of North America and Canada. In 2009 she was extensively refurbished and had fin stabilizers, a bow thruster, stabilizers, an ice-strengthened hull and carried nine Zodiac Heavy Duty Mk5s. In December of that year she was briefly renamed as *Cldloq II* and registered at Malta, but by the following May had reverted to *Clelia II* once more before becoming the *Orion II*. She sailed extensively for Orion Expedition Cruises and also with Polar Cruises to Antarctica. She was acquired by V-Ships Leisure, Monte Carlo, Monaco, on 25 September 2011. In January 2013 under the Travelscope branding she was renamed as *Corinthian*.

Corinthian has all-suite accommodation for one hundred guests in fifty suites. She has a dining room, two sun decks, a library with internet access, two lounges with audiovisual facilities, a jacuzzi, a gym/spa, beauty salon, boutique, swimming platform and a hospital. She has a crew of seventy and is registered at Malta.

The 4,200-GT *Corinthian II* (IMO 8802882, MMSI 538004274, callsign: V7WD8) was the former Renaissance Mega Yacht *Renaissance Seven*, built in 1991 by Nuovi Cantieri Apuania Marina di Carrara, Italy. She has a length of 91 m and beam of 15 m and a 4.3 m draft. Renaissance went bankrupt in September 2011 and in December she and her sister were both laid up at Marseilles where she was renamed as *Renai I*. She was sold to Mauritius Island Cruises in November 2003 and renamed by them as *Sun* until May 2004 when they renamed her *Island Sun* until February 2005. She was chartered out from 2005 to Noble Caledonia and she became *Corinthian II* with Travel Dynamics International.

She is an all-suite yacht fully refurbished in 2005. She is fitted with fin stabilizers, a bowthruster, an ice-strengthened hull and carries Zodiac

Yorktown suite.

Yorktown bows.

inflatables. She can accommodate 114 guests in fifty-seven suites. The penthouse and veranda suites have private balconies and butler service. Her amenities include The Club, a library with internet access, a lounge with audiovisual facilities, a dining room, a wraparound sun deck with jacuzzi, an exercise room, a beauty salon, swimming platform and a medical centre. She has a seventy-five strong crew and is registered in Majuro, Marshall Islands. She is currently owned and managed by International Shipping Partners, Miami, Florida.

The 2,354-GT *Yorktown* (IMO 8949472, MMSI 368373000, callsign WDG3446) was built by First Coastal Shipbuilding, Green Cove Springs, Coral Springs, Florida, in 1988 as the *Yorktown Clipper* for Clipper Cruise Line, St Louis, Missouri. She had a length of 68 m, a beam of 12 m and a 3 m draught. (218ft). She later served on the Great Lakes from 1992 between Charlottetown, Prince Edward Island and Rochester, New York.

In 2006 she was acquired by Cruise West, Seattle, renovated and in May 2007 she became the *Spirit of Yorktown*, serving in Alaska and off the West Coast. When Cruise West went into administration on 18 September 2010 the ship was laid up in Seattle. Her owner and operator was Yen Lee's Explorer Maritime Cruises, New York, NY. In August 2011 General Electric Capital Corporation sold the ship to Travel Dynamics International. They gave her a renovation early in

2012 and began operating her as *Yorktown* in May 2012. Under charter to V-Ships Leisure she ran aground in Detroit River on 25 August 2012 with 120 guests aboard, but no damage was done and no injuries incurred.

She can carry 138 guests in sixty-nine exterior cabins. For public areas she has the lounge, dining room, sun deck, library with internet access, swimming platform, medical facilities. She is American-manned and US Coast Guard regulated. She has a draught of just nine feet enabling close-in access

TUI Cruises

Touristik Union International (TUI) is a vast tourism and travel group, originally set up in 2002 by the renamed Preussag AG and based in Hamburg, Germany. It has entered the cruise ship industry through its absorption of both the German Hapag-Lloyd (in 1998) and the British Thomson Company. Not content with that in 2009 it established its own cruise subsidiary, TUI Cruises, in association with Royal Caribbean Cruises Ltd. It concentrates almost exclusively on German-speaking guests. The current CEO is Richard J. Vogel. The company has two vessels, the 76,522-GT *Mein Schiff* 1 (ex-*Celebrity Galaxy*) and the 77,713-GT *Mein Schiff 2* (ex-*Celebrity Mercury*).

This company was launched as a joint 50:50 staked venture between TUI AG and Royal Caribbean Cruises on 10 December 2007. It was aimed squarely at the premium end of the 906,000-strong German cruise market, which had hitherto been so successfully nurtured by AIDA. Similarly, the new company is based in Hamburg and has been operating from May 2009. The target audience for the new line is stated to be, 'above all younger couples and families, which value ample room to move around, generous surroundings coupled with high quality and attentive service'.

TUI has contracted with STX Finland for the construction of two new cruise ships, named, with remarkable lack of originality, *Mein Schiff 3* and *Mein Schiff 4*, but, at 99,300 GT, they, like the first pair, are outside the scope of this volume other than as the parent organization for the ships listed here respectively under Hapag-Lloyd and Thomson Cruises.

Un-Cruise Adventures

This company is based at Fishermen's Wharf, Seattle, Washington, and combined the former Un-Cruises and InnerSea Discoveries organizations. It traces its origins back to the founding of American Safari Cruises in 1996 which pioneered small yacht cruising in Alaska, previously the preserve mainly of the largest vessels. This company thrived and in 2001/2008 its Chief Executive Officer was Dan Blanchard. Blanchard had considerable experience with both Cruise West and Glacier Bay Lodge Cruises. In 2008 Blanchard and Tim Jacox, also previously with Cruise West, formed a new company, InnerSea Discoveries, a limited liability company (LLC), which bought the original American Safari Cruises. In January 2013 the company formally became Un-Cruise Adventures. The present-day board includes both these founders, Blanchard and Jacox, as the combined Principal/CEO and the Vice-President, Sales and Marketing respectively.

The company offers alternate choices of afloat/ashore activity. The first, Active Adventures, commenced cruising the Inside Passage from 2011 extending the normal cruise programme to include active explorations ashore with hiking and kayak expeditions to the interior. Three small vessels were employed for this, the *Wilderness Discoverer*, *Wilderness Adventurer* and *Wilderness Explorer*. The Luxury Adventures arm of the business uses three further vessels, the *Safari Endeavour*, *Safari Explorer* and *Safari Quest* and these cruises also allow guests to similarly extend themselves if so desired. A third facet is Heritage Adventures, a new branch commenced in summer 2013 which follow the routes of the early Alaskan pioneers, gold prospectors and adventurers who open the land up. The *S.S Legacy* a replica vessel of a typical nineteenth century steamer is the main vessel used for these voyages. Some of the ships also cruise the Columbia and Snake Rivers, which this author has enjoyed immensely, British Columbia, the Sea of Cortés in Mexico and even Hawaii.

The *Wilderness Adventurer* was built in1986 by Blount Boats, Rhode Island, as the *Caribbean Prince*. She was owned successively by Sealodge II LLC, Washington Mutual Bank and GB Vessel Acquisition LLC. In May 1998 she was acquired by Glacier Bay Tours & Cruises, Seattle, and renamed. In 2004, while cruising Tracey Arm, Alaska, the ship struck ice, which punched a 3-inch diameter hole in the hull. The ship was evacuated without any casualties and was beached on the rocks before it sank and was later salvaged. In 2011 she was fully renovated for Un-Cruise. She now accommodates sixty guests in three classes of cabin, Navigator, Trailblazer and Pathfinder. She has a sun deck, which houses the bridge, a lounge, observation deck and main deck, with the lounge, dining room and galley. She carries inflatable skiffs, paddle boards and Necky Kayaks. She has a hot tub, sauna and fitness equipment.

Wilderness Discoverer is the former *Mayan Prince*, also a Blount-built boat launched in 1992. She was owned by Sealodge I LLC, Sitka, Alaska, Washington Mutual Bank and GB Vessel Acquisition LLC before passing to Glacier Bay Marine Services Inc. She was renamed *Wilderness Explorer* when acquired by InnerSeas six years later. She was refurbished in 2011 and now has space for seventy-six guests in four cabin types, Navigator, Trailblazer, Pathfinder and Explorer. She has a sun deck with sauna and fitness equipment, two hot tubs, a main lounge and bar and she is equipped with Necky Kayaks, paddle boards and inflatable skiffs.

Wilderness Explorer was built in 1976 by Eastern Shipbuilding, Panama City, Florida, or West Travel Inc., for the Cruise West Line and originally named *Spirit of Discovery*. She is owned by Sealodge V LLC, Sitka, Alaska. She was fully modernized in 2012 and houses 76 guests in three categories of cabin, Trailblazer, Pathfinder and Explorer. Her three passenger decks have a sun deck, a lounge with an Alaska Hot tub, a dining room and galley, a bar a sauna and fitness equipment and she carries Necky Kayaks and paddle boards.

Safari Endeavour was built by Jeffboat Inc., Jefferson, Indiana, for West Travel Inc. for Cruise West. She was originally named *SeaSpirit* and later became *Spirit of Endeavour*. She carries eighty-six guests in elegant splendour with forty-three staterooms with the following categories, Master, Commander, Captain, Admiral and Commodore. She has four passenger decks with a sun lounge and bow viewing area, a dining room with galley and a salon. She is equipped with a wine bar, a spa with two hot tubs, a sauna, fitness equipment and a massage suite. She carries sea kayaks, paddle boards and inflatable skiffs.

Safari Explorer was built in 1998 by Freeport Shipbuilding Inc. for Safari Explorer Charters LLC and named *Rapture*. She was then owned by Certified Marine Expeditions. In November 2009 she became the *Safari Explorer* and underwent a major overhaul in 2007/2008, with interior upgrades, new generator, HVAC installed, galley upgraded etc. She now embarks thirty-six guests in six categories of stateroom, Single, Master, Commander, Captain, Admiral and Commodore. Her amenities include a sauna, on-deck hot tub and masseuse room/table, exercise equipment, wine library, and she carries sea kayaks and high-speed skiffs.

The *S.S. Legacy* was built by Bender Shipbuilding, Mobile, Alabama, in 1984 for West Travel and Cruise West and is designed as a replica of a Victorian steamer. Originally she was to have been

Kayaks aboard *Safari Explorer*. (*On-Cruise*)

named *Pilgrim Belle*, but became *Victorian Empress* and finally *Spirit of '98* . She is owned by Sea Lodge III LLC, Sitka, Alaska. She was acquired by Un-Cruise's InnerSeas predecessor and became *Safari Legacy*. She was completely renovated in 2012 when she becaome the *S.S. Legacy*. She can accommodate eighty-eight passengers in six categories of stateroom, Master, Commander, Captain, Admiral, Junior Commodore and Owner's Suite. There is a grand salon with dance floor with bar and the Klondike dining room and Victorian-inspired decor throughout. She has a wine bar and library, plus a hot tub, sauna, fitness equipment and a massage suite.

Safari Quest is a motor yacht and was built by PCP Inc., DBA Sheer Yachts, in 1991 for Alaska Charters LL, Kirkland, Washington, and is owned by them. She was originally named *Obsession*. She carries twenty-two passengers and has eleven staterooms in three categories, Captain, Mariner and Commander, and a crew of nine. She has four decks with a sun lounge, hot tub, and fitness equipment, a library, bar, salon and dining area. She carries kayaks, paddle boards and inflatable skiffs.

Voyages of Discovery

Voyages of Discovery was itself founded in 1994 to supply educational cruises for school children and in 1997 it was acquired by All Leisure Group, which brought in additional cruises for mature professional adult passengers. From then until 2001 Voyages of Discovery operated historical and cultural voyages and initially concentrating on the Eastern Mediterranean, Red and Black Seas, the company has become a worldwide cruise player. From 2001 the cruise itinerary was extended to include Northern Europe and Scandinavia and in 2001 was conducting these tours by short-term leasing of various cruise ships, but the following year a five-year lease was signed to operate the *Discovery* between May and November from May 2003. Two years later, however, the opportunity was taken to acquire the *Discovery* along with her winter cruise programme and its Fort Lauderdale sales office. The company now operates in the UK, USA, Canada, Australia, New Zealand and South Africa and its ships visit as diverse a group of destinations as Russia, France, the Caribbean, Central and South America, India, Antarctica and the Far East.

The company is now based at Lynnem House, Burgess Hill, West Sussex, with Alan Murray as Managing Director and as part of the All Leisure Group plc (ALG), which includes Page & Moy Travel Group,

Swan Hellenic and Discover Egypt Holidays and Hebridean Island Cruises. The company received the accolade of Best for Lectures in 2010 and Best Niche Cruise Line in 2011.

The group fleet now comprises four ships, *Discovery Sailaway*, Swan Hellenic's *Minerva*, *Voyager* and Hebridean Island Cruises' *Hebridean Princess*, details of the latter being found in their appropriate sections.

The former 15,271-GT *Voyager*, began operations in 1990 as the *Crown Monarch*, as previously mentioned in the Voyages of Discovery section.

The *Discovery Sailaway* has an equally complex history. She dates back to 1972 when she was built as the *Island Venture* for Kommandittselskapet Cruise Venture A/S & Co, for Norwegian Cruiseships A/S and operating from New York .When the Oslo company of Fernley & Eger acquired US company Princess Cruises and dissolved the Norwegian partnership, its share of the company was *Island Venture*, which was promptly renamed as *Island Princess* to fit into the new scheme of things in 1972. By 1974 Princess had been absorbed into the British P&O and *Island Princess* went with her. After more than two decades of service, in 1999 they in turn disposed of her to the Korean Hyundai Corporation who gave her a new name, *Hyundai Pungak*. The concept was to ship South Koreans north to visit Mount Kumgang. However, the idea collapsed with Hyundai's demise in 2001 and she was purchased by Orient Lines, a subsidiary of Norwegian Cruise Lines – the wheel seemed to have turned full circle. By 2001 she had became the *Platinum* and received a $15 million upgrade. A charter was arranged with Voyages of Discovery and the ship was re-christened as *Discovery* at Harwich in 2003. For a brief period she became the *Andaman Victory* a floating education centre for the Indian-based Pailan School of International Studies operated by Yogi Seaways of Kolkata, but reverted to *Discovery* once more on 1 November 2004. Two years later ALG purchased her outright. She now sails under the name *Discovery Sailaway* as from August 2012 All Leisure and Cruise and Maritime Voyages, UK a Booking Agency, agreed a partnership deal that transferred *Discovery* to CMV from February 2013.

She has two restaurants with open-seat dining, two swimming pools, one with a retractable magrodome roof, and two jacuzzis, night clubs, a cinema, and a spa. She has thirty-five suites including thirty with balconies. Her facilities also include two swimming pools, one with a retractable roof, two jacuzzis, four lounges, five bars, a library, card room gymnasium and health centre, lecture theatre and cinema, internet centre, two restaurants, a Medical centre, a gift shop, a photo gallery, and a beauty salon. She carries four high-speed passenger tenders and six Zodiacs for Antarctic duties.

Voyages To Antiquity/The Aegean Experience Maritime Company Ltd

The owner is The Aegean Experience Maritime Company Ltd, with offices at Siraggiou Street, Piraeus, Greece, and Mayflower Court, Msida, Malta, and the operator is Voyages to Antiquity, with registered officer at Leatherhead, Surrey, headquarters at Summertown, Oxford, established by Gerry Herrod, who had founded Orient Lines fifteen years previously and which was itself an early pioneer in themed cruising. The new philosophy was to concentrate on the eastern and central Mediterranean area and bring to big ship sailing the luxury river cruise concept of new sights and wonders each day. The company is now part of the All Leisure Group plc, which also includes Voyages of Discovery, Page & Moy, Travelsphere, Swan Hellenic, Hebridean Island Cruises and other specialist cruise firms. The Managing Director is Alan Murray, with Mitchell Schlesinger as Vice-President Sales, Daniele Rocha Marketing Manager and Andrea Corman as Guest Services Director.

The *Aegean Odyssey* (11,563 GT) was originally a Ro-Ro ferry built in 1974 by Santierul Naval Galatz, Romania, for Zim Integrated Shipping Services Ltd, Constanta and named *Narcis*. She served thus until 1985 and was then purchased by Dolphin Hellas Cruises and renamed *Alkyon*. In 1986 she was converted to a cruise ship, with a 29 m extension inserted. She operated between 1986 and 1989 as *Aegean Dolphin* and between 1989 and 1990 as *Dolphin* and then from 1990 to 1996 as *Aegean Dolphin* once more. She underwent a refit in 1992 and in 1995 was chartered out to Epirotiki Line. In 1996 she was under charter to Renaissance Cruises as the *Aegean I* and in the period 1997–1998 was chartered to Golden Sun Cruises. She underwent another refit in 2002. Louis Hellenic Cruise Lines sought to purchase her in 2005 but this was aborted and she was de-commissioned until in 2008 she was acquired by Aegean Experiences. Subsequently she had a massive refit in 2009/2010 at Keratsini and Salaminas Shipyard, Ermoupoli, Syros, Greece, and in May 2010 was renamed as *Aegean Odyssey*. Ownership passed to Samos (Island) Maritime Company Ltd, Piraeus.

She features a range of suites, including Concierge Class, Junior, and staterooms with and without balconies. The ship amenities include two eating establishments, the Marco Polo Restaurant and Tapas on the Terrace, as well as the Terrace Café, three lounges, three bars, a lecture theatre, a library, a souvenir shop, a photo gallery, an internet centre, an outdoor pool, a spa and jacuzzi, a beauty salon, a medical centre. She is registered at Valletta, Malta.

A second vessel, the *Voyager*, commenced operations in December 2012 with an inaugural season in the Caribbean and circumnavigated Central and South America via the Panama Canal Cape Horn, the Falkland Islands and the Amazon.

The 15,271-GT *Voyager* first commenced service in 1990 as the Commodore Cruise Line vessel *Crown Monarch* being built by Union Naval de Levante, Valencia, Spain. From 1994 she became the Crown Cruise Line ship *Nautica* serving under this name for two years and again, between 1996 and 2007, she became *Walrus*, but still with Crown Cruise Line. For a brief period in 2007/2008 she was named *Jules Verne* owned by Champ Elysees MV and operated by the German Phoenix Reisen organization.

She was docked at Bremerhaven Sockgesellschaft GmbH, Bredo shipyard, for a rebuilding and was then again chartered out to the Bonn, Germany-based Phoenix Seereisen Company as the *Alexander von Humboldt from* 2008. The Club Cruise company of Veenendaal, Netherlands, was the next to operate her briefly in 2008 and then from November that year to November 2009 she was out of service while disputed outstanding claims were resolved for unpaid bills owing and were paid by V-ships of the Isle of Man, to where the tug *Englishman* towed her in September 2009 for auction where All Leisure Group acquired her. They chartered her once more to Phoenix Seereisen, Bonn, Germany, in 2010 and she was also chartered to the Turkish Bamtur group, all without name changes. In July 2012 Voyages began as her operator and as *Voyager* she started operating for the company in December 2012 after another major $20 million makeover at Portland, Dorset. The whole interior design was changed to reflect the 'Explorer Theme'. She emerged with seven passenger decks, Sun, Bridge, Promenade, Discovery, Columbus, Livingstone and Raleigh, and carries 556 guests and has thirty-six balcony suites and 90 per cent outside cabins. She also now features the new Scott's Lounge, and the Explorer Club restaurant.

V-Ships

This is another of the large ship management companies that encompasses Ship Management, Ship Leisure, Ship Manpower, Ships Marine and

Ships Capital divisions on a worldwide basis. It currently has more than 980 vessels on its books, including several cruise ships already mentioned in these pages including the *Albatros, Alexander von Humboldt, Akademick Nikolay Ayugin* and *Orion-II*. The group was established in 1984 and is based at 'Les Industries', Rue Dugabian, Monaco. The Managing Director is Alessandro Ciocchi. The Chairman of V-Ships is David Hoare, and the President is Robert Giorgi, with Bob Bishop as Ship Management CEO, Lorenzo Malvarosa as Ships Leisure CEO and Keith Parsons as a Director. The group has a staff of 24,000 on its books.

Windstar Cruises

This long-established specialist cruise operator is based at Suite 210 4th Avenue, Seattle, Washington, and is now owned by TAC Cruise, operated as a wholly owned subsidiary of Xanterra, Greenwood Village, Colorado. The current CEO of Windstar is Hans Birkholz. The company was founded in 1984 as Windstar Sail Cruises to operate a fleet of unique masted-sail yachts. Built to a design by Marc Held and with interior design by Archiform Design, Paris, they have a new type of alternate propulsion units. The four 62-m (204-ft) high masts have six triangular 1.986sq/m Dacron sails that are operated from the bridge via a computer control system and unfurl in two minutes. They can accommodate 148 guests over four decks with a crew of eighty-eight. They proved a great success, so much so that in 1987 the Holland America Line (HAL) Chairman, Nico van der Vorm, authorized the purchase of 50 per cent of the company and the following year purchased the remaining share outright, only for HAL to be subject to the same treatment themselves when Carnival Corporation absorbed them in 1989. Two somewhat larger vessels, *Wind Surf* and *Wind Saga*, with a 312-guest capacity, were at that time at the design stage for HAL, but, with French Government input to keep the shipyard viable, they

were completed for the Club Méditerranée (Club Med). One ship was initially named *La Fayette* until January 1990, when she became *Club Med I* while her sister was named *Club Med II*. In 1998 Windstar took over *Club Med I* and re-assigned to her the original name *Wind Surf*. In March 2007 the Carnival Corporation divested itself of the Windstar brand and fleet, and sold it lock, stock and barrel for $100 million to Ambassadors International.

In 2011 the Anschutz Corporation, Denver, Colorado, itself first founded in 1959 and now a multi-billion dollar conglomerate, acquired the company for £39 million via its TAC Cruises LLC after Ambassadors International filed for bankruptcy and now Xanterra Parks and Resorts acts as the parent company and operates Windstar as a wholly owned subsidiary. Details of the trio still in service are detailed below.

Wind Star and *Wind Spirit*'s accommodation comprises seventy-three deluxe staterooms and one owner's cabin. The public rooms are the veranda with seating for eighty, the veranda terrace with a forty-guest capacity, the restaurant and the lounge, both of which seat 148. There is a small Casino with seating for just thirty-five players, a library and a pool bar and deck area.

The larger, 5-masted, seven-sailed, *Wind Surf* can carry 312 guests in 123 deluxe ocean-view staterooms and has thirty-one deluxe ocean view suites and two deluxe ocean view bridge suites. She has seven passenger decks and has a crew of 191. Facilities include the reservation-only restaurant, Degrees, in addition to The Restaurant itself and the Veranda restaurant. She has a Casino, a lounge, a salon and The Yacht Club, and also has a library that features internet access. There are two swimming pools and two hot tubs.

Windstar purchased Seabourn Cruise Line's *Seabourn Pride, Seabourn Legend* and *Seabourn Spirit* on 19 February 2013 and renamed them.

The 9,975-GT *Star Pride* was built in 1988 by SSW (Schichau Seebeck Werft) Schichau Seebeck shipyard, Bremerhaven, Germany, and she accommodates 208 guests. Her all-suite accommodation has the following classifications – Owner's, Classic, Balcony and Oceanview. Her public rooms include the atrium, a boutique, the Casino, The Club, a computer centre, a gym, a library, a marina, the observation lounge, a pool, The Restaurant, the show lounge, the Sky Bar and Grill, The Spa at Seabourn, the Veranda Café, Restaurant 2 and whirlpools.

She is registered at Nassau, Bahamas.

The *Star*, (9,975 GT) was built by SSW Schichau Seebeck Werft GmbH, at Bremerhaven in 1989. Her public areas include the Constellation Lounge, the Sky Bar, the Veranda Café/Restaurant, a swimming pool with whirlpool spas, the Spa at Seabourne, The Club, the casino, the boutique, a library, the Magellan lounge, a computer centre, the Forward Whirlpool Spa, a launderette a water sports facility and a medical facility. Her crew number is 164.

She is registered at Nassau, Bahamas.

The 9,961-GT *Star Legend* was built by SSW Schichau Seebeck Werft GmbH, at Bremerhaven in 1991. Her featured public area includes the Midnight Sun Lounge, for morning and afternoon tea/coffee, quizzes and relaxation, the Sky Bar for open air drinks and the Sky Grill, the veranda and café/restaurant for buffets or bistro dining, there is a swimming pool with whirlpool spas, the Spa at Seabourn, with gym and beauty salon, saunas, steam rooms, treatment areas and massage, and The Club bar and lounge with live DJ in evening. There is also the Casino, the boutique, a duty-free shop, a library, the King Olav Lounge, the main show lounge with lectures, demonstrations, films, live dancing or cabaret. Other facilities are the computer centre with four workstations, a launderette, whirlpool spa, a restaurant that is an elegant main dining room, the water sports marina for water-skiing, and kayaks plus a stainless-steel mesh enclosure for sea swimming and a medical facility. She has a crew of 164.

She is registered at Nassau, Bahamas.

The range of cruise options includes one hundred ports in areas as diverse as the Baltic, Costa Rica, the Greek Islands, the Mediterranean, Northern Europe and Panama Canal.

Chapter Three

Running the Ships

As an exercise in pure logistics the cruise industry is a model of the need for extemporary planning and administration. With the average vessel making up to six ports calls a week, and given the sheer scale of both the range of products, basic and luxury, required to satisfy the needs of both passengers and crews, it is a task that can only be tackled with military precision. From the captain of the ship to the anonymous cleaner who ensures your cabin is pristine from the time you leave until the time your return, each crew member has a task that must be fulfilled satisfactorily and discreetly day-in, day-out. Everything that is involved with the running of a high-class hotel ashore is added to the complex business of keeping a huge ship viable, mobile and efficient, and with the further tier of responsibility of providing the entertainment capacity of a dozen theme parks or a mini Las Vegas-style resort operating smoothly over a 24/7 time-scale. From malls full of boutique shops crammed with designer gear, to medical centres, libraries, art galleries, restaurants, casinos and organizing off-ship activity, a cruise ship is a highly demanding mistress to maintain. Fuel, food and drink levels must be maintained, laundry and cleaning rotas fulfilled, the navigation and safety of the ship often in crowded waters must be vigilant with so many lives at stake, the weather along the planned routes must be watched carefully, ports-of-call with different requirements and restrictions monitored, and every whim of the passengers catered for,

both spiritual, mental and physical. Despite all this, and the enormous cost of building and outfitting, it has been maintained by observers in the banking world that the modern 'megaship' has the potential to pay for itself within a five-year window.

Then there are the environmental considerations and they, like today's ships, are vast. The daily waste generated by so many passengers and crew aboard a single cruise ship is considerable. As one would expect in this hyper-socially conscious world the correct disposal of such extraneous matter has been carefully broken down and classified into groups. As on all ships the used liquids generated by the ships' engines and motors themselves continue to be known as bilge water, and its disposal at sea and in harbours has been carefully monitored for decades to avoid the harming of wildlife and their habitats. The many examples of the calamitous effect of oil discharge have led to some prosecutions of cruise companies in the past for similar bad behaviour. But this is just one aspect of the problem and cruise ships being, in effect, hotels at sea generate a great many other waste products on a daily basis.

The ships' ballast tanks, which are filled or discharged to stabilize the vessels at certain cyclic stages of their voyage, can have a harmful effect on oceanic life at the most basic level introducing alien elements into areas many miles away from where they were inducted. Human effluent is euphemistically known as black water while normal waste water from baths, showers, pools, cleaners, kitchen appliances and the like is termed grey water. Then there are tons of solid waste products from consumption, such as plastic food packaging and metal containers, bottles and jars, reams and reams of paper and the like, most of which is incinerated and reduced to ash. Most cruise companies are acutely aware of the 'trail' left by their vessels and apply strict rules to minimize it, extending these to the passengers' responsibility as well, afloat and while ashore, for the descent of several thousand people from a single ship can 'swamp' many small destinations that may not be able to cope. Much research and money is currently being ploughed back by the industry into the cleansing of operational functions and reducing the other big polluter, hazardous waste, chemicals, solvents and the like, before they enter the discharge chain. While total elimination of such a footprint may be impossible the industry is definitely hard on the track to, most literally, clean up its act.

Ports of Registry

All ships have a port of registry, more commonly referred to as their hailing port or home port, although in the cruise industry this latter term is frequently misapplied to the departure port. A ship's registration documents are held here and if she is a recreational ship, she is identified 'clearly and visibly' along with her name, in clearly legible letters, on the ship's hull, by tradition on her stern and on the port and starboard of any exterior part of her forward structure. The IMO maintains that all ships 'engaged in international trade' are required to have a country of registry before they can sail in international waters. The IMO adds, 'A ship is considered the territory of the country in which it is registered.' Different countries apply different standards and rules on board the ships registered to them and companies choose those that suit their organization best.

Registration and Regulatory Bodies

With so many people packed aboard cruise ships it is inevitable, and to be encouraged, that such vessels are highly regulated both as ships and also in how they are operated and run. Major international treaties ensure the maximum compliance with regulation and good practice; the first of these followed the *Titanic* disaster of 1912, and resulted in the setting up of the ice patrol. But it was the Safety of Life at Sea (SOLAS) convention that enshrined the guiding principles into the major treaty concerning maritime safety. This was followed by the Marine Pollution (MARPOL) conventions of 1973 and 1978 aimed at minimizing the pollution effects of ships upon the world's oceans, which came into effect in 1983; and Standards of Training, Certification and Watchkeeping for Seafarers (STCW) of 1984 (amended 1995), which seeks to lay down and maintain the highest standards of training for seagoing personnel. Two major bodies existing to maintain the maximum safety of ships at sea are Lloyd's Register of Shipping and the International Maritime Organization (IMO), both headquartered in London. For the companies there is also the Cruise Lines International Association (CLIA), set up to promote the North American cruise industry, which, as approximately over 70 per cent of cruise line passengers are American, has considerable influence. The focus of the CLIA is dedicated to the laudable ideals of ensuring the cruise industry provides a safe, healthy and secure shipboard environment for both passengers and crew; minimizing the environmental impact of its vessel operations on the oceans, marine life and destination ports; adhering to regulatory maritime initiatives and heading the effort to improve such policies and procedures; creating a regulatory environment that will foster continued growth in the industry and delivering a reliable, affordable and enjoyable cruise experience.

IMO

IMO's Maritime Safety Committee (MSC) met at the organization's London headquarters for its ninety-first session from 26 to 30 November 2012.

The busy agenda included discussions on passenger ship safety; the adoption of amendments to the International Convention for the Safety of Life at Sea (SOLAS); and consideration of matters related to piracy and armed robbery against ships and other items submitted by the IMO sub-committees.

Passenger ship safety

The MSC established a working group on passenger ship safety to consider relevant issues, including the action plan drawn up at the last session following the *Costa Concordia* incident in January 2012 with the deaths of thirty-two people.

The MSC had quickly agreed on a number of operational measures to be implemented immediately, on a voluntary basis, prior to the adoption of any measures following the analysis of the official marine investigation report into the loss of the *Costa Concordia*.

The MSC also received an update from the Government of Italy on the status of the *Costa Concordia* casualty investigation at which the IIMO was represented, as an observer, on the body overseeing the casualty investigation.

Adoption of SOLAS amendments

The MSC studied for adoption the following recommendations:
- Draft amendments to SOLAS regulation III/17-1 to require ships to have plans and procedures to recover persons from the water, as well as related guidelines for development of plans and procedures for recovery of persons from the water. Also, there was a related draft MSC resolution on implementation of SOLAS regulation III/17-1 to ships other than those engaged in international voyages;
- A draft new SOLAS regulation II-1/3-12 to require new ships to be constructed to reduce on-board noise and to protect personnel from noise, in accordance with the draft revised code on noise levels on board ships, also set to be adopted, which sets out mandatory noise level limits for machinery spaces, control rooms, workshops, accommodation and other spaces on board ships, and will supersede the previous code, adopted in 1981 by resolution A.468(XII); and
- Draft amendments to SOLAS regulation II-2/10 on fire fighting to require a minimum of duplicate two-way portable radiotelephone apparatus for fire fighters' communication to be carried; and draft amendments to regulation II-2/15 on instructions, on-board training and drills, to require an on-board means of recharging breathing apparatus cylinders used during drills, or a suitable number of spare cylinders.
- SOLAS amendments to mandate enclosed-space entry and rescue drills to be approved.

The MSC approved, for subsequent adoption, draft amendments to SOLAS regulation III/19, on emergency training and drills, which would required crew members with the appropriate responsibility to participate in enclosed-space entry and rescue drill at least once very two months.

The draft amendments are aimed at enhancing the protection of seafarers' lives by requiring drills be held to ensure that seafarers are familiar with the precautions they need to take prior to entering enclosed spaces and also with the most appropriate action they should take in the event of an accident.

There initially were ten new policies that addressed the need for early muster drills, bridge access and procedures, the availability of life jackets and their positioning, the loading of lifeboat and drills. Also addressed was the need to keep proper records of the nationalities of passengers to help the on-shore emergency services and the safe securing of heavy objects aboard. The evacuation procedures from passenger ships was also overhauled. The very basis of the design of future new cruise ships has been examined. As regards the wider practicalities, the immediate result of such a colossal loss, and the £400 million salvage bill, has been an enormous 125 per cent rise the excess of loss reinsurance renewals.

Piracy and armed robbery against ships

Following a high-level policy debate on arms on board ships at the last session, the MSC reviewed the latest statistics on piracy and armed robbery against ships and discussed current initiatives to suppress piracy and armed robbery. The number of attacks launched by Somali-based pirates is reported to have decreased. However, the number of reported attacks off west Africa has risen.

Following the work done by MSC 90 to develop guidelines for private maritime security companies using armed security personnel, MSC 91 received an update on the progress made by the International Organization for Standardization (ISO) to develop international minimum standards for the deployment of such personnel, for use by flag states if or when appropriate.

Goal-based standards implementation work to continue

The MSC will continue its work on goal-based standards. It is expected to consider the report of a correspondence group, established to develop draft guidelines for the approval of equivalents and alternatives as provided for in various IMO instruments.

A working group will be established to further consider the draft guidelines and the continued development of the safety level approach.

IMO audit scheme code and amendments set to be approved

The MSC approved the draft IMO Instruments Implementation Code (III Code), which sets the standard for the IMO audit scheme, and approved draft amendments to the following treaties to make the III Code and auditing mandatory: International Convention for the Safety of Life at Sea, (SOLAS), 1974, as amended; the International Convention on Load Lines, 1966 (LL 1966) and its 1988 Protocol; the International Convention on Standards of Training, Certification and Watchkeeping (STCW), 1978, as amended and the Seafarers' Training, Certification and Watchkeeping (STCW) Code; the International Convention on Tonnage Measurement of Ships, 1969 (Tonnage 1969); and the Convention on the International Regulations for Preventing Collisions at Sea, 1972, as amended (COLREG 1972).

The aim is to adopt the treaty amendments in 2014, once the III Code has been formally adopted by the IMO Assembly, in 2013.

Code for Recognized Organizations (ROs) set to be approved

The MSC approved the draft code for Recognized Organizations (ROs) and related draft amendments to SOLAS, 1974, and the Load Lines 1988 Protocol, to make it mandatory, for adoption at a future session. The code provided a consolidated text containing criteria against which ROs (which may be authorized by flag states to carry out surveys and issue certificates on their behalf) are assessed and authorized/recognized, and gives guidance for subsequent monitoring of ROs by administrations.

The MSC was updated on developments in relation to the establishment and testing of long-range identification and tracking (LRIT) Data Centres (DCs) and the operation of the LRIT system.

Other issues

In connection with other issues arising from the reports of IMO sub-committees and other bodies, the MSC were invited to adopt amendments to update the performance standard for protective coatings for dedicated seawater ballast tanks in all types of ships and double-side skin spaces of bulk carriers (resolution MSC.215(82)) and the performance standard for protective coatings for cargo oil tanks of crude oil tankers (resolution MSC.288(87); adopt amendments to annex B to the Protocol of 1988 relating to the International Convention on Load Lines, 1966 (1988 Load Lines Protocol), as amended related to Regulation 27(11) initial condition of loading and Regulation 27(13) condition of equilibrium; adopt amendments to update the International Code for Fire Safety Systems (FSS Code), as amended, including revised specifications for breathing apparatus and revised chapter 14 on fixed deck foam systems; adopt amendments to chapters 17, 18 and 19 of the International Code for the Construction and Equipment of Ships carrying Dangerous Chemicals in Bulk (IBC Code), which have been concurrently adopted by the Marine Environment Protection Committee (MEPC); approve a draft COMSAR circular on guidance on smartphone and other computer devices, which points out the potential safety concerns in relation to the use of applications for 'smartphones' and other computer devices that relate to Search and Rescue (SAR); adopt a number of new and amended ships' routeing measures; consider the Secretary-General's report on a number of countries whose independent evaluations have been completed since the previous MSC meeting and to confirm if those parties continue to give full and complete effect to the provisions of the International Convention on Standards of Training, Certification and Watchkeeping for Seafarers (STCW), 1978, as amended; approve revised Guidelines on the Medical Examination of Seafarers (STCW.7/Circ.19); approve a draft STCW.7 circular providing guidance on Electronic Chart Display and Information System (ECDIS) Training; approve guidance to STCW parties, including draft revised circulars on procedures regarding the consideration of information communicated in accordance with article IV and regulation I/7 of the STCW Convention (MSC.1/Circ.796/Rev.2); provide guidance on the preparation, reporting and review of independent evaluations and steps taken to implement mandatory amendments required by regulations I/7 and I/8 of the STCW Convention (MSC.1/Circ.997/Rev.1); and guidance on arrangements between parties to allow for recognition of certificates under regulation I/10 of the STCW Convention MSC.1/Circ.950/Rev.1); approve draft amendments to the International Management Code for the Safe Operation of Ships and for Pollution Prevention (International Safety Management (ISM) Code), intended to improve its efficiency and user friendliness; approve a draft Assembly resolution on revised guidelines on implementation of the ISM Code by administrations; approve a draft Assembly resolution on revised guidelines for the structure of an integrated system of contingency planning for shipboard emergencies; approve draft amendments to the International Convention for Safe Containers (CSC), 1972, for subsequent adoption. The draft amendments incorporate amendments to the CSC Convention adopted in 1993 by resolution A.737(18), which have not yet entered into force: approve the draft MSC-MEPC circular on the Revised Guidelines for Formal Safety Assessment (FSA) for use in the IMO rule-making process (Revised FSA Guidelines), and the draft MSC-MEPC circular on guidelines for the application of Human

Element Analysing Process (HEAP) to the IMO rule making process (HEAP Guidelines); and approve a draft revised MSC.1/Circ.1350 on unified interpretations of SOLAS regulation V/22.1.6 relating to navigation bridge visibility, to include a new paragraph covering the use of a remote camera system as means for achieving the view of the ship's side from the bridge wing.

Lloyd's Register of Shipping

This venerable institution, recognized and respected the world over, originated in a coffee house owned by one Edward Lloyd in Tower Street and then from 1691, Lombard Street, both in the City of London. At Lloyd's shipping merchants and agents would meet informally to discuss business and opportunities, and would be joined by insurance underwriters in negotiations to cover both the cargoes and the vessels themselves in case of loss en route. The actual Lloyd's Register of Shipping itself, as it is officially titled, but more generally known simply as 'Lloyd's Register', was originally a handwritten document listing the ships and placing them into certain categories for easy reference and comparison, evaluating them for insurance purpose according to their tonnage, dimensions, equipment and other relevant criteria. As a handy standard reference at a time when British trade was booming as the Empire expanded and British ships carried 90 per cent of the world's trade, this Register quickly became an essential tool. The earliest known surviving volume dates back to 1764 but it had been 'The Bible' of the shipping world many years prior to that. Some friction arose between the shipping magnates on one hand and the insurance underwriters on the other that saw two separate editions (the Red and the Green Books) of the Register appearing for a period of thirty years, but this was increasingly confusing. Thankfully commonsense eventually prevailed and an independent society, Lloyd's Register of British and Foreign Shipping was set up in 1834. (It should be noted that Lloyd's of London, equally famous underwriters founded in 1871, has *never* had any connection with Lloyd's Register). The scope of this annually issued publication is now so great that it is issued in several volumes each year.

Lloyd's Register of Shipping with its headquarters in Fenchurch Street, London, maintains a network of 240 offices around the globe and employs in excess of 2,500 highly skilled maritime personnel who assess and certify merchant vessels, their systems and their facilities to exacting uniform standards. The specific service it conducts for cruise ships is classification, almost 50 per cent of such ships being classed by Lloyd's Register. The period covered is from conceptual design appraisal, through design approval, the construction process and surveys during the service life of the vessel, including passenger safety surveys that assess passenger and crew accommodation comfort. Lloyd's has its own noise and vibration criteria with which it monitors and evaluates these factors objectively. Lloyd's Register also has a fire engineering service with which it evaluates alternative proposals for the appropriate SOLAS compliance.

Updating the IMO specification

This organization was first established as the Inter-Governmental Maritime Consultative Organization (IMCO) following the 1948 international conference held at Geneva under the auspices of the United Nations. The IMCO first met a decade later and by 1960 had agreed an updated version of SOLAS. The organization then turned its attention to pollution, which resulted in the International Convention for the Prevention of Pollution from Ships in 1973, which was subsequently modified in 1978 as MARPOL. This covered accidental and operational chemical, garbage, sewage, air pollution as well as oil pollution. Measures to ensure a fair system of compensation for those affected by such pollution were also addressed in 1969 and 1971, and have since been twice updated. In 1982 the IMCO was renamed the International Maritime Organization (IMO). Other safety factors tackled were the setting up of the International Mobile Satellite Organization (IMSO) and the Global Maritime Distress and Safety System (GMDSS), which initiated fully automatic distress signalling, and became fully operational in 1999. The guiding principles of the IMO remain its declared mission statement – 'Safe, Secure and Efficient Shipping on Clean Oceans.'

Cruise Line International Association (CLIA)

This is currently composed of twenty-five of the world's major cruise lines and was first established in 1975. It merged with the similar International Council of Cruise Lines (ICCL) in 2006 and currently represents about 97 per cent of the North American cruise capacity. There are also around one hundred executive partners, strategic business allies that provide services to and are reliant upon, the industry in the USA, plus more than 16,000 stateside travel agencies. The CLIA has its headquarters at Fort Lauderdale, Florida, with another office in Washington DC. Whereas the CLIA was originally founded to promote and market the fast-growing industry, the ICCL, which originated in 1990, was dedicated to participating in regulatory and policy development. The aims of the combined Association are stated to be, '… to promote all measures that foster a safe, secure and healthy cruise ship environment, educate, train its travel agent members, and promote and explain the value, desirability and affordability of the cruise vacation experience.'

Identification Codes

International Maritime Organization (IMO)

From January 2009, under SOLAS regulation XI-1/3 Company and Registered Owner Identification Number and associated amendments, 'every Company and registered owner shall be provided with an identification number which conforms to the IMO Unique Company and Registered Owner Number Scheme'. The IMO number comprises seven digits always with the prefix IMO followed by a unique seven-digit code, which is solely assigned by Lloyd's Register – Fairplay (LRF) during the ship's construction, and this respected organization also has sole responsibility for monitoring and managing the scheme for the IMO itself.

Maritime Mobile Service Identity (MMSI)

This is a unique international electronic ship-recognition identity code. It consists of nine digits in total, with the initial three digits comprising the Maritime Identification Digits (MID) with a regional range of 2 to 7, inclusive. Thus Europe has the numeral 2, North and Central America, 3, Asia , 4, Oceana 5, Africa 6 and South America 7. Cruise ships are fitted with London-based Inmarsat's geosynchronous telecommunications satellite ship earth stations, and such vessels always have the final three digits as 000.

Each MMSI number is assigned to an individual ship and allows each vessel to be automatically called via the worldwide radio frequencies and can help with the automatic connection of telecommunications networks. Once assigned the MMSI stays with the ship throughout its lifetime. Even after a ship has been scrapped or lost, its number is never reassigned to any other vessel. The system is also used to systemize the IDs of group ship stations.

Chapter Four

Funnels Features

As long as there have been liners, shipping companies have used their most prominent feature to highlight the company via their colour or the logo affixed to it. Nowadays the very shape of the funnel casing usually marks out the identity of the vessel's owner, though often these structures merely mask the true outlet stacks or can be totally bogus appendages retained to pay tribute to past traditions. Costa's upright clusters; Cunard's distinctive kneed-appendage, the Mickey Mouse ears of the Disney ships, all instantly mark a ship. Here are some samples currently to be seen across the world's oceans.

Seabourn Sojourn.

Thomson Celebration.

Funnel Styles

Salamis Filoxenia.

Astor.

Silver Spirit.

Sea Adventurer.

Glossary

ABB Asea	Brown Boveri company of Billingstad, Norway
AG	Aktiengesellschaft – Corporation
A/S	Aktieselskab – Joint Stock Company (Danish)
BEST	Business Excellence Sustainable Task
BIG-BAU	Bremen InvestitionsGesellschaft Mbh
CCP	Controlled Pitch Propeller
CEO	Chief Executive Officer
CGT	Compaignie Générale Transatlantique
CLIA	Cruise Lines International Association
CODED	Combined Diesel-Electric and Diesel-Mechanical
COGES	Combined Gas and Steam
cp	controlled pitch (propellers)
DF	Dual-fuelled
DSC	Dalien Shipbuilding Complex
ENI	European Number of Identity
Flag	Indication of country a ship is registered in
ft	feet
FCT	Flexible Camshaft Technology
FTSE	*Financial Times* Stock Exchange Share Index
GmbH	Gessellschaft mit Beschränkter Haftung – Limited Liability Company
GMDSS	Global Maritime Distress and Safety System
GRT	Gross Registered Tonnage
HAL	Holland America Line
HFO	Heavy Fuel Oil
ICCL	International Council of Cruise Lines
IEF	Installed Engine Power
IMO	International Maritime Organization
IMCO	Inter-Governmental Maritime Consultative Organization
IMSO	International Mobile Satellite Organization
IRI	Istituto per la Ricostruzione Industriale
kW	kilowatts
LLC	Limited Liability Company
LNG	Liquid Nitrogen Gas
LNG	Liquefied Natural Gas
LPG	Liquid Petroleum Gas
m	metres
MaK	Maschinenbau Kiel
MAN	Maschinenfabrik Augsburg Nürnberg AG
MARPOL	Marine Pollution
Mbh	Massenbachhausen – Limited Liability
MMSI	Maritime Mobile Service Identity
MSC	Mediterranean Shipping Company

MW	Megawatts
NCL	Norwegian Cruise Lines
NDL	Norddeutscher Lloyd
NYK	Nippon Yusen Kaisha
OD	Oil Distribution
Oy	Osakeyhtiő – Limited Company (Finnish)
PANAMAX	The largest ship that can traverse the Panama Canal *ergo* 'Post-Panamax' a vessel too large to traverse.
Pax	Passengers
plc	Public Limited Company
P&O	Peninsular & Orient
RCI	Royal Caribbean International

RCCL	Royal Caribbean Cruise Line
RINA	Royal Institution of Naval Architects
Ro-Ro	Roll-on, Roll-off
rpm	revolutions per minute
SE	Societas Europaea
SOLAS	Safety of Life at Sea
SpA	Società per Azioni – Shared Company (Italian)
STCW	Standard of Training Certification and Watchkeepers for Seafarers
TUI	Touristik Union International
vp	variable pitch (propellers)
WHRS	Waste Heat Recovery System